Intimate Bonds

THE EARLY MODERN AMERICAS

Peter C. Mancall, Series Editor

Volumes in the series explore neglected aspects of
early modern history in the western hemisphere.
Interdisciplinary in character, and with a special
emphasis on the Atlantic World from 1450 to 1850,
the series is published in partnership with the
USC-Huntington Early Modern Studies Institute.

INTIMATE BONDS

Family and Slavery in the French Atlantic

Jennifer L. Palmer

PENN

UNIVERSITY OF PENNSYLVANIA PRESS

PHILADELPHIA

Published by
University of Pennsylvania Press
Philadelphia, Pennsylvania 19104-4112
www.upenn.edu/pennpress

Printed in the United States of America on acid-free paper
1 3 5 7 9 10 8 6 4 2

Library of Congress Cataloging-in-Publication Data
ISBN 978-0-8122-4840-1

To David, Henry, and Benjamin
In honor of my parents
And in memory of Amy.

CONTENTS

ADCM   Archives Départementales de la Charente Maritime

AMLR   Archives Municipales de La Rochelle

ANOM   Archives Nationales d'Outre-mer

AN   Archives Nationales de France

BN   Bibliothèque Nationale de France

All translations, unless otherwise noted, are my own.

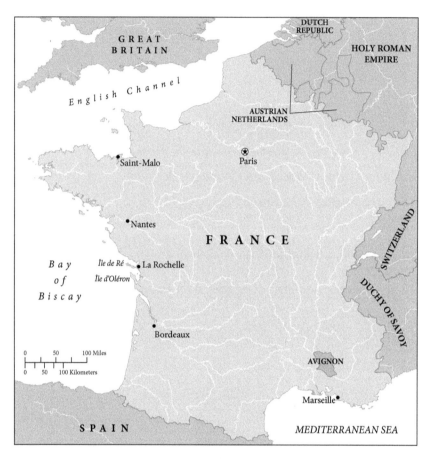

Map 1: France.

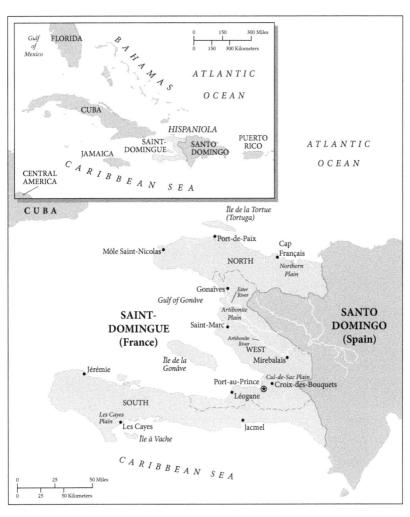

Map 2: Saint-Domingue.

Interracial Intimacy in the French Atlantic

On 31 July 1755, the ship *Le Théodore* arrived in the port town of La Rochelle, having sailed from Port-au-Prince, Saint-Domingue, calling at the smaller, river-bound city of Léogane along the way. To Hardy and Lizette, two slaves arriving in France for the first time on board *Le Théodore*, La Rochelle must have appeared startlingly unlike Saint-Domingue as they sailed into the harbor. Far more than four thousand miles and a voyage of two or even three months separated the departure and arrival points: climate, customs, social interactions, and even language were all different. The city's multistoried townhouses, hôtels particuliers, and elegant arcades, all made of gleaming golden sandstone, doubtless looked grand in contrast to the wooden structures and muddy streets characteristic of Port-au-Prince and Léogane. Everywhere in the city they would have encountered seas of white faces looking at them curiously. Unlike the colony, where people of color outnumbered whites by a huge majority even in the cities, La Rochelle had but a small community of color.[1] Yet common elements also linked these ports. Port-au-Prince and its environs, located on the west coast of the western province of Saint-Domingue, and La Rochelle and its hinterland, situated on France's Atlantic seaboard, shared ties of commerce, strengthened by connections of kinship and friendship that spanned the ocean. For some, the intimate bonds between the two locales truncated the distance, making it seem closer and more familiar than it actually was; many involved in transatlantic trade had friends, family, and business associates on the other side of the ocean. For those who traveled back and forth between La Rochelle and Port-au-Prince, slavery was simultaneously a point of continuity and of profound difference. Numerous slave owners and slaves who traveled together expected that crossing the ocean would not change their daily intimacies or relationships. However, these two ports were literally and figuratively an ocean apart, and experiences, expectations, and laws governing slavery posed unexpected challenges—and opportunities—to traveling slave owners and slaves alike.

Although alienated from their homes and networks an ocean away, Hardy and Lizette nonetheless arrived in France as part of the families and households of their owners. The daily structures and practices of slavery in La Rochelle differed dramatically from those in the western province of Saint-Domingue, where laws, social practices, and living situations all revolved around the project of maintaining hierarchy between slave owners and their slaves. In La Rochelle, slave owners and officials built on evolving ideas of race and gender to reinforce their version of social order. As Hardy and Lizette arrived in La Rochelle in the company of their white owners and likely their owners' children as well, they came already embedded in families where hierarchies occasioned by slavery were the norm. Even in La Rochelle, four thousand miles from Saint-Domingue, few slaves could break these intimate bonds.

While Hardy and Lizette were both slaves, important differences in their lives, backgrounds, and the families with whom they lived point to the varied and multiple experiences of slavery. Hardy, about twenty-seven when he arrived in France, was born in Africa.[2] He likely had an understanding of, and conceivably experience with, African systems of slavery that differed markedly from slave systems in the New World. Although practices of slavery naturally varied greatly by region, time period, and individual, the status of African slaves could change over the course of an individual's life or across several generations.[3] Further, acceptance into a family unit could offer slaves opportunities to reduce their marginality in everyday life.[4] Hardy could have used this knowledge to his advantage, purposely setting himself apart in ways that his owner would notice. His African roots, after all, made him unusual among house slaves in Saint-Domingue as well as slaves in La Rochelle: owners generally chose créole slaves, those born in the colony, to live and work closely with them. Hardy must have done something to attract attention from among the considerable number of slaves belonging to his owner in order to be chosen for such a personal role.[5] More typically, Lizette was a créole.[6] At forty-five on her arrival, she would have been an appropriate age to wet-nurse her owner's eighteen-month-old son. She probably also cared for the mother, who was pregnant again.[7] No other people of color journeyed with her. If she had children of her own, they stayed in Saint-Domingue.

While it is easy to assume that the enslaved position of the two rendered their lives similar, the intimate bonds that linked them to the families with whom they traveled led to different experiences within slavery. Although Hardy and Lizette journeyed together, likely knew each other, and perhaps occasionally met in the streets of La Rochelle, their enslavement meant that their lives were oriented toward the households of their owners, not toward each other or indeed any other people of color. Their families form two of the in-depth case studies investigated in this book. Hardy's owner, Aimé-Benjamin Fleuriau, arrived in France not only with Hardy, but also with five of his mixed-race children. This household, which initially included a white man, five free adolescents of mixed race, and a black male slave, soon expanded to incorporate Fleuriau's white bride, and eventually their legitimate children. This group brought a nuanced understanding of gradations of race and status with them. They used this knowledge to enact and dispute these hierarchies in their household and in the broader French context where race and status increasingly were conflated. Hardy lived the rest of his life under Fleuriau's roof, serving the merchant and presumably his family.[8] Hardy's enslaved status separated him from Fleuriau's mixed-race children, even though they too had African blood.

Lizette's household looks less complicated: she was the only person of color, at least at first, serving a white woman and her children. Yet her owner Marie-Magdelaine Regnaud de Beaumont was no ordinary white woman. Married but living alone, Madame Regnaud de Beaumont possessed her husband's power of attorney, which empowered her to conduct business for him and sell the produce he sent from their plantation near Léogane. He also sent her at least two other slaves.[9] In this household devoid of a patriarch, Madame Regnaud de Beaumont consistently struggled to assert patriarchal authority, including over her slaves.

By focusing on household relations across lines of race in France and Saint-Domingue, this book establishes that intimacy shaped the institution of slavery and, equally importantly, that family formed a platform to resist racial categorization. As the experiences of Hardy and Lizette indicate, slavery in France was, at its heart, domestic and intimate. Domestic relations fostered intimacy in a variety of ways. In the context of the family and the household, people of all different skin tones, whether slave or free, interacted on close, quotidian levels in France and Saint-Domingue. Highlighting the French metropolitan experience unearths new ways of understanding the colonial context of slavery by bringing intimate relations to the fore. These interactions were exploitive in nature, and reinforced, rather than undermined, a hierarchy that had race and slavery at its core. White owners ate food cooked and served by slaves with dark skin, white men raped women of color, white women used black boys as luxury objects that highlighted their own status. Occasionally, however, the family and household also acted as loci of resistance to racial categorization, and even to slavery. White fathers of mixed-race children sometimes evinced the same type of concern for them as for white children, offering them freedom and material advantages. White men on occasion freed their enslaved sexual partners, at times providing them with economic benefits as well.[10] Thus, the very people who apparently had the most at stake in maintaining racialized patriarchal authority—that is, white men—occasionally undermined the system by exercising that authority.

Intimacy reveals how empire transformed gender roles. As the divergent paths of Hardy and Lizette will show, gender continued to usurp race as the primary category that structured household relations. In families that included children of mixed race as well as families with only white children, fathers treated daughters one way and sons another—their concession was to race instead of gender. Similarly, in France, male and female slaves and free people of color performed different work. People of color, both slave and free, also used their family positions as a means of articulating their place within French society, adopting French gender norms to do so. Men emphasized their status as heads of household, while women adopted the feminine privilege of avoiding contact with officers of the state when they could, leaving such interactions to their husbands. These European gender ideals conflicted with what slaves would have known in Saint-Domingue, where women worked the fields proportionally more than men, men were thought incapable of exercising masculine restraint or authority, and domesticity remained a chimera for women. They also diverged markedly from Africans' understandings of women's key economic roles, particularly in the commercial sector.[11] When Hardy, Lizette, and other slaves traveled across the ocean, therefore, they added to an existing repertoire of ideas about what gender meant.

Yet empire also caused gender hierarchies to break down and transformed gender roles within the family. When white men left France to seek their fortunes in the colonies, leaving their wives in charge of families and businesses, women stepped into unaccustomed roles as heads of household. Resistance to racial categorization, though, was not simply a patriarchal prerogative; people of color, both slave and free, also manipulated the fuzzy delimitations of race to their own advantage when they could. Over the course of the eighteenth century, definitions of race solidified and dark skin was increasingly equated with enslaved status. On the surface, this change appears a unified, though complex, process, with officials and slave owners working in concert to gradually restrict the boundary between slavery and freedom, as well as roles and opportunities available to free people of color. Yet in reality this process was far from smooth and seamless, generating new forms of resistance as well as new norms and hierarchies. Focusing on intimacies across racial lines illuminates where challenges to emerging racial categories were strongest. Additionally, interracial personal connections opened up spaces where people of color could explore and assert alternatives to a dichotomous black and white hierarchy, as imagined by French and colonial officials. This exploration took place within the family.

This study sheds new light on the history of empire and slavery in the early modern French Atlantic by looking at the relations and institutions that anchored this world: the family and the household. By closely considering individual families and the personal connections that entangled the lives of whites and people of color in La Rochelle and the western province of Saint-Domingue, this work shows how intimate choices defined and transformed the French transatlantic empire and trade. Personal relations, whether lived through everyday interactions and intimacies or over long periods of absence and overseas correspondence, shaped the opportunities for men and women, free and slave, to renegotiate gender roles. This in turn created space for rethinking race as a social category. Families had transatlantic connections, and moved between metropole and colony. This movement was the essential factor that created opportunities for engaging with and challenging these categories. Tracing connections across transatlantic spaces demonstrates how individuals and family units were affected by, responded to, and transformed family, gender roles, slavery, race, and empire. Race and enslaved status were not firm, inevitable categories, but fluid constructs open to interpretation and reinvention. Focusing on households and intimacies that spanned the ocean, this work shows how transatlantic and interracial personal connections created spaces where people could explore alternatives. People of all skin tones for whom race was a dynamic, fluid, lived category knew that it was a negotiated process, and that intimate relations across racial lines were a vital part of this negotiation. The institution of the family was the primary site for racial negotiation and exploration, and focusing on intimacies across racial lines reveals where opposition to emerging dichotomies was the strongest. Following the intimate bonds that crossed the Atlantic's currents, then, reveals that family and household relationships played a central role in the creation of and resistance to race as an emerging category.

From La Rochelle to the Western Province

La Rochelle is a particularly intriguing city from which to launch an investigation of race, family, and households for three reasons. First, its close-knit and largely Protestant network of merchants made ongoing, concerted efforts to create and reinforce transatlantic family ties. Second, a legal anomaly meant that it was the only major port city to which laws regulating slavery in France did not technically apply. Third, while heavily imbricated in the slave trade, its lifeblood came from direct trade with the Antilles. Slavery and commerce therefore were not synonymous. Examining racial practices and attitudes of the residents of this city consequently opens up opportunities to gauge acceptance of and resistance to official racial policies as they unfolded over the course of the eighteenth century, and in turn to consider the range of responses these policies provoked.

While a small city by metropolitan standards, La Rochelle was always a gateway to France's empire. Samuel de Champlain was baptized there as a Protestant in 1574 and from the point of the famous explorer's departure on, the city's Protestantism and its imperial position intertwined.[12] The religious strife of the seventeenth century had reduced La Rochelle's population to about 10,000 in 1728, and it increased slowly over the course of the eighteenth century to about 17,250 in 1787. The city was geographically small, bounded by walls (or their remnants) that enclosed an area of only about 1.5 square miles. Beyond the walls stretched farmland, and on market days farmers rubbed shoulders with fishmongers and dockworkers in the crowded, noisy, smelly *centre-ville*. As in most French cities, rich and poor commingled, with the large, gracious residences of wealthy merchants standing elbow to elbow with the more humble quarters of artisans and shopkeepers and the squalid residences of the urban poor.

In the eighteenth century, La Rochelle prospered as a port seemingly against all odds. Ships had to enter the old port through a narrow channel, carefully circumventing the sunken ships filled with stones that formed the basis of the dykes set up by Richelieu during the famous siege of 1627–1628. They then had to pass precariously between two medieval towers, the Tour St. Nicolas and Tour de la Chaîne, and into a small harbor hardly three

Figure 1. Joseph Vernet, *View of the Port of La Rochelle*, 1762. Musée de la Marine, Paris. © RMN-Grand Palais/Art Resource/NY.

hundred yards long and one hundred fifty yards wide that only allowed a limited number of ships, and those of a limited tonnage. This basin was subject to severe tides, and at low tide ships could neither enter nor exit. Because of the restricted space, rather than mooring alongside the quays, ships had to pull nose in to the quay, making loading and unloading merchandise difficult and dangerous. To top it all off, the port was slowly silting up.

In spite of these disadvantages, La Rochelle offered some advantages over its larger rivals, Nantes to the north and Bordeaux to the south. Its location in the Provinces des Cinq Grosses Fermes, a large free trade zone that also encompassed the wealthiest areas of France including Paris, Burgundy, and Normandy, made it an attractive point of entry for transatlantic shipping.[13] With its ocean-facing port and protective islands, the entry to La Rochelle was far easier and safer than either of its river-bound rivals. Its economic isolation made it all the more oriented west, toward the Atlantic. Because of this seaward proclivity, La Rochelle, more than other Atlantic ports, served as a clearinghouse for long-distance shipping, with the Antilles as its main point of trade. Its largest imports and exports were sugar and indigo, and in contrast to other ports, La Rochelle's economy depended almost solely on trade with the French Caribbean colonies. Indeed, for most of the century over 65 percent of ships leaving from La Rochelle had the West Indies as their destination. In comparison, the percentage of exports destined for the Antilles from Bordeaux and Marseille during the eighteenth century hovered from about 15 to 20 percent. Most ships bound for the West Indies from La Rochelle had Saint-Domingue as their primary port of call, with Guadeloupe and Martinique as secondary choices. Although Nantes dominated the slave trade, La Rochelle ran second for most of the eighteenth century in terms of the number of slaving vessels outfitted.[14]

La Rochelle's peculiar legal situation also distinguished it from Nantes and Bordeaux in ways that had important implications for the struggle for authority over slaves that played out between slave owners and royal officials. In retaliation for its role as a center for Protestant rebellion during the French Wars of Religion, the crown placed the city under the jurisdiction of the Parlement of Paris, making it the only major port to fall under Parisian control.[15] This quirk had important ramifications for slaves and slave owners in La Rochelle: because the Parlement of Paris failed to register the first French laws pertaining to slavery in France, the Edict of 1716 and the Declaration of 1738, the royal officials of the Admiralty, not the courts, had jurisdiction over slaves in La Rochelle.[16] The Paris Parlement's refusal was intended as a rebuke against slave owning and a denial of its existence on France's shores. However, in La Rochelle, *belle et rebelle*, as the local saying goes, residents used this repudiation for their own ends, to strengthen the claims of slave owners who wanted to bring their human property to France. Slave owners most directly confronted royal attempts to regulate slavery in port cities such as La Rochelle, where owners were supposed to register slaves in their port of arrival. The conjunction of the "legal limbo," in Sue Peabody's terminology, created by the failure of the Parlement of Paris to enregister these key laws and the large number of slave owners, slaves, and free people of color who entered the port opened up a space in which slave owners affirmed their authority while people of color articulated their autonomy. Appeals to intimate bonds formed the core of this significant contestation over authority because intimacies simultaneously offered the rationale for slave-owning practices, ways for owners to exercise their dominance, a platform for slaves to resist their enslavement, and a vocabulary for people of color to claim inclusion in their community. In all these situations, slave owners, slaves, and free people of color alike worked around and manipulated laws, purposefully maneuvering their conformity or defiance to suit their own purposes.

The long history of religious tensions between Catholics and Protestants had other repercussions as well, and La Rochelle's history of Protestantism loomed large over the city. For centuries a cosmopolitan center for trade, the 1685 Revocation of the Edict of Nantes actually strengthened the city's international ties by dispersing around 200,000 Protestants around the Atlantic world, creating a Huguenot diaspora.[17] This mass migration actually facilitated the creation and strengthening of commercial ties abroad, including in the French Antilles.[18] Nearly 40 percent of French Protestants who settled in the Antilles came from La Rochelle and its environs, some 15 percent of the total number of emigrants by the end of the seventeenth century.[19] Religious tensions in La Rochelle cooled somewhat by the 1720s and Catholics and Protestants existed in a careful détente, but occasionally animosities flared up.[20] For example, when authorities discovered a Protestant school in 1735, several girls from Protestant families were forced into convents.[21] This simmering acrimony gave Protestant merchants a particular motive to direct their commercial efforts westward toward the Atlantic world rather than eastward toward Paris, and also provided incentive to undercut metropolitan authority when they could. Although by the eighteenth century Protestants no longer dominated La Rochelle's population—they had fallen to about one quarter of the total population by 1730—those who remained tended to be wealthy merchants, economic and political leaders of the city. They cultivated an unusually cohesive community, intermarrying among themselves and reinforcing business and kinship ties across generations. Merchants self-consciously extended these networks, based on family and cemented by religion, to Saint-Domingue.

All of the families and most of the slaves whose stories fill the subsequent pages had roots in the western province of Saint-Domingue as well as in La Rochelle. La Rochelle and the Antilles had a long history of association. Colbert chose the city as a supply base for the Caribbean colonies in the 1660s. In 1664, Rochelais bankers supplied capital for the establishment of the Compagnie des Indes Occidentales.[22] As a result, the port had become the main point of embarkation for trade with the Antilles by the end of the seventeenth century.[23] Soon the demand for colonial goods in Europe prompted merchants, traders, and would-be planters to turn their attention to Saint-Domingue, hitherto a colonial backwater and a secondary port of call to the more established Guadeloupe and Martinique.[24] By the 1720s,

Saint-Domingue emerged as a major profit center, and the Rochelais were well placed to take advantage.[25] Rochelais men poured into the colony bearing a colonial dream of getting rich quick, a difficult feat in tradition- and hide-bound Ancien Régime France.[26] The most successful of these emigrants established sugar plantations and did indeed make fortunes. Other lucky ones, especially those with family backing, connections, and mercantile experience, established merchant houses. Most, however, went the way of many poor whites in the colony, becoming plantation managers or overseers working for pay or exercising trades in Saint-Domingue's towns. Numerous men from La Rochelle, drawn by ties of kinship or neighborliness, settled in the western province, clustering in and around Port-au-Prince, Léogane, Saint-Marc, and Croix-des-Bouquets.[27] There were, of course, exceptions to this general geographic rule. Some Rochelais families certainly had links to other parts of the island and other colonies, the largest merchant houses even had multiple branches tying these places together.[28] Rochelais clustered in the west, making and losing fortunes alongside and in partnership with their neighbors from home, thus binding the city and the province tightly together.

This migration was motivated in part by the Revocation of the Edict of Nantes in 1685, which meant that opportunities for Protestants in La Rochelle were closing off just before Saint-Domingue became a French colony and as Rochelais commercial interests became increasingly westward facing. Religious persecution combined with economic need or the search for economic opportunity.[29] Rochelais migrants were generally landless laborers from the port's rural hinterland. They were joined by artisans whose skills were in high demand in plantation society such as carpenters, blacksmiths, joiners, and barrel makers, but also tailors, cobblers, masons, and cooks.[30] Large-scale events like bad harvests and declining industry or simply ongoing penury spurred some toward the Atlantic. Family and individual needs—for example the death of a parent, the practice of primogeniture, or a relative already established in the Antilles—impelled others.[31] After this initial generation, migration tended to follow lines of family and community, growing out of the practical comfort of knowing someone in a new place and the inscription in family memory of the possibility of emigration.[32]

Those migrants who arrived in the western province would have found multiple differences from France. Instead of the flat, marshy hinterland characteristic of La Rochelle, they encountered mountains and volcanic soil. While they left behind the frigid gray waves of the Atlantic, the cerulean

Caribbean, pleasantly warm, greeted them. In the summer, these migrants faced stifling heat and oppressive humidity; occasional earthquakes rocked the ground they stood on while hurricanes uprooted trees and caused mudslides and flooding. Even Port-au-Prince, the largest city in the west, stood in unfamiliar contrast to French cities of the west coast. Planned by military engineers, the streets were laid out at strict right angles and lined with mostly wooden houses and shops. Streets were unpaved, and habitually muddy. Yet Port-au-Prince, the administrative capital from 1752, was a secondary port of call to the larger, wealthier cultural and social center, Cap Français. With a population of about 6,200 residents in 1789 (plus an additional thousand soldiers and two thousand plus sailors), Port-au-Prince, was small but dynamic: the number of houses grew 31 percent between 1764 and 1778 (see Figure 2).[33] Other towns included Saint-Marc, surrounded by the fertile Artibonite Plain, a regional administrative center that boasted public amenities including a central square, a church, a prison, a public promenade, and a theater troupe.[34] "No place," claimed Moreau de Saint-Méry, "is an honest stranger welcomed with as much enthusiasm and affability as in Saint-Marc."[35] Léogane, with its fertile, well-irrigated plain, was slightly larger, boasting a church that was deemed "the most beautiful of the colony" until its ruin in the 1770 earthquake, a prison, a hospital, and at various times a theater troupe and garrisons of soldiers.[36] The Cul-de-Sac plain around Croix-des-Bouquets provided rich opportunities for cultivation, while its proximity to Port-au-Prince opened up commercial prospects. These, perhaps, attracted its higher than usual proportion of free people of color.[37] The town remained small, partly because legislation aiming to promote the development of Port-au-Prince forbade establishing businesses there.[38]

Of course, the most visible and notable element that distinguished the western province from La Rochelle was slavery and the presence of a large population of people of color, slave and free. By 1788, Saint-Domingue's population of 21,808 free people of color nearly equaled the population of 27,717 whites. Both were dwarfed by the over 405,500 slaves, who comprised nearly 90 percent of the populace.[39] By the end of the eighteenth century, Moreau put the population of the western province at 14,000 whites, two-thirds of whom were men; 12,000 free people of color, about 56 percent men, and 168,000 slaves, with men comprising slightly more than half.[40] This put the proportion of slaves to free people at about fifteen to one, 50 percent higher than the ten to one average in the colony as a whole.[41] This meant that for whites in Saint-Domingue, newly arrived immigrants and island born créoles

Figure 2. Nicolas-Marie Ozanne, *Vue du Port-au-Prince*, 1791. Engraving for Moreau de Saint-Méry, *Recueil de vues des lieux principaux de la colonie françoise de Saint-Domingue* (Paris: Ponce and Phelipeau, 1795). © Bibliothèque Nationale de France.

alike, interactions with people of color were an everyday occurrence. While the few whites who lived on plantations were surrounded primarily by slaves, in urban areas, particularly Port-au-Prince, free people of color made up 15 percent of the population and lived in highly integrated communities with whites.[42] They were each other's neighbors, patrons, clients, business associates, and customers. Whether in cities or on plantations, people of color and whites formed a variety of intimate associations.

In spite of their differences, La Rochelle and the western province shared a common marginality in the French empire. La Rochelle, a metropolitan city that was nonetheless peripheral, took its place as a port behind Nantes and Bordeaux; the western province took a backseat to the more productive and established north. Yet this common peripherality actually allowed networks to entwine in the two locales, weaving them together with personal ties to an extent that shifts the view of core and periphery, center and margin. The family was a nexus for this contestation, and closely examining family ties calls into question conceptions of empire as a top down enterprise emanating from the core. What emerges is an empire of multiple layers, entangled connections, and personal relationships built on bonds of intimacy.

Family, Household, and Intimacy

What exactly was intimacy in the eighteenth century? "It is said of the physical and of the moral," according to the *Encyclopédie*, which lays out two related but different meanings of the term: "These bodies enter into an *intimate* union; so it is synonymous with *close* and *deep*. They are *intimates*; they live in the greatest *intimacy*, which is to say that they do not have anything hidden nor any secret from one another. It is also related to the interior."[43] Historians have taken their cue from this last phrase, influenced by a distinction between private and public life that emerged in the nineteenth century.[44] Doing so has allowed scholars to construe the private sphere broadly and opened the door to critiques that questioned the public/private divide, particularly framing patriarchal power as both a public and a private concern.[45] Yet this critique has generally remained confined within interior spaces, which in the eighteenth century were rapidly taking on modern contours: dining room, parlor, and, most significantly, bedroom.[46] It has been about constructing the self and the self's relations with others, particularly the family, in private or semiprivate ways.

Yet intimacy in the eighteenth century existed far beyond the self, the nuclear family, and the four walls of a home. Within households that comprised multiple generations, blended families, servants, and others, it was difficult to "have anything hidden nor any secret from one another," even as private space was rapidly becoming a bourgeois ideal. Physical intimacy within the household was the rule, and family members and servants would have been intimately, sometimes forcibly, acquainted with each other's bodies in ways that are unfamiliar today.[47] They saw each other's bodily secretions, smelled each other's sweat, and knew each other's most personal peccadillos. Intimacy extended into the street, especially in cities where neighbors lived in close proximity, overheard each other's conversations, and knew each other's business. In urban areas bodily waste flowed freely in the gutters, and seeing men or women relieving themselves publicly was a far from unusual sight. Sexual intercourse, too, did not always occur within the privacy of the home.[48] Bodily and interpersonal intimacy thus permeated workplaces, professional organizations, and business networks, which themselves overlapped with households. Intimacy coexisted with collegiality.[49] It crossed lines of age, as children and adults lived and worked side by side. It transcended social status, as the rich and the poor lived in close proximity and interacted on a daily basis. It persisted across time and space, as correspondents shared personal thoughts and feelings, conversing with those who were absent through letters.[50] It ranged to communities based on religion, mutual interest, or common experience. Colonial practices complicated intimacy even more, highlighting how it confounded social and legal categories. It could cross lines of race, springing up in a variety of forms between whites and people of color. It could traverse status, existing between slaves and their owners. Intimacy was simultaneously private and public, familiar and strange, comfortable and uneasy, and sometimes terrifying.

While the family did not always delimit intimacy, family and household were important sites for intimate relations. Households, however, were not only affective units; they were also, perhaps even primarily, economic ones, where servants, employees, and other non-family members all contributed to making the household a productive economic unit. Indeed, in La Rochelle, households and businesses overlapped, and families did not separate household and business expenses.[51] Colonialism further complicated the family economy in appalling ways, as family members could be property; in the context of slavery, productive household labor took on a whole new meaning.[52] At the same time, colonial practices pushed the boundaries of French households at the very moment when historians have posited that they were contracting and shifting to less complicated nuclear families based on mutual affection.[53] Households in France included individuals of multiple generations, different social statuses, and a variety of bloodlines. Antillean households included all these, plus racial diversity that cut across all categories.

This study focuses closely on the "tense and tender ties" formed across lines of race in the context of empire to argue that these ties could be used to push against or maneuver around ruling practices, particularly policies that regulated racial categorization.[54] While sexual intimacy across racial lines in imperial contexts (and indeed in slave societies in general) is well established and an important category of cross-racial contact, it was by no means the only one.[55] Historians have generally equated intimacy with sexual congress between white men and women of color. Yet a multiplicity of intimate connections, including sexual service but also ranging from relations of trust based on common masculinity and shared labor, to kinship, to neighborliness, informed not only family choices and strategies, but also practices of colonial rule. What emerges is a broad catalogue of intimate experiences that extended well beyond either familial or sexual connections, and that sometimes rubbed uneasily against rapidly homogenizing ideals of the nuclear family. These intimacies were far from uniform or stable.[56] This book reconceptualizes intimacy to extend beyond blood relations or even the household, considering a broad array of ways in which individuals came into contact and built *"close* and *deep"* personal relationships with each other. Focusing on intimacies thus broadly defined reveals the "unsuspected ties" between the history of empire and the Atlantic world, on the one hand, and the microhistories of families and individuals, on the other.[57] It also offers the possibility of rethinking the role that intimacy and family played in the construction of gender and racial norms in the late eighteenth century.

History of Racial Thought

In 1797 Moreau de Saint-Méry published his *Description topographique, physique, civile, politique et historique de la partie française de l'isle Saint-Domingue* against a backdrop of bloody revolution and calls for equality and citizenship for all men on both sides of the Atlantic. Moreau has become famous for his pseudoscientific explication of 110 different racial combinations, even though the specific categories he elaborated never were actually used in Saint-Domingue.[58] However, he also laid out a much simpler taxonomy that has continued to influence how historians approach race in the French Atlantic world. He introduces readers to "three classes, almost physically distinct, that make up the population of the French Colony, rendering this population very different from that of European lands:" whites, slaves, and "affranchis," "more universally known by the name of *Gens-de-Couleur* or of *Sang-mêlés*."[59] It is these three classes that historians continue to use to study and categorize different social groups in Saint-Domingue, and more broadly in the French empire.[60]

Yet even Moreau points out the insufficiency of these categories. He continues, "This may even give a quite skewed idea of this Colony, to attribute to each of these classes a particular character, which serves to distinguish it completely from the other two."[61] Here, he emphasizes to readers the complexity of race as a social and cultural category not wholly linked to biology. A créole himself, he understood the subtle racial and social gradations whereby free people of color blended imperceptibly into whiteness, and he knew that gens de couleur entered into different types of intimacy with whites, making them valuable business associates, marriage partners, and allies. His readership in France would not have understood these subtleties.

The French social hierarchy had its own nuances, and there was little room for free people of color in it. Considering the disjuncture between colonial and French understandings of race nevertheless is essential because it helps to explain why French racial policies differed from colonial ones.

Exactly when racial thinking and racial categories began to emerge in the French empire has proved a controversial subject. Intellectual and legal historians point to a long history of French racial thinking that predates the emergence of plantation society in the French Antilles, generally dating it to the end of the seventeenth century.[62] Social historians have generally agreed that race solidified as a category over the course of the eighteenth century, although some highlight later time periods, especially after the Seven Years' War (1756–1763), as critical to this process.[63] Dominique Rogers has begun to question this chronology altogether in her careful study of free people of color in Saint-Domingue, positing instead a greater level of integration and flexibility in racial categories that persisted through the eighteenth century in spite of legislation aimed at regulating colonial society.[64] In multiple ways the debate among historians of the French empire recaps earlier debates among scholars who have attempted to trace the genealogy linking slavery and racial thought.[65] While fruitful, in focusing on chronology this debate nevertheless obscures key aspects of this emerging racial hierarchy.

This book posits that studying day-to-day life within the household complicates narratives of race as a solidifying category by demonstrating that individuals habitually crossed racial lines throughout the ancien régime. Intimacy across racial lines was a site of racial production and its profound disruption. This study shows that individuals approached and understood race as a fluid category with extremely unstable boundaries that they could adapt and subvert. In this, those who engaged with racial categories as a lived experience often pushed directly against legal and intellectual understandings of race. This opposition cut across racial lines and was the purview neither solely of whites nor of people of color, a fact that also attests to the ongoing flexibility of race as a category. In fact, not until the French and Haitian Revolutions did collapsing the distinction between slave and free status lead to solidification of racial categories.

This book moves between metropole and colony, focusing on individuals and families with connections in La Rochelle and the western province of Saint-Domingue. It alternates between case studies based on individual families (Chapters 1, 3, and 5), and chapters that use a wider lens to investigate how racial hierarchies were accepted, modified, and resisted (Chapters 2, 4, and 6). The case study chapters rely on family papers, including letters, business correspondence, plantation records, marriage contracts, and wills. The papers families chose to keep reveal how they saw themselves as a collectivity, in relation to others, and in relation to the world. Here, they show how families, households, and their individual members constituted and resisted formulations of race through interracial intimacies. The chapters focusing on racial hierarchies draw on sources that have more traditionally been used in studies of race and slavery in France and its colonies. These include laws, notary records, parish records, and administrative records of people of color in France. Chapter 1 explores the relationship between planter Paul Belin des Marais and his slave Alexis, an intimacy that crossed racial lines but depended on common masculinity. Chapter 2 reinterprets laws about slavery as a framework for investigating how slave owners established and maintained authority over their slaves in France. Chapter 3 looks at the Regnaud de Beaumont family to consider how families used contracts to try to prepare for the contingencies brought about by colonialism, and how colonial intimacies sometimes rendered these preparations useless. Chapter 4 argues that money and power were the determining factors in shaping white women's relationships with people of color. Chapter 5 examines how and why various members of the Fleuriau family defined the category of family differently. Chapter 6 considers people of color in France and how patriarchy shaped their articulations of their roles and justifications for their presence. The Epilogue brings the analysis into the Haitian Revolution, arguing that the conflict's politicization of race had the effect of solidifying racial categories.

As for Lizette, Hardy, and their owners, all of them had opportunities to shape what race meant on an intimate, daily level. This is their story.

CHAPTER 1

Proximity and Distance in Plantation Society

Until the day he died in 1769, Rochelais ship captain-turned-planter-turned-man of leisure Paul Belin des Marais ran his plantation as an Old Regime business, relying on and fostering personal connections based on family, place, and religion with people up and down the social ladder. For him, these bonds, founded on familiarity and shared experience, were more important than the emerging social category of race. This is not to say that Belin did not perceive social distinctions; he did, of course, with the fine-tuned eye of a parvenu, a merchant-*cum*-landowner whose wealth was of his own making. He also realized that his social inferiors, as well as superiors, could ease his path to success, and that it could only benefit him to build bridges across the social spectrum, bridges that could cross lines of race and even slavery.

His deathbed legacies to his live-in servants attest to his generosity, but also his keen awareness of what befitted a man of his social position. A cook, housekeeper, porter, lackey, coachman, gardener, concierge, and his wife's servant and chambermaid all benefited from his largesse, to the tune of 150-500 livres each, more than a year's salary for most servants.[1] He did not leave legacies to his coterie of slaves on his plantation in Saint-Domingue. This is not surprising: for a man of his wealth and position it would have been even more startling for him to include legacies to slaves in his will than to leave his servants out. Nonetheless, he did express a wish that his trusted slave Alexis be freed.

On the surface, the concrete monetary remuneration Belin left to his servants and his vague wish that one single slave receive his freedom seem exceedingly different legacies. Both bequests, however, demonstrate that Belin's approach to his relationships with his inferiors was firmly rooted in Old Regime practices. They were clients to his patron; they benefited from his largesse, maybe inflating his ego in the process, but he, too, benefited from these unequal vertical social ties.[2] His most intimate familiars included servants, certainly, as one would expect of a well-to-do man in the Old Regime, but as a plantation owner who had spent his prime in Saint-Domingue, they also included slaves.

Taking a close look at the workings of the Belin plantation in Saint-Domingue opens a window onto changing colonial and metropolitan understandings of race, slave ownership, and labor relationships. Over the course of the eighteenth century, all these categories underwent important shifts, although metropolitan and colonial viewpoints did not always keep pace with each other. In general, as race as a social category ossified, the state increasingly claimed a monopoly on policing the ever-solidifying boundary between slavery and freedom. At the same time, personal relationships grew less important as the economy moved towards an abstract rational calculation in which economic relations and the market mattered more than intimate connections. Plantations grew more factory-like, as did economic enterprises in France.[3] Belin and his trusted slave driver Alexis had to negotiate all these changes, yet throughout their reliance on each other changed little.

While interracial intimacy has usually been conceptualized along sexual lines between white men and black women, men of different races also had opportunities to form intimate bonds. Especially in the early years of a plantation, the day-to-day demarcation between the labor of owner and slave would have been muddy. French men eager to establish themselves might have spent much of their time working the land. Although unlikely to engage in hard field labor, they certainly would have supervised it as well as performed work such as keeping accounts and finding markets for their produce that in later, more prosperous years they might leave to agents or overseers. All these activities would have brought these white men into close contact with slaves, especially slaves who ranked highly in the plantation hierarchy, such as *commandeurs*, or slave drivers. Thus black slaves and their white owners sometimes labored side by side, though clearly their relationship—and the work they did—remained unequal. It would not be surprising, under such circumstances, if a slave owner identified one or two men alongside whom he had sweated and whom he knew and trusted as favorites.[4] Such an intimate relationship looked quite different from sexual intimacy between white men and enslaved women.

Such long-term intimate connections across lines of race also posed a more insidious problem than sexual intimacy from the perspective of officials attempting to regulate racial boundaries and slave society in general: it could disrupt rapidly solidifying acceptance of race as a social and legal category. While the same could be said of cross-racial relationships between men and women, relationships between black and white men posed a particular challenge to the social order because they did not have a gender hierarchy at their core. In the face of shared labor and experiences, racial distinctions did not, perhaps, seem as stark as they appeared to those without such personal bonds, including metropolitan administrators and observers. Intimacy, then, could operate as a platform from which slave owners and slaves could push against changing understandings of race, slavery, and plantation labor.[5] The long history of trust that existed between Belin and Alexis opened opportunities for the slave to act in ways that by the end of the eighteenth century slave owners not only would disavow, but also simply could not understand.

Belin's death in 1769 signaled a shift in management practices on his plantation, but it also was emblematic of a shift in plantation ownership on Saint-Domingue as a whole. As the century wore on, plantations passed from the hands of their original owners, many of whom had lived on the land themselves, at least for a while. Opportunities for cross-racial intimacy between men of different races diminished as absentee ownership became more common and colonial landowners frequently lived thousands of miles from their plantations.[6] Moreover, as generations shifted and a new cohort of owners inherited colonial property, they were increasingly unlikely to have even set foot on colonial land themselves. To such heirs, plantations were little more than columns of assets and losses; they approached plantation ownership in the rational spirit of capitalist production. In the absence of intimate relations with people of color engendered by a generational shift in colonial land ownership came a calcification of attitudes correlating dark skin and slavery.

Networking the Atlantic: Family Business

Belin's origins in La Rochelle well placed him to take advantage of the profitable possibilities of empire, first as a ship's captain and later as a plantation owner. As for many in La Rochelle, Belin's transatlantic trade was a family business. There were solid pragmatic and economic reasons behind this. With an ocean between a Rochelais merchant and his colonial trading partner, it was prudent to have someone on the other end that each could trust. It became common for the large Rochelais trading houses to have offices in Saint-Domingue, overseen by collateral kin such as cousins or nephews of the principal partners. So much the better, then, if this enterprise could extend to plantation ownership, thus comprising supply, distribution, and sale. Plantation ownership also provided a lucrative outlet for younger sons. Although merchants in La Rochelle did not practice primogeniture as did nobles, they kept their principal assets together to the greatest extent possible. This might mean, for example, leaving an estate in the hands of an older son and trading house under his direction, while providing a younger son with less consequential properties, *rentes*, or cash. Owning a plantation had the benefit of removing younger sons from competition with *frères aînés*, while still enabling them to contribute substantially to family assets, thus furthering fortune and position. This exact situation arose in the Belin trading house.

The Belin family had been merchants in La Rochelle since the sixteenth century. Ozée Belin, the patriarch of the clan in the early eighteenth century, held the office *ouvrier de pleine part de la monnaies royale*, as had his father and grandfather before him, and as would his eldest son. He was also a director of the Compagnie Royale de Saint-Domingue.[7] Ozée's second son, Paul, had to look elsewhere to make his fortune, although his prominent father's contacts and resources certainly paved his way. The Belin family's Protestantism may have also opened doors for the young Paul. While in the eighteenth century religious dissenters were excluded from numerous aspects of public and political life, they created commercial niches for themselves. The mass exodus occasioned by the 1685 Revocation of the Edict of Nantes actually facilitated Protestants' move into transatlantic trade by reinforcing trade networks created in the seventeenth century.[8] While multitudinous Huguenots left the Francophone world altogether, some sought refuge in the less stringent religious atmosphere of the French colonies.[9] Religious and trade networks thus overlapped, and the same merchants poised for involvement in Atlantic trade often already possessed colonial contacts among their *coreligionnaires*.

Thus, Paul Belin's reliance on family and religious connections as he embarked on a transatlantic career comes as no surprise. He began as a transatlantic ship's captain, a post that evokes a life of swashbuckling adventure on the open seas. While Paul did tend to make choices that reflected a strong streak of independence, such a position also necessitated backing and contacts on both sides of the ocean. He relied on his merchant relatives in La Rochelle and their extensive business connections all along the Atlantic coast of France to fund and outfit the ships he sailed to the French Caribbean. Although he had already been captaining ships for the Admiralty of La Rochelle, the young Paul got his big break in 1722, when his cousin Allard Belin formed a partnership with Sieur Guillemaut de Beauleau, a Protestant in Saint-Malo, to equip a ship to sail for the colonies.[10] They hired Paul Belin as their captain.[11] Belin strengthened the ties between the two merchant families when he married Françoise Guillemaut, Guillemaut de Beauleau's sister, in or shortly before 1722.[12]

While the precise date of his departure is uncertain, Paul Belin left France for the western province of Saint-Domingue in the late 1720s, leaving his wife his power of attorney and an extensive network of business contacts, including his merchant kin and hers.[13] In 1727 he purchased a plantation in the parish of Cordes-à-Violon on the Artibonite Plain, near the town of Saint-Marc and in the vicinity of other Rochelais planters.[14] From there he shipped indigo and cotton to his cousin Étienne Belin, a prominent merchant in La Rochelle who helped Paul maintain close ties with the extended Belin clan in the city. Paul's return to France in 1740, having made his fortune, further fortified these connections. Even after he settled in Paris with a much younger second wife, he expressed his explicit preference to have his colonially produced products sent to his cousin. His agents complied with these wishes and regularly sent Étienne Belin indigo and cotton produced on the plantation.[15]

Little information is available about Belin's score of years in Saint-Domingue and even less about the establishment of his plantation, but what remains implies his reliance on personal connections and networks, in the colony and La Rochelle. A letter Belin received from a business associate of his acquaintance, for example, illustrates the habitual overlap between business and family. He wrote, "I passed all the days of last week in La Rochelle. I saw there a part of your respectable family; M. Seignette your brother-in-law, [and] Messieurs Étienne and Allard Belin your cousins. They showed me much courteousness but I did not have the time to cultivate these excellent acquaintances. I was deprived of the honor of seeing Madame Seignette your sister, [as] she was a little indisposed. I stayed with M. Benjamin Seignette who is also your relative and with whom I have a business relationship."[16] Although not all French business letters so explicitly emphasized personal connections, doing so could only prove an advantage. Belin brought an assumption of the desirability of this intersection with him to Saint-Domingue.

Plantation Networks

In Cordes-à-Violon, Paul Belin encountered a social milieu quite different from that he had known back in La Rochelle. In the French port his family had a secure position, well-established reputation, and extensive connections. In contrast, he likely knew few people in Saint-Domingue when he first arrived in the 1720s, a decade of booming population and sugar production. In this context, carefully built networks of personal contacts could shift in a moment, as colonists returned to France, succumbed to the unfamiliar tropical climate, or merely continued roaming in pursuit of elusive fortune. Additionally, the prevalence of slavery and the sheer size of the enslaved population, which outnumbered whites in Saint-Domingue nearly eight to one, meant that Belin likely had extensive interactions with slaves, probably for the first time, although some of his Rochelais kin counted slaves among their households.[17] His habitual modes of making connections yielded little benefit for his interactions with this population. Yet in spite of the distance and ocean of differences that separated Saint-Domingue and La Rochelle, Belin continued to rely on his family and the people who knew them. Not only did they constitute his metropolitan trading partners, he also made efforts to associate with individuals who had connections with the Belin and Guillemaut clans back in France. Even in the cash-hungry colonies the captain-turned-planter persisted in prioritizing personal and family connections rather than financial outcomes when making business decisions, highlighting the persistence of Old Regime priorities even in the emerging plantation economy.

This reliance on family connections led Belin to Pierre Paumier, his neighbor and possibly his overseer, who originally hailed from Saint-Malo and had connections with the Guillemaut family.[18] The pair owned adjacent property. They took their association a step further, and agreed to a business transaction that would benefit them both: they contracted to share slaves. The specific conditions surrounding this agreement demonstrate the advantages personal connections could offer. Belin and Paumier entered into a partnership that would last for five years. Belin would contribute twenty-one slaves. Paumier would have the use of the slaves' labor immediately, but would pay his neighbor annual installments of 2,450 livres. After the term ended, each planter would keep half the slaves and half of any offspring they produced. In addition, their neighboring strips of land would merge and they would hold it jointly.

This agreement posed considerable advantages for Paumier, and suggests the possibility that Belin was doing him a favor. Paumier received the immediate use of twenty-one slaves, which he never could have afforded on his own.[19] Slaves were valued at two to three thousand livres for healthy men who worked in the field; skilled laborers could be worth over six thousand livres. The total sum Paumier paid his neighbor would scarcely have bought him five slaves, yet when the contract ended he would own ten. All he sacrificed was sole ownership of a strip of land, yet even that he would continue to hold jointly. Belin's motivations prove harder to discern. He seemed to reap little benefit from the society; he potentially could have sold a single slave for more than the 2,450 livres Paumier paid him annually for the use of twenty-one. What did he get out of the deal? Certainly the more prosperous man may have wanted to help out a less fortunate acquaintance. Belin's reasons for entering an agreement that perpetually left him holding the short end of the stick only became clear upon Paumier's death the following year. Close examination of Paumier's will demonstrates that the partnership agreement was a creative means of estate planning, a kind of insurance policy that equally benefited the two parties and rested on transatlantic connections.

When Paumier made his will, his widowed mother in Saint-Malo was certainly foremost in his mind. Transmitting money from one side of the ocean to the other was a difficult and messy business. Letters of credit could be lost or stolen in transit, unscrupulous credit holders might refuse payment, and the exchange rate between colonial and French livres proved challenging to calculate accurately. Completing the transaction through a contact who was established on both sides of the Atlantic proved an elegant solution, and Belin was well placed to do this because he and his wife presided jointly over common assets. Funds paid to one of them could be disbursed by the other without any other transfer of credit.

When Belin and Paumier made their partnership agreement, then, they took transatlantic circumstances into account. Already ill, Paumier made Belin his primary heir, leaving only one legacy of two thousand livres to his mother.[20] After his death Belin took possession of Paumier's estate, the land they held in common, and the slaves they owned jointly. The planter's wife, back in Saint-Malo, paid the legacy to Paumier's widowed mother.[21] Belin thus profited from their curious agreement after all.

At the crux of this unusual arrangement lay personal connections. Belin and Paumier could help each other because of the complex ties that made them mutually accountable within and beyond the reach of plantation society. Their association was cemented by common colonial experiences. Although their circumstances differed, they frequented the same places, ate the same type of food, knew the same people, and engaged in similar types of labor. If these experiences were the mortar that held their relationship together, their family ties back in France constituted the bricks from which it was built. The personal ties they shared formed the basis for their business relationship, and opened paths for them each to benefit in unusual ways that would not have been possible otherwise.

This vignette spotlights the importance of family connections, personal acquaintances, and common business interests in the complex enterprise of transatlantic trade. However, once Belin left Saint-Domingue, he could no longer rely as heavily on personal connections for running his plantation. Most of the contacts he had carefully amassed during his years there had died or moved. When he needed a new overseer for his plantation in 1768, nearly thirty years after his return to France, he therefore had to rely on his agents in Saint-Marc to choose a suitable man. An essential shift occurred, then, on Belin's plantation. Management by a resident owner who had its prosperity very much at heart differed considerably from oversight by a salaried overseer, supervised by agents who received a set commission. The difficulties that ensued on the Belin estate made clear the risks posed by transatlantic business unmoored from personal connections. As will be seen, the interests of white owners and overseers did not always coincide in spite of their common race. In contrast, the interests of absentee owners and the black slaves who worked the plantation could and sometimes did overlap.

Problems with Provisioning Plantations: Prunier and His Pigs

Belin returned to France around 1740. By the 1760s, he had settled in Paris with his youthful second wife. On the occasion of his marriage he wrote to his *procureur* in Saint-Domingue, "At my age one can take women or leave them, but in this country in old age one is vulnerable to the servants and poorly cared for."[22] After twenty years away from his plantation, Belin was out of touch with shifting colonial ideas. Although he maintained frequent contact with colonial business associates, his personal understanding of race and labor relations on plantations was dated, mired in the 1730s, when he had left Saint-Domingue as a man in his forties. Yet a lot had changed in

Saint-Domingue during his absence. When he left, Saint-Domingue's sugar boom was in full swing. By 1740 the colony alone exported as much sugar as all the English islands combined.[23] The tantalizing prospect of social mobility proved possible to a lucky few, like Belin, who arrived at the right time and before inhabitants had consolidated most of the region's desirable land into large plantations. At this point, race was a fluid concept in daily life. Free women of color with property were desirable marriage partners for white men, and free people of color of means studiously avoided racial labels.[24] People of color contributed to Saint-Domingue's economic well-being and social order, owning property, working for wages and as entrepreneurs, and living side by side with whites, particularly in urban areas.[25] Few laws restricted the actions or opportunities of free people of color; the Code Noir accorded them the same rights as whites, and explicitly authorized slave owners the right to manumit slaves as they wished.[26] Race, while certainly an important social category, was also a fluid one understood in relation to family and lineage as well as skin color, and mutable over an individual's lifetime.[27]

By the 1770s, the social organization of Saint-Domingue had changed dramatically. While the white population had only doubled since the 1730s, the free colored and enslaved populations had nearly tripled; slaves on the island outnumbered whites nearly thirteen to one.[28] The economic slowdown occasioned by the Seven Years' War led colonial elites to emphasize their commonalities with the metropole, leading to "a more explicitly biological racism" and increasing restrictions on people of color.[29] Moreover, manumission laws had tightened considerably, showing that slavery was increasingly understood as a permanent rather than a mutable state.[30] Yet Belin's understanding of colonial life stagnated. His association with Paumier in the 1730s was based on an Old Regime model of mutual interest, not an emerging colonial order defined by race. Belin continued to hold this view as evidenced by his reaction to the trouble that arose on his plantation in 1768, when he was an elderly gentleman of almost seventy-five years of age. At this moment Belin clashed with agents whose ideas about slavery and race had been shaped by the events of the intervening thirty years.

This gap in perspective, intensified by time, distance, and the difficulties of communication, led to problems when a newly appointed overseer, one Prunier, allegedly began to mistreat Belin's slaves and abuse his position on the plantation. At this point, Belin's more flexible concept of slavery as a changeable state that could end in manumission came into conflict with his agents' more rigid idea of the importance of maintaining a plantation hierarchy. The slave driver and *indigoteur* Alexis was at the heart of the controversy.[31] Belin's understanding of race as a flexible category and slavery as a state that could come to an end, compounded by his long personal relationship with Alexis, created a disconnect with his agents, and opened up an opportunity that Alexis himself could exploit.

Although Belin's agents de la Vincendière and Berard and his overseer Prunier provided him with regular reports, Belin continued to tap into his own personal networks as well. Even from the other side of the Atlantic he mobilized his relatives, friends, and associates to supplement the information his agents sent about his plantation. He relied on contacts who traveled to or lived in the colonies for first-hand accounts of his estate. Consequently, when a "very truthful" friend of Belin's passed through La Rochelle after returning from the colonies and told him that the new overseer Prunier was mismanaging his resources, he took the report extremely seriously.[32] Belin wrote immediately to his procureurs in Saint-Domingue, saying, "I know this gentleman particularly, and I have as much confidence in him as if I had seen it myself. 'Our overseer Prunier,' he told me, 'may think of your interests, but he thinks even more of his own; he has a quantity of livestock on your plantation, in any case, which he sells, and he also sells grains of all kinds that come from your plantation, while your slaves lack it.'" Belin continued, "I do not charge him [Prunier] with embezzlement, but his interests, which he has at heart, are very contrary to mine, and even very detrimental."[33] Consequently, he asked his procureurs to replace Prunier with an overseer "who did not have his own plantation [and] who was a sensible man, not violent towards my slaves, and who does not have poultry and livestock at my plantation[.] In order to make his life agreeable [he will have] a *négresse* and a *nègre* to serve him and a little hunting without employing anyone else in it, or selling anything."[34]

Belin made clear here that he expected that his interests and his overseer's would align to their mutual benefit and profit, as befitted patrons and clients. However, Prunier violated this expectation by milking what revenue he could from the plantation; he saw their relationship simply in terms of money and his own financial interest. With this irreconcilable difference in mind, Belin reiterated his wishes to dismiss Prunier in his next letter to his procureurs, and charged them particularly with visiting his plantation regularly to ensure that his specifications about its management were followed. For good measure he asked an old friend in the colonies to ensure that his wishes were carried out.[35]

Although Belin did not say that his informant accused the overseer of abusing his slaves, he nonetheless expressed particular concern about their well-being, an understandable worry considering that slaves formed a considerable part of his wealth.[36] "Make sure that my slaves have small pleasures," he instructed, "like raising pigs and poultry." He continued, "Make sure that the overseer drives them well and that he does not mistreat them except when they deserve it." Showing his vulnerability and conceivably a tinge of nostalgia, he added, "If I were on my plantation, I would take more care of it than ever[;] humanity must lead you all to that."[37] Although Belin viewed that "he [Prunier] drags from the plantation the most that he can, . . . I do not complain about my revenues."[38] Money, often framed as plantation owners' biggest concern, played no role in his complaints, emphasizing that this conflict centered on a growing disconnect over plantation management and the system of slavery that underwrote it.

This conflict over Prunier and his pigs points to the ongoing difficulties of provisioning plantations in Saint-Domingue. It also cuts to the heart of questions of responsibilities of slave owners by raising the issue of who was in charge of feeding slaves. The Code Noir specified quite precisely the provisions owners were required to furnish for their slaves: "Two and a half pots . . . of cassava flour or three cassavas weighing at least two and a half pounds each or equivalent things, with two pounds of salted beef or three pounds of fish or other things in proportion." This points to the different diets of slaves and Europeans, who preferred wheat to cassava, manioc, or yams.[39] Cane brandy could not be given as a substitute for food, and the Code "forbade them [owners] from unburdening themselves of the food and subsistence of their slaves by permitting them to work a certain day of the week on their own account."[40] Owners who did not follow these injunctions could face prosecution.[41] In contrast, for example, the Code Noir made no provision for the lodging of slaves. While possibly a protective measure on the part of the crown intended to guarantee a certain level of subsistence for slaves, these requirements also firmly positioned slaves as property, their labor working cash crops much more valuable than their efforts to grow food, and any labor on their own account seen as deeply suspect. However, leaving the provisioning of slaves in the hands of owners rendered slaves extremely vulnerable. At the end of the seventeenth century, the Dominican Jean-Baptiste Du Tertre observed, "As the nourishment of the *nègres* depends on their masters, it is [as] different in each case as the mood of those they serve. Some are better nourished than others, but to tell the truth they are all nourished in an absolutely pitiful manner, so if they do not have the means to provide for themselves, they suffer endlessly."[42]

Pigs offered a solution. Cheap to feed and occupying little valuable space, they could provide slaves with relatively affordable protein. In spite of the Code Noir's restrictions, many owners either required slaves to raise their own food or gave them tacit permission to do so. Priests reporting their journeys to the islands had long noted the centrality of the practice of raising pigs to feed slaves. In 1722, the Dominican Jean-Baptiste Labat identified potatoes as slaves' major source of nutrients, but added that "they are permitted to raise pigs, and they can do it very easily with the branches or the stalks and leaves of potatoes, the head of the sugar cane, and the heavy foam when they can have it."[43] Half a century earlier, Du Tertre explained how slave owners could turn this practice to their own benefit as well.

> They [the slaves] in the past were permitted to feed pigs, but the great amount of care they require made them [the slaves] neglect those of their Masters which they left to die of hunger; [masters] were obliged to take this privilege away from them. Sieur d'Ontage who is loved by his slaves, feeds them in a manner, that in place of costing him is quite useful to him: because he gives them [his slaves] from time to time five little piglets to feed, of which he takes three of his choice for himself, and leaves two for them: this makes it be that they raise all with the same care, and as they all have an interest in seeing them well fed, it is up to him who feeds them, I'll be dashed if there is not one among them who does not bring them a brew of creeper leaves, or potato stalks, when they return from work at midday and evening. After they are killed, he gives them others, and thus the slaves are well nourished and it does not cost him anything.[44]

For slaves and overseers, then, raising their own livestock could have important nutritional and potentially financial benefits. While Belin apparently accepted his slaves' customary right to raise pigs, he viewed his overseer's similar attempts as poaching on his property and prerogatives as an owner.

Belin's explicit instructions to dismiss his overseer elicited no response from his agents in Saint-Marc. Although he sent letters in June, July, August, and October 1768 reiterating his wishes, by November he still had not received confirmation that his orders had been carried out. This was a difficult situation indeed. Over four thousand miles separated Belin from his plantation, and his economic prosperity lay in the balance. Faced with their possible negligence, he urged his agents to choose an overseer who met with the approval of one person he knew: his slave Alexis. He wrote to his procureurs, "As you know, I have my slave Alexis, subject of trust; the overseer must have a certain regard for him. Messieurs Fulliot and Raulin there [in Saint-Domingue] stress this confidence; I beg you to have it also, and to commend to him a new overseer."[45]

Slave drivers such as Alexis occupied positions of responsibility on large plantations like Belin's. Regularly the most highly valued male slaves, they worked closely with overseers or resident owners.[46] Belin's attitude toward Alexis, combined with Alexis' relatively advanced age, intimates that the slave had been working the plantation for a number of years, likely since Belin's own days in Saint-Domingue. Given subsequent events, Belin and Alexis probably developed a working relationship, perhaps even a degree of familiarity beyond that which normally arose between male slave owners and male slaves. This relationship was undoubtedly incredibly complex. We can imagine that Alexis may have carefully curried his owner's favor, playing into a paternalistic form of patronage that Belin wanted, waiting for carefully culled moments when he could tap into Belin's framework to ask for favors or benefits. If this was his plan, it worked; Belin viewed Alexis as a worthy "subject of trust."

At long last the agents responded to Belin; his final letter crossed their tardy response mid-journey. Yet in spite of the plantation owner's multiple injunctions, his agents hesitated to follow his orders to replace the overseer Prunier. They took a delicate approach that attempted to keep their own relationship with Belin intact. Hesitating to defend Prunier outright, they warned that "good men are scarce, and most rare."[47] Although they acknowledged Belin's ultimate authority by promising to carry out his wishes to replace Prunier, they raised doubts about the veracity of the accusations against the overseer—accusations which, by implication, charged them with the mismanagement of the plantation as well. In so doing, they worked to keep plantation hierarchies intact. "Without laying claim to authorize or excuse S[ieu]r Prunier," they wrote, "we cannot, Sir, excuse ourselves from saying to you that the wrongs he has done to you have been much exaggerated." They quickly put to bed any thoughts of their own laxity by reassuring Belin that "M. de la Vincendière [one of the agents] has often been on your plantation, where he has always found everything in a very good state," and even that "the slaves never lack for anything."[48] The agents, therefore, quickly closed ranks with the overseer along racial lines.

They did not disavow the alleged abuses altogether, for to do so would have been to contest Belin's authority directly and thus to challenge the plantation hierarchy from a different quarter. Instead, the agents subtly turned the suspicion to another possible culprit. "The number [of Sieur Prunier's pigs] is less than that of S[ieu]r Porte, the doctor," they slid into their letter. After defending Prunier and casting suspicion elsewhere, the agents casually let drop, "incidentally, all your slaves have pigs. They have as gardens not levees because they are too labor-intensive to maintain, but a quite large terrain next to Madame Fouchard. In a word, they lack for nothing."[49] The agents also clearly saw Alexis as a key player on the plantation, for they began to levy accusations of his misconduct even before they received Belin's commendation of the commandeur. Belin's letter of 22 November 1768 recommending Alexis and the agents' letter of 21 November censuring his conduct were written just one day apart and crossed each other mid-journey. Although Prunier was accused of keeping forty-four pigs, they said that "among that number there are six that belong to your slave driver Alexis, and four to another of your slaves."[50] This last accusation may have been born of desperation, as the agents sought to cast blame everywhere but on themselves. However, given Belin's letter expressing his faith in Alexis, this was the shot that came closest to home. "These," the agents swore, "are the facts taken from the plain and exact truth."[51]

The conflict over Prunier and his pigs points to the ways distance shaped the fraught relationships between plantation owners, overseers, and slaves as old understandings of hierarchies and relationships confronted new. Overseers occupied an ambiguous position on the plantation as wage earners, the equals of neither the owners nor the slaves.[52] Distance complicated these difficult relationships, inhibiting owners from keeping tabs on rivalries or making their own judgments about whose word to believe. In this case Belin had to weigh the communications he received by letter against his own fading impressions, trying to make decisions based on limited evidence about what course of action would best benefit his current and future interests and the plantation as a whole. Belin's insistence that his slaves be allowed to "raise pigs and poultry" even while he wanted to dismiss his overseer for the same practice drives home that he viewed similar actions by his slaves and his overseer quite differently. At the root of these differences lay his consistent assumption that everyone on the plantation should act for its—and his—good. For his slaves, he assumed that raising livestock fit into this rubric because they had immediate, personal need for the food they raised. Not so his overseer Prunier; Belin saw the overseer's use of anything grown on the plantation as illegitimate, tantamount to embezzlement. From this point of view, Belin had no choice but to dismiss Prunier.

Belin spent the winter laid up with gout, during which time he realized that battling his agents in Saint-Domingue was not in his best interest. When the new year dawned, he reaffirmed that "I have made my choice to discharge S[ieu]r Prunier. My intention has always been that my slaves should have abundant supplies and even little pleasures." Yet in the end he underwent a change of heart, forced by circumstances to accept his agents' recommendations, at least in part. He agreed to keep Prunier as overseer, and even to raise his wages five hundred livres per year "on the condition that, as he promised, he decrease his herd of pigs, which he must have only for his own consumption; an overseer should not sell anything for his own profit."[53]

To his agents and his overseer putting such faith in a slave, particularly at the expense of a white overseer, was an egregious violation of the plantation hierarchy. To them, personal relationships and trust mattered less in a changing colonial social order. His agents only knew half the story; when they learned the rest, years later, their outrage likely was further incensed. This was just the beginning of a long controversy over Alexis that brings into high relief the extent to which concepts of race and slavery changed in Saint-Domingue from the 1730s to the 1760s. This case also implies that the presence of former colonists in France unexpectedly staved off broad metropolitan acceptance of those changes until a new generation of absentee owners, heirs of the former colonists, took over running the plantation.

Alexis: Slavery and Patronage

By the late 1760s a new conceptualization of slavery as a strictly hierarchical relationship with racial difference at its core began to solidify in Saint-Domingue. Legal measures increasingly classified individuals by race rather than enslaved or free status.[54] At the same time, colonial courts occasionally prosecuted owners for the abuse of slaves.[55] This development points to an increasing effort by colonial administrators to regulate race and relations of slavery. "Renegade planters" who abused their slaves to excess put the entire plantation system at risk, so the thinking went, because their cruelties might prompt slave marronage or even revolt.[56] This marked change coincided with a rise in absenteeism after the Seven Years' War. By the war's end, Belin had already been an absentee landowner for over two decades. Yet as long as he owned his plantation, his way of conducting business changed little. After Belin died in 1769 at the age of about seventy-five, a struggle over the estate ensued that highlighted the contrast between Belin's old fashioned proclivities and newer, more rationalized approaches to plantation management. Alexis found himself stuck in the middle. Emancipation, as promised by Belin, frequently was seen as the ultimate reward for a slave's loyal service, but Alexis was also subject to the deep suspicions of Belin's heirs on whose goodwill his freedom rested.

As Belin was childless, his nieces and nephews inherited the estate. Half went to his sister's children, the Seignette nieces and nephews in La Rochelle, and the other half to the children of his wife's sister in Saint-Malo, named Hallays.[57] This was an extremely valuable inheritance. Decades later, even after the upheavals of the Haitian Revolution, the French government judged the property to be worth more than any other in the parish Saint-Marc.[58] Yet with the sole exception of Alexandre Hallays, the Belin heirs would never set foot on this valuable piece of property. As would become common as ownership shifted from a generation of men who had lived in the colonies to their children, Belin's heirs had no firsthand experience with Saint-Domingue or colonial slavery. This meant they went about managing their plantation extremely differently from their uncle. Whereas Belin visited the colonies as a ship's captain before setting up residence as a plantation owner, his heirs may have read travelogues about Saint-Domingue to learn about their new property. While Belin experienced the hardscrabble difficulties of starting a plantation, his heirs might have heard dinner table stories from their uncle about the far-away land. The heirs certainly read the letters sent to them by the plantation's procureurs and overseer, but they could not picture the place as their uncle could, nor did they understand the rhythm of plantation labor from first-hand experience as he had. Their views on colonialism and slavery were formed in France, not forged through colonial life.

Their views on the issue of plantation management would become clearer after a close inspection of their late uncle's papers, which revealed that Alexis had played a much larger role in the accusation against Prunier than anyone except Belin himself had previously suspected: *he* was the correspondent in whom Belin expressed "as much confidence . . . as if I had seen it myself." This discovery prompted a flurry of correspondence between the Seignettes in La Rochelle and the Hallays in Saint-Malo. Belin's nephew Pierre-Henry Seignette, who acted as the spokesperson for his siblings and cousins, wrote to his Saint-Malo cousin Alexandre Hallays to inform him of a particularly interesting turn of events. "There turned out to be a stir on the plantation," he wrote excitedly.

> Alexis the slave, slave driver with whom my uncle took the most extreme care, wrote to him a year ago, and raised with him complaints against M. Prunier, who is the overseer. He [Alexis] accused him [Prunier] of embezzling the [labor of the] slaves to have them work his own plantation, and that he made off with their supplies for his animals, which he raised in great quantity. My uncle wrote to Monsieur Payen and Messieurs de la Vincendière and Berard, without saying from where he was informed, to send this overseer packing. They did not do it and wrote that although he had had some lapses, that he had reformed. He [Alexis] must have been suspected of complaining at some point, for [before the incident] everyone said that he was a good slave, [but] it was added after that he was an insolent who was spoiled by the friendship that he had been shown.[59]

In the 1780s, colonial officials and the Conseil supérieur in Port-au-Prince were taking accusations of slave abuse seriously in an attempt to stop planter brutality, even going so far as to permit slaves to charge their owners before a prosecutor. A number of slaves accused their overseers of mistreatment, though with mixed results.[60] Slaves on the Fleuriau and Cazeau plantations, for example, denounced their overseer for excessive abuse, particularly against new and pregnant mothers, and forcing them to work on his own plantation at the expense of their owner.[61] Yet the conflict on the Belin plantation, which occurred in the late 1760s, reveals that even before officials cracked down on "renegade planters" slaves took advantage of absenteeism to drive a wedge between planters and owners. Trusted slaves such as Alexis could raise their owner's suspicions, placing themselves on the same side against overseers who, in abusing slaves, went counter to owners' interests. By taking this action, Alexis subtly shifted the terms of his relationship with Belin. The letter informing Belin of Prunier's alleged treachery positioned Alexis as someone who had his patron's best interests at heart—the place Belin believed Prunier the overseer was supposed to occupy. This allowed Alexis to approach Belin less as a supplicant than as an informant, knowing he had access to information Belin wanted. Alexis thus also operated within a model that allowed flexibility within a multilevel hierarchy.

While Belin apparently trusted Alexis implicitly and took him at his word, the planter's heirs were less willing to do so. This indicates that they were influenced by changing ideas about race in France, unburdened, unlike their uncle, by personal ties to the colony. Although the heirs viewed Alexis with suspicion, they were also, perhaps, swayed by their uncle's trust in him. Absent a trustworthy associate in the colony to help them discern fact from fiction, the heirs needed a way to obtain more information. Alexandre Hallays was dispatched to Saint-Domingue, charged with taking stock of their newly acquired colonial asset.[62] As he prepared to depart, Seignette implored him to "inform yourself in secret, my dear cousin, of the truth of this affair when you are there."[63]

As the ongoing conflict over Alexis reveals, the "truth of this affair" may have been harder to establish than the heirs supposed. From their comfortable hearths in France, it would have been easy to assume that slavery and freedom were absolute states, but in Saint-Domingue many formerly enslaved people of color lived as if emancipated, even if their owners had not taken the legal steps necessary to formalize their free status. Shortly after Belin's death, his agents sent his widow a letter that confirmed his intention to free Alexis. "The *nègre* Alexis," they wrote, "will . . . enjoy the fruit of the attachment that his late master had for him[.] He [that is, Belin] had previously given the order to the late M. Raulin [the agent] to give him his liberty."[64] Alexis, then, trusted by Belin, likely lived as free even before Belin's death, even though administratively and legally he remained a slave.

Belin took steps in death that he had not taken in life to secure Alexis's administrative freedom, feasibly recognizing that his heirs would not understand the fine-grained distinctions of freedom familiar to colonists. Belin expressed his wish that Alexis be freed, and endowed "the slave Alexis with the right and ability of the said slave to take from the plantation whichever *négresse* he would like to choose."[65] This in itself showed how out of touch Belin had become with Saint-Dominguan cultural norms: in the 1770s and 1780s, slave owners freed less than three tenths of a percent of their slaves annually.[66] Furthermore, as early as the 1760s planters increasingly ceded control over manumission to the state, a development of which Belin was likely unaware.[67]

It is possible that Belin used the promise of freedom as a carrot to manipulate his slave, or alternatively, as the heirs believed, he really did feel "friendship" towards him. In either case, Belin unknowingly undermined rapidly solidifying categories of race by reinforcing masculine solidarity across racial lines. Giving Alexis "a *négresse* of his choice" did much more than reinforce masculine ties by reaffirming patriarchy. For Alexis, choosing a woman meant he was not only a free man, but also a head of household. When Belin's agents in Saint-Domingue wrote "the slave Alexis will . . . enjoy the fruit of the attachment his late master had for him," they referenced not only his freedom, but also his masculine authority over his wife.[68] This was a powerful gift indeed, as contemporary ideas about slave masculinity emphasized their virility but never their responsibility, the main measure of manliness in France.[69] By giving Alexis a woman, Belin made him a man.

While Belin's will assumed the conditions of an earlier decade still applied and framed Alexis' freedom as a personal matter between slave and owner, his heirs came to realize that it was no such thing. Freeing a slave was not as simple as their uncle's breezy wishes suggested. As a result of the colonial struggles between elite planters, the crown, and *petits blancs*, slave owners alone did not have the power to transform slaves into freedmen; the regulating oversight of the colonial bureaucracy modulated this authority. Manumission laws charged colonial administrators with policing the boundary between slave and free, taking the demarcation of status out of the possibly capricious and easily influenced hands of slave owners. This bureaucratic intervention meant that informal ties between slaves and owners carried progressively less weight as slavery intensified in the second half of the eighteenth century.[70] In order to formally manumit a slave, owners had to obtain permission from colonial administrators. After 1769 the hefty manumission tax typically amounted to around one thousand livres for a female slave and five hundred livres for a male slave, the disparities in these amounts reflecting that manumitting a female slave also meant freeing her descendants.[71] Although administrators liberally granted permission for manumission, these substantial taxes could discourage all but the wealthiest and most determined manumitter. In the shadows of the official manumission process there emerged a continuum of liberty where some former slaves lived as if free even if they had not been formally manumitted, the so-called *libres de fait*.[72] The Belin heirs adhered to the letter of their uncle's wishes and began the manumission process soon after his death. Although a severe earthquake in Port-au-Prince destroyed the Intendant's offices, rendering him unable "to ratify the liberty of the slave Alexis," the former slave driver finally received his formal manumission in 1771.[73] Two years had passed since Belin's death. During this time he evidently continued to make trouble by upsetting hierarchies, because when the manumission process reached completion Belin's nephew Seignette wrote, "We are quite relieved to see the affair of the slave Alexis finished."[74]

For Alexis, it is possible that emancipation did not bring the benefits Belin may have assumed it would. Slave owners could use manumission not only as an incentive to inspire loyalty or hard work, but also as a way to avoid supporting slaves who were old or infirm.[75] By this time, Alexis must have been quite aged, maybe around the same age as Belin himself; as early as 1765, plantation records classified him as asthmatic and infirm.[76] If this were the case, his opportunities for supporting himself—and the "*négresse* of his choice"—would have been limited. He may have felt that remaining on the plantation was his only or best option, and some evidence intimates that he sought to stay there. His new owners back in France did not really understand how a free black man could fit into a plantation framework. After Alexis' freedom was finally ratified Seignette wrote to the procureur, "If you believe him [Alexis] useful to the plantation, do not neglect to attach him to it. We believe however that one must only have a limited confidence in these people. They are almost all rascals and liars. They are naturally enemies of those who command them. You must know better than us, and know what degree of confidence one can accord them."[77] Finally formally free, Alexis remained attached to the plantation, subject to the whims of his former owner's heirs and at the mercy of their overseer.

The Heirs and Rational Profitability

Belin's heirs knew little about running a colonial plantation or life in Saint-Domingue. Although one could imagine this younger generation gathered around their gouty uncle, listening eagerly as he related tales of adventure or perchance not so eagerly as he bloviated on about his colonial experiences, their knowledge of plantation life was secondhand, at best. Moreover, as residents of France, not Saint-Domingue, their ideas of land management, slavery, and racial difference reflected metropolitan thinking. From the outset, the heirs adopted a system of rational land management that approached racial categorization and enslavement as binary categories. This was a far cry from their uncle's more personal approach, which had for years laid the groundwork for the plantation's economic success. If they encountered people of color outside the overseers' reports, it was only a rare happenstance, not a daily occurrence. For them, people of color figured only in the context of profit and loss. Their reliance on overseers' reports put them in alliance with their colonial representatives, but as Belin's problems with Prunier had shown, overseers' and owners' interests did not necessarily align. Further, overseers were not the only inhabitants of plantations with access to the written word, as Alexis' letter vividly illustrated. The heirs looked to these reports as their primary and possibly only source of information on plantation life. This had profound effects on how slaves were treated.

After Belin's heirs took possession of the plantation, they managed it in a markedly different way from their uncle. With no colonial experience themselves, they drew instead on theories of rational land management emerging in France, particularly physiocracy, and proved susceptible to literature calling for ameliorated treatment of slaves, not as a humanitarian measure but as a way to maximize profitability.[78] The changes in plantation management that took place in the late 1770s and 1780s signified that by the time absentee landownership became more prevalent, understandings of race began to ossify. Landowners with direct colonial experience continued to take a flexible approach to race, viewing race and slavery as two separate and fluid categories and even understanding racial categorization as something that could change. In contrast, absentee owners such as Belin's heirs approached race and enslavement as absolute categories, purely a matter of black and white.

A series of long-overdue reforms to the Code Noir took effect beginning in 1784, a century after the first promulgation of the laws. This overhaul aimed to prevent the types of abuses of which Alexis accused Prunier, including brutality against slaves and managing more than one plantation.[79] In an effort to hold overseers accountable, the Code mandated that once a month overseers send absent owners a careful accounting of the births and deaths of slaves and livestock, as well as financial accounts, the names of any other workers employed on the plantation, and a report on anything else affecting its administration. It also made provision for removing overseers and agents who did not follow these provisions, and put legal mechanisms in place to ensure that these new laws were followed. Planters in Saint-Domingue vociferously and effectively objected to these reforms. The Conseils supérieurs in Cap Français and Port-au-Prince delayed registering the laws, issued remonstrances, and held debates.[80] In response, the 1785 amendments softened the 1784 measures by offering overseers an opportunity to appeal allegations of abuse, legitimizing the physical punishment of slaves, and emphasizing that slaves owed "respect and obedience" to overseers as well as owners.[81]

Changes in how the Belin plantation was managed often anticipated the revisions to the Code Noir, implying that the law aligned more closely with metropolitan understandings of plantation management than with colonial ones. The major division that prompted the pushback against the reforms, then, was not between plantation owners and overseers, but rather between French and colonial understandings of how plantations should be run. By 1777, it had become standard practice on the Belin plantation for the overseer to send the heirs comprehensive reports that included the numbers, occupations, and values of slaves, well in advance of the 1784 revisions to the Code Noir that required such measures.[82] These reports sketched only a sparse picture of plantation life, focusing primarily on the plantation's assets, a concern that had slaves at its center because of their market value and the value of their labor. Each annual report laid out slave demographics, the process and seasons of cultivation of crops, and the types of livestock raised on the property. The reports provided little insight into the texture of plantation life or relationships, information Belin would have already known but his heirs did not. A characteristic report, drawn up by the overseer of the Belin plantation in October 1777, included a complete list of the slaves sorted into categories according to sex, with separate lists for men, women, boys, and girls. The overseer numbered each slave and listed their names, "nations," and ages.

The Belin heirs also introduced other reforms that they may have seen as progressive, including the practice of tipping slaves for exceptional service. Owners had long hired out slaves for their own profit, and sometimes slaves could even work on their own account, enabling self-purchase, but this new practice was different, anticipating similar measures in other parts of the Caribbean by several decades.[83] Rather than authorizing a slave's ownership over his own time to make a profit as he could, they remunerated slaves either for actions deemed out of the ordinary, or for doing their own work well. In 1786, for example, the overseer listed a payment of 8.5 livres "to a slave of Lemere for capturing a maroon slave," and another payment of the same amount "to the slave of Madame Couturier for a maroon slave."[84] More notably, the 1786 overseer's report lists "tips for the two indigo makers" of thirty-three livres each.[85] Indigo makers occupied privileged positions among slaves; as skilled men, they were among the most costly slaves on a plantation.[86] On the Belin habitation, the two indigoteurs, men in their late twenties at the height of their strength and skill, were valued at 6,600 livres each.[87] Their sheer worth explains why it might have been necessary to offer them incentives: their rebellion, from work slowdowns to marronage, could spell disaster for the plantation. Monetary rewards given for the labor of slaves also highlight the ways in which absenteeism changed labor relations between slaves and owners. Monetization of this relationship was not necessary in earlier days, when personal connections provided both carrot and stick. Tipping became a necessary policy only when absenteeism erased daily intimacies between owners and slaves.

Women, whose labor tended to be considered less skilled and therefore less valuable than men's, had fewer opportunities to accrue cash rewards.[88] Nonetheless, owners did set great store by enslaved women's reproductive potential. By the 1760s, rising concerns about slave demography coincided with two key trends: criticisms of abusive treatment of pregnant women and mothers of newborns by slave owners, and changing ideas about European women that increasingly emphasized the importance of their roles as wives and mothers.[89] Perhaps in response to these evolving ideas, the 1784 revisions to the Code Noir included provisions offering pregnant women some measure of protection.[90] Pregnant and nursing women were to have reduced work hours, and mothers of six or more children would progressively gain exemption from field labor based on the number of children they had.[91] These provisions closely followed the critic of slavery Abbé Guillaume-Thomas-François Raynal's injunctions to "break the irons of mothers who had raised a considerable number of children to the age of six years."[92] In the wake of these reforms, planters offered mothers hospital care, gifts of food or clothing, or honorific distinctions more frequently.[93]

The Belin heirs had measures rewarding women for their fertility firmly in place by 1774, twelve years before legal requirements were established to ameliorate the labor conditions of pregnant and nursing women. In a letter to his agent in Saint-Domingue, Belin's nephew Seignette wrote, "we think as well, Sir, that it would be good to recompense the women who raise their children with care; humanity requires that one treat them positively; it is further in the interest of the Proprietors, [as] Créole *nègres* have a greater value than *nègres* brought over by boat."[94] By 1786, women who successfully birthed infants systematically received payments of thirty livres.[95] Two years later these payments were still being made.[96] The consistency of these payments reveals a coherent policy rewarding slave women's fertility. The fact that this policy anticipated the law by more than a decade hints that the Belin heirs were more influenced by metropolitan ideas about slavery, including criticisms of it, than by colonial fears of slave revolt. It also points to the importance of these metropolitan ideas and absentee practices in shaping the 1784 Code Noir revisions.

Seignette and the other Belin heirs must have emphasized that they considered the birth rate a primary measure of the plantation's success to their colonial agent, for he went to great lengths to reassure them that their slave population was increasing in a satisfactory manner. In one of his regular letters to the Belin heirs, he wrote, "I see, Sirs, that the details that you were given about the plantation . . . brought you great pleasure, as did the inventory with which you were provided[.] On that occasion I observed to you that it was considered superfluous to repeat in the report the deaths and births." In spite of his stated reluctance to repeat himself, the number of births evidently was so noteworthy that he felt the need to reiterate it several times in the same letter:

> The births between 31 January 1790 and 8 October 1790 are included in the inventory under the articles "*Négrillons*" and "*Négrittes*" as you will realize in glancing attentively over it. You will find under the heading of *négrillons* St. Philippe, son of Heleine, born 15 February 1788, classified as number 14, as well as the other four [slave boys] who follow[.] [Each slave was numbered and listed by name in this inventory.] Under the heading of *négrittes*, Charlotte, daughter of Monique born 21 February 1788, classified as number 21, and the four others [slave girls] who follow, until number 25. These, then, are the births in order.[97]

Although the Belin heirs may have been the driving force behind this scrutiny of women's fertility, their colonial agents certainly responded to it, maybe in the end impelled by the 1784 revisions to the Code Noir. This shift signaled a new interest in reproduction as part of the plantation's productive labor, one that could have been responding to abolitionist calls for ameliorated conditions for slaves, but one that also had productivity and profit at its core.

This case exemplifies how absenteeism might have changed owners' ideas about how best to manage their overseas plantations. Because second-generation owners were more likely to live in France, this generational shift in plantation ownership brought with it the increasing influence of metropolitan ideas on plantation management. While changes in the management policies on the Belin plantation seemed to accord with the 1784 revisions to the Code Noir, this shift was not inspired by law. That the policies anticipated the law indicates that by the 1780s the deepest divisions in management philosophies ran between metropole and colony, not between owner and overseer.

From the 1720s to the 1780s a profound shift took place in the relationships that could evolve between plantation owners and slaves. The example of the Belin plantation shows that this transformation stemmed in part from a generational shift in plantation ownership as an initial generation of owners who had lived in Saint-Domingue on plantations in close personal proximity to their slaves gave way to a second generation with no personal colonial experience. Paul Belin des Marais and many of his contemporaries lived and worked alongside slaves and free people of color. Although they were clearly firm supporters of the racial and racist hierarchies inherent in the plantation system, their personal experience meant that they had a complex, nuanced understanding of race. Belin himself formed intimate relationships across lines of race, notably with his slave Alexis. For absentee owners, such opportunities disappeared. Absenteeism thus had significant repercussions for how a plantation was run and, above all, how hierarchies of race were understood and enacted.

For Paul Belin des Marais, personal relationships took precedence. This strategy worked well for him, enabling him to profit while also supporting those with whom he was connected. Yet time and distance stretched the limits of his networks, and when conflicts arose on the plantation long after his departure, his personal connections ultimately proved of little use. Prunier stayed, as his agents pressed, and Belin had little choice but to accept their actions.

The next generation of owners, Belin's heirs, approached plantation management in a very different way. For them, personal interactions with slaves were not even in the bounds of possibility, and they accepted long-distance oversight by proxy as the norm. This distance allowed the heirs to remove personal favoritism, obligation to others, and reciprocity from the equation, replacing them with more coherent policies based on practical calculations of profit that incentivized certain types of labor. Drawing on Enlightenment ideas about rationalized labor and humanitarian amelioration of the conditions of slaves, they exhibited a fundamentally different attitude towards slaves than their uncle. As his connection with Alexis demonstrates, Belin fostered reciprocal relationships with at least some slaves, acknowledging that he, as well as they, could gain from such an association. For his heirs, slave/owner relations were much more one-sided, and they approached

slavery and freedom, black and white, as binary categories. While they undoubtedly saw their rational policies as providing advantages for slaves, the
only way they thought their slaves could benefit them was through productive or reproductive labor.

The slave Alexis was caught in the middle of this shift. He managed to
squeeze through the cracks, his manumission guaranteed by Belin's heirs' desire to carry out their uncle's wishes. The conflict Alexis's intervention caused
and the heirs' inability to understand the relationship between Belin and the
slave vividly accentuate how shifts in understandings of race and slavery had
begun to foreclose certain opportunities for personal connections between
slaves and slave owners.

CHAPTER 2

Legitimating Authority

Slave owners perceived the ways intimacy across racial lines could open opportunities for slaves to challenge their chattel status, sometimes legally but other times simply by extending their networks beyond their owners. Such networks could include individuals who were willing to do slaves favors or speak for them, or institutions that provided an alternative locus of authority. In France, slavery was relatively uncommon and owners' control more tenuous than in Saint-Domingue. Additionally, slaves' relative freedom of movement in the metropole meant most had ample opportunity to develop contacts with people or institutions that might be sympathetic to their plight. This posed a challenge for slave owners, who sought at all costs to prevent slaves from forming intimate bonds of friendship, mutual dependency, obligation, or respect with anyone but them. At the same time, they struggled to maintain their authority in a legal climate in which the monarchy increasingly sought to regulate owners' control over their slaves. This led to contested and conflicting interpretations of laws that regulated slaveholding in France.

By the beginning of the eighteenth century, slavery had become essential to Caribbean colonial prosperity. Like any nouveau riche group, colonists who made their fortunes wanted to show off their wealth to those back at home. Much of colonists' wealth was wrapped up in the bodies of their slaves, and when they traveled they wanted to take representatives of their fortune in human chattel with them without threat to their property rights. This desire posed a legal problem, for the free soil principle held that slavery could not exist in France. This legal tradition, dating back as far as the fourteenth century, was based on the idea that slaves brought into the kingdom would be freed.[1] For colonists who wanted to bring slaves to France, ancient legal traditions that positioned the monarch as the guardian of freedom and a

Christian bulwark against illicit enslavement directly conflicted with emerging beliefs in the sacrosanctity of personal property.

The French crown ultimately abrogated the free soil principle and allowed slavery on French shores after intense pressure from colonists, who constituted a powerful interest group. The stakes in making and carrying out this decision were high, and a conflict soon emerged between individual and royal authority over whether the state had the right to regulate this particular type of private property. Colonial law, including the Code Noir, classified slaves as *meubles*: unlike serfs, they were "moveable" property untethered to any particular estate and could be divided among heirs. Although several legal challenges to this classification emerged over the next few years, meubles slaves remained.[2] In general the crown lacked the authority to regulate personal property of this sort. Individuals could buy, sell, move, or alienate meubles as they wished, while in contrast *immeubles* were subject to some legal restrictions. Yet in an effort to reconcile slave owning in France with the free soil principle, royal authorities claimed jurisdiction over regulating slaves. Slave owners hesitated to cede this authority, and instead construed laws regulating slavery for their own purposes.

Efforts to resolve this tension gave rise to the legal fiction that slavery was only in and of the colonies. Maintaining this fiction involved some legal gymnastics and allegedly tight control over precisely who could bring slaves to France, for what reasons, and how long they could stay. Starting with the Edict of 1716, legislation permitted only people coming from the Caribbean colonies to bring slaves to France, and only under certain conditions. Even then, the clear implication was that slaves would return to the Antilles with their owners when their metropolitan business had been completed. By definition, slaves and slave owners were just passing through. However, many slaves were *not* just passing through France. Numerous owners kept their slaves with them in France for years, even decades, and a few slaves received their freedom and lived out their lives as free people of color in the metropole. Given the legal fiction that there were no slaves in France, the actual persistence of slavery caused difficulties for authorities and slave owners alike.[3] Royal authorities scrambled to close loopholes that enabled owners to keep their slaves in France, while simultaneously defending the legitimacy of the crown's authority to regulate this particular type of private property. Consequently, slave owners in France had to devise creative means of asserting authority over their slaves. To do this, they turned to the provisions of the laws themselves and worked around the legal limits placed on slavery in ways that preserved the colonial institution and consolidated their own authority over their slaves.

In addition to these legal battles, slave owners also faced challenges to their authority within their households. By and large, the slaves who came to France were an elite group. They knew their owners intimately, and lived in close proximity with them. In the Antilles slave owners could use this proximity to reinforce a slave's chattel status in different small, intimate, quotidian ways that they probably used without thinking. What owners called their slaves, how they spoke to them, touched them, and treated them alone and in front of others all signaled a slave's enslaved status in ways both public and private. In France such personal tactics, played out between two individuals, were insufficient. Given the weight of the free soil principle and the tenuous legality of slavery in France, owners also had to justify their ownership, mark their property to a population unused to the idea of chattel slavery in their midst, and make their slaves so clearly theirs that no alternate avenues of authority seemed to exist. To do this, they unexpectedly turned to the laws that permitted slavery in France. Although the laws aimed to regulate slavery, not justify it, the colonial lobby had been instrumental in persuading royal authorities to pass these laws. Slave owners pushed at their boundaries, reinterpreting them in ways that expanded—rather than limited—owners' control over their slaves in France.

This chapter explores the mechanisms that slave owners used to legitimate property rights and exert authority over their slaves in La Rochelle and, by extension, in the metropole. Slave owners used legal frameworks intended to limit slavery in France and to increase royal control over the institution in order to bind slaves into stiff hierarchies instead. For owners, the common first step in this process was following the law that required all slave owners, without exception, to record their slaves' arrival in France with royal Admiralty offices. The Edict of 1716 positioned religious instruction as one of the only valid reasons for slaves to enter France. It was to baptism, then, that slave owners turned as an institution through which they could assert their own control over their slaves. Thus by ostensibly trying to regulate slavery in France, laws paradoxically laid the groundwork for legitimizing it.

Slaves and Owners in France and Saint-Domingue

When slaves such as Lizette and Hardy first disembarked from La Rochelle after a long voyage from the colonies, they had few immediate connections except with their owners. Like slaves taken from Africa to the Americas, slaves brought to France were ripped from their social networks, removed from their loved ones, and immersed in a largely unfamiliar culture. Although a select group used to interacting with white French men and women, slaves brought to France found that much of their expertise on colonial life meant little in their new surroundings. Power structures, relations with authority, and even the French spoken in the streets were all different from what they knew in the Caribbean. Aside from a few acquaintances made on their voyages, most slaves likely knew no one outside their owner's household. This social isolation put them in extremely vulnerable positions.

Slave owners also found multiple differences between France and Saint-Domingue, especially in the legal and social limits of their authority over their slaves. In the Caribbean, the Code Noir placed judicial limitations on the physical abuse of slaves, explicitly prohibiting "torturing them, or any mutilation of limb," and also making killing a slave a criminal offence.[4] However, these limitations on owners' authority were virtually never enforced, and the de facto condoning of torture served, in the words of Malick Ghachem, "to legitimate the sovereignty of masters over slaves."[5] For all intents and purposes, owners in Saint-Domingue could torture, beat, rape, starve, and otherwise abuse those they called their chattel essentially as they wished, as part of an ongoing individual and collective effort to delineate the boundary between slave and free. Harsh treatment went unnoted for the most part, and even killing a slave seldom occasioned more than a fine.[6] For practical purposes, owners had almost unlimited control over their human property.

In France, layers of legal, social, and intellectual expectations combined to dissuade owners from using overt violence as a means of asserting their authority over their slaves. Although it likely was expected that owners used some force against slaves, as they would against servants, wives, and other members of their households, torture was the province of the crown and extrajudicial torture directly challenged royal authority. Furthermore, Enlightenment philosophes increasingly condemned torture as a crime against nature.[7] Thus royal authority alongside a rising tide of educated opinion forced slave owners to seek other ways to exercise control.

Slave owners in France also had a personal interest in making their authority over their slaves look as natural and benign as possible, for slaves in France held a different position from slaves in the colonies. As conspicuous displays of wealth, slaves were likely to appear with their owners in public, and they attracted particular notice. This attention conferred a priceless cachet, and owners would not have wanted to do anything that threatened their own prestige. Violent discipline certainly would have ruptured the figment of effortless superiority over exotic others that owners sought to confer. Additionally, colonists had an interest in conveying an impression of slavery as a mild and even benevolent institution, particularly in the face of threats posed by Enlightenment discourses of natural law, royal attempts to regulate people colonists clearly saw as their property, and the slight disdain for the nouveaux riches sometimes displayed by wealthy metropolitan residents. Owners thus needed to look for ways other than physical coercion to assert their wills—and their property rights—over their slaves. Moreover, they needed to find mechanisms to assert their authority in ways that made slavery look relatively anodyne.

Slave owners received little help from the law; laws that regulated slavery in France did not clearly delineate the extent or the limits of slave owners' authority. By implication, certainly, laws permitting slavery in France conferred upon slave owners the same license over their slaves' bodies as they exercised overseas. However, things in France worked a bit differently, at least partly because of the historical weight of the free soil principle and the reluctance to condone slavery tout court. The Admiralty, an arm of royal authority, had jurisdiction over the enforcement of laws regulating slavery and slaves themselves. These laws put the burden of compliance with regulations firmly on slave owners who ultimately bore the financial loss should the crown confiscate their slaves if they failed to follow all policies.

None of the laws made provisions for how owners should handle recalcitrant slaves. Owners certainly could have beaten slaves in an effort to enforce their will, just as masters beat servants and husbands beat wives, or withheld resources. But should these tactics prove ineffective, owners lacked recourse to one major colonial option—sale to another owner—which was not legal in the metropole. Slave owners could ship recalcitrant slaves back to the colonies, but this would have been an option of last resort, since the owner would lose the services of the slave in question—and also have to pay the steep price of passage. For slave owners, this meant they needed to find ways of controlling and exerting authority over their slaves within the bounds of metropolitan legal and social expectations. Consequently, in La Rochelle slave owners looked for ways to bind their slaves more closely to them, making them more dependent and cutting them off from powerful outside influences, especially the Catholic Church. In doing so, they had to carefully skirt legal boundaries regulating slavery, staying just on the right side of royal authority.

Slave owners found that keeping their slaves socially isolated was a remarkably effective tactic. This proved a tricky project, as slaves showed themselves exceptionally adept at gaining knowledge of their new surroundings and those who peopled it, and using this familiarity to extend their own liberties and make their own social positions.[8] Connections outside their owner's household could make slaves particularly bold, even prompting them to seek freedom. For example, Pauline Villeneuve in Nantes won her freedom through the courts in 1716 after finding a home in a convent, while Jean Boucaux won his in 1738 after marrying a white woman.[9] Owners attempted to close off potential avenues through which slaves could make contacts and establish relationships outside the household, especially connections with individuals whose stature in the community rivaled—or even surpassed—a slave owner's own authority.

Edict of 1716

In response to growing pressure from wealthy, slave-owning colonists, the Edict of 1716 gave slave owners the right to bring slaves to France. This new law, which followed on the heels of Pauline Villeneuve's successful freedom suit, extended the classification of slaves as meubles, or moveable property, as under the Code Noir, to France.[10] Although this new law essentially undermined the free soil principle, it did not mean that slave owners could just transport slaves to France as they wished. In return for allowing colonists the privilege of bringing their slaves to the metropole, royal officials appropriated for themselves the authority to regulate the terms and conditions under which they could do so. Before slave owners left the Caribbean, they were required to obtain a letter of permission to transport individual slaves from the colonial governor. Within a week of their arrival in France, they had to register the slave and show this permission to Admiralty officials. They also would state the name, age, and place of origin of their slave, along with the name of the ship on which they had sailed, its captain, and the date of their arrival in France. Finally, they would give the reason why they had brought the slave to France.

The law delineated only three licit reasons for colonial slave owners to bring their slaves from the colonies: to receive instruction in the Catholic religion, to receive training in a trade, or to serve their owners in the capacity of a domestic servant on the voyage.[11] The clear implication was that, having fulfilled their duties and their training, the slave would return to the colonies. The law put the burden of compliance squarely on the shoulders of slave owners, but specified no penalties for noncompliance. This lack of incentive to comply opened the possibility that slaves of owners who failed to follow these formalities might be freed. Instead of primarily benefiting slaves, this provision gave royal officials an ace up the sleeve and served as a reminder to slave owners that the crown had the upper hand. Indeed, several key success-ful emancipation suits of the early eighteenth century hinged on the owner's failure to follow correct registration procedure.

According to the law, permission to bring slaves to France only applied to colonists. Although slavery itself was classified as a permanent condition, slaves and slave owners in France were considered to be transient; the law did not authorize metropolitan residents to own slaves. The fiction that slavery did not exist in France was especially clear in Article 15 of the Edict, which mandated that colonists in France who sold their colonial properties and of-ficers who were no longer posted to the colonies had one year to send their slaves back across the sea. If they did not, their slaves were to be freed.[12] In practice, however, colonists and former colonists not only routinely kept slaves in France for years, but some French residents who had never set foot in the colonies also owned slaves colonial family, friends, or associates had sent to them. That Admiralty officials routinely acceded to or turned a blind eye to this practice suggests that while the Edict may have been intended to regulate slavery in France, in practice it legitimized its extension onto metro-politan soil.

The law also placed several specific restrictions on the liberties of slaves while they resided in France, thereby sharply demarcating them from French subjects who performed similar labor, such as domestic servants. These pro-visions also closely followed the Code Noir, thus highlighting the continuities between the legal status of slaves in France and in the colonies, in spite of the persistent fiction that slavery was only a colonial institution. Any wages or goods slaves received belonged to their owners, and slaves could not enter into civil lawsuits. If a slave's owner died the slave became part of the estate and passed to the heirs, along with other goods and property. Slaves could not marry without their owner's consent (although if the owner did consent, the slaves were freed). This final provision prevented hierarchies of gender and race from clashing by ensuring that women could not serve both masters and husbands, and that men could not be heads of families if enslaved. In a pale echo of the free soil principle, the law also placed some restrictions on the property rights of owners over their slaves: slaves could not be bought or sold in France, nor could they be seized in payment for debts. Only these anemic provisions differentiated slaves from other forms of property. The Edict of 1716 thus worked to protect the property rights of slave owners who brought their slaves to France. Provided they followed the law, slave owners could travel to the metropole with slaves without fear of their confiscation.

This legislation took some time to pass through the bureaucratic channels of the Admiralty. Due to a legal quirk that made La Rochelle the only major Atlantic port under the jurisdiction of the Parlement of Paris, the law technically never went into effect because the Paris Parlement had not registered it, a likely effort to protest what they saw as an obvious violation of the free soil principle. This murkiness of the law's status presented a clear opportunity for slave owners, potentially enabling them to justify not registering their slaves, thus escaping royal surveillance and regulation. Yet Admiralty clerks in La Rochelle began keeping records of slaves who entered France in August 1719 in spite of the Parlement's failure to register the Edict. In contrast, the Admiralties of Nantes and Bordeaux began keeping registration records only after the enregistration of the law by local Parlements in 1717 and 1723 respectively.[13] In La Rochelle, though, slave owners began to comply with the Edict even though there were no consequences if they failed to do so and the law made several mandates that proved time-consuming and inconvenient to slave owners.

Indeed, in spite of the law's ambiguous legal status, slave owners in La Rochelle not only went out of their way to comply with it but also sometimes went beyond its requirements, at least at first.[14] For example, virtually all slave owners departing from the colonies brought with them the requisite permission from the colonial governor. From August 1719 through April 1725, slave owners initiated 175 records pertaining to slaves with the Admiralty.[15] The bulk of these were the required slave registrations, although some slave owners renewed registrations, confirmed that they had sent slaves back to the colonies, or stated that slaves had died. Only twenty-nine (16 percent) did not include a letter of permission or any other type of permission. Of the remainder, one hundred seventeen did include the letter (66 percent). These high numbers are unsurprising, for from the perspective of colonists, this requirement was authoritative law. However, thirteen additional slave owners in this sample, all arriving from Saint-Domingue, carried an excerpt from a colonial Admiralty register authorizing them to transport slaves instead of a letter of permission, bringing the total that had permission to 74 percent. This option was not delineated by the law, but apparently accepted by Rochelais Admiralty officials nonetheless. This illustrates that colonists approached these requirements flexibly, perhaps with the collusion of the local administration.

By the late 1720s providing a letter of permission was the exception, not the rule; word apparently spread to the colonies that as far as Rochelais officials were concerned, at any rate, this was an unnecessary formality. Of the two hundred one slaves recorded arriving in La Rochelle from July 1729 to October 1737, for example, Admiralty officials indicated that owners of only sixty-six, less than one-third, had presented such a letter.[16]

The remainder of these records hint at the ways slave owners could use the law for their own purposes in order to extend their authority over their slaves in France rather than to limit it. Fifteen of the records are not registrations of slaves at all, but renewals that purported to extend the stays of slaves in France, even though the law made no provision for this. For example, Sr. de Linier initially made declarations for his slaves Toyay and Magdelain on 31 May 1721. He renewed these declarations three years later, 5 May 1724.[17] This practice was still common twenty years later when Theodore La Croix first declared his slave, a fourteen-year-old boy whose name was not given, on 12 February 1732. He renewed the declaration on 16 February 1735 and 1 June 1736.[18] This ostentatious compliance left little room for slaves and their allies to challenge slaveholding practices. Indeed, after the 1716 freedom suit of Pauline Villeneuve, no slaves again used the courts to petition for their freedom until 1738.[19]

In the ten years after the Admiralty began registering slaves in La Rochelle, owners entering the port city declared approximately two hundred fifty slaves, all people of color of varying descriptions.[20] Although most arrived from Saint-Domingue, they also disembarked from colonies as far flung as Guadeloupe, Martinique, Sainte-Croix, Cayenne, Madagascar, and Canada. The vast majority of these declarations complied with the Edict of 1716 to the letter. They included a copy of the letter of permission sent from the colonies, and every declaration specified that slaves would be instructed in the Catholic religion and learn a trade. Although it is possible that not all slave owners fulfilled the registration requirement, the number of those who did and the level of detail they provided in the declarations demonstrates that they found utility in the registrations in ways that went beyond a simple question of compliance with the law.

One particular practice suggests that slave owners used the declarations to expand and legitimize opportunities for slave owning in France. The Edict of 1716 specifically restricted the privilege of owning slaves to colonists, colonial officials, or transatlantic ship's captains, all individuals who presumably passed through France only temporarily. Yet many slaves actually entered France alone. They were sent to France, not brought, by colonists to relatives or friends, often for the purposes of ostentatious gift giving or resale in spite of the illegality of these practices. Colonists began sending slaves to France almost immediately after officials began to enforce the Edict of 1716, and by mid-century this had become routine in La Rochelle and elsewhere. In the minds of slave owners and prospective slave owners, the Edict thus extended slavery to French soil.

This practice extended to the highest levels of Rochelais society. In 1725, the Contrôleur Contre-garde of the mint registered a slave that a ship's captain had brought to him.[21] In 1756 the practice was still common; the boy Arlequin, only eight years old, arrived in La Rochelle alone, sent by his owner in Saint-Domingue to a merchant in Rochefort.[22] One slave owner, Gérôme Faure, who was not and never had been a colonist, experienced some uneasiness about maneuvering around the law, and engaged in some fancy footwork to justify what amounted to, in essence, illegally importing a slave into France. In 1724, Faure sent his power of attorney to an agent in Saint-Domingue, who in turn obtained the necessary permission from colonial authorities on his behalf. A slave named Marie duly arrived in La Rochelle several months later.[23]

In spite of the clear illegality of this practice, colonial governors routinely gave overt permission for it in their letters, illustrating a certain level of collusion between slave owners and colonial officials. Even early in the century, these two groups realized that their concerns did not always line up with metropolitan ones. The governor of Cayenne, for example, explicitly gave a militia captain permission to send (*envoyer*) a slave to France.[24] The case of Sieur Baudin des Morattes provides a typical example. On 2 December 1720 the merchant stated to the Admiralty that he had received a slave from Sieur Baudin (probably a relative) in Cap Français. The letter of permission he provided explicitly confirmed that the Baudin in the colonies *sent* his slave Cupidon to France. Similarly, on 26 June 1723 Jeanne Chevallier of La Rochelle made a statement that Paul Cebe of Saint-Domingue had sent her a ten-year-old girl named Catin. On the same day, Antoine Carré stated that he had received a thirteen-year-old enslaved *mulâtresse* named Marie-Roze from Sieur Allaire du Langot of Cap Français.

Two things stand out about all these examples. First, all include permissions from colonial authorities, though in every case this permission took the form of an extract from an Admiralty record in Saint-Domingue, not the mandatory and more usual letter from the governor. Second, none of these permissions included the name of the person receiving the slave, indicating that slaves were sent to France without specific destinations or owners.[25] Acquiring slaves in France therefore may not have been as difficult as metropolitan royal officials would have liked to believe. Furthermore, Admiralty officials, bureaucrats who almost certainly had more ties to their locale than the royally appointed governors, colluded in this deception, helping slave owners to evade royal restrictions.

The networks of cooperation that made such evasion possible ranged across the ocean. In France, the demand for slaves surely extended beyond those with colonial connections. If a resident of France desired a slave but did not have a convenient colonial relative to provide one, certain Rochelais merchants with colonial associates could provide such a service, seemingly engaging in what amounted to an informal traffic in slaves. Such merchants, all prominent citizens, routinely helped colonial and metropolitan slave owners navigate the Edict's requirements and create the proper paper trail to legitimate their slaveholding. Whether they received payment for their services or simply did favors to friends or relatives, some merchants had emerged as clear intermediaries between the Admiralty offices and slave owners by the 1730s. For instance, Jean Gilbert made fifteen declarations of slaves at the Admiralty office between August 1730 and January 1735.[26] It is highly unlikely that he owned all fifteen slaves, which would have flown in the face of social conventions. Returning colonial governors or other high officials did sometimes travel with several; colonial intendant Mithon must have stunned the local populace when he arrived in La Rochelle with seven in 1720, far more than any other single slave owner.[27] A surplus bespoke superfluity for the purposes of the voyage and as objects of display. Rather than keeping all fifteen slaves, Gilbert likely acted as an informal clearing house. He received slaves sent from Saint-Domingue, made declarations for other slave owners, and renewed slave registrations. Similarly, from 1730 to 1737 Jacques Rasteau made eight declarations, declaring slaves and renewing declarations for slave owners and on his own account.[28] The names Belin, Seignette, and Vivier also appeared frequently in Admiralty registers.

All these families had branches well established on both sides of the Atlantic. Using this network, their colonial members sent unsupervised slaves to France while their metropolitan counterparts received the slaves and helped to steer new owners through the registration process, frequently making declarations for them. Their transatlantic families provided these merchants with the connections necessary to act as informal slave brokers, although this was certainly outside the intended boundaries of the law. They carefully complied with the letter of the Edict of 1716, while completely violating its spirit.

Slave owners' facility in maneuvering around the law limited the scope and weakened the force of the Edict of 1716. Not only did owners keep slaves in the metropole indefinitely, numerous people sent or brought to France as slaves did not return to the colonies at all, as the spirit of the Edict intended they should. Increasingly, some officials perceived this practice as a problem that threatened the fabric of French society because it challenged royal authority by going against the king's law. In the end, they worked to address it by giving increased legitimacy and authority to the exact individuals who had caused the difficulty in the first place: the slave owners.

Declaration of 1738

In contrast to the earlier legislation, the Declaration of 1738 explicitly counterpoised France as a land of freedom against the hierarchical plantation culture of the colonies, and identified slaves as the agents who threatened this dichotomy. Slaves returning from the metropole allegedly became "dangerous" after "contract[ing] a spirit of independence, which could have unfortunate consequences."[29] These "abuses," the Declaration maintained, were "so contrary" to the "growth of [the] colonies" that the king could "not permit to allow [them] to remain [unaddressed]."[30] It also specified additional restrictions on slaves that spoke to growing fears surrounding slavery in France. It expressly forbade slaves from "pretending to have acquired their liberty, under the pretext of their arrival in the kingdom."[31] Slaves could no longer marry at all, and could only receive their freedom by their owner's testament; even then, the newly emancipated slave was required to leave France.

The law thus weakened protections for slaves while giving slave owners more latitude to exercise their authority. Moreover, the Declaration placed increased limitations on slave owning in the metropole in an effort to consolidate the crown's prerogative to regulate slavery. Specifically, the Declaration required slave owners to explicitly state which trade slaves would learn and the name of the master craftsman charged with their instruction. It also restricted the length of time slaves could remain in France. Owners could no longer leave slaves in the metropole if they themselves journeyed abroad, and could not keep their slaves in France for more than three years. If owners failed to follow any of these formalities their slaves would not be emancipated, as under the earlier Edict, but confiscated by the crown and shipped back to the colonies. Owners might also have to pay a 1,000-livre fine. Under this legislation owners faced stiffer requirements and penalties, but the Declaration of 1738 continued to protect their property rights while maintaining the fiction that slavery did not exist on a permanent basis in France.

Like the Edict of 1716, a freedom suit also prompted this legislation.[32] The slave Jean Boucaux came with his owner to France from Saint-Domingue in the late 1720s. After working as a cook for over nine years, he married a white woman. According to the 1716 law, slaves who married with their owners' consent were emancipated. Although Boucaux's owner evidently had not consented to the union, the slave may have believed himself free. Certainly from that point on his owner's wrath poured down on the unfortunate slave.[33] After his imprisonment in the Châtelet, Boucaux and his attorneys brought a suit for the slave's freedom to the Admiralty of France. He ultimately received his freedom, although it remains unclear whether his attorney's elaboration of the legal history of the free soil principle or his owner's failure to strictly comply with the Edict of 1716 carried the day.[34] Regardless, this suit made some of the holes in the earlier legislation evident, and the Declaration of 1738 aimed to close some of these gaps.

As with the first law regarding slavery, the Parlement of Paris did not register the Declaration of 1738. This meant that in La Rochelle the Admiralty instead of the courts had charge of enforcing it.[35] Perhaps the Minister of the Marine had an inkling of the tacit cooperation among Rochelais and colonial authorities and slave owners, for he took a personal interest in its local enforcement.[36] Upon his request, the Intendant sent him a report on the number of people of color in La Rochelle, including slaves as well as a free family of color who worked at the mint and three *mulâtresses* who worked as laundresses. However, the Intendant claimed that the city of La Rochelle had never received a copy of the Declaration of 1738. It had not been registered by the local Admiralty office, and the Intendant himself denied ever having seen it; thus it could not be enforced.[37] Without evidence that the Rochelais Admiralty deliberately refused to enforce this law, the minister was unable to do more than fulminate. Slave owners were quick to take advantage of this discrepancy.

Article X of the Declaration upheld the fiction that slavery was relegated to France's colonies by requiring owners to specify what trade their slaves would learn in the metropole. The implication and intention was that slaves would acquire artisanal skills such as barrel making and smithery, which were essential to colonial enterprise, and would return to the colonies to exercise these trades. In reality, only four of one hundred and one owners who registered slaves in La Rochelle 1737–1747 complied with Article X and specified the trade that their slaves would learn in the metropole. Of these, only one would allegedly learn a trade that would actually facilitate transatlantic commerce.[38] This is in direct contrast to Nantes, France's major slave trading port throughout the eighteenth century, where the Declaration prompted a change in slave owners' behavior. In the northern city, under the jurisdiction of the Parlement of Rennes, which had enregistered the law, slave owners consistently listed the name of the *métier* their slaves would learn and also the name of the craftsperson charged with training them.[39] In comparison, Rochelais owners continued their previous practice of stating in exceedingly general terms that they brought slaves to France to learn a trade and for religious instruction.

However, far from ignoring the law altogether, Rochelais slave owners took great pains to register and re-register their slaves, turning up like clockwork at the Admiralty offices to justify keeping them well beyond the three-year limit imposed by the Declaration. For example, Dame Margueritte Suzeanne Huet first declared her slave Louis-François in 1742. She renewed this declaration in 1745, 1748, 1751, and 1755, saying that he "had not yet been sufficiently instructed in the Catholic religion and does not know the *métier* to which she had put him. She will keep him," her declaration stated, "until he is in a state to be sent back to the colony."[40] The Declaration made no provision for such behavior. This outward conformity to but actual subversion of the law suggests that white slave owners actually manipulated the law to justify long-term slave owning in France. Further, it affirms that officials in La Rochelle tolerated slavery as a matter of course, to an extent beyond that strictly allowed by law, and approached the issue with a flexibility that erred on the side of protecting human property and the interests of colonists rather than enforcing strict limitations on slavery, as mandated by the crown.

In an even more surprising twist, owners also used the Admiralty registers to record their manumission of slaves. This practice directly contravened the Declaration of 1738, which specifically forbade owners from freeing slaves except by testament, and then only under the condition that the owner died before the three years allowed for slaves in France expired.[41] Nonetheless, starting in 1739 and for the next few years the Rochelais Admiralty records certified at least four manumissions of people of color brought to France as slaves.[42] Because owners generally manipulated Admiralty records in ways that reinforced their own authority, it seems doubtful that they had the best interests of their slaves at heart when recording such manumissions. Indeed, some of these manumissions may have been prompted by a 1741 letter from the Minister of the Marine to the Intendant of La Rochelle, which ordered the return of all slaves to the colonies within six months.[43] In response, the Intendant asked the Minister if free *nègres* were exempt from the mandate. Although the Intendant gave no reason for his query, it soon became clear that owners who freed their slaves could continue to benefit from their service. "The majority of these people [who have slaves]," he wrote, "seem to me to have the intention of giving them their liberty, and [I] ask if this circumstance changes anything regarding the lot of these slaves."[44] Although the Intendant never criticized the Admiralty's regulation of slavery, he readily obliged slave owners looking for a way to keep their slaves. Thus, he obtained special exemptions for two slave owners to keep slaves in La Rochelle.[45]

Using manumission for their own ends, owners worked to bind former slaves into patriarchal households in a way that maintained their slave-like status. Henriette, commonly known by the name Zulima, was one dubious beneficiary of this trend. Her owner certified to the Admiralty his intention to emancipate her for her "good and agreeable service," but only after she had served him as a slave for five more years. Not until 1 January 1743 was she free to "serve whom she wished."[46] By simultaneously freeing her and making her freedom contingent on her continued service, Henriette's owner effectively used manumission as a way to defend his control over his slave against the encroachments of royal authorities. Emancipated people of color, even those emancipated under dubious circumstances, could not be confiscated by the crown, even if the owners had not followed all the legal requirements of the Declaration of 1738. By enabling owners to technically free slaves while actually continuing to claim their labor, manumission offered a shield from laws regulating slavery.

The slave Pierre found himself in such an ambiguous situation, suspended somewhere between slavery and freedom. In 1741, Pierre of the "Anglois nation" was in the service of René Roulleau, archdeacon of the Cathedral of La Rochelle. Likely aware of the 1738 law, Roulleau informed the Intendant that Pierre lived in his household, adding that he was old, infirm, and not of much use.[47] He presented an extract from Pierre's former owner's will to support his own claim that the slave was free when he entered his service. This document highlights the indistinct line between slavery and freedom, emphasizing that for a person of color in a patriarchal household headed by a white man, the distinction may have made little difference. The testament of Nicolas Rigault of Artibonite, as presented by Roulleau, said, "I also give liberty to the said Pierrot, domestic slave belonging to him [exactly who is unspecified in the excerpt], of the Anglois nation, on the condition that he go to France to serve the Dame and the Demoiselle Rigault, wife and daughter of the testator, with all the affection and the fidelity possible."[48] When Roulleau finally registered Pierre with the Admiralty in 1742, he stated that Pierre, then forty-six (not as old as Roulleau's letter to the Intendant may lead one to think), had been living with him for six years. He does not explain how this came to happen, other than offering that he "was sent from Saint-Domingue a *nègre* named Pierre." For good measure, Roulleau also stated that "he regarded him as free" and that Pierre "had never had the title of slave."[49]

Nevertheless, Pierre's exact status and his position in Roulleau's household remained unclear. Given that no Admiralty declaration exists for Pierre before 1742, although he had arrived in La Rochelle at least six years before, the archdeacon may simply have been trying to protect himself. He thus "gave him his liberty again," according to the text of the record, although he had no authority to do so. Pierre's example emphasizes the Admiralty's inability to entirely control the porous boundary demarcating slavery and freedom, and, conversely, the ability of slave owners to manipulate it for their own purposes.

The dangers of the ambiguity between slavery and freedom for slaves and the opportunities slave owners had to exploit this uncertainty became even clearer in the case of André. In 1742 André lived with the family of the merchant Élie Vivier. Members of the Vivier family, who were heavily involved in colonial commerce, often made slave declarations as a service to owners. One member of the Vivier clan who lived in Cul-de-Sac, Saint-Domingue, even supplied slaves to owners in La Rochelle on a regular basis.[50] Élie Vivier's connections to this informal and specialized slave trade suggests a lack of complete altruism in his motivations for registering the liberty of his own slave André. In this emancipation record, Élie Vivier stated that he had out-fitted the ship the *Aimable Besonne* to engage in the slave trade off the coast of Angola. The ship's captain successfully procured six hundred slaves, and from among that number he chose "a little *négrillon* who attached himself to him on the voyage from Angola to Saint-Domingue." Keeping one slave among their human cargo for their personal use was a privilege customarily accorded to captains by the merchants who outfitted vessels, and the Edict of 1716 and the Declaration of 1738 made allowance for it by extending to ship's captains the privilege of bringing slaves to France. The captain of the *Besonne* took advantage of this authorization, and the "little *négrillon*" came with him to France. He did not seek the requisite permission to do this in Saint-Domingue, Vivier claimed, because he "regarded him as a free servant." When the captain fell ill and died on the return voyage, charge of the child fell to his second-in-command, one Baillon. According to Vivier, Baillon had his small ward baptized and named André, and he engaged the *curé* of the parish of Saint-Sauveur in La Rochelle to "take care of his education, which he did, and to instruct him in the Catholic, apostolic, and Roman religion to the point that he is an example of wisdom and of piety." Since André had be-come such a paragon, he had worked as a domestic whom his master "had never had the intention to hold under the title of slave."[51] But in spite of his alleged freedom, André passed from master to master, working as a domestic in patriarchal households as if he were a slave. For him, Vivier's attestation of his freedom had little effect.

In a situation where owners exercised tenuous authority over their slaves and had very different motivations from royal officials for wanting to control them, they used every means possible to legitimize their own influence over those they saw as their property. They manipulated legal requirements to reg-ister slaves and used Admiralty records to reinforce their property rights. They subverted the laws meant to restrict slavery, drawing instead on their force, which rested on royal authority, to expand control over their slaves. Nonetheless, these were not the only means available to slave owners at-tempting to solidify their property rights over slaves in a legal environment that continued to put restrictions on their authority. They also turned to

French cultural institutions, weaving their slaves into bounded networks that began and ended within the owners' households, and limiting slaves' opportunities to make connections outside this intimate circle.

"To Instruct Them in the Roman, Catholic, and Apostolic Religion"

Like the law, the Catholic Church had long been used to inscribe social authority. In France, the Church had a broad reach: it welcomed people into the world through baptism, guarded the gates of legitimate marriage, and performed last rites that sent believers into the afterlife with pure, cleansed souls. For most people who lived in France, Church festivals marked the seasons of the year and religion permeated daily life. With the rise of Gallicanism and the increasing sway of Louis XIV over Church affairs in the late seventeenth and early eighteenth centuries, church and state authority became increasingly entwined. It is not surprising, then, that the laws regulating slavery in France drew on Church authority by requiring that slaves receive religious instruction; after all, the 1685 Code Noir similarly required that all slaves be baptized in the Catholic faith.[52]

In Saint-Domingue, slaves newly arrived from Africa already had undergone shipboard baptism, at least in theory. Richelieu and Colbert each gave orders that companies with slave trading monopolies should offer religious instruction and baptize slaves.[53] Later, after the breakup of these monopolies, the burden shifted squarely to slave owners. Some took this charge seriously. One habitant, for example, instructed his *gérant* to "do his best to instruct [the slaves] in the Catholic, apostolic, and Roman religion," and to "engage the priest as much as he can to baptize the *nègres, négresses, négrillons,* and *négrittes* who have not [yet] been [baptized], above all having attention when [we] buy new *négrillons* and *négrittes* to have them taken to the priest to baptize them."[54] Overall there was little consistency, particularly in terms of what constituted the religious instruction required by Article II of the Code Noir. In principle, all slaves who arrived in France should have already been baptized. In practice, the law's ambiguous phrasing allowed slave owners to define what religious education meant, including teaching slaves the catechism themselves, and thus offered another opportunity to inscribe their authority over their slaves. As a result, slave owners regularly baptized slaves they brought to La Rochelle.

Because of the port city's unique history as a Huguenot stronghold, Catholicism had a different meaning there than in most French cities, particularly among the Protestant-heavy merchant class, the same group that tended to own slaves. In the Catholic kingdom of France, Catholic baptism played a religious and a civil role: in the essential moment of baptism, an infant's soul was accepted into the church at the same time as its person was declared to legally exist by the state. Protestants thus regularly faced a crucial choice: to follow their religious tenets and avoid Catholic rites, or to set aside their own religious beliefs in favor of the civil legitimacy that Catholic sacraments provided. Officially the law prohibited Protestants from baptizing their children in the Catholic Church.[55] Yet for La Rochelle's Protestant merchant elite, the civil benefits conferred by Catholic baptism outweighed the doctrinal drawbacks. Urban Protestants, commonly prosperous and well-educated members of their communities, were highly likely to submit to outward pressures to conform to Catholicism while maintaining private Protestant worship, and those in La Rochelle were no exception. Wealthy, upwardly mobile Protestant families habitually married and had their children baptized in the Catholic Church.[56] Although some of their co-believers reviled the practice, wealthy Protestants found Catholic sacraments necessary processes to establish legitimacy and ensure inheritance rights.[57]

Protestants thus approached traditional Catholic practices, especially baptism and godparentage, differently than their Catholic peers. In the eighteenth century Catholic parents of all social statuses usually looked upon the occasion of baptism as an opportunity to cement relationships of patronage or clientage, habitually appointing prosperous or powerful kin or community members as godparents to their children. Choosing kin as godparents reinforced family ties, a potentially significant act, particularly if the relatives in question were wealthy or well placed: choosing prominent patrons could provide children valuable contacts down the road.[58] In turn, godparents were expected to look out for their godchildren, guide their spiritual development, and offer them opportunities that the children's parents could not.

Rather than looking up the social scale to find godparents, as most Catholics did, Protestant merchants who baptized their children in the Catholic Church looked down, choosing social inferiors, particularly servants, instead of wealthy associates to fill this important religious and social function. For example, at the 1760 baptism of Suzanne Catherine Fleuriau, daughter of wealthy merchant and plantation owner Aimé-Benjamin Fleuriau, the child's parents chose their domestic servant Jean Gilbert as godfather. Their servant girl Marie Metay was godmother to their next child, Louis Benjamin.[59] In the next generation, Aimé-Benjamin Fleuriau was named godfather of his grandson of the same name, but he did not attend the baptism ceremony; his servant Jean-Denis LeFevre represented the merchant at the church.[60] Godparentage therefore acquired meaning in this Protestant community that was the inverse of its traditional use as a form of patronage among Catholics. In lieu of binding a child to a social superior with greater resources, Protestants bound their inferiors to them by conferring upon them the privilege and responsibility of inclusion in this important ceremony. Protestants thus wove a network of servants and tradespeople around them that further secured their own social position and the loyalty of those who knew them intimately. At the same time, they went to great lengths to avoid crossing the threshold of Catholic churches themselves.

In some cases slaves even were appointed godparents to the children of their Protestant owners, embedding them in their owners' families. Such a case arose in the Fleuriau family in 1766 when Hardy, "servant in the paternal household," was named godfather to Marie-Adélaïde, Aimé-Benjamin Fleuriau's daughter.[61] Although Hardy was not identified here as a slave, this must have been the same Hardy who arrived on *Le Théodore* at the same time as Lizette, accompanying his owner from Saint-Domingue. Similarly, twenty years later in 1786, François, "domestic *nègre* in the household of the maternal grandmother," represented the Protestant merchant Charles Macarthy at his godchild's Catholic baptism.[62] These examples do not indicate that owners held slaves in high esteem; although becoming a godparent may have been an honor for Catholics, this was not the case for these Protestant families. Naming a slave as a godparent could even be construed as mocking Catholic ritual. Nevertheless, this practice also had the effect of binding slaves more closely to their owners through public performance of the connection. In such cases Protestants forced slaves to demonstrate loyalty to their owners by literally standing in for them when their own religious beliefs inhibited their presence.

Baptizing slaves was a different story, because both Protestant and Catholic religions could potentially provide slaves with an alternate locus of authority away from their owners. In England, Protestants commonly saw baptism as a ceremony equated with manumission.[63] The Catholic Church also had the capacity to challenge slave owners' authority over their slaves.[64] Catholic baptism, therefore, potentially opened new avenues for slaves to make connections and claims that could even lead to freedom.[65] Paradoxically,

Rochelais slave owners turned to Catholic baptism in order to close off such avenues. On first glance this may not seem an effective choice, particularly because neither the Edict of 1716 nor the Declaration of 1738 explicitly required slaves to be baptized. Ironically, the terms of these laws, which established religious instruction as one of the only legal reasons for bringing slaves to France, also lay the groundwork for this practice. In Saint-Domingue, missionaries and priests had long struggled over the question of the appropriate content and amount of religious instruction for slaves. In 1731, one Jesuit in Saint-Domingue wrote, "When I learn that some [slaves] have arrived in my district, I go to see them, and I begin by having them make the sign of the cross, guiding their hands, then I do it myself on their foreheads. . . . The *Nègre*, who does not comprehend what I do, nor what I say, opens wide eyes, and seems completely stupefied; but to reassure him, I address to him through an interpreter the words of St. Peter, 'You do not know what I am doing but you will eventually.'" The priest laments, "and it is here where the science of the most able Theologian will come up quite short; but a Missionary must think twice, before leaving a man to die, whatever he is, without baptism."[66] Another Jesuit added, "they are very little capable of understanding Christian Truths. . . . They are rarely judged capable of communion, even at death."[67] Conscientious priests, then, agonized over the tensions between their belief in the benefits of conversion and doctrinal mandates about the necessity of knowledge of Catholic ritual and beliefs for those accepted into the fold.

Similarly, priests in La Rochelle struggled with how to evaluate the previous religious instruction of slaves. When a priest of the parish of Notre Dame in La Rochelle baptized the slave Pierre-Jacques in 1727, he worried about whether he was violating doctrine by baptizing Pierre, possibly for a second time. In the end, Pierre's owner "assured [him] by a letter that the said *nègre* was never baptized and that it is doubtful that he was born of Christian parents."[68] These words assuaged his doubts, for the priest baptized Pierre without further ado. This slight twinge of conscience was atypical for priests baptizing slaves in La Rochelle. In general, priests performed the ceremony on request and did not raise concerns about the slave's religious instruction.

This custom was not indicative of Catholic practice in general. In France, new converts to Catholicism had to exhibit solid knowledge of the catechism. For most slaves, on the other hand, a simple baptismal ceremony likely proved the extent of their religious education. The different expectations for slaves in terms of what constituted a manifestation of faith limited slaves' access to an institution that was potentially a powerful ally. Owners' willingness to baptize slaves who had little knowledge of religious doctrine and the Church's compliance with this strategy foreclosed a potential space of contestation over slavery.

Slave owners' incentive to have their slaves baptized therefore went well beyond straightforward compliance with the law; they also created closed circuits of domination by layering religious over temporal authority in unexpected ways. Godparents, for example, had the potential to act as powerful counterpoints to the supremacy of slave owners, as they were charged with guiding the religious development of the newly baptized. Consequently slave owners had to choose godparents for their slaves carefully so these spiritual role models would not challenge their own secular power over their human chattel or, for Protestants, the spiritual sovereignty of their delegitimized faith. As a result, owners often named themselves godparents to their slaves. In the case of Étienne, a sixteen-year-old slave baptized in 1724, his owner and godfather were one and the same.[69] The Protestant ship's captain Pierre Bonfils approached the problem slightly differently, naming his wife his slave's godmother.[70] Decades later, Bonfils' brother Jean acted as godfather to his own slave Jean-Marie, and his sister-in-law again acted as godmother.[71] Catholic and Protestant slave owners alike named themselves godparents to their slaves, suggesting that the benefit of religious sanction of their authority over their slaves appealed to slave owners no matter what their religious affiliation.[72]

Just as the process of commodification erased slaves' personal histories, the sacrament of baptism also erased past relationships.[73] Baptism records demonstrate the process owners used to reinforce the subordinate positions of slaves within a household and to negate any existing intimate bonds, whether social or kinship ties, that a slave might have had previously. The 1739 baptism record of Pierre Augustin shows the ceremony's usual procedure. "The twelfth of November 1739," the priest wrote, "by me priest [and] parson of the parish of Notre Dame undersigned, have baptized a *noir*, aged about thirty years, brought from the coast of Léogane, . . . belonging to M. Pierre Gautrier Gilleson, merchant on the said coast of Léogane, who has promised to bring him up in the Catholic, apostolic, and Roman religion. The godmother and godfather are Pierre Gilleson and Geneviève-Agnès Picard. The said *noir* is named Pierre Augustin."[74] The priest expressed no doubts about Pierre Augustin's need for baptism. Through the baptismal process, Pierre Augustin's owner also became his godfather and, as was habitual, named him. While Protestants and Jews converting to Catholicism took an active part in the ceremony, Pierre Augustin and other slaves did not. He did not make his own mark attesting his faith; his owners did so for him, as if he were an infant. While in Catholic doctrine baptism cleansed original sin, for slave owners baptizing slaves in France the sacrament acted as a form of rebirth, expunging an adult's former self and previous connections.

Godparentage became a particularly important nexus in owners' efforts to exercise control over their slaves in France because the institution had already assumed the position of a discursive trope in writings on slavery by the early eighteenth century. From the seventeenth century onward, almost every priest who offered a public account of their travels to the Caribbean asserted the great respect slaves held for their godparents until it had become a truism. The Dominican Jean-Baptiste Du Tertre, writing in 1667, alleged that owners habitually used the institution of godparentage as a tool for reinforcing their authority over slaves. He claimed that "the godfathers and godmothers [of slaves] are ordinarily French, friends of their masters."[75] In such a situation, religious authority reinforced racial, social, and juridical hierarchy. Similarly, in 1722 the Dominican Jean-Baptiste Labat emphasized, "It is difficult to imagine the extent of the respect, the obedience, the submission, and the regard all the *nègres* have for their godparents. Even the Créoles, that is to say, those who were born in the country, regard them as their parents. I have been surprised an infinity of times to see how they discharge these duties."[76] Here, racial and religious hierarchies had become so entwined that slaves' alleged respect for their godparents was accepted as surprisingly natural.

By the end of the eighteenth century, the dominant regard for Catholicism crumbled in the face of Enlightenment secularism. As ideas about the inferiority of Africans took shape and solidified, secular authors took up the naturalization of this religious hierarchy to criticize what they began to see as unthinking devotion that supposedly confirmed slaves' inferiority, rather than praiseworthy regard. In 1777 Hilliard d'Auberteuil criticized, "people of mixed blood have, like the *nègres*, much filial piety; they have a superstitious respect for their godmothers."[77] Similarly, créole historian and jurist Moreau de Saint-Méry, writing in the 1790s, claimed that "the respect of the *nègres* for the godfather and their godmother is pushed so far, that it takes away from that which they have for their father and their mother."[78] While in the seventeenth and early eighteenth centuries priests saw Africans and people of African descent as potential converts, by the end of the century superstition took the place of simplicity and devotion in priestly descriptions of slaves. Whether with praise or with censure, authors nevertheless consistently emphasized the importance of the bond between slaves and their godparents.

Given the persistence and pervasiveness of this belief in god-filial loyalty, slave owners had a compelling reason to step into the role of godparents themselves. Acting as godparents to their slaves or calling on close kin or associates to fill this role enabled slave owners to consolidate their personal authority over those they saw as their property. In this context, the baptism ceremony, usually a way to extend contacts, actually cut slaves off from their own networks and situated them firmly under the authority of their owners.

As laws circumscribed the circumstances under which slavery was allowed in France, slave owners carved out opportunities to assert authority over their slaves through the same French legal practices intended to limit the institution. In the process, they adapted well-established French methods of social organization, including baptism, in ways that laid the groundwork for the extension of slavery to France. By following the letter of the law and skirting its intentions, slave owners drew on the legitimizing authority of the crown to expand their own power over their slaves, making it more and more difficult to maintain the fiction that slavery was only in and of the colonies. Slave owners' success in appropriating Old Regime institutions for their own purposes highlights the flexibility of the institutions themselves, and also the complexity of the ongoing clash between royal and individual authority, on the one hand, and metropolitan and colonial authority on the other.

It also speaks to the intricacies of relationships between slaves and their owners. While metropolitan laws tended to approach these relationships as clear-cut, in reality they were extremely complicated affairs influenced by slaves as well as by owners. Owners were well aware of this, which was why they felt the need to so firmly inscribe their authority in the metropole in the first place. As these intricacies became evident, royal legislation sought to clarify and crystallize ties between slaves and their owners as well as between owners and the crown. These efforts culminated after the Seven Years' War in strict limits over slaves and free people of color in France and, by 1784, also over colonial slave owners' legal authority over the bodies of their slaves.

Yet even as metropolitan laws attempted to regulate slavery in France, it became clear that colonial relationships were far more complex than French legal architects had imagined. Relations between whites and people of color ranged far beyond imagined master/slave dichotomies, sometimes developing into intimate connections that entailed affection as well as power and domination. Further, as individuals moved between France and Saint-Domingue, they prepared themselves to negotiate different legal systems as well as different local customs and understandings of slavery. In Saint-Domingue race and slavery had long been adjacent categories, simultaneously joined to each other but not always overlapping. As legislation intended to regulate slavery actually had the paradoxical effect of legitimating slavery on French soil, race began to emerge as an important category in France as well. This in turn raised more anxieties about slavery and race.

As race became an increasingly important category in France by the second half of the eighteenth century, intimate relationships were key in determining how individuals approached and resisted racial categorization. Resistance sometimes came from surprising quarters: plantation owners and white patriarchs could object to lumping free people of color alongside slaves as fiercely as free people of color themselves. The next chapter closely examines family relationships and the multiple issues at stake in articulating them, ultimately interrogating the complex motivations behind racial categorization, including family strategies such as marriage and inheritance.

CHAPTER 3

Navigating Transatlantic Separations

Intimacy and business may initially seem at odds. Yet like Paul Belin des Marais, French men and women involved in colonial trade did not solely consider it a business venture, but rather a personal enterprise that shaped how they approached intimate, familial questions about inheritance, wealth, property, name, and legitimacy. Doing business in Saint-Domingue commonly meant sending at least one male family member across the sea, whether for merchant families with established trading houses or for those looking for opportunities to get rich on the land. The overwhelming majority of French emigrants to Saint-Domingue were men, and when they traveled family members stayed behind in France.[1] Single men left parents, siblings, and extended kin; married men left wives and children. Yet family as well as individual ambition motivated emigrants' journeys. They took with them the vague shining hope that one day they would return to France wealthy, able to sweep their families into the lap of luxury—or more modestly, that they could pay debts, provide for widowed mothers, and give their children a start in the world.

As a result, the French imaginary conceptualized the Caribbean colonies as a temporary place: an El Dorado where they could get rich by growing cash crops through slave labor, but not a permanent spot to settle. Unlike in France, the produce, not the land itself, was considered the principal resource. This idea persisted in spite of early efforts to promote traditional patriarchal families. In the 1630s, the Compagnie des Îles d'Amérique offered a bonus of twenty-five pounds of tobacco to men who brought women with them to the Caribbean, and to men who married women of any race in the colonies.[2] Yet because of the assumption of impermanency, even married men who sought their fortunes in the islands tended to travel alone.[3] In the long term this demographic gender imbalance had profound repercussions in Saint-Domingue, where white men formed alliances with women of color, and the free colored population rivaled the white population.[4]

But what of those they left behind? While the preponderance of single white men in Saint-Domingue certainly affected the island's demographic and economic development, the same men's absence also shaped social and economic practices in the metropolitan cities where male fortune seekers left behind their mothers, wives, sisters, and daughters.[5] As women's social positions were largely defined by their relations to men, the absence of their closest male relatives changed women's roles, allowing them to engage in activities customarily reserved for men, including transatlantic commerce. Families foresaw and planned for how these long-term separations would affect women's social, economic, and cultural positions. While customary laws limited women's economic and legal autonomy, families used contracts to expand women's roles in ways that enabled them to occupy the somewhat unusual position of married women who were heads of household.

This is not to suggest that the advent of transatlantic trade and the absences it entailed ushered in a period of unfettered liberation for wives left behind in France. Rather, their gender limited women's abilities to step neatly into their husbands' roles. Furthermore, when an ocean lay between husband and wife, traditional nuclear family relationships began to change. Spouses formed other attachments and forms of intimacy, and priorities shifted. Many men in the colonies felt less constrained by conventions of sexual propriety than women and entered into long-term relationships with women of color, whether legitimated by church weddings or essentially as common law partnerships. As male colonists' families shifted in shape and appearance, wives sometimes had to watch as assets flowed from their husbands' estates to illegitimate mixed-race children. The potential conflicts between blood relations and socially constructed concepts of the family, and between metropolitan and colonial understandings of the family, came to a head when death pitted the interests of legitimate and illegitimate families against each other. Even with the careful preparation families put into planning marriage and inheritance, provisions such as these often came as an unwelcome surprise. Such was the case with Jean-Severin and Marie-Magdelaine Regnaud de Beaumont.

This chapter uses a case study of the Regnaud de Beaumont family to explore how families in La Rochelle planned and prepared for transatlantic separations as a matter of course. To do so they used contracts—especially marriage contracts, powers of attorney, and wills—to weave between and around the customary laws of La Rochelle and Paris. In a transatlantic age in an ocean-facing city, individuals looked to family members in the colonies as business partners, with the assumption that kin shared interests and would safeguard each other's financial welfare. Likewise, in a commercial seaport women frequently were involved in their husbands' maritime ventures; after all, who could have more interests in common than a husband and wife? Yet the assumption of shared marital interests proved to be founded on sand, easily eroded by the waves of the Atlantic as separation redirected the interests of husband and wife into different channels. In such situations, and in spite of the protections of common law and the safeguards of contracts, women had little recourse when their carefully laid plans went awry.

Common Law and Contracts

Because neither French common law nor the bureaucratic ideal of the family as the basic political unit took long-term separations—or their contingencies—into account, families themselves adapted well-established strategies to provide for the long absences and changing family roles necessitated by transatlantic trade. Specifically, they tailored legal provisions in contracts, especially marriage contracts, testaments, and powers of attorney. Families worked to shape these documents to give themselves safety and flexibility in the event of a transatlantic separation. In particular, such contracts aimed to protect the welfare of women.[6]

In the normal course of things, husbands represented the interests of married women. This became a significant challenge when an ocean separated husbands and wives. Laws governing marriage generally assumed husbands and wives lived in the same place. Geographical separation could complicate the legal situations of transatlantic couples because women with husbands in the Caribbean found themselves caught between the customary laws of La Rochelle and those of Paris, which governed the colonies; the two customs treated women's property and inheritance very differently.[7] Aware of these potential legal obstacles looming on the horizon, families planned ahead, using contracts to empower women and give them options. These options proved particularly critical at the two moments that most affected all women in the Old Regime: marriage and death. A third moment, a husband's departure, similarly shaped the lives of women in Atlantic ports.

When Jean-Severin Regnaud de Beaumont and Marie-Magdelaine Royer married in 1735, their families would have been particularly conscious of strategies of marriage and inheritance. Her deceased father had been a planter in the colony of Saint-Domingue; his father held a royal post in La Rochelle. Jean-Severin himself was a transatlantic ship's captain, a lucrative occupation that commonly served as a stepping stone, as it would for Jean-Severin, to owning a colonial plantation. Both families had amassed a significant amount of capital, and had poised themselves to climb the social ladder. If this was their goal, their match was a good one, as it brought together the royal contacts of the Regnaud de Beaumont family with the enormous profit potential of the Royer plantation, which Marie-Magdelaine stood to inherit eventually from her mother. Yet it was evident to the families that to maximize this fortunate confluence of assets they needed to take colonialism into account.

Jean-Severin's role as a ship's captain and Marie-Magdelaine's prospective inheritance of an indigo plantation meant the couple were well aware of the financial importance of empire to their union, and made it almost certain that long separations lay in their future. Marie-Magdelaine's family, with their colonial experience, would have been particularly conscious of the challenges such a separation could pose for women. Accordingly, they designed the marriage contract to safeguard Marie-Magdelaine's interests and to open room for her to exercise choices in the case of a transatlantic separation, or to maximize profits and protect her from creditors if her husband died overseas. In doing so, they used the marriage contract to dance around the limits customary law placed on women's roles.

Marie-Magdelaine Royer was a fine marriage prospect for the young trader Jean-Severin Regnaud de Beaumont. An only child, she stood to inherit her parents' colonial plantation and all the commercial possibilities it promised. Although she was born in La Rochelle in 1714 and returned there when she was approaching marriageable age, she spent her childhood in Cul-de-Sac, Saint-Domingue, not far inland from the capital Port-au-Prince, and an area well situated because of the confluence of several rivers that facilitated irrigation.[8] The economy of this area of Saint-Domingue expanded rapidly during the sugar and coffee booms of the eighteenth century, and colonists cleared the plain to make way for vast plantations. Sugar cultivation, in particular, expanded in the western province, which boasted some of the largest plantations in the colony.[9] The value of land skyrocketed, and it leased for up to twice the cost of similar plantations on other parts of the island. This region also was an enclave for Rochelais merchants and planters, including members of the Belin, Fleuriau, and Seignette families.[10] At the time of her marriage, Marie-Magdelaine's widowed mother still lived in the colony and oversaw the family's prosperous indigo enterprise.

But the Royer family, like many colonists, did not view Saint-Domingue as a permanent abode for themselves, and certainly not for their daughter. Instead, it was an important part of a multipronged strategy for family advancement. After the death of her father when she was a young child, Marie-Magdelaine remained with her mother for some years in Saint-Domingue. Her mother never remarried, so her financial interests were overseen by a male guardian chosen by "relatives and friends."[11] Colonists commonly sent their children to France for the final polish they thought only a metropolitan education could provide, and the widow Royer proved no exception. Once she approached marriageable age, Marie-Magdelaine's mother sent her back to La Rochelle, where she lived under the chaperonage of an aunt, her mother's sister. This family of women traversing an ocean was unusual even in these transatlantic times. The aunt would have been familiar with expectations for women's education, and Marie-Magdelaine's mother trusted her sister to make sure her daughter acquired the finish a gentleman well versed in the *politesse* of the metropole would require in a marriage partner. The network of male "relatives and friends," so ready to help the widow and young girl in Saint-Domingue, evidently did not extend to La Rochelle, for the office of carefully vetting prospective marriage partners, typically the purview of men, fell to her aunt as well.[12] This aunt must have approved of Jean-Severin Regnaud de Beaumont and his family, for plans for the marriage proceeded.

As Marie-Magdelaine had not yet reached twenty-five, the age of majority for women, her marriage required her mother's permission. In yet another attestation of the careful detail with which transatlantic families approached marriage, the bride's mother sent her sister a power of attorney months in advance for just such a purpose.[13] This document authorized the marriage and gave the bride's aunt the authority to make the contract in her mother's stead. Her aunt, then, apparently negotiated Marie-Magdelaine's marriage contract, although this responsibility usually fell to fathers or other senior male kin. As a native of La Rochelle and resident of Saint-Domingue, the bride's mother knew firsthand the challenges transatlantic families posed.[14] This knowledge evidently extended to her aunt, who, through the marriage contract, demonstrated a remarkable awareness, especially for a maiden aunt, of possible circumstances that transatlantic separation could create within a marriage. Contracts thus shaped this union from beginning to end. Merchant families appreciated the power of such legal documents, and knew how to use them either to conform to the law or to bend customary law to their own best advantage, as did the marriage contract between Marie-Magdelaine Royer and Jean-Severin Regnaud de Beaumont.

Couples of all social stations entered into marriage contracts, prepared by and signed before notaries, before actually getting married by a priest.[15] Terms of the contract could go well beyond the amount of a dowry and include provisions for a woman's widowhood, the distribution of her estate after her death if the marriage produced children or did not, or even place limits on the couple's inheritance of their parents' estates. Such contracts provided families with opportunities to safeguard the particular interests of their children. For sons, this might mean negotiating a larger dowry or laying claim to an especially appealing piece of his wife's prospective inheritance. For daughters, it could entail ensuring her livelihood as a widow and safeguarding her family property for her heirs, challenges that customary law in La Rochelle addressed. Merchant families also made marriage alliances that advanced their trading connections.[16] Wives and widows played direct roles in keeping merchant houses solvent, particularly in marriages that entailed transatlantic separation. It behooved all parties, therefore, to provide options in the marriage contract that would facilitate women's involvement, including after the death of their husbands.

Managing transatlantic holdings posed distinct fiscal and personal challenges, particularly for women. Husbands' personal oversight of colonial interests, while potentially a sound business move, could entail years, even decades of separation of husband from wife. During this time the wife had little sway over his business decisions, even those pertaining to property she had brought into the marriage. Moreover, transatlantic crossings and colonial life posed countless perils: hurricanes and disease claimed innumerable lives in the sweltering tropics. Were the young bride widowed, particularly without children, she could encounter difficulties managing or even keeping her property. The Royer-Regnaud de Beaumont marriage contract anticipated these extremely possible sets of circumstances by carefully circumnavigating legal traditions and including provisions that ensured that Marie-Magdelaine Royer would have choices, especially in the event of her widowhood.

The couple's marriage contract, signed and notarized in La Rochelle on 29 March 1735, specified that it would follow the *Coutume de Paris* rather than that of La Rochelle.[17] Although this might initially seem like a surprising choice, Parisian customary law prevailed in France's overseas colonies, high-lighting that Marie-Magdelaine and Jean-Severin anticipated a colonial so-journ. The two systems of law had much in common: they similarly vested a husband with control over his wife's property, giving him a broad amount of power over both her person and any community property as well as the use of assets she brought to the marriage.[18] Both also prohibited the husband from alienating property specifically belonging to his wife, including her dowry.[19] Common law took particular care to protect dotal properties from spendthrift husbands, as their intent was to provide for widows and children and prevent women from laying claim to portions of their husbands' estates.[20]

For families involved in transatlantic trade, the differences between the customary laws of Paris and La Rochelle mattered more than the similarities. In La Rochelle common law positioned women as generators of common marital property, with half this property rightfully going to their descen-dants. In Paris, any property a wife brought to or generated within a marriage was hers only for her lifetime. After her death, it generally passed irrevocably to her husband or his heirs. In order to provide for Marie-Magdelaine in the face of any of the challenges of transatlantic separation, premature death, and bankruptcy, her family used the marriage contract to enable her active par-ticipation in her husband's trading activities and even to continue them after his death, a move they made with Jean-Severin's full knowledge and willing consent.

Property was at the heart of this careful balancing of Rochelais and Pari-sian common law. Though technically claiming that it operated under Pari-sian common law, the marriage contract rejected many of the advantages this legal regime could pose for wealthy families, including consolidation of mar-ital assets. Only about one-third of the assets the bride and the groom brought to the marriage entered into community property to purchase furniture and personal possessions.[21] This was typical practice among wealthy families in La Rochelle.[22] The rest of their assets, including real estate, prospective inher-itances, and lump sums of cash, remained strictly separate. This division of assets at the outset would provide concrete benefits for Marie-Magdelaine were she left alone in France while her husband traveled overseas. At least in theory, she would have access to resources that were in her name, funds that could support her and their future children were they to live apart from her husband.

The legal customs of Paris and La Rochelle diverged most notably over inheritance, and the Royer-Regnaud de Beaumont marriage contract worked to incorporate elements of each to allow Marie-Magdelaine the choice and flexibility to continue running her husband's enterprises in the event of her widowhood. It was not easy to create this room to maneuver, as most customary laws governing marriage viewed women as carriers or custodians of wealth instead of generators of wealth in their own right, and most married women lacked the legal capacity to devote their labors to expanding their own fortunes. They brought wealth into the family when they married, and their labor within the family contributed to the expansion of their husbands' estates, which his children or other kin would eventually inherit. In La Rochelle and the rest of the western portion of France, the family of birth took precedence over the family of marriage, and property flowed through wives' families as well as husbands'. In this tradition of preserving lineage property over conjugal property, even the dowry would eventually be inherited by a woman's descendants, not her husband's.[23] Only assets acquired or generated during the marriage remained under the purview of the husband. In contrast, Parisian customary law considered inheritance of either immeubles or meubles part of community property, the couple's joint estate.[24] Further, in Paris and most other parts of France, the wife only had a life interest in her dowry, which ultimately reverted to the husband's heirs, lost to the wife's family forever.[25]

The Rochelais system of inheritance opened opportunities for women as generators and bearers of wealth. Each spouse inherited half the couple's community property on the death of the other, with the other half going either to their children or to the deceased's next-of-kin in their family of birth.[26] This opened possibilities for widows to continue running a business by going into partnership with the children, for example.[27] If a couple did not have children, intestate property might go to siblings, nieces and nephews, or parents. Wills generally followed the patterns established by common law. Family resources always remained within the lineage; the marriage of a child was a temporary alliance designed to facilitate flow of property from one generation to the next, not an irrevocable loss of capital.[28] Although in some trades it became rarer for wives to play an active role in running their husbands' businesses, in port cities such as La Rochelle, families actively worked to make room for wives and widows to participate in commerce.[29]

Rochelais common law integrated women into the economic life of the family by mandating equal inheritance for all children, boys and girls. Wills generally followed this pattern, although parents could use testaments to override the requirement of equal inheritance. The equal division of parental property worked well in urban port towns such as La Rochelle, where wealth was largely comprised of small or liquid assets such as urban property, income from *rentes*, and profit generated from trade. The diverse holdings of a wealthy merchant or a modest shopkeeper could be divided easily among heirs. Among the rich, the family home typically went to the oldest son, while younger sons inherited less imposing pieces of property, and daughters acquired cash or *rentes*.[30] The Rochelais system bound generations and branches of families more closely together; grandparents, aunts and uncles, sisters and brothers, parents and children all had a common interest in fostering and preserving family property. Nonetheless, Rochelais common law possessed one distinct disadvantage for families involved in Atlantic trade or couples anticipating a transatlantic separation: it did not apply to the colonies. Families therefore turned to contracts to negotiate the differences between Parisian and Rochelais common law, resorting to aspects of each as they provided opportunities or advantages.

In this particular case, the marriage contract drew upon the inheritance laws of Paris and La Rochelle in equal measure in order to provide Marie-Magdelaine the most flexibility in the event of widowhood. It delineated three options. First, she could maintain control over the couple's joint assets herself, a good option if her children were young or if trade was strong and profits high. Second, she could follow the custom of La Rochelle by passing her husband's half of their joint estate immediately to their children, an excellent choice if they were grown and ready to enter into a trading partnership. Third, she also could renounce their joint estate altogether, leaving her "free and clear of all debts," thus protecting herself and her family property from creditors, and preserving intact the assets she had brought into the marriage to pass along to her children.[31]

Under customary law in La Rochelle, a woman generally chose at the time of her marriage if she would have use of a fixed amount of the joint estate if her husband predeceased her, or if she would inherit half of their joint estate, as specified in customary law.[32] This option provided a valuable escape clause for a widow who, as a wife, had no formal control over the contracts and decisions made by her husband.[33] In this case, the expansiveness of these detailed provisions allowed Marie-Magdelaine Royer the option of continuing a thriving transatlantic business on her own as a widow. Her colonial upbringing, her merchant father, and her correspondence with her mother about colonial products hint that this was indeed a strong possibility.[34] As suited to a woman of her assets, even if she renounced the estate in favor of her children she could keep a furnished room in the family home or receive an allowance with which to rent a room, along with her jewelry, clothing, personal effects, and the considerable sum of ten thousand livres.[35]

In the face of an anticipated transatlantic separation, the Royer-Regnaud de Beaumont marriage contract's careful legal navigation makes sense, as the couple married under the jurisdiction of the Custom of La Rochelle, but the Custom of Paris could potentially apply to any inheritance. Marie-Magdelaine proved acutely aware of the difference between the two, and of the relative advantages each could offer her.[36] Numerous families of migrants from France's west coast to Saint-Domingue or other colonies faced this latent legal tangle.[37] A marriage contract could work out possible contradictions ahead of time. Parisian customary law offered the couple some potential benefits. In particular, it allowed flexibility in advantaging one heir over the others, thereby opening up the possibility that a son or the widow herself could continue operating the family business in the event of the husband's demise. The custom of La Rochelle also offered the couple attractive options, namely, allowing them to keep some of their assets strictly separate—at least in theory. Only a few assets specified in the marriage contract and any assets they generated during their marriage became part of their *communauté de biens*. Although Regnaud de Beaumont had some control over his wife's property during his lifetime, it was earmarked to pass intact to Marie-Magdelaine's heirs on her death. He did not have the right to sell it, mortgage it, or alienate it in any way.[38]

This separation of property meant that each spouse maintained a degree of financial autonomy and security. At the same time, only by augmenting their joint property could they better their own social and financial position, and that of their children. While the assets they brought into the marriage remained separate and would be passed discretely to the heirs of each as per the custom of La Rochelle, any money they made while married would belong to them jointly. Jean-Severin and Marie-Magdelaine thus had strong incentives to work together to increase the property they held in common. This meant that Marie-Magdelaine could play the role of a producer of wealth as well as a bearer of wealth, a role she definitively stepped into during her decades-long separation from her husband while he labored in Saint-Domingue and she remained in France.

Powers of Attorney

Not all couples anticipated long separations in their marriage contracts, but they all had recourse to other legal mechanisms to help women manage quotidian financial issues. The explosion of the Atlantic economy did not impel the first instances of marital separation, and for centuries French women had coped when separated from their husbands.[39] However, this practice became quite common in Atlantic ports such as La Rochelle in the eighteenth century, when ship's captains and sailors departed on long transatlantic voyages and other men flocked to France's Caribbean colonies in search of fortune, leaving their families behind them. Women throughout France routinely managed the day-to-day financial challenges of keeping a family afloat, including establishing lines of credit, making purchases, paying bills, and running family businesses.[40] In La Rochelle, families prepared for anticipated absences of husbands by providing wives with powers of attorney. This practice was particularly common among seafaring folk, where it extended up and down the social scale, from ship's captains to common sailors.[41] It had the advantage of explicitly empowering the wife, at home in France, with a measure of fiscal and legal authority she might otherwise lack, particularly over joint marital assets. According to the standard formulation of such documents, this included the "power to appear in court for them both [the husband and wife] and their agents, to represent [them] before all judges, commissioners, notaries, clerks, and other public and private persons . . . , to make decisions, to govern their goods and affairs either in this town, province, or anywhere else in the manner in which [they see] fit," all with the same authority as her husband.[42] Through powers of attorney, women melded traditional obligations to guard, preserve, and augment the family estate for their children with more modern ideas about expanding wealth by engaging in commerce.[43]

Even during the first years of their marriage Jean-Severin was regularly absent on merchant voyages.[44] Nonetheless his wife gave birth at regular intervals, and by the time he left La Rochelle for good, around 1743, he was already father to seven children. He never met the youngest of these French-born children, his namesake; before his birth in 1743, Jean-Severin *père* departed for Saint-Domingue.[45] At the time the colony was in the midst of a cash crop boom kindled by increased European demand for colonial products, and Jean-Severin did his best to take advantage of it. Although for unknown reasons he did not settle on his wife's family land, he owned and managed a plantation near Léogane that specialized in indigo, and he also produced some sugar, the quintessential Caribbean cash crop.[46] He saw his wife one last time when she made a final transatlantic journey to Saint-Domingue in the early 1750s, perhaps in response to a long illness Jean-Severin suffered in 1751.[47] A late-life son was born to them there in 1753, and she was pregnant again when she left the colony.[48] She gave birth to their ninth and final child, a daughter, on her arrival in La Rochelle in 1755.[49] With the exception of these few years passed together in the Antilles, Marie-Magdelaine and her husband spent most of their married lives apart, and she wielded his power of attorney from the time of his initial departure for the colonies in 1743 until his death in 1775.[50]

Throughout their married life, Jean-Severin continued the pattern begun in their marriage contract of giving his wife a substantial amount of control over their joint affairs. The power of attorney provided the primary legal mechanism through which he did this. Holding her husband's general power of attorney gave a woman a greater than usual amount of legal and fiscal control over their joint estate. Through this mechanism, Marie-Magdelaine Royer Regnaud de Beaumont wielded control over this joint estate under the authority of her husband's name, but in her own right. She ran his affairs and her own from her house on the rue des Maîtresses in La Rochelle, corresponding with merchants in Nantes, Bordeaux, Paris, and Saint-Domingue, arranging for shipment and dispersal of the indigo and other products sent from her husband's plantation, signing contracts and making business arrangements, and filing lawsuits to recover profits from sunken ships or crooked deals.[51]

Because of the large number of men who migrated to the Antilles from La Rochelle, on either short- or long-term bases, a woman wielding her husband's power of attorney became a common legal circumstance in the seaport. Yet this created fewer opportunities for women to engage in commerce than one might initially suspect. Although a husband gave his wife some measure of authority by granting her power of attorney, this move cannot be interpreted as empowering wives with control over family resources equal to that of their husbands. Because of its temporary nature, the power of attorney in fact emphasized husbands' power over their wives' civil life or death. In all cases, men controlled the gateway to their wives' civil authority. They could bestow it, but they could also take it away. For practical reasons many men involved in transatlantic trade chose, during their absences, to legally invest

Regnaud de Beaumont Family

Legend:
- ≡ = unmarried union
- — = married union
- ‖ = illegitimate children
- | = legitimate children

Jean-Severin Regnaud de Beaumont, 12 February 1706–27 July 1775, Léogane

m. 29 March 1735, La Rochelle

Marie-Magdelaine Royer, 24 April 1714, La Rochelle–27 Vendemiaire an IV (18 October 1795)

Presumed Marie-Anne, Free Negress, After 1743, Léogane

Children:

- Jean-Severin Nicolas, 22 December 1735–? (before 1775)
- Marie-Magdelaine, 25 April 1737–14 October 1811
- Jean Louis, 8 May 1740–? (before 1775)
- Raymond-Étienne, 8 or 9 September 1741–23 May 1754
- Marie-Brigitte, 8 October 1742–? (after 1804)
- Jean-Severin, 20 November 1743–25 November 1748
- Jean-Marie-Olive Regnaud, 11 December 1753, Léogane–? (after 1786, in or around Léogane)
- Marie-Severin-Augustin, 25 October 1755–9 February 1768

Children of Marie-Anne:

- Marie-Claire
- Marie-Olive

their wives with much of the influence that belonged to male heads of household. Married men on the point of departure seldom named anyone except their wives as *procurateur*, emphasizing the assumption that the couple shared a common economic interest. Madame Regnaud de Beaumont, then, found herself in the same legal situation as other women of varying social statuses whose husbands undertook the perilous sea voyage for the notably insalubrious Caribbean, unsure of their return.

Although power of attorney conferred legal authority on women, cultural limitations sometimes circumscribed the ways they could use this authority. While shopkeepers might have willingly set up lines of credit for household accounts, businessmen proved less amenable to accepting shipments of colonial goods from or contracting partnerships to outfit merchant voyages with a woman. In entering the male-dominated arena of transatlantic trade, Marie-Magdelaine Royer ran into difficulties her husband would have been unlikely to encounter. Her agents forestalled her requests, and her letters of credit were not honored. In spite of the indigo and other luxury goods her husband sent to trade from the colonies, she struggled to obtain the necessities required to care for her family—she simply lacked the clout possessed by a man involved in transatlantic trade.

As she strove to muster the influence required to exercise the legal authority the power of attorney gave her, Madame Regnaud de Beaumont turned to personal relationships and drew on the credibility of men besides her absent husband to persuade other merchants she was a force with which to reckon. She looked to a web of associates and acquaintances that stretched from the Atlantic ports of Bordeaux to Nantes, from Paris in the east to the Antillean colonies in the west, with La Rochelle at its center. She called on these contacts as she needed them, acting as a conduit for her husband's authority and empowering them, in turn, to represent her in situations where her femininity made it difficult to represent herself.

The Incident of the *Bellonne*

Plantation agriculture was a capricious business, relying on the vagaries of weather, crop yields, the market in colonial goods, outbreaks of disease, and even the political and diplomatic alliances of France, which in turn affected the stability of transatlantic shipping. Monsieur and Madame Regnaud de Beaumont cagily diversified their financial holdings, including ownership of a portion of a slaving ship, the *Bellonne*, in which Marie-Magdelaine took an active interest. As a former captain himself, Jean-Severin knew firsthand the potential profit margin of transatlantic trade. Accordingly, they went into partnership to buy this vessel, refit it to suit the purposes of the voyage, hire a captain and crew, and gather and load the merchandise to be traded.[52] If the ship returned laden with colonial produce, each partner reaped a percentage of the profits commensurate with the percentage of the capital they had invested in the enterprise. If the ship was lost, the partners each lost the money they had initially invested, a dispersal of risk that minimized the likelihood the venture would prove financially ruinous.

Established merchants owned shares of multiple vessels, thereby increasing the likelihood of returns and decreasing the possibilities of a disastrous loss. The Regnaud de Beaumonts only invested in the *Bellonne*. It proved seaworthy, and it brought in profits from the trade in slaves and colonial goods beginning in the early 1740s.[53] This venture had the potential to be doubly profitable for the couple, as Jean-Severin provided at least some of the colonial products the ship carried back to France.[54] Marie-Magdelaine little suspected that she would see none of the returns when this profitable partnership was dissolved and the ship sold.[55]

For a while, their joint ownership of the *Bellonne* proved a lucrative venture. Saint-Domingue was the preferred destination for the average of more than thirty-three slave ships per year that arrived in the French Antilles between 1712 and 1755.[56] The *Bellonne* was part of this flotilla. While owned by the Regnaud de Beaumonts it made two slave trading voyages, departing from La Rochelle in 1738 and 1741, and possibly subsequent journeys in the direct trade.[57] Although little information is available for the first crossing, what is known suggests that these voyages were typical for the period. The ship had a cargo capacity of one hundred eighty tons. On the first trip, it transported two hundred seventy-one Africans, a number slightly below the average of three hundred twenty-five for the middle of the eighteenth century.[58] On the second, three hundred forty-one slaves embarked from the Windward Coast and the Gold Coast, mostly from Anomabu, a trading post on the coast of what is today Ghana.[59] As was typical, nearly two-thirds of the slaves were men.[60] Even with a collective mortality rate of 13 percent (78 slaves dead—also a typical proportion), the owners could expect to make a hefty profit. In Cap Français in 1778–1779, male slaves sold for an average of 1,960 livres, and women for 1,763.[61] The only truly surprising element of the voyage was that instead of disembarking first at Cap Français, the commercial center of the colony, the second voyage sailed directly to Saint-Marc, more commonly a secondary or tertiary port of call.

Although the trajectory of the ship in the 1750s and 1760s is unclear, the Seven Years' War undoubtedly affected its transatlantic profitability.[62] In the decade after the conflict, pent-up wartime demand for slaves made the slave trade a lucrative investment, and as ship owners the Regnaud de Beaumont family was well positioned to take advantage. Yet instead of capitalizing on this demand, the partners in the *Bellonne* dissolved their association and sold the ship in the late 1760s. If this decision came from a need for ready money, their intentions were thwarted; the funds remained in the hands of just one of the partners, who lived in Bordeaux and refused to disburse their share of the profits to the other members of the society.

In this situation, Madame Regnaud de Beaumont had few choices in spite of the power of attorney. How could she, a woman with children and family responsibilities, force a merchant in a different city to cough up her family's share of the profits? She had business and family commitments in La Rochelle, and women traveling alone faced practical difficulties and deep suspicion. Consequently she entrusted her suit to Jacob de Griselles, a merchant and officer of the king in Bordeaux, rather than travel there to take care of the matter herself.

Madame Regnaud de Beaumont's letters to this merchant differ markedly from the usual terse epistles of business associates. Instead, both she and Griselles emphasized their personal connections and wrote the gracious news-filled letters of acquaintances. This departure from common business practice implies that in this age of letter writing, Madame Regnaud de Beaumont used letters to emphasize the importance of personal connections in commerce as in social situations. Griselles reciprocated in kind, even touching on the ways in which personal relationships could ease the way toward a favorable judicial decision as he brought her case to force the disbursement of the profits from the sale of the ship before the Parlement in Bordeaux. He emphasized his own connections with the judges, which he guaranteed Madame Regnaud de Beaumont would help him settle the case in their favor with due speed. He assured her, "be very persuaded, Madame, of my zeal and my haste to solicit for myself and my friends the Judgment of the lawsuit that is in our Parlement." By using his connections to gather as much information on the case as he could, he promised that he would gain "a familiarity with this affair to be able to act more effectively."[63] For two and a half years he assured her that their case was about to be heard and that her share of the holdings of the society would be distributed to her forthwith.

Finally, after months of such communication without seeing a single *sou* of the profits, Madame Regnaud de Beaumont ran out of money or patience. She was involved in other deals for which she needed cash.[64] She finally asked Griselles for an advance on the profits she knew she was owed, drawing on her business acumen to sharply insist on her rights. This move emphasized the limits she faced in exercising the authority given to her by the procuration. As her letters grew more and more insistent, Griselles finally admitted that "I do not know what to think of his [Monsieur Prevost, a partner in their enterprise who lived in Saint-Domingue] delay in getting the capital to me, knowing quite well that he has on hand more than 100,000 francs in capital of our society concerning the ship the *Bellonne*."[65] He went on to deliver the real blow—that Prevost had already paid her husband the share of the profits Madame Regnaud de Beaumont thought would be coming to her. As small consolation, Griselles continued, "I do not know if he also remitted to him the seven thousand eight livres that I found owed to Monsieur your husband."[66] Backpedaling somewhat on his extravagant promises to successfully present her case at the Parlement, he offered his sincerely phrased regrets on not being able to advance her any of the funds she was owed. Madame Regnaud de Beaumont's special legal rights and privileges came to naught: in spite of her work, responsibilities, and best efforts, the hard-earned profits she needed desperately were dispensed directly to her husband, without even a word to her.

This casual assumption of patriarchal privilege shows that while the power of attorney offered Madame Regnaud de Beaumont some practical power, when serious financial matters were at stake other merchants frankly preferred to deal with her husband. At this point in her correspondence with Griselles, the letters underwent a striking transformation. Perhaps realizing Madame Regnaud de Beaumont's dire financial straits or responding to her increasingly insistent and detailed queries as to the efficacy of his accounting, the merchant abandoned his avuncular tone and went on the defensive. "I can easily prove to you," he snapped, "that I had in advance for Monsieur your husband from the 25 April 1766 until 10 February 1767, a sum of more than eleven thousand francs, and from the following 5 October until 5 May 1768 more than sixteen thousand livres." However, since Griselles had overseen and received the profits for the sale of the ship, he said, "I find myself at present his debtor . . . of seven thousand francs."[67] He finally agreed to send her a bill of exchange for two thousand francs, which she could draw from a firm in La Rochelle.[68]

Yet when she received the bill and took it to the merchant in question, he refused to disburse the funds.[69] In Griselles' next letter, he defended himself against what must have been her bitter recriminations. "I will send [another] to you," he says, "in spite of the reasons that I had the honor of sharing with you in my preceding [letter], that must by their validity engage you to not hound me as you do."[70]

Her letters in turn combined careful business accounts of what she was owed with astringent reproaches of his way of conducting business. She berated him, "my last [letter] of the 5 June has been until the present without response on your part, about which I am very surprised." She went on to ask, "what [do] you intend to do on the subject of the sum that you must remit me? You complained wrongly, Monsieur that I hound you; but I complain rightly that you lead me on, and you mock me in every way." Her indignation rested not only on her want or need for the sum of money, but also on careful research and calculations. "I received," she continued, "a letter from my husband, and [another] from M. Prevost, who credited me as having received that sum." She went on to threaten that either he provide her with the sum she asked for—2,000 francs—or she would withdraw all her accounts with him. After giving him a careful statement of expenses incurred on the lump sum he still held for her, including a bill of exchange he had previously remitted to her, she said, "it still seemed to leave me with 4,308 livres." She also refused to pay postage for letters he sent on her behalf.[71] Her threats worked; with his next letter, he sent her another bill of exchange for 2,000 livres.[72] Having gotten what she wanted, she sent him a nice note of thanks.[73] In spite of her *politesse*, her claims still proved only partly successful: the profits from the sale of the ship remained in the hands of her husband, and she received not even half the additional amount she was owed.

This correspondence demonstrates that the actual authority conferred by the power of attorney was far less sweeping than the text of the document implied. Although the document invested Madame Regnaud de Beaumont with the same rights, privileges, and legal abilities as her husband in a court of law, just getting her case into a courtroom proved to be a trial. Probably aware of these difficulties, she first set out to settle her business disputes in more informal ways that were more easily accessible to women, particularly by fostering and trading on personal relationships. Only when this strategy proved unsuccessful did she bring her considerable business acumen to bear; with the evidence of her cold figures, supported by the accounting of her associates, her claim brooked no denial. While the power of attorney gave her claims muscle, it remained in the background, a last resort, and she used it rather to pass along her husband's authority to others than to appropriate and wield it herself.

When the case finally came before the court, she again empowered Jacob de Griselles to make her claim. He wrote to her, "I do not fear winning this suit with expenses, if I have merchants for judges, who know all the nuance and force of my presentations; but if it will be magistrates who must judge a question that they do not perhaps consider, as if they were in the place of merchants, in the end we must wait until the time which the judgment is rendered, after which I will sigh heavily."[74] Madame Regnaud de Beaumont no doubt sighed heavily as well when her delicate correspondence with Griselles came to a close. It had been an exercise in carefully negotiating where the responsibility for her business lay, who had authority over her finances, and ultimately the manner in which she lived her life as a woman responsible for a household throughout her husband's long absence. This control was extremely important for maintaining the wellbeing and position of her family.

The incident of the *Bellonne* brings into relief one way that empire shaped the lives of women in port cities. Like many other women faced with a husband's extended absence, Marie-Magdelaine Regnaud de Beaumont occupied the roles of both wife and head of household. As a head of household, she was responsible for her and her children's welfare and for working to assure and improve the position of her family. As a wife, she not only remained under the authority of her husband, he also could—and did—undercut her directives with his own. The long separation of this husband and wife therefore caused a rift that affection, if it remained alive, could not surmount. The distance across the Atlantic and the time it took for letters to travel back and forth—six weeks to six months—meant that even in the best of circumstances husbands and wives could not always communicate effectively about their common goals or how they intended to reach them. While their economic partnership, cemented by their marriage, continued, husband and wife by this point each were working toward their own separate ends.

The incident of the *Bellonne* may have been Madame Regnaud de Beaumont's first inkling that she and her husband, supposedly united in the common goal of increasing their wealth and position for the good of their children, actually had extraordinarily different intentions indeed. But this was only the beginning of her money troubles, and exactly how far their interests had diverged did not become clear until after her husband's death.

Illegitimacy and Inheritance

White men who sojourned in Saint-Domingue frequently had families with women of color, thus complicating their family situations. When these men were already married, such alliances thwarted family strategies, especially inheritance, and also challenged notions of what comprised a family. Inheritance, then, became a means of constituting, attacking, or defending competing understandings of family and familial relationships. Transatlantic distances weakened official family ties formed in France, while colonial practices complicated notions of family as lineal blood relations. New types of family relationships gave rise to new means of transmitting wealth, which were often hotly contested by kin who felt themselves slighted. At stake here was the meaning of family as an economic and affective unit.

When Jean-Severin Regnaud de Beaumont died in 1775 in the town of Léogane, Saint-Domingue, he had been physically separated from his wife for most of their forty years of marriage and had not seen her in over twenty years. In the meantime, he had formed another family. This was hardly unusual in Saint-Domingue, where white men commonly engaged in sexual relationships with enslaved or free women of color, practicing "de facto polygyny."[75] Such liaisons generally remained outside the civil and religious adjudications of family that governed intimate relations in France, and white men had no legal responsibilities to mixed-race offspring born out of wedlock. Nevertheless, numerous men, including those who also had legitimate families, made efforts to provide for their illegitimate children of color. Men routinely gave such children gifts of money, land, livestock, or slaves, set them up in business, or provided them with dowries, although there was no legal obligation for them to do so.[76] Regnaud de Beaumont went beyond most in that he provided for his mixed-race daughters, Marie-Claire and Marie-Olive, to the exclusion of his legitimate family back in France, a move that went against common law, his marriage contract, and assumptions about slavery and the family.[77]

As in France, colonial law mandated that men leave the bulk of their estates to legitimate children or kin. Fathers could not disinherit their legitimate children, and French common law generally held that they could only leave adulterine children legacies that filled their basic needs, and that only in usufruct.[78] Although in France illegitimate children whose parents were free to marry generally could inherit substantial legacies, in Saint-Domingue the law went further, stipulating that mixed-race children could lay no claim to their white fathers' estates unless their parents married.[79] Contracts provided means to skirt such provisions.[80] Fathers could give illegitimate children money or property through *donations entre vifs*, and could leave sizable legacies to them in the form of cash, livestock, personal possessions, and annuities. Such gifts in fact contributed to the social and economic power of free colored people in Saint-Domingue.[81] These practices had the potential to wreak havoc among families in France. Jean-Severin Regnaud de Beaumont's wish to provide for his illegitimate *mulâtre* daughters drove his legitimate white family apart.

Shortly before her husband's death, Marie-Magdelaine Regnaud de Beaumont realized that something was amiss. Consequently, in 1774, maybe aware of her husband's ailing health and certainly cognizant of his advancing age, she sent her youngest and only surviving son Jean-Marie-Olive to Saint-Domingue, the colony where he was born twenty-two years before. In the thirty-nine years since their marriage, Jean-Severin and Marie-Magdelaine Regnaud de Beaumont had failed to realize the colonial dream. Jean-Severin had grown old on the land he worked, but his fortune had not increased with age. While some planters grew rich on colonial products grown by their slaves, his fortune, of a promising size at the time of his marriage, had dwindled to practically nothing. Like numerous planters in the 1770s, he also was deeply in debt. He owed E. L. Seignette, a transatlantic merchant in La Rochelle, nearly 14,000 livres, and he had other debts as well.[82] Although his wife had also faced financial challenges, his son was shocked to witness the depths to which his father had sunk.

Jean-Marie-Olive's letters to his mother and sisters back in France reinvigorated the ties among the transatlantic members of the family. As testament to the difficulties of transatlantic marriage and to the broken trust that had distanced them, Monsieur and Madame Regnaud de Beaumont seldom exchanged letters. When young Jean-Marie-Olive arrived in Saint-Domingue, therefore, his father's poor health and meager finances came as a surprise. He wrote to his mother, "you would not be able to believe, dear Mother, how my dear Papa is in despair to not have and to not be able to send you any [financial] relief. He has been, and is more than ever, in a physical state which makes it impossible to do it, lacking himself a good number of things, he needs money of which he has been deprived for a long time, and [he] hardly has what is necessary." According to his son, Regnaud de Beaumont found himself "in a situation as critical as that in which we all found ourselves in France, and he has had the worst illnesses, passing whole nights without sleeping, and is even persuaded that he is losing his sight, which is irreparable."[83] The son complained that even his father's "linens were already old," insinuating that Regnaud de Beaumont senior could not afford even the most basic necessities.[84]

In spite of his son's return, Regnaud de Beaumont was hardly a figure that inspired reverence in or respect for patriarchal authority. He was old, sick, partly blind, and pitifully poor. Nevertheless, he still had the right and power to make his will. In doing so, he decisively undercut the marriage contract he signed forty years before and the expectations of his legitimate family. For his wife, safeguarded, as she thought, by the marriage contract and customary law, the testament came as a series of surprises. First was the revelation of his second family, a woman of color and their two daughters, a common enough circumstance she may have surmised but did not know beforehand. Second and more shocking, her husband's entire estate and her own had dwindled to practically nothing. Not even her son's letters had prepared her for the extent of her husband's penury. Regardless of the protections of the marriage contract and the customary laws of La Rochelle and Paris, all of which forbade her husband from alienating her property, her wealth and her plantation were nonetheless gone, apparently without her knowledge or consent. Finally, Regnaud de Beaumont left the pittance that remained of the estate to his illegitimate daughters in the form of legacies, effectively cutting off his three surviving legitimate children completely.[85]

These legacies affirm that Regnaud de Beaumont's emotional connections lay with his family in Saint-Domingue, not with his legal family in France. He left "a life pension of one hundred livres" to each of his "natural daughters, free *mulâtresses*" Marie-Claire and Marie-Olive, "daughters of Marie-Anne free *négresse*."[86] Such a legacy in itself was not rare. It was more unusual, however, for a father of "natural" children to acknowledge his paternity in his will. While fathers might recognize mixed-race children at their baptism as a way of ascertaining their freedom, they generally gave them gifts or left them legacies without specific acknowledgment of their familial relationship. Regnaud de Beaumont's daughters were to be paid in installments of fifty livres every six months, beginning on the day of their father's death, and payments

---

were to continue throughout their lives. In addition, the girls and their half-brother Jean-Marie-Olive each inherited a mahogany chest filled with their personal belongings, suggesting that the whole family, legitimate and illegitimate, white, mixed-race, and black, lived under one roof—a circumstance the son, perhaps naturally enough, had failed to mention in his letters to his mother. Regnaud de Beaumont specified that his son, still a minor, would stay on the plantation as overseer. His legitimate daughters and his wife, back in France, he did not mention at all.

He appointed his neighbor Michel Samuel DeColon his executor, conceivably hoping that his friend, familiar with life in the colonies, would work to ensure that Marie-Claire and Marie-Olive received their annuities. In principle these legacies were in line with what many mixed-race children could expect: they provided enough to live on but did not, on the surface, seem overly exorbitant. In this instance, though, Regnaud de Beaumont's assets had disappeared to such an extent that these legacies comprised the bulk of his wealth.[87] Even his plantation was mortgaged to the hilt, and his considerable debts ate up his lean assets.

Regnaud's burial took place on 27 July 1775 in the parish church of Sainte Rose in Léogane, the same church where his son had been baptized twenty-two years before.[88] His death precipitated a flurry of transatlantic correspondence and paperwork: his assets had to be valued, his wife had to determine how best to protect herself and her children from her husband's creditors, and the estate needed to be portioned out accordingly. Regnaud, never a good businessman, had proved astoundingly optimistic in judging the value of his estate. The unexpectedly small size of his holdings led to conflicts over its apportioning and disputes that divided parents from children and siblings from each other.[89]

DeColon, as executor, began the sticky process of liquidating his friend's assets, while keeping the widow informed by letter. His news was seldom good. The plantation was in "appalling confusion," and what he called the "cursed place" produced little revenue in the year between Regnaud's death and its sale.[90] They hardly had enough to keep body and soul together. DeColon wrote that "the slaves here are dying of hunger, and all naked." Finally, he wrote, "I have sold the plantation, the slaves, and the few beasts that remained for the sum of 34,000 livres," a considerable amount, which, however, included "12,000 livres in letters of credit . . . and 18,000 livres cash."[91] Colonial letters of credit were notoriously difficult to collect, and the entire sum amounted to scarcely more than the substantial thirty-thousand-livre dowry

Marie-Magdelaine Royer brought into her marriage.[92] He wrote, "The most difficult thing will be to get paid, and I fear a terrible suit."[93]

The biggest point of contention, of course, was the annuities Regnaud de Beaumont had left to Marie-Claire and Marie-Olive. In spite of their ongoing relationship with their father, little is known about these two women. As urban, free women of color, they were most likely to work as housekeepers or shopkeepers, both potentially lucrative trades that required high levels of skill.[94] Even though their father's life ended in penury, as daughters of a planter they may have enjoyed some advantages based on his connections: well-placed godparents, for example, or a certain amount of respect in the community. As young women, they likely planned on marriage and perhaps were amassing dowries for that purpose, either in cash or in the form of household furnishings. Items desirable for well-placed women of color included cedar or mahogany beds complete with coverlets and mosquito nets, wooden armoires, tables, chairs, mirrors, mattresses, pillows, bolsters, and counterpanes.[95] For Marie-Claire and Marie-Olive, the legacies left by their father might have made the difference between a good marriage and a mediocre one, or may have provided the means to set themselves up in business. The stakes, therefore, were high.

Thus began a long financial battle over the course of which Marie-Magdelaine Regnaud de Beaumont tried to preserve her family's legacy, her children worked to safeguard their own financial interests, and her husband's natural daughters struggled to secure their way of life. The success of each depended on their ability to articulate their own version of their family relationship with the deceased Regnaud. Seemingly what was at stake here was not race but legitimacy, but of course in the colonies, the two categories overlapped so much that they were often interchangeable. Legitimacy, however, provided the legal framework for Madame Regnaud de Beaumont and her allies to contest her husband's will. As a result, DeColon, with the tacit approval, if not the explicit instruction, of Madame Regnaud de Beaumont, worked to prevent Marie-Claire and Marie-Olive from inheriting the legacy left by their father by emphasizing their illegitimacy. DeColon wrote,

I have sold the land in town . . . the *négresse* who occupies it is desolated but I do not know what to do. She obtained an official copy of the will by which the late M. Regnaud gave to his two natural daughters an annual pension of one hundred livres each, for a total of two hundred livres. There is every appearance that I will have to act; I will always respond that he has nothing, that first the privileged debts must be paid, then the others, and that it is not natural, although there may be a small pension to provide food, that the natural children have a pension in a situation in which the legitimate ones have nothing, and in which they are obliged to work to earn their bread. We will see what is decided.[96]

In this extraordinary passage, DeColon made quite clear that lineage and legitimacy trumped affection and even testamentary intentions.[97] Legally, he was right: not only did common law consolidate the rights of legitimate children over their parents' estate, Regnaud de Beaumont's marriage contract confirmed his future children's inheritance. But his years in the colonies changed his family situation. While his wife back in La Rochelle had three surviving children, he had five, and he wanted to provide for his mixed-race daughters in Saint-Domingue. He tried to do this through the legal means available to him by making them legatees in his will. This recognition of their relationship, in an official document signed, sealed, and registered by a notary, offered Marie-Clare and Marie-Olive a portion of social and financial legitimacy, even if legally they had none. Their father, wielding his prerogative to make a will, thus tried to use the force of the law to protect the inheritance he felt was theirs by right of their relationship to him.

According to the letter of the law, Regnaud de Beaumont's strategy had been sound. All debts and legacies would be paid out of the estate before it was divided amongst heirs.[98] DeColon and the widow knew that only if the estate were bankrupt would the annuities fail to be paid. What's more, the unnamed *négresse* in DeColon's letter realized this as well (likely Marie-Clare and Marie-Olive's mother Marie-Anne). Upset at having her house sold from under her, she turned to Regnaud de Beaumont's will. By obtaining an official copy she demonstrated herself familiar with not only Regnaud de Beaumont's wishes, but also the legal process by which they would be enacted. DeColon clearly thought she would take the case to court, and feared, as long as any money at all remained in the estate, that she would win. His strategy, therefore, drew on moral as well as legal definitions of family. He emphasized the injustice of the situation for the legitimate children, and the father's "natural" obligation to assure their future first.

In the end, Marie-Magdelaine Regnaud de Beaumont renounced her right to her husband's estate.[99] This option, delineated in their marriage contract, protected her property from her husband's creditors and ended her liability for his debts. Her younger daughter Marie-Brigitte joined her in her renunciation, thereby giving up all her claims on her father's estate, although she still would retain the right to one-third of her mother's. This did not mean that Marie-Magdelaine could simply walk away. She still had to oversee the appraisal of the assets and to give authorization for the day-to-day expenses of running the plantation while the legal battle unfolded. To that end she gave DeColon her power of attorney, thereby authorizing him to sell slaves and other forms of property, probably in an effort to liquidate the assets and to help her children salvage what they could from the estate.[100]

Her other two surviving children, Jean-Marie-Olive, still in Saint-Domingue, and his sister Marie-Magdelaine in La Rochelle, more optimistic or more desperate than their mother or sister, continued to fight for their father's estate. They looked everywhere they could to recuperate some of the assets their father had lost, and to a limited extent they succeeded. DeColon, acting as their representative, tried to collect debts of over three thousand livres from a merchant in Bordeaux who owed money to their father.[101] They also brought suit against a free black man who was his debtor, and later tried to sue DeColon himself.[102] They evidently still were trying to recover their father's estate in 1786, when Jean-Marie wrote his last letter to his mother. In it he complained about his dire financial straits as he had before, and some of his bitterness about the hopelessness of his situation comes through: "there is no money," he said; "youth passes, and we are no further along."[103] After that, the young man disappeared. His aging mother never heard from him again, or learned of his fate.[104]

The provisions of Regnaud de Beaumont's will, the surprising paucity of his resources at his death, and the unexplained disappearance of his wife's property all highlight the difficult contingencies colonialism raised for families, and the lack of options available to women. In the end, when faced with her late husband's near bankruptcy, the result of his own mismanagement, Marie-Magdelaine could only protect the assets over which she had control. She spent her married life legally empowered by her husband, managing business deals and assets, yet as a widow she struggled to recoup any of the fruits of these labors. She had continued operating under the assumption that her husband shared her idea of what constituted a family: a husband and wife legally married and their legitimate children, all working toward the common goal of the betterment of all. He had come to a different understanding of family, one based on shared daily life and, presumably, affection.

Establishing an economic foothold in the colonies frequently occasioned a long separation between husband and wife, and these circumstances gave rise to a specific set of opportunities and constraints for women left behind in France. Families tried to prepare for such challenging circumstances through contracts. Customary law, while affording women some protections, did not account for long marital separations that in ports such as La Rochelle came as a matter of course in the eighteenth century. Families did their best to peer into the future, writing into marriage contracts provisions that would allow a married couple separated by an ocean the flexibility they would need to work singly toward their assumed joint project. Couples continued this strategy on the eve of husbands' departures; powers of attorney offered wives the legal license to operate businesses, manage property, and generally contribute toward their mutual assets, even in their husbands' absences. Contracts such as these filled the gaps in customary law while not necessarily undermining or going against it. Contracts and custom aimed to allow families to accumulate and pass on assets, making provisions for the welfare of women and children, particularly in the case of a husband's death.

Testaments also generally endorsed this goal, offering the testator an opportunity to indicate appreciation, affection, or benevolence through small legacies, while ratifying the flow of wealth from one generation to the next. Yet the case of the Regnaud de Beaumont family reveals the power that colonial circumstances had to interrupt this flow. When white men formed new alliances, they upset assumptions of what constituted a family and how families should act, particularly with regard to the accumulation and transmission of wealth. Contracts, therefore, proved ways to disrupt as well as protect family assets.

On the surface, the case of the Regnaud de Beaumont family suggests that the circumstances of transatlantic separation opened up a wealth of opportunity for women. Marriage contracts wrote in choices and drew on multiple common law traditions to ensure women maximum flexibility to continue engaging in profitable commercial activity. Powers of attorney gave them authority as heads of household, while the absence of husbands gone to the Antilles impelled a number of women into the thick of business deals. However, contracts proved to be limited tools. Power within the family continued to flow from white French men, who gave women the permission to act in their names. Husbands could take away this authority as easily as they bestowed it. While women's cultural position could stand in the way of their participation in colonial commerce, men's cultural position enabled them, at least on occasion, to alienate their wives' property without raising questions in spite of the multiple prohibitions against this.

While women's sexual propriety was of utmost concern in a marriage, men could and did form second families, and sometimes, as here, indicate through their testamentary allocation of assets that their regard for them surpassed that which they held for their legitimate children. Patriarchal authority, therefore, operated on both sides of the ocean: white women, women of color, legitimate children, and illegitimate children all depended on the will of the father. Other family members could only do their best to protect their own interests and privileges.

While on first glance intimacy pertained little to transatlantic commerce, the Regnaud de Beaumont family makes plain that intimate relationships profoundly shaped commercial interactions. Marie-Magdelaine Regnaud de Beaumont's uncommon status as a woman fully empowered by her husband opened up opportunities for her to engage in business dealings on equal legal footing with her male associates. However, her gender limited the cultural authority she could actually wield in the transatlantic marketplace. At the same time, by virtue of his masculinity her husband exercised patriarchal authority in commerce and in domestic life. By providing for his mixed-race second family at the expense of his legitimate wife and children, he undermined ideals of the nuclear family, and also of racial hierarchy.

Yet white women as well as white men had intimate relationships with people of color, including Marie-Magdelaine Regnaud de Beaumont. Closely examining these interracial relationships contests the assumption that intimacies across racial lines necessarily had sexual congress at the core. Focusing on relations between white women and people of color, slave and free, gives texture to households complicated by slavery, and offers an opportunity to consider family and household separately from interracial sex.

CHAPTER 4

_____

Economies of Race and Gender

As Marie-Magdelaine Regnaud de Beaumont doubtless knew, having grown up in Saint-Domingue, white women constituted a distinct minority in the colony. In 1700, there were two white men for every one white woman, a proportion that remained consistent through much of the eighteenth century due to the continuation of heavily masculine immigration.[1] As a result, contemporary and historical accounts of Saint-Domingue primarily have portrayed white women in sexual terms. Metropolitan commentators characterized white women, like all colonists, as sexual creatures turned torrid by the tropics.[2] Hilliard d'Auberteuil called them "fecund, passionate, and jealous. . . . The desires in them ordinarily survive youth and beauty, they still seek voluptuousness when age advances and pleasure flees." He continued, "Innocent joy and amiable modesty rarely shine in their glances. . . . Voluptuousness is in their eyes, and seduction in their hearts."[3] Simultaneously, colonial defenders of white creolité portrayed the sexuality of white women as the foundation of the virtue of colonial society.[4] Portrayed by Moreau as "spiritual" and "sensitive," doting mothers and faithful wives, white women's loving yet chaste nature grew from the colonial experience itself.[5] While colonists and metropolitans debated the nature of white women's sexuality without ever questioning them as fundamentally sexual beings, they were in agreement about the destructive and consuming nature of the sexuality of women of color.[6] Whether constructive or destructive, redemptive or lethal, contemporary discourses generally portrayed women in one-dimensional, sexualized terms.[7]

Yet white women played a much more integrated role in colonial life than such accounts imply. Although, as Hilliard d'Auberteuil posits, some white women may have been plantation ladies "lolling limply among their slaves," scores of white women in Saint-Domingue were—like their counterparts in

France—active producers and consumers, buyers and sellers, lessors and les-sees, owners and slaves, mistresses and servants.[8] They were embedded in networks of personal and intimate relations that extended across race and status.

Examining the roles and relationships of white women in colonial Saint-Domingue therefore prompts a reconsideration of common narratives that portrayed white women as neglected, jealous wives, cast aside by their hus-bands in favor of *mulâtre* mistresses and particularly brutal to their slaves as a result.[9] White women and people of color actually formed a variety of inti-mate bonds as they came into close daily contact with each other. In Saint-Domingue, slavery complicated households, families, and the relations among those who comprised them. Gender and race played crucial roles in defining and structuring hierarchies within these households. Negotiating such an intimate context, where hierarchy was simultaneously reinforced and broken down, required a specialized skill set and knowledge that, in turn, shows that distinctions between house and field slaves, those who lived closely with whites and those who did not, went beyond differences in living conditions, labor, and abuse. Seriously considering knowledge acquired by slaves and free people of color who lived in close proximity with whites and interacted with them on a daily basis prompts rethinking intimacy and inti-mate relations across racial lines.

Focusing closely on white women's relations with people of color gives a much richer sense of how people in colonial Saint-Domingue understood the household not exclusively as a site for sex and affective relationships, but also—and perhaps primarily—as a site for economic relationships. Consider-ing white women as economic actors emphasizes their integration into colo-nial life, on plantations and in urban centers in the western province. Colonial circumstances may have presented opportunities for women to assert eco-nomic autonomy in ways not available to them in France. Colonial practices and relationships, however, complicated changing dynamics of power in the metropole. Hierarchies that may have seemed crystal clear in one place could prove difficult to assert in the other. A focus on white women, then, not only disrupts stereotypes, it also offers a new view on how race, gender, money, and power operated in Atlantic France.

Household Relationships

In the Old Regime, households were first and foremost sites of production. Slavery, too, was an economic relationship, and for slaves, as for servants, households were sites of labor. They were likewise places of violence, of domination and vulnerability based on patriarchy and race.[10] They were also intimate spaces where individuals existed side by side. Such coexistence bred intimacy, whether sexual, deep, indifferent, or one-sided. Focusing on white women's intimate relationships with people of color helps to rupture the fantasy that cross-racial relationships were exclusively sexual in nature. Although it is important to note that some relationships between white women and women and men of color certainly were sexual—Hilary Beckles has found instances of sexual intimacy between white women and men of color in early eighteenth-century Barbados—by the mid-eighteenth century white women faced increasing ostracism and men of color brutal punishments for such intimacy.[11] These consequences make it difficult to imagine that sex was at the bottom of all relationships between white women and people of color, as historians and contemporaries tended to assume of white men. Rather, paying close attention to how white women constructed and reinforced their networks with people of color, slave and free, offers an opportunity to consider the complexity, reciprocity, and multiple motivations behind interracial relationships.

In the western province of Saint-Domingue, particularly in urban enclaves, whites and free people of color lived, worked, and traded in extremely integrated communities.[12] They were neighbors, renting or owning houses on the same streets and even sometimes sharing the same residence. Although conflicts inevitably arose, sometimes leading to litigation, neighborliness often prevailed. They did business with each other, buying and leasing land, purchasing necessities, making loans, and even trusting their affairs to each other.[13] While such urban relations did not seem to reflect racial hostilities between whites and free people of color, things were different, of course, for slaves: hierarchies between slaves and their owners were legally encoded and enacted with obsessive regularity. Yet slavery too bred intimacy, especially between owners and house slaves or body servants. Such interactions would have led to familiarity of habit, ways of thinking, and body. Examining white women's emancipations of slaves as well as gifts and legacies they made across racial lines begins to outline the possibilities for quotidian familiarity in creating intimacy, and intimates that everyday interactions, not sexual commerce, lay at the heart of interracial relationships. Seriously considering such interactions prompts a reassessment of the complicated relationship between gender and race and the ways that gender shaped these correlating hierarchies.

Unsurprisingly, white men emancipated slaves more frequently than white women; white men's simple demographic preponderance combined with married women's legal invisibility makes this an expected outcome. In turn, most historians have assumed that white men's motivations for granting emancipation stemmed from family feeling, and that they usually freed their sexual partners and their mixed-race children.[14] Most recently, Dominque Rogers' careful culling of emancipation contracts in Port-au-Prince and Cap Français has borne out earlier figures that on the surface support this assumption: approximately 70 percent of slaves emancipated from 1776 to 1789 were female.[15]

However, white women, like white men, primarily emancipated enslaved women and children. A small sampling of emancipation documents registered with notaries in the western province is suggestive rather than comprehensive. Yet of eleven acts in which white women emancipated slaves, drawn up by three notaries in three different towns over the course of nine years, only one of twenty-two slaves emancipated was a grown man. Ten were women and eleven children, five of the children were boys and three girls, and for the remaining three the sex was not specified.[16] There are several possible explanations for this numeric imbalance. Gender expectations emphasizing white women's chastity and sexual continence conceivably constrained them from forging intimate relations with enslaved men that might lead to manumission. This may have been particularly true for the single or widowed women who tended to settle their own contracts. Further, the number of female slaves in urban areas in Saint-Domingue exceeded the number of male slaves.[17] Free women of color in Cap Français bought and sold female slaves twice as often as male slaves, a surprising statistic as the overwhelming majority of slaves imported to Saint-Domingue were male.[18] White women may have been more likely to own women slaves as well. On a practical level, such gender unity must have simplified daily interactions and relations of authority. However, taken in conjunction with white men's preference for emancipating women and children, it also implies that expectations for and roles of women of color made it more possible for them to form personal bonds across lines of race. The relations forged within the household, typically based on accepted gender roles, shaped pathways to emancipation and interactions across racial lines.

The emancipation of Manite, the slave of Dame Julienne Guilladeau, illustrates the cumbersome legal process and demonstrates some of the potential reasons white women may have had for emancipating slaves. On 30 January 1784 Dame Guilladeau, widow of a planter, went to a notary's office in Léogane to ratify that she had given liberty to Manite, a *mulâtresse*.[19] This had been a long process. By the 1780s, owners who wished to emancipate their slaves had to receive permission from high authorities. Accordingly, the widow had received an ordinance from the intendant of Saint-Domingue, dated the previous November, which authorized her to emancipate Manite, whose baptismal name was Marie-Françoise. She likewise had to present a certificate of permission given by the Audiencier of Port-au-Prince, who held jurisdiction over Léogane. She then had to publish her intent to free Manite three times.[20] As no one objected to her intention, she certified that fact to the officials in Port-au-Prince, and finally paid a fee of 2,000 livres, and additional taxes of 40 livres.[21] This high fee was due to Manite's gender; after 1766, owners paid a freedom fee of 2,000 livres on female slaves of childbearing age, much more than the market value of most enslaved women. This was an acknowledgment that not only the woman but also all her descendants would receive their liberty; men were taxed at only half that rate.[22] Part of a broader effort to inhibit emancipations in general, this provision particularly aimed to prevent white men from freeing their mistresses. As the case of Manite makes clear, though, not all manumissions were effected by men seeking to free their lovers. Whites, including white women, could have other compelling reasons to free their slaves.

Once Manite was officially declared free, she received a new surname, "Zoe, in the African idiom," conforming with a law that aimed to draw clear distinctions between whites and free people of color, in part by forbidding slaves or free people of color from taking the surnames of whites.[23] Finally, the seneschal of Port-au-Prince ratified the document, which he did over a year after the fact. There is no hint that Manite took any part in this process, although many slaves played active roles in self-emancipation and in the actual process of having the correct emancipation documents drawn up.[24] This is unsurprising, as she was only ten years old at the time.

By demonstrating the extensive bureaucratic formalities and considerable expense necessary to free a slave, particularly a female one, this contract hints that by the 1770s whites who pursued formal emancipation for their

slaves must have had significant motivations to do so. Although emancipation acts give little insight into slave owners' reasons, they do provide occasional flashes that present some evocative possibilities. A number of white
women freed mixed-race children, who may have been the offspring of their
husbands or sons. This may have been the case when the heirs of Marie-
Thérèse Joummeaux freed Joachim, the three-year-old *mulâtre* son of her
slave Romaine.[25] It is possible, of course, that these children belonged to the
white women themselves, but such a scenario is much less likely. Yet actually
either instance seems a bizarre stretch, an effort to read the stereotype of un-
bridled colonial sexuality onto all interracial connections. When Dame Ju-
sienne Cobert freed the slave Marie-Lomie who had belonged to her deceased
son, it is possible that she may have been respecting his wishes to free his
mistress.[26] More likely she emancipated the forty-nine-year-old slave for her
faithful service to her son, as the emancipation document indicated, or even
that she simply no longer wanted to be bothered with an aging slave whose
most productive years of labor were already behind her. Similarly, white
women who freed enslaved children may have done so as a reward not to the
children but to their mothers, because they felt a fondness for them independent of blood relations, or because they did not want the expense or bother of
bringing them up.

Not all owners who intended to free slaves went through the formal process. A number of slaves lived "as free," the so-called "libres de savane," a
condition in which Alexis, in Chapter 1, may have lived before his liberty was
ratified.[27] Some owners even considered the existence of an emancipation tax
an affront to their own claims to property rights in their slaves.[28] On plantations, slaves could live "as free" with little interference from authorities, although in many cases their conditions differed little from those of slaves.[29]
However, this was an exceptionally precarious way to live. Any slave accused
of even a minor infraction and unable to produce a manumission record
could be sold back into slavery. In towns, where people of color were an active and visible population, the line between slavery and freedom was not as
easily blurred.[30] Going to the trouble and expense to procure a formal manumission, therefore, signaled that white owners wanted to protect their erst-
while slaves from re-enslavement by making their legal freedom clear.

Magdeleine Rossignol's decision to free nine of her slaves by testament
outlines the complexity of households and the relations within them in Saint-
Domingue. In large part, Rossignol appears quite conventional. A native of
the colony, she was twice widowed and seventy years old at the time she made

her will in Petite Rivière in 1779. Like many créole widows, she had amassed quite a bit of property; she left a good-sized estate and detailed instructions on how she wished to dispose of it.[31] She was an old woman apparently without children; her primary beneficiaries were a niece and nephew who lived close by, but did not comprise part of her plantation household. She considered herself a good Catholic. Like other testators, particularly women, she gave generous legacies to the parish church "to be employed in the adornment and decoration of the main altar," provided her executor would distribute a substantial sum to the poor of the parish, and stipulated that a third sum would be used to say masses for her soul for a year after her death.

Her will followed strict conventions in that she addressed religious obligations first, then specified a few legacies, and finally disposed of the bulk of her estate. She proved less typical in that she left legacies to her slaves, a significant departure from most wills that make it important to consider. Although not unusual for a woman with no children of her own to make provisions for members of her household, in this instance her household comprised her slaves, again emphasizing how slavery could complicate household structure and relations. She "freed from all servitude and slavery immediately after her death" nine slaves: Hypolite, a twenty-five-year-old *mulâtre* whom she termed her "*mulâtre* domestique"; Rose, a créole *négresse* of forty-five whom the widow identified as her "servant"; Rose's six children Joseph, Claude, Nicolas, Paul, Justine, and Barthélémy, "all *noirs*"; and Françoise, a twenty-two-year-old *négresse* whom she also called a "servant."

Her choice to emancipate Rose's children highlights household arrangements that distinguished Saint-Domingue from France. In the metropole, it would have been unusual for domestic servants to have children, particularly who lived under the same roof as their employer. That Rose's children did so accentuates that, in some ways, this was a peculiar blended family. Even the terms she used to describe these slaves implied their status as close familiars: Rose and Françoise she termed servants, while only for Hypolite, set apart by his sex and his mixed race, does she employ the euphemistic but usual term "domestic." By the late eighteenth century, domestic slaves habitually were termed "*nègres domestiques*" no matter what their race. As racial laws hardened, "*nègre*" came to express enslaved status. While one term alone would have denoted enslavement, Rossignol used both.

Rossignol gestured toward mitigating that classification by labeling Hypolite a *mulâtre*; at the very least, it suggests her familiarity with his parentage or how he classified himself. This epithet also undercut his classification as a slave, as numerous free people of color had mixed-race ancestry. Calling him a "domestique" thus could have testified to his subordinate status and also, contradictorily, grouped him with free people of color, whose ranks he would soon join. In a situation that did not necessarily call for nuanced vocabulary, she nonetheless employed it.

Rossignol realized that this mass emancipation would prove quite an expense, and she made provision to muster the necessary funds to "render the said emancipations authentic." She first authorized her executor to sell her furniture and other effects. If this sum did not prove sufficient, she gave him permission to sell some field slaves in order to pay the steep fees. In so doing, she sharply demarcated the boundaries of her household. She approached field slaves as property, investments that could be converted into cash when necessary like other property. In contrast, this provision attests that she considered the nine slaves she intended to emancipate not as property, but as people. This underscores that differences between house and field slaves went beyond the material.

Yet the lines distinguishing the lucky servants to be emancipated from the majority of her slaves were not merely drawn at the threshold of the house. Although her twelve field slaves (plus one child, who did not count towards that number) went to her nephew along with her plantation, several house slaves remained enslaved as well. She willed two children, Victoire, four years old, and Marie-Pierre, aged two, to her great-niece Louise Cotherau. The girls, "créoles and *noirs*," were daughters of her "servant" Jeanette, whose own fate is unspecified. Of course, Jeanette could have been free, but if so, why were her young children not only enslaved but also excluded from the widow's broad emancipation? Although Jeanette's classification as a servant implies that she indeed labored in the household, her exclusion from the group emancipation makes clear that Rossignol chose to free only certain members of her household; merely working as a house slave proved insufficient.

Rossignol also left Hypolite an annual income of one hundred fifty livres. This legacy suggests that Hypolite played a particularly important role in her household. Although not as large a sum as white men commonly left to their *ménagères*, or housekeepers, this amount was directly in line with legacies testators in France left to faithful servants. While not necessarily enough to live on, this sum would have provided Hypolite with an important start.[32] Why would she leave a legacy to him and not to Rose or Françoise? Rose, in particular, had children to support. This choice may be less indicative of their relative need or the closeness of their relationship to their mistress than of Rossignol's assumptions about normative gender roles and patriarchy. In fact, rather than singling out Hypolite for his good deeds, she points to Rose. She recognized "the fidelity and good service that the said Hypolite and the *négresses* Françoise and Rose had shown her, notably the last, in consideration of which she intends to give *bonheur* to her six above named children." Likewise, there seems little reason to believe that Hypolite and Rose formed a conventional nuclear family; she was twenty years older than him, and it is unlikely that he could have fathered her six children. As peers in age, he more plausibly may have formed a romantic attachment with Françoise, although the will makes no mention of such a relationship. Whether or not these nine individuals intended to maintain an association as free people, Rossignol conceived Hypolite as a sort of *père de famille* by virtue of his sex.

Although the terms of their relationships remain elusive, these ten people—one white, eight black, and one mixed race—must have had sustained, consistent interactions that endured for a period of time and led to a certain amount of intimacy. Even if this intimacy was only the physical familiarity that comes from long cohabitation, these were relationships the widow took seriously. She "declar[ed] to have extremely at heart that this disposition regarding them [that they be emancipated] be exactly accomplished." An old woman, she likely needed company and care. Although for her "servants" any interaction with their owner was grounded in hierarchy and force, these ties were also real and, for these nine slaves, enduring through their freedom, which she provided for in her testament. Authority in this household was not always or even primarily patriarchal. After all, Rossignol was the slaves' owner, and, in the end, benefactor. Her position certainly may have been based on hierarchies themselves founded on patriarchy—of white over black, free over enslaved. However, there remains the possibility that this household also worked out other avenues of authority dependent on other factors—age, for instance, or health—that culminated in Rossignol's unusual final wish to free such a large number of slaves. Ultimately, her role as head of household enabled her final assertion to determine the inheritance of household members.

Slave owners frequently cited "good service" when singling out slaves for emancipation. The formulation's vagueness made it so porous it could include virtually anything, ranging from sexual service to loyalty, exceptional acts, or working for one owner for multiple years. The phrase became a conventional way for slave owners to justify emancipation, enabling them to skate over complex relations in which the subjective desires and actions of enslaved people played a role, using a framework that was acceptable to the colonial bureaucracy. Furthermore, the opacity and formulaic nature of most legal documents providing for emancipation make the motivations and actions of slaves and owners difficult to read.

It is possible to understand such emancipations as based on daily intimacies between adults, which, in some cases, prompted slave owners to reward slaves with whom they had close relationships. Thus, when Madame Veuve Bourgogne, who lived in France, gave liberty to her slave Madelaine, a *négresse*, "in consideration of the services that the said Madelaine had rendered to her mistress," the action could have denoted affection, appreciation, or recognition that owning a slave on the other side of the ocean brought hassles without the benefits of slave ownership.[33] The complexity and the expense of the process, however, illustrates that freeing a slave was not done on a whim, and that owners must have felt a real desire to emancipate those for whom they went through the process.

Unsurprisingly, women in charge of their own legal affairs were most likely among female slave owners to emancipate slaves. After all, husbands usually administered married women's property so men may have been on record as emancipating slaves that de facto belonged to their wives. Even some independent women, such as Madame DuVivier Bourgogne, empowered men to complete the necessary paperwork for them, whether because it posed an inconvenience, a difficulty, or because they felt unequipped to negotiate the necessary layers of bureaucracy.[34]

Nevertheless, some women took charge of the process themselves. Jeanne Mathurine Drouillard is a case in point.[35] Although married, she was "separated in dwelling" from her husband, Monsieur DeVolunbrun, a king's counsel at the Conseil supérieur of Port-au-Prince. She lived with her father on a plantation on the outskirts of the town. Styling herself as the "benefactress" of the slave Catherine, an elderly *négresse* who had been a domestic slave, she completed the paperwork to emancipate Catherine herself. Similarly, Demoiselle Marie-Françoise Santo-Domingue, the widow of a planter and a woman of considerable means, negotiated a second marriage contract that specified that her property would remain separate from her new husband's. This separation of property included her slaves; although a married woman, she herself gave liberty to Charlotte, an elderly *négresse* who had been a domestic slave.[36]

White women also gave slaves to free people of color as gifts, an action that defies interpretation as the analogue of white fathers giving slaves to their own mixed-race children. When Dame Elisabeth-Nicole Levy, the widow of M. Augustin Guillier, chevalier and conseilleur du roi, gave two slaves to the mixed-race children of "Madeleine *dite* Halva, *négresse*," she must have had reasons beyond blood relations for doing so.[37] The widow evidently knew this family and its history especially well indeed, for she had emancipated Madeleine *dite* Halva and her two children five years before.[38] This family thus had an ongoing relationship with their former owner, an intimacy that even extended to "le *nommé* Claude," Madeleine's young son who had been born free after her emancipation. The widow emphasized that, although she gifted the slaves because she "wanted to testify her amity to the *nommés* Louis-Augustin and Marie-Louise *dite* Zabeth, *mulâtre* and *mulâtresse*," Madeleine *dite* Halva and Claude also would receive the benefit of the slaves' labor. The emancipation followed by the gift of slaves establishes an ongoing personal relationship as well as a financial one. In France, widows slipped down the social scale notoriously quickly, unable to bring in income that allowed them to continue their standard of living. Here, perhaps, the widow Guillier found a creative way around that problem. Although her overall financial situation is unclear, she clearly owned multiple slaves, and Madeleine *dite* Halva and her children evidently continued to work for her even after their emancipation. The gift of slaves, then, may have been payment for their labor, which itself ensured that the widow had continued access to the conveniences that Madeleine and her children provided, even though they were free.

Although economics surely formed part of the connection between the widow Guillier and Madeleine and her children, elements of the deed of gift connote a more personal dimension to this relationship as well. For one thing, Madeleine *dite* Halva was present in the notary's office when this deed of gift was drawn up, and she personally accepted the gift of an Arada slave woman named Lenore and her twelve-year-old daughter Thérèse on her children's behalf. Her presence was unnecessary and somewhat unusual, and it attests that, even if she and the widow had not arrived to see the notary together, at the very least the widow had told her former slave where to go and asked her to meet her there. Through her attendance at the notary's office and her acceptance of the gift, Madeleine positioned herself as a head of household. Moreover, the widow also gave Madeleine's three children 1,200 colonial livres. With this money Madeleine promised to purchase "a *négrillon* or a *négritte*, in favor of her three children." Significantly, this generous gift crossed generations; jointly possessing, essentially, three slaves could set Madeleine's children up well in the world. It also bespoke the widow's personal knowledge of their family and situation as it aimed to ease the life of Madeleine by provisioning that she, too, would have access to the labor of Lenore and her child.

The case of Jeanne Millet reveals that interracial relationships between whites and free people of color extended down the social scale and that petits blancs engaged with them as well as planters.[39] On 1 October 1782, Jeanne Millet, a white woman with few financial resources, "infirm of the body but nonetheless healthy in spirit," sent for the nearest notary to make her will.[40] At eighty-three, the widow had outlived most of her contemporaries, and she had survived more than one husband. Although she ended her life far from her natal town of La Rochelle, she had a network of friends and family in her adopted town of Léogane.[41] Her nephew, Antoine Naudet, a sacristan at the parish church, lived with her. His presence in her household attests that for those of modest means, as well as merchants and plantation owners, transatlantic family was an important resource. Family members in Saint-Domingue could help provide a start for collateral male kin. In this case, Antoine Naudet held the place of a surrogate son: in her will, Jeanne made him her executor and universal legatee. This attests to the importance of kinship in inheritance, but also paints a picture of the somewhat remote life the widow and her nephew lived in a small town on the edge of the French empire, far from any family networks they may have had in La Rochelle.

Jeanne came from humble origins—her father was a tailor—and her estate did not amount to much. She left her nephew all her furniture, including her bed, an armoire, a table, and some "mauvais" chairs. Her modest estate evoked her social milieu: a "bourgeois" and a locksmith witnessed her will. Jeanne made only one other bequest, eschewing common legacies to parish churches or religious groups. Instead, she left all her personal belongings to the "natural children of the free *Négresse* Catherine, for them to share out in equal portions."

This legacy demonstrates that in spite of her relative lack of blood kin in Léogane, the widow was not alone. Indeed, a family surrounded her: Catherine and her children. The widow's will gives no precise indicator of their relationship, but it was close enough for her to give them her most intimate possessions, possibly including clothes, linens, toiletries, and household items for personal use.[42] Legacies such as these ordinarily bespoke quotidian interaction, such as that between master and servant; they connote intimate, bodily familiarity. Although the value of such items likely would have amounted only to a pittance, especially divided among Catherine's children, the significance of this gift should not be dismissed. The economic worth of a few personal effects could provide a financial boost, either by preventing the outlay of cash for such necessities, or by bringing in an infusion of cash when they were sold. Even more importantly, this legacy fortified a personal connection between Jeanne Millet and Catherine's children. Martha Howell has argued that personal legacies acquired significance beyond their actual value by cementing personal relationships between legator and legatee.[43] The fact that the widow chose to leave her personal possessions equally to the unnamed children of a free woman of color implies that their relationship went beyond that of servants and mistress. Most likely Catherine herself took care of the widow in her old age; surely if Catherine's children had cared for her directly, she would have named them individually. Yet if her relationship was only with Catherine, why not simply leave all her personal effects to her? Instead, her reference to "the natural children of the free *Négresse* Catherine" almost paradoxically suggests that she had taken an interest in their whole family, not just an individual.

Leaving legacies of personal property outside one's immediate lineage could, in Martha Howell's words, "destabiliz[e] the social and commercial order."[44] In this case such destabilization carried particular significance, for Jeanne Millet left her legacy across lines of race at a time when legal racial categories were rapidly solidifying. By the 1780s, in Saint-Domingue new racial codes restricted free people of color's participation in public life.[45] Although the social impact of sumptuary laws and prohibitions against interracial sociability may have been minimal, the clear intent mirrored metropolitan efforts to regulate all people of color separately from whites.[46] Yet individuals crossed imaginary racial divides all the time, undermining social hierarchies that in Saint-Domingue were increasingly based on race. In households, official regulations did not always dictate actions and behavior, making them sites that had the potential to thwart official initiatives.

Jeanne Millet died six days after she made her will, on 7 October. Her body was interred in the parish cemetery the following day. Her nephew attended the burial, signing the parish register in an elegant and educated hand.[47] If Catherine or her children were in attendance, there is no record of it. Maybe this emphasizes the pecuniary nature of their relationship. In spite of that the ties between Jeanne Millet and Catherine's children continued, cemented by Jeanne's personal effects, a legacy that destabilized racial hierarchy by showing that something could cross it: emotion, gratitude, affection, or bribery. At any rate, Jeanne's personal goods crossed this divide, and for a while, at least, Catherine's children would remember them as having belonged to an old white woman.

The fact that white women gave legacies or gifts to free people of color and freedom to slaves attests that interracial relations were not founded on sexual intercourse alone. White women, like white men, tended to liberate women and children and to make gifts that benefited women and their children. Taken together, this preference signifies that women of color, particularly women with children, were most able to form interracial bonds with whites. This may have resulted partly from gendered expectations of labor that meant that women of color were most likely to come into close contact with whites in their capacities as house slaves or personal attendants. It also signifies that gender expectations for women of color allowed them to form and foster these relationships in ways unavailable to men of color and that extended beyond the bedroom. Intimacy, then, did not always have to unfold within the privacy of the home, either confined within the bounds of legitimate marriage or illicitly unfolding beside it. Rather, intimacy could grow quite publicly, based on labor or economic exchange.

Intimate Economies

To many contemporary observers, white women in Saint-Domingue threatened whiteness by becoming like people of color. Dominant tropes of colonial white women emphasize their languor, sexual promiscuity, and violent jealousy, painting a picture of colonial femininity very much opposed to the qualities of economic industriousness, purity, and devotion to family deemed necessary for a good wife in France.[48] Although colonists pushed back against this depiction, they tended to do so in Rousseauian terms by portraying white colonial women as closer to nature and better wives and mothers because of it.[49] Across the board, contemporary critics and defenders of white colonial femininity described white women in cultural rather than economic terms.

In reality, white women were extremely integrated into the colony's economy as buyers, sellers, and owners of property and other assets, and as such, they upheld slavery instead of threatening it by blurring racial lines.[50] Widows, unmarried women who had reached the age of majority, and *marchandes* all had the legal capacity to administer their own affairs, and, as in La Rochelle, women in Saint-Domingue with absent husbands often were empowered by sweeping powers of attorney. Occasionally, too, women's marriage contracts gave them the right to have and to hold property as wives, particularly in second or third marriages. White women thus empowered frequently bought, sold, and rented property, including land and slaves, and entered into contracts with people of color, white men, and other white women. They formed and dissolved businesses, lent and borrowed money, issued receipts, and held and issued powers of attorney. In short, they engaged in the same types of business transactions as white men and free people of color, albeit with less frequency.

The high remarriage rate for white widows and low average age at first marriage meant that in 1753 in the southern city Les Cayes, for example, only 3 percent of white-headed households or stores were headed by women.[51] However, in the 1780s white women participated in 18 percent of urban land sales and 11 percent of rural land sales, and in the 1760s they participated in 21 percent of urban leases.[52] These figures pose a marked contrast to the high proportion of women among free colored notarial clients, which Dominique Rogers puts at 62 percent in Cap Français and Port-au-Prince.[53] Such figures should come as no surprise given married white women's legal incapacity. Moreover, married women frequently acted legally in conjunction with their husbands, a fact these figures may not take into account.

In addition, white women, particularly those at the bottom of the social scale, engaged in contracts beyond those pertaining to property. Examining some of these transactions paints a picture of a vibrant colonial economy in which white women were active participants. In spite of its male-dominated white population, then, the circumstances of colonialism in Saint-Domingue actually may have opened opportunities for white women to be more integrated into the economy than they were in France.

Nevertheless, it is easy to understand why white women's economic roles were seldom discussed. Women, even those who owned property in their own right, commonly preferred to empower men to conduct business for them. Cultural expectations about masculinity and femininity may have barred some white women from forming contracts or engaging in business, including land management, themselves. Yet close examination of notary contracts determines that assumptions that white women simply left business matters in the hands of male relatives or agents does not hold water. All white women did not flee the tropics for more temperate climes as soon as

their ties to the men who had presumably brought them there were severed
by death. Instead, white women made Saint-Domingue their home, adminis-
tering resources and amassing assets just as women did in France. They did
this before they were married, as married women, and as widows. They entered into contracts with family members, friends, and also business associates outside their immediate social circles.

Even so, the evidence suggests that white women thought differently than
white men and free people of color about what constituted valuable property.
Even though land ownership was a key element that determined colonial
wealth, some white women actually divested themselves of real estate property soon after it came into their hands, even prioritizing quick cash sale over
maximizing profits. Selling land would have made it easier for white women
to pick up and leave, certainly a consideration for women who were newly
widowed and eager to join extended family in France. Managing real estate
from a distance was notoriously difficult, as Belin's example made clear, and
even more so for women. Given white women's social and legal position,
moveable, personal property may have offered them more autonomy over
their assets and their lives than real estate property, and this desire for control
as much as financial necessity or financial disability brought on by gender
expectations may have prompted them to sell or rent property quickly after it
came under their authority. The experience of Madame Regnaud de Beaumont, where her wealth disappeared under the watch of her husband, offers an
additional reason women would have preferred assets they could easily keep
under their direct control. Although laws protected women's property in theory, patriarchy undermined these provisions, thus posing the possibility that
land wealth would be dismantled without much recourse to legal action.

The business dealings between the widow Gaston Prou and Sieur Jean-
Marie Bion, a merchant in Port-au-Prince, provide an illustrative example of
white women's involvement in the colonial economy. On 6 March 1779, the
widow lent Bion the enormous sum of 22,000 livres on the eve of her journey
to France.[54] Possibly she had no need of the sum during her travels, and
thought she might as well put it to good use. He would pay her back in four
payments of 5,500 livres over the course of four years; they drew up a contract to that effect in the offices of a notary in Port-au-Prince. Although
transatlantic letters of credit regularly went unpaid, the widow likely saw this
as a safe investment because she intended to return to Saint-Domingue. She
entrusted her affairs to a firm of property managers while she was away.[55]
Taking advantage of her absence, Bion did not repay the loan as promised,

although he did pay her interest of 1,100 livres per year "to maintain the use of the said capital." Four years later the widow was back in Saint-Domingue and ready to access the principal, feasibly prompted by Bion's own impending return to France. He still did not have the cash he owed her, so she accepted property as payment. He transferred to her a house in Léogane that had three rooms and an open gallery, an attached store of four rooms, a second two-room store on the same property, a detached oven for a bakery, and a well. He also gave her a forty-five-year-old female slave named Cuba, and various "furniture and effects like beds, bureau, table, and others." Even after this transfer, Bion still owed the widow 5,030 livres.

In this case, the widow Gaston Prou clearly considered Léogane her home, a place to which she would return: she defied the notorious colonial dream of returning to France with fabulous wealth by going back, indeed, but leaving again. Once she arrived home she collected on her debt in a way that provided her with financial stability and flexibility. Such an urban property, typical of Saint-Domingue with several dwellings grouped around a central courtyard with a kitchen and a well, often brought several families together under one roof.[56] She and her son could live there, use the premises for a business, or could rent out all or part of it. The fact of her initial loan and her acquisition of this property affirm that the widow had a financial and business savvy that her husband lacked. Acting for her minor son, she renounced the boy's portion of his deceased father's estate, as it was "more costly than profitable."[57] In contrast, she had plentiful cash, always an advantage in cash-strapped Saint-Domingue, and she acquired an urban property situated on rue du Gouvernement that offered her a fairly reliable source of rental income and personal financial autonomy in her own community, Léogane.

In fact, the urban milieu was where white women, like free people of color, thrived economically.[58] In the towns of Saint-Domingue, women leased apartments, rooms, and stores, set up businesses, found tenants, and turned profits. Although some women clearly divested themselves of property in preparation for a return to France, notary records indicate that white women were quite at home in colonial Saint-Domingue and made long-term economic plans for themselves and their families to remain there for the foreseeable future. Thus, when Marie-Françoise Desmarets, widow of colonist Claude Coquilleau, rented a two-room apartment with an office in Saint-Marc for a period of two years, she quite probably intended to set up a business, even though she was illiterate and could not sign her name.[59]

Contracts for purchase, sale, and rental of property demonstrate that free people of color and whites generally acted as social and economic equals in business transactions. Economic ambitions regularly outweighed concerns about race and social status in parts of Saint-Domingue in the 1770s. Marie-Agnés Desgas, white widow of a surveyor, rented a plantation planted in cotton and manioc from a man of color and his children for a period of seven years.[60] The contract's length avers her intention to play an economic role in this community comprised largely of free people of color, even though it is not entirely clear she actually lived on the plantation full time. Her neighbors on the plantation were Bastien, a free *nègre*, whose land bordered the rental property on the south, Marie Gratia, a free *négresse* on the north, the free *négresse* Thérèse Cavalier on the east, and the free *négresse* Marotte on the west. The rental contract included much that the widow would need to live there and cultivate the plantation, namely a house, a slave hut, a dovecote, tools for cultivating the cassava, a sieve for preparing manioc flour, two small cotton mills, and a forty-five year old slave named Margueritte. These goods affirm that she intended to spend at least some time on this property during which, it can be assumed, she would have engaged in economic and social commerce with her neighbors, perhaps even selling them the manioc grown on her plantation. Conversely, Marieanne Lecocq, a widow of a planter near Saint-Marc, rented her usufruct interest in a plantation to a free *mulâtre* named Jean-Pierre called Morin, a wigmaker.[61] Together these examples emphasize that while some white women divested themselves of the responsibilities of managing property when they could, others sought out property and the economic opportunities it presented. When white women did so, they—like their male counterparts—became members of an economically integrated community where profits and prosperity mattered more than racial or social hierarchies.

Furthermore, some white women with property not only kept it but acquired more, looking out for their own economic interests as well as those of their households. In Petite Rivière, twice-widowed Étiennette-Louise Montare found herself in the position of making economic decisions for herself, her two children by her second marriage, and her second husband's five children from his first marriage.[62] Self-identified as a "habitante," or planter, Montare coinherited with his children as well as her own an indigo plantation from her late husband, which was well situated on the Artibonite Plain near the river. "With the view of extracting a better proportion of the work of his slaves," her husband "had formed the plan to withdraw from the top of the plantation" and "cultivate that which he was going to buy from Sieur

Abeille." Although it is not clear whether this sale materialized, her neighbor Catherine Rondeau (possibly a relative of her late husband), the widow Montas, offered to rent her some land. Étiennette-Louise Montare asserted that she wanted to "execute the plan of the deceased and to not miss out on the deal proposed by the said Dlle. Montas."

Another widow owned property bordering this plantation on the west, making this section of Artibonite a veritable enclave of white widowhood. Although it is not stated specifically that any of these women lived full time on the land they owned, at the very least they lived nearby as the lease was signed "in the principal house of the plantation." Although neither woman signed the document, they were there in person as "they had declared they did not know how to write or sign." Clearly their illiteracy did not prevent them from engaging in economic activity. Montare had long-term plans to extract a profit from her land that would benefit her and the couple's children. She signed a lease for six years, paying 2,700 livres for the first year and 3,000 for subsequent years, a substantial sum that would go in the widow Montas's pocket and comfortably sustain her on her plantation or in any town in the western province of Saint-Domingue.

As in France, family proved an important economic category, and family members did what they could to improve each other's economic positions. The case of the widow Jeanton and her son in Saint-Marc illustrates mutual obligation between mothers and children. The two clearly had a business arrangement, for although she lived separately on a plantation of which she had "the enjoyment," she gave him money and he paid her debts, including a considerable bill to a surgeon.[63] A year later he rented five slaves from his mother, all branded "Jeanton St. Marc," for a period of five years.[64] By this point she lived with her son, hinting possibly at a change in fortunes, but more likely her own physical deterioration. The son paid his mother a fair market price for this rental, as determined by neighboring planters: 900 livres per year "while hostilities lasted," and 1,400 thereafter. It does not appear that the mother cut the son a break, using the rental as an opportunity to give him a financial boost.

The agreement may have worked the other way around, offering the son a way to support his mother while allowing her to maintain her dignity. She owned these slaves, all of whom had been born in Africa and therefore likely field hands rather than house slaves or personal attendants. By renting them from his mother, the son ensured her an independent income. Provided that "hostilities lasted" for a couple of years and none of the slaves died, he profited from their labor while paying less than he would have to buy them outright. Two years later the son continued to pay his mother's bills, including her surgeon and apothecary. The income he owed her from leasing her slaves was deducted from this accounting.[65]

White women also entered into business partnerships, particularly with white men, thereby implying that they had economic and social choices, position, and leverage.[66] Family interests as well as entrepreneurial enterprise could be wrapped up in such arrangements. Marie-Victoire Méance entered into a partnership with her husband and brother to share "the revenues and products of their [two] plantations."[67] In this instance, husband and wife owned property separately, a provision that must have been in their marriage contract, although their economic interests closely aligned. Her husband owned half of the partnership and she and her brother a quarter each, a ratio indicating that they probably had jointly inherited a plantation from their parents. In this case, pooling resources benefited both plantations. It is significant that Marie Victoire Méance owned one-quarter of the partnership and participated in it in her own right. Méance's position affirms that in Saint-Domingue, white women were viewed not only as vehicles for transmitting property across generations, but also as property owners themselves.

That widows worked creatively to manage property reinforces the conclusion that widows' circumstances did not force them to leave Saint-Domingue, remarry, or sell their land immediately. They had choices, as the case of the widow White highlights. Marie-Louise Haurin, the widow White, entered into a society with Jacob St. Macary, a savvy merchant who knew the ins and outs of plantation life.[68] She had inherited a plantation from her parents before her marriage, suggesting that she was a créole, a native of the colony who had been reared on a plantation herself. Newly widowed with a child, she put her indigo and cotton plantation, its buildings, and thirty-two field slaves into the partnership. St. Macary contributed fifty slaves. He paid Haurin 3,000 livres per year for use of the premises, and they would split the revenues of the plantation. The widow planned to live on the plantation at least part time and was allocated two house slaves to serve her during her residence. While the contract might initially make it seem as if the widow White turned over her assets to a male associate to manage, a closer reading avouches that she likely intended to be more involved in the day-to-day running of the plantation than he. Above all, she anticipated living there while her partner only had the right to visit any time he liked. Moreover, the contract stipulated that they would hire an overseer and specified that the overseer would keep account books whether she was there or not. This implies that while the widow White was there, she meant to keep so close an eye on the plantation's production it might seem unnecessary for the overseer to keep accounts. The fact that she chose not to remarry and instead minimized her financial risk by taking on a partner in production highlights that women in Saint-Domingue were not only carriers, but also producers of wealth.

Property ownership was not the only way white women could amass wealth. They also drew on their own skills and labor to form business partnerships and generate revenue. When Demoiselle Françoise Chabert Beaulieu entered into a partnership with Sieur Guillaume Audebert, he put up 6,600 livres in capital, while she "brought nothing but her industry."[69] As a *marchande de modes*, she would bring in income through her skill and labor. Similarly, Charles Magnant and Suzanne Coulon entered a partnership in which they each would contribute according to their ability, and they would share the profits and losses.[70] He was a fisherman; she, a single woman over the age of majority, would sell the fish. Together they bought three boats (one named *La Suzanne*, presumably after its half-owner). Coulon also contributed a lump sum of cash as startup capital, which would be returned to her after the partnership ended.

Marie-Anne Hyver, widow of a "bourgeois," proved a particularly active entrepreneur. Sometime in 1776 she made a "verbal partnership" with Pierre Poupin to run a hotel and pension.[71] Their business apparently prospered. Five years later she bought out her partner, paying him 40,000 livres for assets including cutlery, pots and pans, silver coffeepots, candlesticks, bottles for oil, furniture, eleven slaves, and mirrors. By 1783 she was ready to enter into another partnership, this time with Sieur Gregoire Fabre, an innkeeper and caterer.[72] Having learned from her earlier experience, she commissioned a notary to draw up this partnership agreement. This elaborate contract stipulated the duties of the common employees and the benefits they would receive from the partnership, including laundry and lodging, who held a key to the till, responsibility for maintaining the accounts, and specified what was excluded from their joint property as well as what went into it.

Taken together, these examples reveal that white women played an active role in the economic integration of Saint-Domingue. Women and men, white and free colored, bought, sold, rented, and traded together. White women had multiple motivations for directly engaging in economic activity, and they did so from different social positions. This challenges prevailing assumptions that their primary function was to reproduce whiteness. Like women in

France, they worked to preserve and better their and their families' social positions. Like men in Saint-Domingue, they pursued the colonial dream of making money, although they sometimes approached that goal in ways shaped by their gender.

Rather than limiting women, then, the colonial milieu may have actually opened up opportunities for economic autonomy in ways that were not available to women in France. Yet in slave societies, economic activity was not the only measure of women's roles; their capacity to exercise authority over their slaves proved another. While in Saint-Domingue systemic mechanisms facilitated slave owner control, in France owners had to rely more directly on patriarchal authority, an authority that white women had difficulty claiming.

White Women and Authority in France

As in Saint-Domingue, in France white women's legal disability meant that their slave ownership left few archival traces. For instance, many white women who owned slaves in France had white men make slave declarations to the Admiralty on their behalf. Considering the different contexts for slave ownership in France and Saint-Domingue sheds light on how white women approached slave ownership in the metropole. Two elements of slave ownership in France distinguished it from slave ownership in the Caribbean and help to situate existing evidence of how interracial relations differed in colony and metropole. First, slaves in France served an important function of display. Second, mechanisms for exercising authority differed, thus shifting the terms of master-slave relationships. Above all, white slave-owning women encountered difficulties exercising essentially patriarchal authority over slaves in France. As in Saint-Domingue, white women avoided interaction with state and legal authorities where they could. Returning to Madame Regnaud de Beaumont and examining how she instead chose to leave a paper trail affirming her authority over her slave Tranchemontagne reveals that when gender authority and racial privilege collided in France, it was neither obvious nor evident which one would prevail.

When owners brought slaves to France, they generally registered their slaves as required by royal mandates, but seldom followed the Admiralty-prescribed process to the letter. While laws required slave owners to register slaves with Admiralty authorities within a week of their arrival, in actuality weeks often passed before many owners complied with this mandate.

Further, owners frequently assigned the task to an agent. This move illuminates the legal privilege of the rich, but also hints that slave owners did not
take this requirement seriously. White women slave owners were notorious
offenders, particularly likely to avoid the responsibility of registering their
slaves in person. There are a range of possible explanations for this. The legal
disability of married women and its attendant prerogative to avoid interactions with authorities may have allowed some women to foist this responsibility off on a convenient male.[73] The masculine physical space of the
Admiralty may have discouraged some women. A royal bastion of patriarchal authority that shared a building with the Chamber of Commerce, the
location symbolized the imbrication of royal and commercial power in early
modern France. Some women, like some men, passed quickly through the
port of arrival where slave registrations were supposed to occur. Rather than
travel back to complete the paperwork themselves, they had someone else do
it for them.

Of the 161 declarations made to the Admiralty in La Rochelle in the decade from 1747 to 1757, white women made 26, or 16 percent, in line with the
percentage of white women who entered into contracts recorded by notaries
in Saint-Domingue. Of these, half made the declarations themselves, while
the other half had a male agent do it for them. One of the women who made
her own statement appeared at the Admiralty twice, the second time to register a second slave. Another appeared three times to renew the registration of
the same slave. Four of these women were widows.[74] Of the remainder, all
had husbands who resided in Saint-Domingue. These numbers sketch an
outline of gender and legal authority that portrays women as marginal figures, commonly unable or unwilling to access the royal legitimacy that registering slaves conferred. Widows, already acknowledged as heads of
household, proved an exception. In general, women's broad disinclination to
register slaves themselves implies their discomfort with or inability to exercise patriarchal control over their slaves.

Yet successfully staking domination over a slave could also bring white
women particular benefits. Slave owners widely recognized registration as
one way to consolidate and legitimate their authority, pushing the practice
beyond its intended purpose of regulating slavery. In this vein, registration
comprised an important element of a multipronged approach to establishing
authority over slaves in a society where slavery was rare and colonial mechanisms for slave control largely absent. Marie-Magdelaine Regnaud de Beaumont realized this: in contrast to the lackadaisical approach of most slave

owners, she turned up at the Admiralty office in La Rochelle to register her slave Tranchemontagne the day after he arrived.[75]

Her husband Jean-Severin Regnaud de Beaumont, a resident of Léogane, sent Tranchemontagne to her in 1751. Tranchemontagne's new mistress stated that he had been sent to France for the purpose of "instructing him in the Roman Catholic and Apostolic Religion, and to have him learn a trade." In accordance with the law and like other slave owners, she promised that when Tranchemontagne's education had been completed she would send him back to her husband's plantation in Saint-Domingue, where the boy had been born and grown up. Tranchemontagne was only about sixteen years old at the time, and likely had never even ventured far from his plantation home, let alone made a long sea voyage to a strange land. He apparently traveled alone: no other slaves arrived on the ship on which he made his journey, and there is no mention of him serving a white master or mistress on the voyage.[76]

Owning Tranchemontagne not only provided Madame Regnaud de Beaumont with a certain amount of cultural cachet, it also offered her an opportunity to exercise authority in a situation where culturally, at any rate, as a woman and a married one at that, she had little. Tranchemontagne proved a safe object for this project; as a newly arrived slave, he had no social connections and was in an extremely isolated and tenuous position. She also had age and experience on her side, as he was a youth of sixteen. All she had to do was to make clear that age, knowledge, experience, social situation, and most particularly race trumped gender: to make it clear in France, where racial hierarchy was not assumed or as deeply ingrained as in Saint-Domingue, that a white woman could exercise authority over a male slave. Part of her campaign to make racial hierarchy obvious and evident rested on following the letter of the law and personally supervising the legal formalities that legitimated Tranchemontagne's presence in France. This process served a dual purpose, demonstrating her own understanding and mastery of the workings of the law, while simultaneously affirming her own position of social and cultural power by asserting her authority over someone else.

A key element of this project was entering Tranchemontagne into an apprenticeship. As Chapter 2 shows, the assumption behind the 1716 legal requirement that slaves in France "learn a trade" was that they would return to the Antilles to become productive and economically useful members of plantation society. The Declaration of 1738 reiterated and tightened this provision, mandating that slave owners in their declarations "make mention . . . of the trade that the said slaves will learn, and of the master who will be charged to instruct them."[77] However, in La Rochelle this basically never happened. Virtually across the board, Rochelais failed to specify what trade their slaves would learn or the name of the master who would teach them, as the law required. The persistence of this willful noncompliance hints, first of all, that Admiralty officials did not stringently enforce this requirement. Second, it also implies that slave owners did not find it a useful way to extend their own influence over their slaves, as baptism could. A master or mistress charged with teaching a slave specific skills could provide a powerful alternative locus for authority and significantly weaken a slave owner's control.

At the heart of the disjuncture between the metropolitan injunction for training and the reasons individuals brought or sent slaves to France in the first place were assumptions about the nature of slave ownership and colonial labor. Lawmakers envisioned slaves as sort of a peasant/artisan underclass of blank slates with France itself the only repository of skilled labor. According to this narrative, productive skilled work could not take place on plantations unless slaves received training in France. Colonists knew, however, that skilled white and free colored artisans already exercised their trades in the colonies; they even sometimes took on slaves as apprentices.[78] Slave owners also knew that the most valuable outcome of taking a slave to France was not artisanal ability; it was the cultural cachet conferred on slave owners in France, and also on owners in the colonies whose slaves had a little metropolitan polish.

Opportunities for apprenticeships in the colony combined with a general failure to enforce the law regarding slaves brought to France left little incentive for owners in the metropole to apprentice their slaves. Yet this is precisely what Madame Regnaud de Beaumont did: she entered Tranchemontagne into an apprenticeship contract to train for one year as a cooper.[79] This was an expensive, cumbersome way to access skilled labor that was already available in Saint-Domingue, where free people of color worked as artisans, and white tradesmen indentured themselves for the price of passage at least into the 1730s. As part of the indenture contract, each usually promised to "teach and instruct his trade in the stated time [of engagement] to a *nègre*," thus augmenting the number of skilled laborers in the colonies.[80] In addition to the cost of his transatlantic passage, she also paid 250 livres for his training, an amount significantly above the average price paid to masters of all but the most prestigious trades for taking on apprentices, particularly considering that he would only receive training for a single year.[81]

This price may have been cheap if the apprenticeship contract is viewed as a way for Madame Regnaud de Beaumont to exercise her authority over her slave. Although an apprenticeship initially may appear to undercut her authority by handing day-to-day control to another, the fact that she even bothered to apprentice him at all—a very unusual move among Rochelais slave owners—intimates that she made every effort to follow the letter of the law, thus legitimizing her claim to slave ownership in the eyes of the authorities. She chose to apprentice him to a woman, Suzanne Vinet, widow of a master cooper named St. Marc.

This arrangement potentially benefited both women. For the widow St. Marc, a slave working as an apprentice certainly provided cheap labor, although this arrangement hardly differed from any apprenticeship in Old Regime France.[82] More important, as a woman working in a man's trade she may have found it difficult to recruit apprentices or journeymen on whose labor she could rely. Widows of master craftsmen could not exercise full guild privileges. Although they continued to enjoy guild membership themselves, they often had limited rights to train apprentices or hire journeymen.[83] For this reason they typically remarried quickly, although they also had the right to continue running their late husbands' workshops.[84] Yet as a master's widow, Suzanne Vinet possessed the power and authority to make contracts and agreements, including those pertaining to her late husband's trade.

In addition to following the law, Madame Regnaud de Beaumont also may have wanted Tranchemontagne out of her household. As a woman living alone, her virtue could be called into question. Stereotypes of colonial women's sexuality were well known, and Madame Regnaud de Beaumont had spent time in Saint-Domingue and was surely aware of them. Potentially more important, she had several young daughters living under her roof, the oldest just fifteen when Tranchemontagne entered his apprenticeship.[85] Protecting their virtue from any perceived dangers that cohabitating with a young man could pose, particularly one of another race, may have motivated Madame Regnaud de Beaumont's decision that it was worth getting him out of the house at any price. Having a sixteen-year-old male slave from Saint-Domingue in her household thus meant, among other things, constraining him to metropolitan norms, particularly regarding sexually appropriate behavior for domestics.

In Saint-Domingue, it was not uncommon for owners' households to comprise slave families. Tranchemontagne, then, may have perceived looking for a mate as entirely appropriate behavior for a young man. In France, in contrast, servants may have been sexually active, but it was frowned on for them to marry or engage in long-term alliances that may have compromised their loyalty to their masters. Madame Regnaud de Beaumont had the added incentive of wanting to close off affective avenues for her slave; any romantic attachment on his part certainly could have compromised her own authority, and provided a powerful incentive for rebellion. This suggests that slave owners actually might have exerted more authority over a slave's private life in France than in Saint-Domingue. Therefore, part of Madame Regnaud de Beaumont's efforts were directed toward ensuring that Tranchemontagne behaved appropriately as a slave and as a domestic.

The widow St. Marc's exceptional and somewhat marginal position as a woman running a workshop alone in a trade typically dominated by men may have actually drawn Madame Regnaud to her. The widow's situation, as a legitimate guild member yet on the edge of guild organization and production, meant that she offered little challenge to Madame Regnaud's authority over her slave. On the other hand, a male master who had the weight of the guilds behind him could have presented a powerful patriarchal presence in conflict with Madame Regnaud's authority as a slave owner. Because she chose a woman to train her slave, hierarchies of race and gender did not collide. Instead, Madame Regnaud de Beaumont reinforced her personal authority while avoiding questions about her gendered position.

The apprenticeship contract emphasized the legitimacy of Madame Regnaud's authority over her slave from the beginning. The source of this authority was clearly stated and left little doubt: it was "based on [her husband Sieur Jean-Severin Regnaud's] general power of attorney by which she is of him well and truly authorized."[86] For his part, Tranchemontagne, by this point sixteen or seventeen years old, was expected to recognize "the aforementioned widow St. Marc his mistress, and to obey her and to agree to everything that she commands that is licit and honest."[87] Madame Regnaud agreed to pay all his expenses, while the widow St. Marc guaranteed "to have him learn, be shown, and be taught the trade of cooper by her master journeyman in the manner in which he exercises it daily, without hiding anything from him, and also well and suitably feeding, providing bedding for, laundering, lodging, and nourishing but only in health, the aforementioned apprentice during the specified year."[88] In remuneration, the widow would receive half of the apprenticeship fee upon the signing of the contract and half after six months had elapsed, which she duly noted receiving on 2 June 1753. The widow, Madame Regnaud, and the two notaries who prepared the document affixed their signatures. Tranchemontagne did not; the contract stated that he did not know how to sign his name.[89]

Patriarchal authority imbued guild hierarchies much as it imbued slavery. Apprentices entering into training generally owed their masters the same obedience and respect minor sons gave to fathers, and in turn masters were legally invested with fathers' prerogatives.[90] Apprentices were supposed to obey their masters in all things, and to follow their guidance in matters of religion and morality as well as in their trade.[91] Most master craftspeople were men, and so it was expected that the roles of fathers and masters dovetailed neatly together, reinforcing paternal authority. Women seldom entered into guilds in their own right, with the notable exception of the all-women guilds such as the seamstresses.[92] Because guild members' identities as practitioners of a trade and as heads of household were tightly bound with their masculinity, the widow St. Marc's authority over an apprentice challenged the paternalistic order so favored by the guilds.

Yet the widow's power over Tranchemontagne posed no challenge at all to the ultimate jurisdiction of his owner. Had the slave been apprenticed to a male artisan, his masculine authority well might have come into conflict with Madame Regnaud's race-based authority. Choosing the widow St. Marc as his master, then, can be read as a calculated decision designed to ensure the authority of his owner as much as to assure his training. In entering into this contract, Madame Regnaud reaffirmed her power over her slave. By explicitly transferring this power to the widow St. Marc, she effectively emphasized that it was hers to give. The contractual nature of this agreement served to legitimize her appropriation of an authority that was patriarchal and masculine in nature. The act of passing this power to the widow St. Marc emphasized Madame Regnaud de Beaumont's absolute authority over her slave, but at the same time served to protect it. The widow, whose own position was based on a tenuous privilege offered to the wives of late masters, was unlikely to pose a real challenge to Madame Regnaud's control over her slave. Madame Regnaud thus consolidated her authority, based on racial privilege, by removing potential challenges based on patriarchy.

Tranchemontagne did not simply accept his position docilely. He would have observed the fuzzy line between slavery and servitude in La Rochelle, and been familiar with patterns of slave resistance in his native Saint-Domingue. He was also an adolescent boy, probably overworked and underfed. Whether by an active effort at resisting his condition or merely negligence, he destroyed some of the widow St. Marc's property during the term of his apprenticeship. She submitted a bill for twelve livres to his owner, stating that it had to be paid for him to continue living with her for the stated period of the contract.[93] Madame Regnaud de Beaumont, of course, paid up, but this act of destruction avers that all her efforts to exert her authority over him were not for the benefit of French authorities alone; Tranchemontagne himself proved less willing to bend to her will than she had anticipated.

Even after Tranchemontagne's apprenticeship ended, Madame Regnaud de Beaumont still worked to bind him to her, showing the difficulties women in France faced exerting patriarchal authority, even over slaves. Just one week after Madame Regnaud made the second payment for his apprenticeship and nearly two years after he arrived in France, Tranchemontagne was baptized.[94] This surprising delay between his arrival and his baptism, a period much longer than for other slaves, indicates that, in contrast to most slaves baptized in France, either he actually received some religious instruction, or, more likely, Madame Regnaud de Beaumont knew that Tranchemontagne, a créole, had been baptized in Saint-Domingue. Perhaps she had compunctions about this, or maybe it took her a while to realize that Rochelais slave owners commonly used baptism as a way to exert authority over their slaves. In a pointed effort to close off any alternate avenues of authority, Madame Regnaud de Beaumont's two oldest children, Étienne-Raimond and Marie-Magdelaine, were named as Tranchemontagne's godparents.

Here, too, Tranchemontagne made his presence felt. Although he signed neither his Admiralty declaration nor his apprenticeship contract, he signed the baptism register with a cross, which generally served as the signature of the illiterate. Very few slaves who received the sacrament of baptism in La Rochelle made any mark at all. His mark in the baptism register affirms his growing awareness of the importance of a signature, and hints at an insistence on his presence and his subjectivity in a situation where he had little control.

Madame Regnaud de Beaumont viewed her efforts to assert her authority over Tranchemontagne as a success: at any rate, she transported more slaves to France. After her final colonial sojourn, she returned to La Rochelle in the company of a créole *négresse* named Lizette, aged forty-five, on 31 July 1755. Lizette served Madame Regnaud on the voyage and likely acted as a wet nurse to her young son as well, roles she almost certainly continued performing after her arrival in France. True to form, Madame Regnaud de Beaumont registered Lizette's presence in the Admiralty within the prescribed week.[95]

At least one other slave must have passed through Madame Regnaud de Beaumont's possession, for a slave named St. Jean, "*nègre* of Sr. Regnaud of Léogane," traveled on the ship *Le Solide* from La Rochelle to Saint-Domingue in 1753.[96]

Women who owned slaves in France could encounter difficulties exercising the types of patriarchal authority necessary to dominate their slaves. In Saint-Domingue, the commonality of slave ownership meant that the dominion of free over enslaved was well established, no matter the race or gender of the slave owner. In France, where slave ownership was much rarer, assumptions about masters' authority closely mirrored assumptions about patriarchal authority. White women who owned slaves, then, had to go to greater lengths to make sure their dominion over their slaves, and their male slaves in particular, was recognized and accepted. Following the letter of the law that permitted slavery in France left few windows to question their domination.

Examining the relations between white women and people of color, slave and free, calls into question the assumptions that white women's primary function in plantation society was to reproduce whiteness. As the examples recounted in this chapter have shown, white women in Saint-Domingue had close personal relationships with people of color that belie the characterization of white women only as sexual rivals of women of color. White women incorporated people of color into their households, living in close, intimate contact with them, and formed bonds with them that they expressed in material ways. Like white men, white women gave slaves, especially enslaved women and children, their freedom and also material gifts that could include cash, goods, or slaves. This emphasizes that white men's motivations, too, may have been more varied than previously assumed.

White women also participated actively in Saint-Domingue's highly integrated economy. They bought, sold, and rented property, businesses, and slaves, engaging in personal and contractual relations with people of color all the while. This opens up the possibility that white women in Saint-Domingue, an atmosphere where economic participation was less tightly regulated, may have exercised more economic autonomy than their counterparts in France. The demographic minority of whites, especially white women, presented ways for them to claim and exert race-based authority in the economic sphere in ways unavailable to women in France. In Saint-Domingue, the hierarchy of free over enslaved, often but not always race-based, was so firmly

entrenched that white women experienced little difficulty exercising patriarchal authority over slaves. In turn, this opened up some flexibility that allowed them to form bonds across race.

In France, on the other hand, white women experienced more difficulty
exercising control over slaves, especially male slaves, as assumptions about
slavery and patriarchy were so closely tied together. Furthermore, understandings of colonial femininity as blatantly sexual undermined the authority
of colonial white women over male slaves in their own households. Borrow-
ing royal authority by following the letter of the laws governing slave ownership could help legitimate their claims. While slave owners in general adopted
this tactic, for white women slave owners the stakes—and the potential
benefits—were particularly high.

In spite of Swiss visitor to Saint-Domingue Girod de Chantras' characterization of white women adopting "imbecilic jargon" that limited their expres-
sion and made them more like women of color, white women actually upheld
slavery, not threatened it.[97] White women in Saint-Domingue were not mere
fragile, imbecilic plantation ladies, isolated from the hustle and bustle of the
commercial life of the colony and protected from the nitty-gritty of race relations in a context where race was becoming an important legal category.
Rather, they were active participants in the burgeoning colonial economy,
and they had personal relationships with people of color, free and slave. At
least in part, colonists accepted these contradictions: white women could be
simultaneously fond of people of color and owners of them, essential economic contributors and guardians of their families. In France, in contrast,
these contradictions posed challenges and caused difficulties for white
women who owned slaves. In fact, even the incorporation of male slaves into
their households could raise questions about white feminine purity, questions already being asked about white women who had lived in the Antilles.

CHAPTER 5

What's in a Name?

While white women such as Madame Regnaud de Beaumont in La Rochelle cast around for creative means by which to exercise their authority over slaves, mixed race families faced different sets of challenges. In Saint-Domingue, white fathers of mixed-race children could, if they chose, acknowledge and provide for these children, as did Jean-Severin Regnaud de Beaumont; such practices were familiar and widely accepted. In La Rochelle, however, the censure of families and communities often precluded such largesse. Thus, after Rochelais merchant Aimé-Benjamin Fleuriau returned to La Rochelle from the western province of Saint-Domingue in 1755 in the company of five mixed-race adolescents, he never once formally acknowledged them as his children. For the children, this posed an immediate and alarming problem. Although children of a wealthy plantation owner and merchant, their position was financially unstable and socially insecure without the protection of his name, and became even more so after he married and fathered legitimate children.

This already precarious situation intensified in 1762 when the French government required all people of color to submit to registration without distinction of slave or free status. The 1762 law effectively drew a color line around families, forcing the categorization of free people of color outside the bounds of French families. It was this classification that both Fleuriau and his children worked to upset.

Thus, when Fleuriau arrived at the *hôtel de ville* in La Rochelle on 5 September 1763 to make a formal declaration of all the people of color in his household, he did his best to hedge his bets. "Under his care," he said, were "three young *mulâtres* and two young *mulâtresses*, all born free, named Joseph, Paul, and Jean, Marie and Charlotte Mendroux, children of the late Jeanne Guimbelot, free *négresse* . . . on the coast of Saint-Domingue." A "nègre domestique" named Hardy also lived with him.[1] Although he did not acknowledge his paternity, his differentiation of his children "born free" and the "nègre domestique" Hardy shows that relationships formed in the colonies, particularly family relationships, did not simply cease to exist after colonists returned home. Family ties linking people of different skin colors and origins persisted, and disrupted both an increasingly facile equation between dark skin and servitude and understandings of the family as a unit. Such relationships, with their roots in Saint-Domingue, reshaped how families were defined, and they brought the exigencies of empire into the daily lives of individuals who never set foot outside the metropole. Although by the mid-eighteenth century race was becoming progressively more important in France, the family remained the primary lens through which most individuals measured their place in society. So when the Ordinance of 1762, the first French law to define individuals solely by their race, threatened the social position of some members of the Fleuriau family, they used their family ties and associations to push back.

While the Ordinance of 1762 was part of a series of laws that regulated racial boundaries more and more stringently over the course of the eighteenth century, it was also an important departure from either the Edict of 1716 or the Declaration of 1738 in that it grouped all people of color together, without regard for slave or free status. The two previous laws aimed to regulate the practice of slavery, delineating and limiting the circumstances under which slaves could be brought to France and the length of their visits. These laws offered basically no protections or privileges to slaves, but did put the burden of compliance—and penalties for noncompliance—on the shoulders of slave owners. They made no provisions for free people of color. By the early 1760s, though, it was clear that slaves and free people of color lived in France. Additionally, official attitudes had begun to change and solidify, leading to policies in France and Saint-Domingue that equated race and status. Historians have focused on the tensions between white colonists and free people of color and concluded that colonial whites drove these changes.[2] However, the case of the Fleuriau family demonstrates that for whites with interracial families, family ties could form a reason and a platform for pushing against the new regulations.

Free people fiercely resisted their categorization alongside slaves as well, and in doing so they had much more at stake than whites. For them, too, family could provide a basis for claiming belonging in France, a claim based not on race but on family position. In order for this strategy to work, though, they had to successfully claim membership in established white French families. This proved the rub, for such families might try to distance themselves legally from any specific connection with colored kin, even while sometimes treating them as members. Moreover, well-placed families in La Rochelle were reluctant to form marriage alliances even with free people of color who had the financial support of their white father, as did Fleuriau's children. This attests that skin color was a social category in France even before it became a legal one.

The case of Fleuriau and his mixed-race children provides an example through which to rethink accepted notions of family formation and to examine how individuals challenged the boundaries of family from the inside. People of color sat uneasily within the usual limits of the nuclear families that increasingly predominated in northern and western Europe, including France.[3] To complicate matters, the growing association of illegitimacy and racial mixture also shaped the position of mixed-race children within the family.[4] Yet many of the characteristics of ancien régime families applied to mixed-race and illegitimate children just as much as they did to legitimate white offspring, particularly patriarchal authority over marriage, inheritance, and discipline.[5] Illegitimacy and mixed racial ancestry also disrupted patriarchal authority because neither category sat easily within the limits of the nuclear family. This opened the possibility that mixed-race children could advance their own interpretations of family relations, even potentially claiming ties that went unacknowledged by their white kin.

Aimé-Benjamin Fleuriau and His Family

Aimé-Benjamin Fleuriau was born and raised in the cosmopolitan Atlantic port city of La Rochelle, yet as a young man Fleuriau had little to do with the crème de la crème of Rochelais society. The son of a bankrupted sugar refiner and one of ten children, he mostly depended on his own resources to make his way in the world.[6] Thus necessity drove him to Saint-Domingue just as much as a quest for wealth. He arrived in the colony around 1729 at about twenty, one of thousands of anonymous young men who emigrated from France's Atlantic coast.[7] Young Aimé-Benjamin's decision to go to Saint-Domingue proved well considered, as he already had colonial connections: his uncle Paul Fleuriau had made the voyage to Saint-Domingue in 1710, and by the time of his nephew's arrival he had established himself comfortably as a plantation owner.[8]

After ten years under his uncle's tutelage young Fleuriau struck out alone as a sugar merchant in the town of Croix-des-Bouquets. His timing could not have been better. By the 1740s, French consumption of "populuxe" goods, including sugar, had begun in earnest.[9] Fleuriau rode the sugar high, and the immense boom in the sugar market, combined with an inheritance from his uncle, enabled him to buy a plantation of his own situated near Croix-des-Bouquets.[10]

In this small town Fleuriau began his relationship with Jeanne "*dite* Guimbelot," a woman of color who apparently had been his slave at one time. Her exact status is unclear, including whether she was enslaved or free when their sexual relationship began.[11] We know little about Jeanne, except that her union with the planter endured for at least ten years. They had no fewer than eight children together: Jean-Baptiste in 1740, Marie-Jeanne in 1741, Marie-Charlotte in 1742, Joseph-Benjamin in 1743, Pierre-Paul in 1745, Jean in 1747, Toinette in 1748, and Marie-Magdeline in 1749.[12] All these children were classified as free people of color at the time of their birth. Their mother certainly had received her freedom by 1741; the baptism record of Marie-Jeanne and all Jeanne's subsequent children refer to her as "Jeanne Guimbelot, free *négresse*."[13]

Although Jeanne may have been enslaved when her sexual relationship with Fleuriau began, she was a free woman for much of their relationship. Although this presumably meant she had some choice in the matter, the continued inequality of their positions and her dependence on him indicate that she actually had few alternatives. She may have relied on the modest monetary gifts he gave her throughout his life. Fleuriau's account books of 1743 include two payments to Jeanne *dite* Guimbelot, the first of three hundred ninety-seven livres, followed by a smaller payment of one hundred twenty-seven livres, "in favor of *sa petite*," possibly referring to one of Jeanne's daughters.[14] In 1777, toward the end of Fleuriau's life when he was residing in France, his plantation accounts record a further payment of three hundred livres to "Jeanneton, former slave of M. Fleuriau, in order to carry out his intentions."[15] Having eight children may have limited her options even more. Although Fleuriau clearly took financial responsibility for them, it is by no means clear that he would have continued to do so had Jeanne brought their sexual relationship to an end.

Contemporaries and historians have well documented the abuse and coercion of female slaves, especially those who lived and worked in close proximity with their owners.[16] This was so common in Saint-Domingue that

Fleuriau Family

= unmarried union
= married union

‖ = illegitimate children
| = legitimate children

Jeanne Guimbelot
Involved
c. 1740–1749

Aimé-Benjamin Fleuriau
24 July 1709–3 July 1787
In Saint-Domingue c. 1729–1755

Married 1756

Marie-Anne-Suzanne Liège

Jean-Baptiste Fleuriau Mandron
1740–10 April 1785, Mirebalais

Children

Marie-Jeanne Fleuriau Mandron
15 June 1741–24 November 1793,
La Rochelle

Marie-Charlotte Fleuriau Mandron
September 1742–1 August 1773,
La Rochelle

Joseph-Benjamin
29 September 1743–?

Pierre-Paul Fleuriau Mandron
8 January 1745–1800

m. Demoiselle Theron

Jean
8 January 1747–?

Toinette
3 August
1748–?

Marie-Magdeline
17 October 1749–?

Marie Mandron
b. c. 1769, Port-au-Prince, d. 20
September 1783, La Rochelle

Daughter

Son

Aimé-Paul Fleuriau
[de Touchelongue]
27 March 1757–1793

François-Charles-Benjamin
17 August 1758–17 September 1759

Suzanne-Catherine
24 February 1760–14 November 1783

Louis-Benjamin Fleuriau
[de Bellevue]
24 February 1761–8 February 1852

Marie-Anne Sara
18 January 1763–1765

Marie-Adélaïde
22 May 1766–3 April 1833

Fleuriau's Slave Hardy
c. 1720, Guinea, Africa–19 August
1771, La Rochelle

Dominican priest Du Tertre put its frequency on par with that of physical mistreatment: "there are plantation owners that have abused their *Négresses* just as much as the slave drivers who make them work."[17] In contrast to episodic abuse, ongoing relationships between free women of color and white men, especially years-long liaisons such as the one between Jeanne and Fleuriau, pose the temptation to look for consent or mutuality. However, in rural Croix-des-Bouquets, Jeanne may have had few other choices.

Sexual service was one way enslaved women could build personal connections with their owners.[18] Being a concubine could lead to concrete benefits for them or their children, including better food, clothing, and shelter than most slaves.[19] Unlike male artisans on whose expertise plantation owners relied, female slaves rarely held skilled positions. Midwives were a notable exception to this rule, yet they would not have had the same level of contact or communication with owners as would skilled carpenters or blacksmiths, for example. Ménagères, on the other hand, housekeepers who had "all the functions of a wife," were highly skilled women who usually had close personal ties with their masters, though they were often free rather than drawn from the ranks of slaves.[20] Although some ménagères certainly were involved in sexual liaisons with the men they served, their daily lives were far from the fantasy of "abandon[ment] to voluptuity" that Moreau de Saint-Méry so strongly indicated.[21] Being a ménagère was a skilled position of authority. They ran households, performing tasks that included cooking, shopping, housekeeping, and even bookkeeping and supervising other servants. Some commanded high wages, and earned a measure of community respect.[22] Whichever "functions of a wife" Jeanne fulfilled, sexual and nonsexual interactions with white men had the potential to yield material benefits that suggest why she may have remained with Fleuriau.

Public opinion in Saint-Domingue condoned white men freeing enslaved women who bore them children; Moreau de Saint-Méry noted "the force that opinion has acquired that the White, father of a child of color, must look to procure him his liberty."[23] Hilliard d'Auberteuil similarly framed such manumission as a common recognition of family ties. He highlighted the appropriateness of owners freeing slave women with whom they had engaged in "illegitimate liaisons," and "the attachment he has for the children issuing from these liaisons." Such attachment, which Hilliard considered wholly natural, would overshadow any pecuniary reservations a slave owner may have had about manumission, for "in the first case, . . . love of money will not prevent him from doing a generous action; in the second case, he will not be swayed from making one more sacrifice to passion."[24] Indeed, two-thirds to three-quarters of all manumissions in Saint-Domingue were of women and children.[25] Fleuriau counted himself among the men who gave mixed-race children freedom and some means of their own.

In Saint-Domingue there was a broad spectrum of freedom and ways to come about it. Some people of color were "born free," such as Fleuriau's children, either of free parents of color or declared as such by their white fathers. Those born slaves could attain freedom through either a cumbersome manumission process, or a variety of informal channels. Given the absence of documentary evidence of the precise circumstances surrounding Jeanne's liberty, her freedom may have been formal or informal. Formal manumission carried the most legal weight. This course of action was difficult, time-consuming, and expensive for slave owners, and after 1713 it required written permission from the colonial administration.[26] Instead, numerous former slaves lived as *libres de fait*, individuals who may have been slaves in the eyes of the law but who lived as if they were free.[27] Given Fleuriau's assent to Jeanne's categorization as a free *négresse* in their children's baptism records, he certainly regarded her as free, whether or not he had taken the formal steps necessary to ratify her freedom. If he had not, lack of manumission papers may have circumscribed her options, tying her to her former owner.

While we cannot know how Jeanne felt about their liaison, the historical records show that each of their children was baptized at their parish church, as mandated by law and custom.[28] That three laws passed between 1737 and 1743 required colonists to baptize all newborn children within forty days of their birth emphasizes that parents often neglected this ritual.[29] Fleuriau and Jeanne's children all promptly received the Catholic sacrament in spite of their father's professed Protestantism, and had their free status duly recorded in the parish register by the priest. These registers, kept by royal decree, included baptism records for slave and free children, people of color and whites, illegitimate and legitimate. The children all received the appellation "fille/fils illégitime," children of Aimé-Benjamin Fleuriau and Jeanne, "*négresse* libre."[30] While Fleuriau acknowledged them as his own, the presiding priest recorded their illegitimacy in each of their baptism records, in accordance with Church practice. All were given the surname Mandron, even though mixed-race children often took the name of their white father, hinting that Fleuriau distanced himself from his children even as he acknowledged his paternity.[31] Fleuriau did not marry Jeanne. Although some white men wed well-off women of color, it would have been highly unusual for a wealthy planter to marry a former slave.[32]

Like other Protestants, Fleuriau used baptism in a mechanistic way. He took the occasion to begin building networks for his children, deliberately weaving them into the elite of Croix-des-Bouquets. In contrast to his Protestant brethren in La Rochelle, he named neighboring planters, merchants, and their wives as godparents, thereby establishing a web of contacts that extended beyond his household and plantation. This practice wove children into the community, an essential consideration for those who, such as the Mandrons, occupied a precarious social position. Fleuriau intentionally created relationships between his children of color and his white neighbors, thereby forging links that cut across notions of race and relied on shared experience and place.[33] For Protestants, Catholic baptism also conferred civil personhood, easing the path to inheritance. In the case of mixed-race children, baptism could prove particularly significant because it acted as a public record of their freedom. Although baptism had no formal legal basis as a means of manumission, planters commonly enlisted the moral authority of the Catholic Church, and the collusion of parish priests, for this end.[34]

In spite of Fleuriau's efforts, his children occupied a liminal status even in colonial life: free but illegitimate, of mixed racial origins but the beneficiaries of whites whose goodwill toward them depended on their regard for their father. In Saint-Domingue mixed-race children of wealthy white planters comprised part of the colonial elite, positioned not at but sometimes near the pinnacle of society. Favored mixed-race sons of white planters enjoyed options. They could become part of the military, practice a trade, work on their fathers' plantations, or even own land and slaves themselves. Daughters of wealthy planters frequently married well and participated in colonial free colored society: light-skinned brides dowered by white fathers would have had excellent marriage prospects, particularly during the sugar boom of the 1730s and 1740s, although interracial marriages happened less regularly as the century progressed.[35] In Saint-Domingue the Mandron children's lighter skin color was, for the most part, a social asset. They were excluded from the highest echelons of society, but their father's wealth and his efforts to embed them in a network of social connections made them better off than most people who lived in France or Saint-Domingue. Once Fleuriau and his children arrived in France, however, their social situation changed dramatically.

After twenty-six years of colonial life, Fleuriau returned to La Rochelle in 1755 at forty-six in a blaze of wealth and glory, a living testament to the possibilities for social mobility offered by the colonies. Because of his new fortune, made from sugar and other colonial products produced by his slaves, La Rochelle's wealthiest families welcomed him as one of their own. Soon after his return he married Marie-Anne-Suzanne Liège, daughter of a wealthy Rochelais merchant, a young woman who, at twenty-two, was less than half his age.[36] The couple, both Protestant, may have married in Bordeaux instead of La Rochelle, possibly to avoid providing the proof of Catholicism necessary to be married in the Catholic Church.[37] While in Bordeaux each had a pastel portrait done by well-known pastelist Jean-Baptiste Perronneau. In these portraits they wear fashionable clothes made of fine fabrics, demonstrating their wealth and their newly attained social position.[38]

Soon after their return to La Rochelle, the couple took up their abode in a house on rue Gargoulleaud, an exclusive street of hôtels particuliers removed from the noise and stench of the port. Fleuriau owned this house, the first but by no means the only one he purchased in La Rochelle.[39] During this time, the living arrangements of his five mixed-race children are unclear. His colonial profits were much diminished by the Seven Years' War, and he owned no other property in La Rochelle during the early years of his return, so it is possible that the quintet lived with their father and his new wife.[40] If this was the case, no record remains of what Marie-Anne-Suzanne Liège, the new Madame Fleuriau, thought of this arrangement. The age differential between the couple helps explain why she accepted the presence of his illegitimate children who were closer to her own age than was her bridegroom; their presence certainly reinforced the patriarchal authority he held in the family. In 1772, he acquired a magnificent hôtel on the street now known as rue Fleuriau.[41] By this point or soon thereafter, his mixed-race daughters, now grown women, lived independently.

Fleuriau's five mixed-race children who traveled to La Rochelle with their father found themselves thrust into a social milieu very different from what they had known in Saint-Domingue and, moreover, in a vulnerable position without the legal protections accorded to legitimate offspring.[42] Used to privileges, they now faced severely circumscribed social opportunities. Rochelais society paid little heed to the colonial commonplace that people with dusky skin could be part of the social elite if wealthy enough. Few free people of color in all France enjoyed the economic resources Fleuriau put at his children's disposal, and the prosperous free colored layer of society that thrived in Saint-Domingue simply did not exist in the metropole. In 1777, the year the greatest number of people of color registered as residents of La Rochelle, their number totaled only eighty.[43] In their new seaport home they had no mixed-race peers of their own social status. And although the people of La Rochelle accepted slavery on French soil without undue compunction, the elite of the city appeared unwilling to absorb these dark-skinned children of one of their most vaunted members. None of the Mandrons married in France, although all Fleuriau's white children, born after he returned to France, married members of other wealthy Huguenot families.[44]

In compliance with the Edict of 1716 and the Declaration of 1738, Fleuriau faithfully surfaced at the Admiralty office in La Rochelle on 2 August 1755, soon after he arrived in France, to register his enslaved manservant Hardy, the same Hardy who arrived on *Le Théodore* with Madame Regnaud de Beaumont's slave Lizette, and who would, in 1766, be named godfather to one of Fleuriau's daughters. In his declaration, Fleuriau stated that Hardy was about twenty-seven years old, and identified him as being of the "Banguia nation," a territory interior to the African Gold Coast.[45] Fleuriau said that he had brought his slave to France to work as his servant on the voyage, to be instructed in Catholicism, and to learn a trade, all as the law allowed.[46] He renewed his slave's registration two years later and again three years after that, thus legitimizing his own continued ownership.[47] Fleuriau did not register his three sons or two daughters with the Admiralty office because their freedom meant they never were classified alongside slaves, their mixed racial origins notwithstanding. Their free status and their wealthy father ensured that Marie-Jeanne, Marie-Charlotte, Joseph-Benjamin, Pierre-Paul, and Jean could go unmarked as *nègres* or *mûlatres* in any official records. This all changed with the Admiralty Ordinance of 1762.

The Admiralty Ordinance of 1762

Although Fleuriau's mixed-race children may have faced social limitations because of their skin color, the social and cultural association of race and slavery in France did not directly threaten their family structures and strategies, unconventional as they may have seemed to outsiders. Interracial families could still produce, accumulate, inherit, and pass on wealth, central goals among the transatlantic merchants of La Rochelle and prosperous families of color in Saint-Domingue. However, the 1762 Ordinance's legal racialization of free people of color clearly posed a serious challenge to the well-to-do Fleuriau clan because it disrupted long-standing and well-accepted

Saint-Dominguan practices of white men providing for their mixed-race children and integrating those children into personal networks based on status and family connections, not race.

Unlike the Edict of 1716 and the Declaration of 1738, the Ordinance of 1762 took aim not only at slaves but at all people of color regardless of status.[48] It collapsed distinctions based on free status, wealth, or social position by making race the only relevant legal category. It mandated that all French residents who counted people of color as part of their households make "precise declarations of *nègres* or *mulâtres* of one or the other sex living with them . . . and from which colony or place they were exported." Moreover, in a departure from previous legislation, the ordinance "mandates . . . that all other *nègres* and *mulâtres* of whatever profession they be, and who are in service to no one, will be obliged to make likewise in person or by an agent, furnished with their special power of attorney, to the said clerks, and in the said time, their declarations of their nicknames, first names, age and profession, place of their birth, date of their arrival in France, and by what ship, and if they have been baptized or not."[49] To prevent what the Ordinance called "excesses dangerous for society" it considered typical of these "dangerous men," all people of color, no matter what their nationality, sex, or status, had to register with the Admiralty.

For former slaves, the Ordinance offered an unprecedented opportunity to record their status officially and in a way that left no question about their present freedom. Multiple free people of color registered with the Admiralty, suggesting that they wanted to take advantage of the occasion to record their differences from slaves.[50] It provided a particularly significant opportunity for former slaves working as servants or day laborers, occupations whose work differed little from that performed by slaves. Yet for people of color who had been born free, the sons and daughters of wealthy planters who in the colonies occupied privileged positions, the Ordinance of 1762 offered little benefit. Furthermore, it forced them to identify as nonwhite. It did give them the possibility to record their free status officially, which may have been attractive in a cultural atmosphere of increasing racial paranoia, but they could only do this by classifying themselves explicitly by race and placing themselves socially alongside slaves. Former slaves may not have objected to this categorization, but relatively privileged mixed-race people likely found this blanket cataloging galling in the extreme, particularly in comparison to the legal and social distinctions made between slaves and wealthy free people of color in Saint-Domingue.[51]

Fleuriau's children had little to gain by having their free status recorded; their father's wealth and position gave them more protection than the registry book. Since their arrival in France the Mandrons had been classified neither as *mûlatres* nor as Fleuriau's children. This offered a modicum of security to their father: Aimé-Benjamin freely acknowledged his children at their baptisms, but his Rochelais neighbors may have looked askance on the presence of five mixed-race children in a way that his colonial neighbors would not, and by failing to officially acknowledge them in France, he could maintain a fiction of distance from his natural children. Keeping his children out of official documents also meant that they had never formally been classified as people of color in France. In a cultural climate where scientists speculated that Europeans and Africans belonged to different species and authors routinely assumed that Africans' dark skin suited them for a life of slavery, well-to-do people of mixed racial origins had considerable incentives to avoid what they likely perceived as demeaning classifications.[52]

Rochelais officials began registering all people of color in September of the following year. When Fleuriau declared his children to the Admiralty in 1763, they had all reached their late teens or early twenties but were still legally minors. At this point, probably for the first time in their lives, these children of privilege, the freeborn sons and daughters of a wealthy planter and merchant, were categorized alongside one of their father's slaves. In spite of making their freedom a matter of public record, then, Fleuriau's declaration also effectively solidified their racial status and made it common knowledge, creating a negative effect for the Mandrons that considerably outweighed any benefit they may have received from having their freedom recorded. Inscribing their race in the 1763 survey weakened the social protection afforded them by their father's status by calling attention to their similarities to slaves and former slaves, and definitively marked them as people of color. Although no physical description remains of Fleuriau's children, this categorization was even more damaging if there was any possibility that they could have passed as whites.

Faced with a mandate to classify his children alongside slaves, Fleuriau nonetheless worked to frame his statement so as to best protect them from this indignity; he did so by accentuating their differences from his enslaved manservant Hardy. Fleuriau's statement about Hardy closely followed the parameters established by the Ordinance and other declarations of slaves made by slave owners in La Rochelle. "I the undersigned declare to have in this town of La Rochelle," Fleuriau stated, "one of my domestic *nègres* named

Hardy, whom I have had learn the trade of saddler." Although he promised to
send Hardy back to his plantation on Saint-Domingue, he also asked—"as he
will need a little more time to perfect his trade, and because it is morally impossible to find, from now until next fifteenth of October the way to send
him to Port-au-Prince to return him to my plantation"—that the court allow
him until the following March or April, at which time he would put his slave
on a ship "bound for the colonies."[53] Few owners who endured the trouble
and expense of bringing slaves to France really wanted to send them back,
and Fleuriau proved no exception. Hardy never got on that ship: he remained
in La Rochelle for another eight years, and died there in 1771 at the age of
about fifty. He was memorialized as "the son of an unknown father and
mother, native of Guinea, a *nègre* belonging to the elder Monsieur Fleuriau,
merchant." In his burial records, as in his Admiralty declarations, his race
and his status were made clear.[54]

In a marked shift from his formulaic slave declaration, Fleuriau immediately differentiated his children by going into detail about their personal history in what is the most elaborate declaration made in La Rochelle in the 1763
survey of people of color. Most declarations only included the name of the
slave, a promise to send him or her back to the colonies, and the owner's signature. The few free people of color who made their own declarations usually
also stated their place of origin and employment history.[55] Fleuriau went
much farther, constructing an elaborate history for the five young people he
still did not claim as his children. He began with the antecedents of the "three
young *mulâtres* and two young *mulâtresses* (all born free), named Joseph,
Paul, and Jean, Marie and Charlotte Mendroux, children of the late Jeanne
Guimbelot, free *négresse*, Créole of the aforementioned place of Cul-de-Sac
on the coast of Saint-Domingue."[56] By detailing their birthplace he signaled
that each had a personal history in a place that belonged to France, not an
unknown African land. By calling them créoles, a term that first appeared in
the 1762 edition of the *Dictionnaire de l'Académie Française* and already signified a person "European by origin who was born in America," Fleuriau emphasized his children's French connections.[57] By naming their mother and
specifying her free status he brought the special circumstances of their liberty
into relief, as they were "all born free." At the same time, by specifying that
Jeanne was deceased, he rhetorically severed their ties to their African roots.
In fact, she still may have been alive: Fleuriau made a payment to "Jeanneton"
fourteen years later.[58] In his declaration, therefore, Fleuriau walked a fine line
between   adhering   to   the   established   formula   and   articulating   the

understanding of social relations he himself had gleaned from decades of living in Saint-Domingue. In the process he underscored the gap between
French and colonial understandings of race and status and worked to bring
French ideas closer in line with colonial ones that allowed a hierarchical continuum based on skin color and social position.[59]

Yet, in spite of these efforts, Fleuriau still slipped into the language of
slavery. This slippage emphasizes that race was indeed a powerful social category before the Ordinance of 1762 made it a legal one, but also makes clear
that Fleuriau himself had conflicting and complicated goals. While he aimed
to shield his mixed-race children, he also wanted to protect himself and his
legitimate family: hence his persistent failure to acknowledge his paternity.
Thus, although Fleuriau had strong incentive to emphasize the Mandrons'
particular situation, he nonetheless fell back into the pattern of slave declarations when he enumerated his sons' apprenticeships. Fleuriau declared that
the first two "young *mulâtres*" were apprenticed to goldsmiths and that Jean
was in apprenticeship to "a tailor of men's suits."

The sons Fleuriau carefully avoided acknowledging in this official document may well have learned these particular trades, but they had no reason
to "perfect [them] to better earn their living," as the merchant went on to
claim.[60] Rather, Joseph and Paul returned to Saint-Domingue for good in
1765, only two years after their father initially recorded their presence in
France. Their brother Jean followed them eight years later. They went back to
Saint-Domingue at a time when opportunities for free men of color were
narrowing. The reforms of the 1760s instituted a more rigid second-class status for free people of color, who were increasingly required to shoulder the
burdens of public service white men did not want.[61] Luckily for the three
brothers, their father's wealth gave them access to land and slaves, and all of
them took an active role in managing their father's plantation.[62]

By emphasizing his sons' apprenticeships to learn trades of which they
had no actual need, then, Fleuriau unwittingly brought the declarations of his
free children in line with the laws governing the presence of slaves in France.
Fleuriau's slip exposes that the collapse of race and slave status, which this
law aimed to achieve, already had begun in France. Fleuriau had never before
classified his children according to their race. Furthermore, he made real efforts to give them the advantages he could. By emphasizing the differences
between the *mûlatres* "under his care" and his *nègre* slave Hardy, Fleuriau
nuanced the categories of race and slavery expressed by the Ordinance, and
may have even been responding to rumors that the government intended to

forcibly return all people of color to the colonies, as 1777 legislation later would require.

Yet his sons' apprenticeships could simultaneously bring them in closer proximity to and distance them from slaves; this antinomy highlights the complicated and entwined nature of race and slavery. The merchant, for example, drew upon gendered understandings of skilled labor to emphasize his sons' conformity with European ideals of masculine skill and authority. French gender roles had little meaning on plantations, where owners demanded field work from women as well as men.[63] The work performed by female slaves directly contradicted European conceptions of gender, which held that only men could engage in hard labor or learn the skills necessary to practice a trade. Likewise, the 1738 law required male and female slaves to learn a trade, though in reality few slaves in France actually entered into apprenticeships. Skilled labor thus remained the province of white French men who were guild members and heads of household.

Fleuriau's children were not slaves, so in his declaration he claimed reasons for them to stay in France that hewed with European expectations of gender roles. For free men, he emphasized, mastery of a trade implied real skill, particularly for a trade such as goldsmith, which Fleuriau claimed Joseph and Paul learned. Goldsmithing required extensive training, justifying their presence in France for a long period of time, and it also involved advanced skills associated with good education and polite society, such as mathematics, taste, and finesse.[64] As a luxury trade, patrons had to possess a certain level of trust in the artisans who pursued it. It also connoted masculine responsibility, for master tradesmen often headed large households comprising wives, children, servants, journeymen, and apprentices. In his declaration, Fleuriau emphasized that his sons had to perfect their trades "to better earn their living," a phrase clearly indicating their conformity with standards of manliness.[65] The claim that the Mandron brothers were training as apprentices, then, placed them in the same category as male heads of household: productive and valued members of French society. Fleuriau also subtly dissociated his children from the stigma of slavery by emphasizing the training and skills only of his sons; he thereby pushed against the rigorous line the 1762 Ordinance drew around race. The position of his sons, Fleuriau claimed, stemmed from their masculine status and their potential to become heads of families, not from the color of their skin. He thus presented his sons as Frenchmen.

Similarly, when it came to his daughters Fleuriau gave reasons for them to remain in France strictly in line with expectations for European women: physical delicacy and family. Fleuriau addressed Marie-Jeanne and Marie-Charlotte separately from their brothers. He begged the court to "have consideration that the aforementioned Charlotte has been for a number of years attacked by a cold distemper sickness, and it has afflicted her sight, from which neither doctor nor surgeon has yet been able to cure her, and that her sister Marie is the only one who can care for her and monitor her in this distressing state that visibly will carry her to the tomb."[66] Here Fleuriau begged for mercy in lieu of resorting to the language of the law. In emphasizing Charlotte's delicate health, which played into tropes of feminine frailty, he also created a role for her older sister Marie-Jeanne as nurse and caregiver, roles that generally fell to women. Fleuriau warned against what might happen "if she [Charlotte] departs for a climate so contrary to the reestablishment of her health; it is for this consideration that the aforementioned Marie and Charlotte require if it please his majesty to dispense them from leaving a climate that is so necessary to their health."[67] By emphasizing the detrimental effects of the tropical climate and the healthful European airs, Fleuriau classified his daughters alongside European women without ever mentioning their race. Both scholarly and popular texts decried the detrimental effects of the tropics on delicate European constitutions, especially for women, while proponents of slavery argued that Africans' toleration of hot climates rendered them suitable for enslavement.[68] By emphasizing the "necessary" benefits of the French climate for Charlotte, Fleuriau firmly distinguished her from the enslaved women who endured tropical heat, supposedly with no trouble at all.[69] He also justified their residence in France in the face of potential rumors of expulsion.

Family played a significant role in shaping shifting understandings and experiences of race and status in France. Fleuriau took responsibility for making declarations for Joseph, Paul, Jean, Marie-Jeanne, and Charlotte Mandron because they were part of his family. He employed European discourses of gender in his statements for the same reason. In doing so, Fleuriau pointed to the insufficiency of the 1762 Ordinance, which grouped all people of color in the same category. Fleuriau held the conviction, based on his own personal experience, that not all people of color could be classified together. Accordingly, he pointed out why his own children should fall into different categories even in the eyes of the law, drawing on how they conformed to gender expectations to emphasize their Frenchness and their family connections over their African ancestry. In employing these rhetorics, Fleuriau made a series of strategic calculations and created a complex web of discourse that, first and foremost, safeguarded his spot at the forefront of Rochelais society.

In contrast to his contemporary Regnaud de Beaumont, he also created a series of buffers between himself and his illegitimate family of color. Although Fleuriau acknowledged his children at their births, he did not give them his name. While he gave their mother money, he had no legal relationship with her. He always had an eye on returning to La Rochelle, and wanted no personal entanglements to impede his goal, maybe particularly once it became clear to him that he was making a fortune.

Yet perhaps in spite of his plans, Fleuriau still ended up with "three young *mulâtres* and two young *mulâtresses*" who lived "under his care." This makes manifest, on the one hand, the powerful force of family. The presence of these children in France brought no possible benefit to Fleuriau. The only reason for him to bring them was because he wanted them close. Yet, in the end, defending these five children against the ever-encroaching reach of the state was one thing; actually treating them like his legitimate children was another. As illegitimate children of a father who never formally acknowledged them once they arrived in France and who also had legitimate heirs, the Mandrons could not know with certainty that their father would provide for them after his death as he had during his life. As Fleuriau's acknowledgment of his children at their baptism expressed, birth was one defining moment in mapping out family relationships. Death provided a similar opportunity.[70] Birth and death offered two of the infrequent occasions where individuals had to officially record their relationships with each other. For free people of color who had few opportunities to make their relationships with their white kin or with each other public, these moments proved particularly important.

Most prosperous Protestant families took the precaution of having baptismal, marital, and funeral services performed in the Catholic Church, which acted as the gatekeeper of civil and religious personhood: only the sacraments could assure the civil privileges of legitimacy and succession. Although Protestants such as the Fleuriau family may not have set much store by the religious tenets of the Catholic Church, they certainly made every effort to ensure their own legal positions. By baptizing all their children as Catholics, legitimate and illegitimate alike, the Fleuriau family safeguarded their ability to inherit. Definitions of family became particularly contentious around the issue of inheritance, where the stakes were highest. Wealthy men in France had long given financial support to illegitimate children, sometimes including sizable legacies meant to provide for offspring after their father's death. Colonists adapted this practice and extended it down the social spectrum, as even some poor white planters such as Regnaud de Beaumont left resources to their mixed-race families, occasionally in opposition to the expectations of family members in France. When wealthy white fathers transmitted assets to their mixed-race offspring, they challenged increasingly prevalent ideas of racial hierarchy and family relationships and responsibilities, particularly assumptions about the roles of fathers as heads of household responsible for husbanding family patrimonies. In the case of the Fleuriau family, Aimé-Benjamin Fleuriau's insistence on leaving legacies to his mixed-race children placed financial resources at the disposal of someone who, at first glance, might appear one of the least likely people of means in all France: his daughter Marie-Jeanne, a woman of color and daughter of a former slave, whom Fleuriau had never acknowledged as kin after he arrived in France.

Race, Family, and Legacies

Unlike their brothers, Marie-Jeanne Mandron and her sister Marie-Charlotte never returned to Saint-Domingue after they went to live in La Rochelle. In the colony social opportunities for free people of color, particularly women of means, were changing, hinting at reasons for their ongoing presence in La Rochelle. Although at or approaching marriageable age for women when they arrived in France, neither ever married. Although in the first part of the century they would have been considered quite a catch for either free men of color or most white men because of their status as daughters of a wealthy white planter, the changing valence of race meant that their marriage opportunities, even in Saint-Domingue, might have been closing off.[71] Instead, Marie-Jeanne and Marie-Charlotte lived together in a house owned by their father in La Rochelle's central Place d'Armes near the Protestant church, not far from where Fleuriau and his new French family resided at a much more exclusive address. For the rest of their lives the Mandron sisters lived in close proximity to their Fleuriau kin and the two branches of the family maintained relations even after their father's death.[72] Although both women lived in the city until they died—Marie-Charlotte in 1773 at thirty and Marie-Jeanne in 1793 at fifty-three—they continued to occupy a liminal position in

La Rochelle, simultaneously part of the prominent Fleuriau clan and very much outsiders.[73]

Aimé-Benjamin Fleuriau thus protected his position at the pinnacle of Rochelais society in a way that sentenced Marie-Charlotte and Marie-Jeanne to remain on its fringes. During the eighteenth century a sense of lineage was wholly alive among the nobility of sword and robe, a status to which the Fleuriau family and other wealthy non-nobles ardently aspired.[74] This implies that Fleuriau made a deliberate choice in his failure to recognize his *mulâtre* daughters so as to exclude them from his lineage. Their race may or may not have played a direct role in this decision; fathers of illegitimate children always had the choice of barring them from their patrimony in an effort to consolidate the inheritance of legitimate heirs. Moreover, over the course of the eighteenth century the number of illegitimate pregnancies and foundlings in France grew dramatically, exposing that fathers increasingly shunned responsibility for their illegitimate children.[75] Unlike many men who fathered illegitimate children, however, Fleuriau went out of his way to provide for his offspring. His explicit failure to recognize them came only at the insistence of the law, which forced their categorization as people of color. Yet it was not their exclusion from their father's money but their exclusion from his *family* that motivated Marie-Jeanne, in particular, to try to claim the Fleuriau name, not the Fleuriau fortune, for herself and her siblings.

Although most women who lived in France in the mid-eighteenth century expected to marry at least once, neither Marie-Jeanne nor Marie-Charlotte ever did.[76] In La Rochelle, elite Protestant families tended to intermarry to create and reinforce ties, and the newly wealthy Fleuriau family surely would have been a desirable target for alliance.[77] Indeed, Fleuriau's legitimate daughter Marie-Adélaïde made an excellent match, marrying a colonel in the army who was a chevalier of the royal military order of Saint Louis, bringing with her a dowry of over twenty thousand livres.[78] Although unlikely to dower his illegitimate daughters so munificently, Fleuriau had repeatedly demonstrated his willingness to provide for them, and there is no reason to suspect he would have refused to give them dowries.[79] However, their mixed race, their illegitimacy, and Marie-Charlotte's illness combined made them undesirable marriage partners. Given these factors, it is not surprising that Marie-Jeanne felt a strong connection with her siblings in Saint-Domingue. She drew on the wealth and prestige of their well-known father by appropriating his name. Then, using his name and his money, she worked to strengthen ties with her remaining family in Saint-Domingue, thereby subverting her father's desires to keep the Fleuriau and Mandron families separate.[80]

The death of her sister Marie-Charlotte in 1773 presented Marie-Jeanne with her first opportunity to have her relationship with her father made public and recorded in official documents. Marie-Charlotte may have died of the "cold distemper" that her father attributed to her in his 1763 statement to authorities.[81] On her death she was buried in the Récollet cemetery. Masses were said for her at two Catholic parish churches, Saint-Sauveur and Saint-Barthélémy, the latter situated across the Place d'Armes from the house the Mandron sisters shared.[82] These masses served an important function for Marie-Jeanne, who survived her sister. In La Rochelle wealthy Protestants practiced their religion in a careful détente with local authorities, and although well-to-do Protestants usually had their children baptized in the Catholic tradition, they avoided darkening the doorways of parish churches when at all possible. Consequently, only Marie-Jeanne and a woman named Elizabeth Morin attended Marie-Charlotte's funerary mass at Saint-Barthélémy Catholic Church, each signing their name in the parish register that recorded the death. Neither Marie-Charlotte's father, nor her stepmother, nor any of her half-siblings, all of whom were Protestants, attended the service. Fleuriau's absence meant that when the officiating *curé* asked for details about Marie-Charlotte's life to record in the parish register, Marie-Jeanne supplied them. Except for this funerary record, no evidence suggests whether the Mandron sisters considered themselves Protestant, like their father, or Catholic. Either way, Marie-Jeanne adopted the Protestant Rochelais practice of using religion for her own ends. She wove a genealogy for her sister that framed her as a member of the Fleuriau family, but she also emphasized her roots in Saint-Domingue.

Marie-Jeanne immortalized her sister as "Marie-Charlotte Fleuriau, *dite* Mandron, daughter of Sieur Benjamin Fleuriau, merchant, and of Jeanne *dite* Guimbelot, native of the parish of Notre Dame du Saint Rosaire of Croix-des-Bouquets, in the canton of Cul-de-Sac, in the jurisdiction of Port-au-Prince, island and coast of Saint-Domingue, in America."[83] In death as in life Marie-Charlotte bore the name Mandron, an everlasting reminder of her difference from her white father. In appropriating the Fleuriau name for her sister, Marie-Jeanne also emphasized the complexity and validity of family connections formed on the other side of the Atlantic. She simultaneously aligned herself and her sister with their father by taking his name and clearly stating their relationship, something he refused to do after he had returned to France, and distanced themselves from their French relations by acknowledging the distinctiveness of their créole origins. She made no mention of race or slavery.

Yet more than Marie-Jeanne's continued presence in La Rochelle testified to Aimé-Benjamin Fleuriau's colonial past and complex family. In 1783, ten years after Marie-Charlotte's death, the names Mandron and Fleuriau again appeared in the La Rochelle parish records. On 20 September, a young girl named Marie Mandron was buried. She was only fourteen, too young to have been fathered by Fleuriau during his colonial youth. Rather, she was his granddaughter, the legitimate daughter of his son Pierre-Paul Mandron Fleuriau and his wife Demoiselle Theron, and she had been born in Port-au-Prince.[84] Like her aunt a decade before, Marie's presence in La Rochelle testifies to the tight transatlantic ties that continued to exist between Fleuriau and his descendants in Saint-Domingue. After her father Paul had returned to Saint-Domingue in 1765, he maintained close enough relations with his father and sisters to want to send his daughter to them, probably for her education. Like her aunts, she arrived in France at a relatively young age. Further, in 1787 Fleuriau communicated with his agent in Saint-Domingue about the possibility of having yet another "daughter and a niece of Paul Mandron" come to La Rochelle, illustrating once again that ties between Fleuriau and his mixed-race children endured.[85] By this time, then, like other prominent people of color in Saint-Domingue, the Mandron clan had come to view time in France as an important polish for a young lady's education; other mixed-race girls, including a young woman named Victoire, had been sent by white fathers to finish their education in La Rochelle.[86] Paul's younger daughter and niece never made the journey to France. One of them fell ill right at the time scheduled for their departure, rendering the trip impossible, to their bitter disappointment.[87]

The solidification of the social position of the Mandrons happened in France and Saint-Domingue simultaneously, illustrating the transatlantic connections that persisted in the family. By 1777, the eldest son, Jean-Baptiste, owned a small plantation, likely growing coffee, for which his father gave him six slaves, purchased from the Rochelais firm Garasché frères.[88] In the mid-1780s, Paul Mandron was a prominent member of society in Saint-Domingue. Even in his daughter's burial record in France he and his wife were given the courtesy titles "Sieur" and "Demoiselle," appellations that in Saint-Domingue traditionally had been ascribed to those of a certain social stature regardless of race, but which by the early 1780s were legally prohibited to free people of color.[89] The fact that these honorific titles were used in French records emphatically broke this link between color and status. His Fleuriau family connections undoubtedly increased his stature in the eyes of the Rochelais cleric who made this record; in her burial record his daughter was identified as "Demoiselle Marie Mandroux," and he was called "Sieur Pierre-Paul Mandroux Fleuriau."[90] Even as late as 1783, in spite of the 1762 ordinance and subsequent measures, race and status were not always linked.

Yet neither this continuing intimate connection nor Marie-Jeanne's insistence on making their relationship a matter of public record moved Fleuriau. In his will the merchant reaffirmed his commitment to provide for his mixed-race children's welfare while at the same time designating his legitimate children his true heirs, in terms of the inheritance they received and in how he envisioned his lineage: among the Fleuriau in La Rochelle there was little room for mixed-race kin. In February 1787, one month before his death, Fleuriau wrote out his will in his own hand. In it he followed Rochelais common law to the letter in specifying that after his wife's portion of the estate had been separated from his, the remainder was to be divided among his three surviving legitimate children: Aimé-Paul, Louis-Benjamin, and Marie-Adélaïde.[91] He clearly considered his plantation in Saint-Domingue his most valuable asset. He specified that his legitimate children should own it jointly, and that each could sell his or her share only to the others.[92] This accorded with general practice and common wisdom in the colonies. The governor-general of Martinique wrote, "if there is a country in the world where the assets by their nature are unsusceptible to division, it is without exception this one, and above all assets such as sugar plantations. Everything in a plantation of this sort is dependent on everything else . . . if one of the objects is separated from the other, nothing exists any longer."[93] Also in accordance with Rochelais custom Fleuriau favored none of the children over the others in terms of the monetary value of their inheritance, but he did allocate specific holdings to his children based on their gender and birth order. He specified that his most important property in La Rochelle, his hôtel particulier in the well-heeled Saint-Barthélémy parish, go to his oldest son, less important properties to his younger son, and sums of cash to his daughter, who had already married and whose dowry comprised part of her inheritance.

Fleuriau excluded his illegitimate children from this apportioning of his estate, although he left generous legacies to Jeanne-Marie and his *mulâtre* children in Saint-Domingue.[94] But his will addressed more than money: as he outlined these sizable legacies, he also sketched his illegitimate children and grandchildren's relationships with each other. In doing so, he outlined a family lineage for his children that extensively explained their connections to each other yet pointedly omitted any reference to his own relationship to them as their father: "I give and bequeath to the children of the late Jeanne Guimbelon, I mean, Guimbelot, free *négresse*, resident while living of Cul-de-Sac, Saint-Domingue, which children are surnamed Mandron, namely Mademoiselle Mandron, Créole, current resident of the Place d'Armes of this town, the sum of twelve hundred livres, money of France, of life annuity, which will begin to run the day of my decease."[95] Fleuriau not only identified his own children as merely the children of "Jeanne Guimbelot, free *négresse*," but even fumbled the name of his long-term concubine the first time he wrote it.

Far from indicating only indifference to the Mandron line, his will took great care to provide for them. He gave generous sums to Marie-Jeanne, or "Mademoiselle Mandron, Créole," his daughter and for thirty years his neighbor in La Rochelle. He also left sizable legacies, 26,000 livres each, to her brother Paul in Saint-Domingue and to the children of the deceased Jean-Baptiste. He charged his son Paul with the continued oversight of his plantation, and, in a backhanded acknowledgement of his own paternity, Fleuriau took the patriarchal privilege of appointing his son the guardian of his brother's children, an arrangement that, in any case, the brothers had already agreed upon.[96] The amount of detail Fleuriau gave about his children's whereabouts, professions, marital status, and births of their children clearly indicates that he maintained contact with his progeny in Saint-Domingue. Yet by emphasizing their lineage through their mother, "Jeanne Guimbelot, free *négresse*," he indelibly marked them as people of color. Failing to mention his own relationship erased his children of color's ties to the Fleuriau name, even as he gave them access to a portion of his fortune.

Paradoxically, then, Fleuriau provided for his children and grandchildren's welfare while cutting their ties to his name and his fortune once and for all. "My succession," he stated, "will be entirely free from obligation toward all of them [Marie-Jeanne, Paul, and Jean-Baptiste's children], whatever titles they have." The Mandron children, if they were to try to claim a larger share of their father's estate based on his acknowledgment of paternity at their baptism, would be cut off "without any of the dispositions previously made nor even any of my same liberalities."[97] This provision made quite clear that, although the merchant valued his children and wanted to provide for them, he did not consider them entitled to an equal portion of his patrimony. This he reserved for his legitimate white children. As his succession netted nearly one million livres, not even counting the value of his plantation, houses in Port-au-Prince, and hôtel particulier in La Rochelle, this discrepancy was enormous.[98] Thus the legacies to the Mandron children had the overall effect of *distancing* them from the Fleuriau clan, in spite of the close connections the two branches of the family fostered throughout Aimé-Benjamin's life. The ties that had bound him to his Saint-Domingue offspring about to be severed by death, Aimé-Benjamin Fleuriau acted deliberately to undo Marie-Jeanne's efforts to claim the Fleuriau name and to exclude his mixed-race children from the Fleuriau family legacy that endured in La Rochelle.

Marie-Jeanne Mandron Fleuriau's Last Will and Testament

Marie-Jeanne took her transatlantic roots seriously. When she made her own will in a clear and even hand in 1788, scarcely a year after her father's death, she again worked to bind the two branches of the Fleuriau family together in name as well as in fortune.[99] She adopted the Fleuriau name and also ascribed it to her brothers, nieces, and nephews in Saint-Domingue, contravening her father's lifelong practice. This subversion, together with the fact that she named her Saint-Domingue relations her sole heirs, avers that Marie-Jeanne aligned herself more closely to her transatlantic siblings than her French ones, in spite of the time and distance that separated her from the former and her geographic proximity to and decades long association with the latter. Through her will she set up her own line of succession, drawn from the wealth and prestige of her father but also separate from the lineage of legitimate heirs he had laid out in his own will.

Marie-Jeanne began her testament by firmly inscribing herself within the Fleuriau family. She opened the document with her full name, thereby announcing her Fleuriau ties to anyone who read it. "I the undersigned, Marie-Jeanne Fleuriau Mandron, maiden, resident of La Rochelle, Place d'Armes, have made and present my will, in case of my death, in the form that follows."[100] Adopting the Fleuriau name in conjunction with her maternal surname, a move she never openly made during her father's lifetime, emphasized her links to the wealthy, powerful, and well-connected Fleuriau clan, and also flouted her father's practice of obfuscating his relationship to his mixed-race offspring.

Marie-Jeanne died 24 November 1793 (4 frimaire year II), just three weeks after the passing of Revolutionary legislation that granted illegitimate children recognized by their parents an equal share in their parents' estates.[101] Although the legislation did not affect her own testament, her efforts to weave the illegitimate and legitimate branches of the Fleuriau family together anticipated the law's intent.[102] Her use of both names, not only the one of her wealthy merchant father, confirms Marie-Jeanne's desire to affirm her family links with the Fleuriau clan and her siblings in Saint-Domingue. Her brother Paul, the only one of Fleuriau's children left living in Saint-Domingue, also continued to use the Fleuriau name; he received letters from his half-brother in La Rochelle addressed to Pierre-Paul Fleuriau Mandron.[103]

Like many women, Jeanne-Marie Fleuriau Mandron reinforced ties of kinship and affection through how she chose to dispose of her estate. In naming her brother Paul and the children of her brother Jean-Baptiste heirs, Marie-Jeanne emphasized the strength of family ties and became a matriarch through whom wealth flowed in her own right: "I instate as my heirs and universal legatees and give them in all propriety and in perpetuity, Pierre-Paul Fleuriau Mandron, currently inhabiting the quarter of Mirebalais of Port-au-Prince, and the children of Jean-Baptiste Fleuriau Mandron, inhabitant of the same quarter, as heirs of their father, all my goods, immeubles, meubles, effects, gold, silver, letters of credit, and other things of a moveable nature that are found to belong to me on the day of my death."[104] She further specified that if her brother Paul should predecease her, his portion of her estate should go to his children. Thus this transfer of cash and goods not only reemphasized ties of kinship but also created ties of heritage by specifying how property would flow from one generation to the next.

By the time she made her will, Marie-Jeanne Fleuriau Mandron had amassed a considerable estate through her father's largesse. Her most valuable items included a black box with silver curiosities inside, fine linens, wines, a gilded mirror with a fine painting above it in the frame, two more mirrors with paintings in grisaille garnished with marble, a dozen cabriolet chairs covered in blue damask, a gold watch and chain, a bed, and a good amount of money in silver and in paper currency.[105] Inheriting such legacies of goods or cash could provide heirs with a valuable start in the world, or add to already sizable holdings.[106] Her estate, then, offered her heirs considerable financial advantages that they apparently needed desperately. Still, her legacy went beyond her immediate beneficiaries. By writing her testament and leaving her property to her nearest kin who shared her family names, Marie-Jeanne Fleuriau Mandron passed along assets that flowed from one generation to the next, building the Fleuriau Mandron heritage.

Across time, distance, and even revolution, the relationship between the white and mixed-race branches of the Fleuriau family continued. Marie-Jeanne never specifically acknowledged her relationship with her white half-siblings in her will, yet she appointed as executor her younger half-brother Louis-Benjamin Fleuriau de Bellevue, a scholarly young man twenty years her junior who eventually became a geologist of some note. The siblings certainly knew each other, as the Mandron women figured in the Fleuriau family papers.[107] Although no record remains of an association between Marie-Jeanne and her half-brother after their father's death, she likely knew of his reputation as a scholar, and that he was trusted and admired in his city.[108]

Naming him as her executor certainly highlighted their family relationship, and her choice emphasizes a final effort to demonstrate that she, too, was a Fleuriau. Louis-Benjamin fulfilled this commission scrupulously, hiring a notary to represent the interests of his half-brothers and their children, the legatees, and arranging for an inventory of his half-sister's goods after her death.[109] This curious situation in which, at the request of his créole half-sister, a legitimate son and heir oversaw the succession of an estate comprised largely of the fruits of his father's largesse to his illegitimate mixed-race children, illustrates in high relief how family relationships complicated seemingly clear-cut correlations between race and status. In appointing her half-brother her executor, Marie-Jeanne Fleuriau Mandron clearly trusted that young Louis-Benjamin would distribute her estate as she wished. He thus became the means through which his father's wealth passed from the Fleuriau lineage and formed the basis of the Fleuriau Mandron heritage, newly established by Marie-Jeanne.

After Marie-Jeanne's death, the interests of the Mandron clan in Saint-Domingue and their Fleuriau kin in La Rochelle irrevocably diverged. From this point on, Paul's destiny became entwined with the unfolding Haitian Revolution, particularly free men of color's struggle to claim political rights. He was the proprietor of a sugar plantation near Mirebalais, a rural area in the central plain of the western province, married to a "quateronne libre" named Victoire; they had at least one son and one daughter.[110] He continued to be involved in Fleuriau plantation affairs, selling sugar on its behalf.[111]

Early on in the Haitian Revolution he threw in his political lot with prominent free men of color such as Julien Raimond, who lobbied for equal citizenship regardless of race. When a group of over two hundred free men of color all over the western province, in Saint-Marc, Mirebalais, Verettes, and Pétite Rivière presented an address to the National Convention in early 1793, Paul Mandron signed it, writing "P. Fleuriau."[112]

In 1800, he was assassinated amidst the purges characteristic of the conflict between Louverture and Rigaud. The gérant of the Fleuriau plantation, Armandeau, wrote to Fleuriau de Bellevue, "Mandron was a victim of the Revolution. It was his son-in-law Miliet who was the culprit. His wife and his children are here in penury, his wife's mind is deranged, and his oldest daughter has begged me to ask you what the succession of her aunt consists of."[113] This desperate plea illustrates that across generations, the Mandrons and Fleuriaus looked to each other as resources in times of need. This story of transatlantic and interracial linkage came to an abrupt and tragic close. Mandron's son reputedly shot himself in 1802, when he was forcibly drafted and the family's plantation requisitioned.[114] As Saint-Domingue transformed into the black republic of Haiti and civil war raged, political allegiance ultimately determined the fate of the Mandron family. Yet Paul's daughter, who died in Saint-Domingue in 1803, went only by the name of Fleuriau.[115] This use of the Fleuriau name alone specifically contravenes the widespread revolutionary and post-revolutionary tendency of children of white planters and their slaves to reject their forefathers' names.[116] The Mandrons' adoption of the Fleuriau name, then, implies their motivation to make their family history public.[117] By doing so they staked their own claim as an important and influential family in Saint-Domingue, by virtue of their ties to France. The Fleuriau name therefore became part of Marie-Jeanne's legacy.

However, there is some evidence to suggest that Marie-Jeanne was not the only member of the Fleuriau family who continued to view the connection between La Rochelle and Saint-Domingue as important. In 1793, Fleuriau's widow and their two sons appear on a list of certified French citizens who owned land in Saint-Domingue.[118] As the upheavals of revolution roiled France and Saint-Domingue, they made an effort to preserve their property by showing themselves loyal citizens of the Republic. Indeed, ownership of profitable land even may have been an incentive to exhibit patriotism toward shifting revolutionary regimes. This shows that Fleuriau's legitimate wife and children saw the plantation in Saint-Domingue as a resource on which they could draw.[119] It also suggests that they too had an expansive view of family.

Ultimately, the connection between the Fleuriau and Mandron branches endured even after their common patriarch had gone.

For Aimé-Benjamin Fleuriau, colonialism changed the meaning of family and whom it included. He chose to acknowledge his mixed-race children at their birth, to bring them to France, and to leave them sizable legacies. These choices indicate that, for Fleuriau, family extended beyond a nuclear unit constituted by law or religion. A flexible entity, family included the mixed-race children with whom he shared ties of blood, personal history, and affection. In his view, however, membership in a family did not entitle all individuals to equal treatment; although he provided for his mixed-race children his legacies to them paled beside the estates his white children inherited. His daughter Marie-Jeanne Mandron also viewed family as a pliable unit, susceptible to shaping and manipulating. Both father and daughter used the elasticity in the concept of the family as a springboard from which they could push back against narrowing legal definitions of race, albeit in different ways and for different reasons. Intimate, familial relations challenged and shaped the meaning of race.

Close examination of the Fleuriau clan offers a compelling vantage point through which to analyze how colonialism shaped the family as a unit as well as the daily lives of its members in eighteenth-century France. Colonialism changed and challenged European ideas and experiences of the family. Family members had different opportunities and levels of authority to delineate what a family meant and who was included in it. Fleuriau, even while keeping his relationship with the "three young *mulâtres* and two young *mulâtresses*" he had "under his care" private, directly intervened with the 1762 Ordinance by shaping what race meant by layering its social meaning over fixed ideas about gender roles.[120] He also fashioned ideas about race and family more privately by delineating family relationships in his will. Marie-Jeanne, a woman and person to whom the 1762 Ordinance applied, turned only to private means to shape ideas about family. Her gender and her race meant that even had she made an official statement such as her father's, it would have carried less weight. Instead she relied on the opportunities presented by family events and private documents to articulate her own version of family relationships. Her practice shows that legal and religious documents provided valuable sites for circumventing and challenging patriarchal versions of family relationships, and for exploring a more expansive and egalitarian view of the family, defined not by a father, but by a band of siblings.

Ultimately, under the letter of the law the correlation between race and status eclipsed the importance of the family in eighteenth-century France. The 1777 Police des Noirs legislation forbade all people of color from entering France no matter what their status, and required those already in the country to register with local police and to carry identification cards.[121] But the law offers only one vantage point for considering how people of color fit into society. Marie-Jeanne's effort to disrupt perceptions of race based on family connections also proved successful, for in 1777, although she still lived in La Rochelle, she was not listed on the register of free people of color. For her, family proved more important than race.

CHAPTER 6

Negotiating Patriarchy

Like Marie-Jeanne and her siblings, most people of color in France had at least a bicultural perspective, with knowledge and experience of France, Saint-Domingue or another slave colony, and sometimes Africa. As a result, they had a deep well of discursive resources on which they could draw when articulating their own positions and relationships. Whether the privileged mixed-race children of white planters or slaves, virtually all people of color in France had, at one point or another, been intimately associated with French households. As a result, all were familiar with French norms of gender and family, household structure, and patriarchal authority. They knew that in such well-to-do families French masculinity was measured by skilled work, emotional capacity, and position at the head of the family, while French women were increasingly idealized as chaste, domestic, and delicate beings devoted to motherhood and wifehood. Most people in the metropole did not have gender expectations that varied by race, although there were some differences according to social status.

People of color with any history in the Caribbean—or even secondhand knowledge of slave society—knew that in the Antilles, on the other hand, gender expectations varied greatly by race and status. They would have been familiar with stereotypes of enslaved men as brutes suited primarily to hard labor and the colonial truism that "female slaves give birth with much ease."[1] They also would have known labels of free men of color as abusive and incapable of love or companionate marriage, while white colonists assumed that "the entire being of a *mulâtresse* is given up to Voluptuity."[2] Those with African origins brought their own notions of family and gender roles, including the assumption that the bond between mothers and children was stronger than that between spouses, and that age and knowledge could allow women to transcend differences based on gender.[3]

Considering their diverse backgrounds and origins, people of color had multiple understandings of slavery and freedom. In France, Enlightenment constructs of slavery and freedom as political categories relative to absolutism began to permeate public consciousness by the second half of the eighteenth century. Some of these ideas crossed the Atlantic and shaped the political engagement of slaves.[4] For most people of color in the colonies, however, slavery and freedom were tangible, lived categories with daily import, although they were by no means clearly distinguished from each other. In Africa, as in the Antilles, gender clearly impacted slaves' experiences of these categories, with sexual service and motherhood bringing value to female slaves, but also investing them with stability and incentives to continue serving the same owner, while male slaves were more difficult to incorporate into existing social structures.[5]

People of color who lived in La Rochelle would have had at least a smattering of knowledge of this broad diversity of understandings. This makes it all the more striking that when the rare opportunities to articulate their own positions presented themselves, individuals chose to emphasize precisely how they fit with French constructions of family, gender, and household. People of color in La Rochelle rarely appeared in official documents. In Saint-Domingue and other colonies, free people of color routinely made efforts to leave a paper trail, and to have their free status, property, and relationships recorded—sometimes at great expense. People of color in La Rochelle, in contrast, rarely employed the services of notaries, a difference stemming either from the cost or difficulty in accessing their services. Two sets of records do exist, though, where the voices of people of color were documented, albeit through a mediated and unequal "exchange" with white authorities.[6] These encounters took place within institutions at the heart of Old Regime authority: the Catholic Church and the Admiralty. Parish records offered people of color the opportunity to articulate and legitimize their most intimate relationships in ways familiar and unimpeachably genuine to those who lived in France. The 1763 and 1777 Admiralty-mandated surveys of people of color were intended to strictly define, regulate, and control the population of people of color in France by delineating race as the primary social category. In making their own declarations, people of color made clear that slavery, freedom, and race remained ambiguous and complicated constructs. What emerges is that, even while individuals drew on different wells of knowledge and experience, free people of color in La Rochelle generally foregrounded how they fit into intimate categories such as family position, gender roles, and individual control of labor in an identifiably French way.

Race and Patriarchy

Although the 1763 and 1777 surveys required that all people of color, whether slave or free, register with local officials, few of these individuals actually made the declarations themselves. Slaves comprised the bulk of the targeted population, and owners routinely registered for them. Employers often did this for employees, and perhaps a good number of people of color slipped through the cracks, never turning up in the surveys at all.[7] However, for freed men familiar with metropolitan mores, these surveys offered an exceptional opportunity to articulate their belonging in a community where official policy increasingly defined them as outsiders and rumors circulated that free people of color were subject to deportation to the Antilles. They uniformly chose to do this by emphasizing their own patriarchal authority.

Pierre Neptune and Antoine Monréal were the only two free black men to make their own declarations in the 1763 survey.[8] Although these two men came from different backgrounds, served owners in distinct circumstances, and came to freedom on divergent bumpy paths, they have two important things in common: they married after their emancipation and fathered children.[9] Because of this, they accorded well with French expectations of masculine patriarchal authority. Both showed awareness of this, and appealed to common ground with French officials as one way to safeguard their freedom and continued residence in La Rochelle.

The life story of Pierre Neptune, as he was known in La Rochelle, takes shape in his 1763 and 1777 declarations in the mandatory surveys of people of color.[10] According to his own testimony, Neptune was born in "Juda, coast of Guinée," a port generally known as Ouidah on the Bight of Benin, around the year 1710.[11] Slave traders captured him and sold him into slavery in or around 1724, when he was about fourteen years old. He claimed to have sailed on the ship *Le Saint Philippe*, a slaver bound for the labor-hungry French Caribbean colonies, captained by one Pierre Cadou.

Here Neptune's story diverges slightly from archival evidence. Pierre Cadou never captained *Le Saint Philippe*, although a ship by that name did make slaving voyages, primarily in the 1750s.[12] It seems more likely that Neptune was taken from Africa on a ship called *Le Neptune*, which in 1729 Cadou captained from Nantes to the Bight of Benin, the area known as Juda or Ouidah.[13] With 345 slaves aboard, the ship sailed for Martinique. On the voyage, the slaves rose up and violently resisted their capture; this revolt left three among them dead.[14] Thus, from the beginning of his enslavement, Neptune had exposure to the possibility of violent resistance. Yet he himself chose conformity, emphasizing the potential and effectiveness of this tactic. Neptune wound up in France because Cadou, exercising a customary privilege of captains of slavers, chose to keep him for his own personal use.[15] The exact circumstances of Neptune's arrival in France remain unclear, as his arrival was not recorded, but *Le Neptune* sailed into the harbor in Nantes in 1730, so likely Neptune and his owner made their way to La Rochelle from there.

In the French climate of changing ideas about race, Neptune served Cadou for over twenty years. He appears, although not by name, as belonging to "M. Cadoux, Capne. de Navire" in a 1740 census of *nègres* in La Rochelle.[16] On his owner's deathbed in 1747, Cadou expressed his intention in his will to free him. Neptune's liberty, however, was by no means assured. When the pair had arrived in France, the captain failed to make the obligatory registration of his slave to the Admiralty.[17] This was not unusual; owners had little incentive to register their slaves, as enforcement of the laws was spotty. Although technically, according to the Declaration of 1738, owners who failed to make the requisite registrations would have their slaves confiscated "au profit du roi" and shipped to the colonies, this rarely, if ever, actually happened. Furthermore, little love was lost between local officials in La Rochelle charged with recording slave declarations, and royal ones in Paris who mandated the registrations in the first place. When local and royal interests came into conflict, local bearers of royal authority were likely to let challenges to the crown slide.

Yet after Cadou's death the Intendant of La Rochelle brought Neptune's irregular position to the attention of the Minister of the Marine, who examined the case himself. His decision seemed to herald the end of Neptune's residence in France. In his reply to the Intendant he wrote, "I have examined the clarifications on the subject of the petition that has come back to me on the part of the *nègre* Pierre Neptune. It is true that the Sieurs Cadou [Pierre Cadou's heirs] do not have a right to claim that this *nègre* belongs to them. Other than that they are not in the case to possess slaves, their father's failure to observe prescribed formalities . . . should have made their father lose the proprietorship over him. . . . But it does not follow that the *nègre* should be regarded as free." This letter stresses that royal policy objected to slavery in France, not to the institution itself, and intimates that in disputes between slaves and their owners, royal officials could not be counted on to defend the interests of either party. In this case, the Intendant sentenced Neptune to be "confiscated for the king's profit" and "sent to the colonies." He enclosed a warrant ordering "the arrest of the *nègre* Pierre Neptune wherever he may be, and that he be conducted under good and sure guard to the nearest prison."[18]

Yet although Neptune may have been arrested, he was never sent to the colonies. Rather, this was the first of several brushes with authorities during which Neptune was threatened with transportation; he proved himself remarkably adept at wriggling out of such tight spots. Finally, conceivably in an effort to avoid additional trouble, Cadou's children gave the African his liberty in 1749, two years after the Minister of the Marine's intervention. If Neptune made any kind of payment, no mention of it was made in the notary act that recorded his emancipation.[19]

Ideas about race had already begun to change by 1741, when Neptune's future wife Lisette arrived in La Rochelle in the context of increased regulation following the Declaration of 1738. On the surface her experiences were much like Neptune's: both were people of color brought to La Rochelle as slaves who spent much of their adult lives there. Nonetheless, their backgrounds were quite different. Lisette, a "*négresse* créole," was born a slave in the French colony of Guadeloupe, and belonged to the Rochelais merchant Isaac Vatable. Like many families in La Rochelle the Vatables had kinship ties and trading interests on both sides of the Atlantic, and for a while Isaac Vatable and his family lived in Guadeloupe. When they returned they brought Lisette with them. Her owner registered her with the Admiralty when they first arrived in France in 1741, when Lisette was twenty-six years old.[20] Although he promised to return her to the colony within three years, as required by the 1738 law, he never did. Lisette remained in La Rochelle and eventually was freed, after which she went by the name Louise.

In the ten years after Pierre Neptune received his freedom, he built a life similar to that of other marginal residents of the port city, although hints of privation and struggle creep into his account. In 1756 Louise and Neptune married and had several children, although none lived past childhood.[21] They both worked as day laborers, highlighting their economic marginality: Neptune occasionally worked as a cooper, and Louise as a laundress. In 1763 Neptune had his second encounter with royal authorities when he made a statement in conformance with the survey of people of color. By this time Neptune had lived in La Rochelle for over three decades, so he had a high degree of familiarity with the city and the position of people of color within it. He probably spoke French fluently, and he had sought Catholic rites for his marriage. Perhaps not wholly integrated, he was at the very least extremely acculturated.

Yet there were still abundant reasons why a person of color in Neptune's situation might not have made such a statement in person. We can imagine that some free people of color may have been relieved to have had the matter taken out of their hands by having others register them, as they may have thought they lacked the understanding of French government and procedure that was necessary to follow the mandates of the Ordinance, or simply may not have known about the requirement. They may have been intimidated to go to the Admiralty offices, or afraid that if they did they might be sent back to the colonies. As it was, the two free black men who made their own declarations in 1763 were of relatively advanced age and had lived in La Rochelle for decades, first as slaves then as free men. Significantly, both had married, were heads of household, and occupied positions of patriarchal authority.

To some extent, Neptune's statement to authorities precisely mirrored those of slave owners. This is unsurprising, as he would have been responding to prescribed questions asked by an Admiralty clerk, who was already well practiced in the routine of soliciting necessary answers. Neptune identified himself and his wife, and stated their ages and places of origin. But then his declaration began to diverge, a reminder that Neptune may or may not have gone to the Admiralty willingly, and may have been surprised at the questions the clerk asked, particularly about the colony to which he would "return" once he left France. While most slave owners vaguely promised that they would return their slaves to "the colonies" when the length of time allowed for their stay in France had passed, Neptune specified particularly that he and Louise would return "to Martinique or to Saint-Domingue."[22] This is curious, as neither of them apparently ever lived in either place, as he had been born in Africa and his wife came from Guadeloupe. This specificity implies that Neptune was attempting to exert some sort of control over a situation in which he had very little, and also hints at discernment in the conditions of slavery in Guadeloupe, Martinique, and Saint-Domingue. Maybe he also wanted to avoid mention of his wife's colonial homeland; he likely thought it would prove more difficult to maintain free status in a place where his wife had been known as a slave.

Further, although the former slave promised to comply with the law by moving his household to the colonies, he undoubtedly had reservations about crossing the Atlantic on a voyage redolent of the Middle Passage, bound for a destination where he certainly knew that the majority of the black population was enslaved. Neptune did not voice these reservations to the officials who recorded his statement. But he did point out the prohibitive cost of travel to the colonies, and he concluded his statement by asking that "someone procure for them" the cost of the passage.[23]

In a distinctive element of Neptune's declaration, the former slave used this opportunity where he was communicating directly to French officials to assert his own patriarchal authority. At first glance, Neptune seems an unlikely standard bearer of patriarchy. As a former slave, he had relatively little social standing, and as a day laborer he had almost no wealth. But as a husband and a head of household, he exerted patriarchal control over his wife. After all, it was he, not Louise, who made their joint declaration, although the law neither stipulated that heads of household should make statements for their entire families nor prohibited either married or single women from making their own statements.

Neptune strengthened his claim to patriarchy by positioning himself as the head of a household made up of women of color. Although childless at the time he made his 1777 statement, he mentioned his three deceased children. He did not refer to these French-born infants in his 1763 statement, but asserted that he and his wife had a seventeen-year-old *mulâtresse* living with them, whom he pledged he would also bring to the colonies when the occasion arose. This girl's identity remains a mystery, as do her reasons for living with the older couple. Neptune only mentioned her once, in his 1763 declaration, and never by name.[24] By including this girl in his declaration as a member of his family Neptune framed himself as a patriarch and head of a household comprising him, his wife, and this girl he presented in the role of a daughter.

In emphasizing his family, Neptune may have been drawing on African as well as French notions of masculinity and adulthood; in some African societies, legal majority was associated with familial authority.[25] He framed their relationship in terms of well-established French notions of family and patriarchy, foreclosing the possibility that officials could interpret it as a vague connection based solely on race. Through asserting his own masculine authority over his household he found common ground with the men recording his declaration. By presenting himself explicitly as a husband, father, and head of household, Neptune drew upon French notions of masculinity and family that diverged markedly from colonial understandings of the masculinity and family life of slaves, which explicitly denied the privileges of patriarchy to enslaved men, including control over wives and children.

Neptune and Louise's tale accentuates the importance of French

definitions of family and gender roles, which free men of color could sometimes manipulate as they sought inclusion in the broader community in La
Rochelle. Neptune clearly understood French concepts of family and patriarchy, and he creatively used them to his advantage. In this way, Neptune actively shaped contested meanings of race in La Rochelle by asserting the
primacy of masculine gender privilege over racial disadvantage. He worked
to underline the similarities between himself and other male heads of household in the town through emphasizing his differences from the women in his
charge. His declaration carried weight because he was a male head of
household.

Neptune demonstrated that men of color could present gender as a fixed
and immutable hierarchy, against which race had only secondary importance. In the way that mattered most to him, Neptune's strategy worked. In
1777 Pierre Neptune and Louise were still living in La Rochelle. They never
made subsequent supplications for financial support for a transatlantic journey, but they also never were shipped back to the colonies.

Although much of Antoine Monréal's story follows a similar trajectory to
that of Pierre Neptune, there was one crucial difference between the two
men: at the time he made his 1763 declaration Monréal had no family, so he
had to find a slightly different rhetorical strategy for positioning himself in
alignment with the officials who recorded his statement. Like Neptune, Monréal emphasized his position as a head of household, a husband, and a father,
although his wife and possibly their daughter had passed away before his 1763
declaration. Thus bereft of a strong claim to patriarchal authority, he also emphasized his long residence in La Rochelle as justification for claiming belonging in the city.

Like Neptune, Antoine Monréal had been brought to La Rochelle as a
boy, arriving in 1717 at thirteen.[26] Also a native of Guinée, he came to France
with a ship's captain whose name he could not recall. He then became the
property of Monsieur Pascauld, a merchant and a former deputy of the powerful La Rochelle Chamber of Commerce, whom he served until his owner
died. He next belonged to Pascauld's widow, but when she wanted to take
him with her to her new home in Paris, Monréal balked. He refused to leave
La Rochelle, arguing with his mistress that at over sixty years old he was too
old and infirm to make the trip, adding that he did not want to live in Paris.

She agreed to leave him behind and gave him his freedom, although exactly when this occurred remains unclear. She also left him a substantial

annual income of two hundred livres upon her death, more money than most servants could expect as one-time legacies from their masters.[27] At a late age Monréal married a white French woman, but his wife and their daughter passed away soon after.[28] On the occasion of his marriage he appears to have been free; at any rate, the officiating priest did not categorize him as a slave. His marriage to a white woman establishes a high level of integration into Rochelais society, and his consistent mention of his late wife and deceased daughter in every declaration he made evinces an effort to assert his patriarchal authority.[29]

Like Neptune, therefore, Monréal served a single owner for years and lived in La Rochelle for decades. The two would have been familiar in a mid-sized town such as La Rochelle, which slightly more than 15,000 souls called home in 1767.[30] Each man received his freedom, and, significantly, married after becoming free. Both natives of Africa, neither had ever lived in France's Caribbean colonies. Monréal particularly indicated that to him, his long-standing membership in the community meant that he merited special consideration when it came to the application of the law. In his 1763 declaration he clearly pointed to his exceptionality, detailing how his particular history in La Rochelle made him different from other people of color. It says, "the above named Monréal, sixty years old and infirm, has lived in this town for many years and has served for a very long time as the domestic of Madame Pascauld, who has left him two hundred livres of annual income. . . . He asks if he is in the same case as the other *nègres* with regard to his age and continuing infirmity, being free."[31] Like Neptune, Monréal put the burden of action on state officials. He complied with the requirement to register, but underneath his statement lay an implied unlikelihood that he would take action to leave France.

It is difficult to imagine who could benefit from the forced relocation of these two elderly men of color, which perhaps ultimately explains why they lived out their days in La Rochelle. These two cases highlight that their familiarity with and conformity to gender norms opened opportunities for Neptune and Monréal to protect themselves and even to strongly suggest that race was a less important social category than gender. However, not all people of color could conform to dominant European gender expectations.

Racial Self-Positioning

While Neptune and Monréal drew on patriarchal authority to align themselves with French expectations of masculinity, other men of color disrupted
the growing correlation between race and enslaved status in different ways.
François Gilles manipulated the boundary between slavery and servitude,
thus calling into question exactly what freedom meant. Jean Nicolas challenged the assumption that dark skin denoted enslaved status, trading on his
mixed race and his roots in the Île de France, not continental Africa, to facilitate his absorption into Rochelais society. Augustin, rather than quietly slip-
ping through cracks in the boundaries between slavery and freedom, grossly
violated his owner's expectations of how slaves were supposed to act.

Examining these three cases confirms that people of color in La Rochelle
created opportunities to position themselves in ways that defied French understandings of racial categorization and enslaved status.[32] The results proved
mixed. Although in some cases crossing boundaries opened up opportunities for men of color to slip into the ranks of those recognized as part of the
Rochelais community, the consequences of miscalculating the extent to
which they could violate these categories could be disastrous. Those most
successful at traversing from slave to free or at evading racial labels—for
themselves or their children—most closely accorded with French expectations of masculinity by marrying and having children. This left few options
for men who did not conform to these ideals.

Free people of color in France frequently occupied ambiguous household
positions, floating somewhere between chattel slavery as understood and exercised in the Caribbean, and servitude as practiced in millions of French
households. Although technically on the "free" side of the boundary demarcating bondage and liberty, employment as a servant could prove precarious
for a man of color because servants in French society were seen as dependents, hence not fully vested with masculine authority. However, the boundaries between slavery and freedom were difficult to ascertain, and sometimes
slaves who performed labor similar to servants could leverage the ambiguity
of their own social position to their advantage.

Servants were ubiquitous in eighteenth-century France.[33] Comprising approximately one-fifth of adult workers, their tasks ranged from the menial to
the ceremonial and the families they served included the highest nobility and
the pettiest bourgeois. In the metropole, much overlap existed between the

household tasks performed by slaves and servants.[34] Some slaves, in fact, occupied somewhat privileged household positions, serving their masters as valets, chambermaids, or hairdressers. Although their exact social situation vis-à-vis white French servants remains unclear, these slaves would have had freedom of movement, nice clothes, and conceivably even spending money.[35] The material similarity of these two states opened up the possibility that slaves could manipulate prevalent ideas about servitude in order to effectively bring an end to their own slavery.

The case of François Gilles reveals the difficulty in demarcating and maintaining the boundary between slavery and servitude in a context where they coexisted intimately, and suggests that slaves could manipulate where this line was drawn. Born a slave in Saint-Domingue and consistently identified as "*noir*," indicating dark skin, Gilles arrived in France in 1741 as the property of the widow d'Assigny. The pair disembarked from their transatlantic voyage in Bordeaux and then traveled to La Rochelle, where the widow had contacts. One of her most important acquaintances was the wealthy Protestant merchant Jean Vivier, to whom she owed some money.[36] Instead of paying Vivier in cash, which was hard to come by for those newly arrived from the colonies, she offered the merchant her slave Gilles in payment for her debt.[37] Although the Edict of 1716 expressly prohibited using slaves as payment, slaves did occasionally change hands in La Rochelle.[38]

When Jean Vivier acquired ownership of François Gilles he was no stranger to the institution of slavery, even though he apparently never traveled to the Caribbean colonies himself. Vivier had previously included other slaves in his household. In fact, the merchant acted as something of a slave caretaker and broker for people traveling between Saint-Domingue and La Rochelle. For example, at the beginning of July 1737 a ship's captain left his slave Jean-Baptiste in Vivier's care while he returned to sea.[39] Jean-Baptiste remained in the Vivier household for over three months, after which the captain presumably returned to collect him.[40] Vivier's son Élie also counted a black servant as part of his household. At least from 1730 to 1742, an enslaved man named André worked for him in the capacity of a domestic. While the young Vivier asserted that "he had never intended for him [André] to have the title of *esclave*," the Admiralty classified him as a "*nègre*," a term with strong overtones of enslaved status.[41] As had their father, Élie and his brother Paul Vivier continued to register slaves with the Admiralty for business associates who had brought them from the colonies.[42]

After his stint with Vivier, François Gilles continued to change hands, circulating among the merchant elite of La Rochelle. Before Vivier's death he gave Gilles to his relative Jacques Carayon, another prominent Protestant member of the Rochelais community and the future director of the Chamber of Commerce, who in partnership with his mother had made his fortune in the slave trade.[43] Gilles remained in Carayon's service for at least the next twenty-seven years, but in the process of passing from one owner to the next his precise status became murky: did he work for Carayon as a slave or as a servant? When Carayon registered Gilles in the 1763 survey of people of color he listed him as free, and insisted that he paid him wages as he would any other domestic. However, Carayon's emphasis on Gilles' wages could have been an effort to avoid the expense of shipping him back to the colonies. Carayon stated unequivocally that because Gilles was a free man he would not pay his way were he required to return.[44]

Although most free people of color took every available opportunity to have the circumstances of their emancipation written down in official documents, Gilles never gave precise information on the events surrounding his liberation, including in statements he made himself.[45] In this light even Carayon's assertion of Gilles' freedom cannot stand undisputed, especially as six years after he made it Gilles continued to classify himself as a slave. In 1769 Gilles attended a burial of the slave Jean-Pierre, called Médor, at the parish church of Saint-Barthélémy. Another slave, Michel-Nicolas, also attended the ceremony. Although Gilles and Michel-Nicolas each signed his name in a practiced hand, itself illustrating a highly unusual degree of literacy for two men identified as "*noirs*," the priest listed Gilles as belonging to "M. Caraillon," surely a variation of Carayon's name.[46] As they were the only ones who attended the burial, Gilles himself must have provided this information. The presence of these two men hints at a fascinating network among people of color in La Rochelle, and it also reveals the permeability of the boundary between slavery and freedom.

Eight years later Gilles was once again recorded as a free man when he made his own statement to the Admiralty in 1777, which he did in the company of another free man of color.[47] Yet even his inclusion in a straightforward list of free people of color does little to clear up the mystery surrounding the conditions of his freedom. Every other free person of color included in the survey gave the name of the owner who had emancipated them, and most stated precisely the circumstances and date they received their liberty.[48] Yet Gilles never offered either piece of information.

In his own statement to authorities Gilles instead painted an elaborate picture of his life in La Rochelle, a picture that connotes a life of liberty. According to his statement, while in the employ of Carayon, Gilles met Elizabeth Prevost, a native of the nearby village Clavette. Circumstances suggest that she was a servant in the Carayon household. With Carayon's permission, Gilles and Prevost married in the summer of 1772, and seven and a half months later she gave birth to a son.[49] Although this brief period insinuates a rushed marriage, it also hints at a level of social acceptance of people of color by whites in the lower ranges of French society. Probably at this time he adopted Gilles as a surname; the marriage record implies that he did this as a tribute to his father, a slave named Gilles.[50] Gilles explained that "Sieur Carayon had given him permission to put himself on his own, and to work for his own profit, which he actually did with his wife, who is also in the service of the aforementioned Sieur Carayon and of several other merchants of this town."[51]

This explanation, clear on first glance, actually leaves out much of the circumstances of his labor. Was this his own choice as a married man and head of household, or did Carayon have a hand in it? Did Carayon hire him out, or could he choose his own masters? Did he remit some of his wages to Carayon, or could he keep all he earned? What does become clear is the contingent and marginal nature of Gilles' labor: either by force or from necessity, he worked for multiple merchants. Yet even in the midst of this bleak economic picture Gilles also managed to suggest freedom even though he offered no documentary proof of it. His ability to earn wages and his marriage differentiated him from slaves, and connoted freedom.[52]

The slippage in Gilles' story between slavery and servitude and the indication of a penetrable boundary between the two broaches the possibility that slaves could enjoy de facto freedom whether or not their owners actually set them free. Here, Gilles' emancipation emerges as a negotiated process, not a clear-cut moment set out in a notarial document. This meant that his freedom was tenuous, dependent on the benevolence of his owners, but also that it was a category over which he had some control. His fragile freedom also rested on a fault line in practices of slavery that Gilles identified and exploited; if no one claimed otherwise, he was, in fact, free.

His success in eventually asserting his freedom stemmed at least in part from his intimate connections, including his long association with the Carayon household and his marriage to a white woman. The Admiralty official's complete acceptance of Gilles' word in his 1777 statement attests to his high level of integration into French society. The official saw Gilles face to face and presumably noted his dark skin and other elements that may have marked him as a person of color in the first place. In further testament to his integration into French society, the priest who baptized his son attached no racial label to the infant, although he categorized the father as a "noir domestique." For Gilles, his intimate familiarities with French ways of life, his acceptance of Catholic rites, and his assumption as patriarch of a family that included a white woman and a child all facilitated his ability to pass as free, to traverse the boundary between slavery and servitude.

The definition of race itself proved another metric that slaves could use to position themselves as free. Documentary evidence consistently identified Gilles as a "*noir*," a label connoting African origin. Yet slaves brought to France were a diverse group with roots in all corners of the globe, including India, the Île Bourbon (presently Réunion), and the Île de France (presently Mauritius), where the majority of slaves were imported from either Madagascar or the East African mainland. Particularly in the wake of the Seven Years' War, which disrupted Atlantic trade routes and redirected much colonial trade to the east, sailors, administrators, merchants, colonists, and their families brought slaves with origins outside of Africa to France. These slaves, of different complexions, features, and cultural backgrounds than slaves of West African descent, posed challenges to emerging systems of racial classification. Sometimes these cultural and phenotypical differences worked in slaves' favor. For example, slaves from the East Indies could use their differences from West Africans to distance themselves from popular French conceptions of what slaves looked like. Indian slaves of mixed-race origin in particular leveraged their physical dissimilarity from Africans to call their enslaved status into question. In doing so they helped to establish Africanness as a defining feature of enslavement by the mid-eighteenth century.

The case of Jean Nicolas, a forty-year-old *mulâtre* whose owner brought him to La Rochelle from the Île de France in about 1755, shows that the growing correlation between Africanness and slavery may have presented the possibility that slaves who did not look wholly African might manipulate an increasingly facile equation between Africanness and enslaved status. Jean Nicolas's owner gave him his liberty upon their arrival in the metropole, and as a free man he worked as a cook to several French families. In 1777 when Jean Nicolas made his Police des Noirs declaration he was in the service of an officer in the king's navy in a small town a few miles from La Rochelle. In the more than twenty years since his arrival Jean Nicolas had married a white woman named Marie-Anne Perraud, and they had one child.[53]

A long-time resident of France and clearly well settled in the town in which he lived, Jean Nicolas' somewhat ambiguous racial and ethnic identity as a man of mixed race and as a native of the Île de France opened up increased opportunities for him to pass unnoticed by authorities attempting to record all people of color. His half-European background likely facilitated his absorption into the Rochelais community.[54] As a native of the Île de France, his European background could have been French, but potentially also Dutch, Spanish, Portuguese, or even English, further clouding the issue of how to categorize him racially. He could have had a European cast to his features, and he may have been reared in close proximity to Europeans, giving him ample opportunity to become familiar with European social mores and conventions. Such familiarity would have helped Jean Nicolas to be accepted as French.

By 1777, to some extent this had already happened: although Jean Nicolas lived in La Rochelle at the time the first survey of people of color was conducted in 1763, his name was not on it. In fact, few free people of mixed race declared their own presence to the authorities in either survey, a lacuna that reveals an opportunity for free men of mixed race to become absorbed into their community.[55] Only two free men of mixed race made their own declarations in the 1763 survey. Both listed their profession as goldsmith, a highly skilled trade more typical of the mixed-race sons of planters such as Fleuriau than of slaves.[56]

Francisque, a slave born in India, used his ambiguous racial identity as the basis for a suit for freedom.[57] Francisque's case before the Paris Parlement hinged on defining his race negatively against Africanness in order to establish his liberty. In 1758, four years before the Ordinance of 1762 moved toward categorization only by race, Francisque's lawyers argued that because he was not an "esclave nègre," the laws of 1716 and 1738 did not apply to him.[58] This case accentuates the slippage in how the French term *nègre* related to color and enslaved status, and also vividly demonstrates that as the eighteenth century progressed, it increasingly referred exclusively to a slave of African descent, collapsing race and slavery into one category. In such a context, the racial origins of enslaved individuals were exceedingly important indeed. In the end, Francisque's lawyers built their case by arguing that he was not in fact a *nègre* because he had been born in India. At least on one level, this argument worked: Francisque ultimately was given his freedom, although the precise legal reason why remains unclear.[59]

Francisque's case exposes a breach between racial otherness and enslaved status, a gap that the Ordinance of 1762 intended to fill. But the experience of Jean Nicolas highlights that this disjuncture persisted at least well into the 1770s, in spite of official efforts to bring the two categories in line. Jean Nicolas had much in common with Francisque. A native of the Île de France and a *mulâtre* to boot, he brought out uncertainties about race and slavery because he was the son of a European and because he was not African. Because of this, the whites who lived around him may not have perceived him as a man of color or as subject to the laws governing people of color in France.

His statement in the 1777 Police des Noirs survey offers evidence of this slippage in racial categorization. Although Jean Nicolas told the official who recorded his declaration that he had a child, his son was not included in the register as a person of color. Jean Nicolas himself may have played a role in this omission by making a conscious effort to have his child left out of the survey. However, the official who took his declaration, knowing what Jean Nicolas looked like, his former status as a slave, and that he was married and had a child, colluded in this exclusion. This establishes that people of color influenced the complex set of decisions that comprised racial classification, and that these decisions depended on a variety of factors including status within the household and the community, not only on the color of a person's skin.

While Gilles played on subtle distinctions between slavery and servitude and Jean Nicolas exploited a gap in the relationship between race and slavery, the slave Augustin directly breached expectations about how slaves should behave toward their owners. Whereas Madame Regnaud de Beaumont's behavior toward her slave Tranchemontagne merely hints at the possible exposure to which owners opened their households, Augustin's case points to the potential for slaves ensconced within households to violate the intimacy such a close relationship entailed, either inadvertently or knowingly. It also intimates the tensions that underlay household relations at a time when the servant/master relationship was evolving from reciprocal loyalty to business-like contract.[60]

While owners still expected loyalty and devotion from slaves, slaves embedded in the household alongside servants likely saw their role quite differently. Mismatched expectations meant that people of color deeply implanted in the households of whites, including domestic slaves, and the whites they lived with could have divergent interpretations of their actions. What slaves recognized as explicable behavior, owners may have perceived as inexcusable. Perhaps the upheaval over the slave Augustin's infraction, an infraction so personal his owner refused to give it a name, grew out of such a "misunderstanding." It is important not to ignore the possibility that slaves may have violated expectations for their behavior purposefully and willfully, for their own reasons. This implies that people of color could accrue power from intimate relations with whites, although exploiting the vulnerabilities such intimacy entailed could come at a terrible cost.[61]

The circumstances under which Augustin arrived in France are somewhat murky. Later developments suggest that he probably disembarked from Saint-Domingue in the 1760s, and that rather than being brought by his owner, as most slaves were, he was likely sent from an old owner to a new one. Although Admiralty registers and surveys of people of color provide the ages, places of origin, and other rudimentary background information of many people of color, Augustin does not appear in any extant document.[62] He led a surreptitious existence, off the radar of Admiralty officials who were responsible for keeping track of slaves in France, a circumstance that evokes a much larger slave population than official records report.

Augustin went from being completely undocumented to exceptionally well recorded upon the death of his owner Isaac Garasché. The Garasché family, like other merchant families, branched out across the ocean, and a Garasché headed a main trading firm based in Le Cap and Port-au-Prince.[63] Upon his death Isaac was the patriarch, and he left a considerable estate to be divided among his eight children. Augustin, as a slave, was part of that estate. Under French law slaves whose owners died became part of their succession, and the heirs were entrusted with sending the slave back to the colonies.[64] Often slave owners circumvented this inconvenience and expense by emancipating their slaves in their wills. Augustin was neither emancipated nor returned to the colonies—at least not yet. In spite of the questionable legality of such a measure, Garasché's heirs assumed his ownership.

Thus in 1770 Augustin found himself the joint property of eight siblings, all children of the recently deceased Isaac Garasché.[65] On 12 May 1773 all eight heirs or their legal representatives convened at a notary's office in the small town of Marennes, not far from La Rochelle, to sort out the question of Augustin's ownership. The resulting document violated French law and custom, and emphasized the permeability of the supposed boundary royal policies drew around colonial slavery and the persistence of colonial practices in France. In the notary's office, Augustin was sold.

Pierre Meynardie, acting on behalf of his wife who was Isaac's daughter Marianne Garasché, agreed to pay each of the other heirs forty livres for relinquishing to him their one-eighth share of the slave they called "Étienne Augustin *dit* Favori." In return for having full proprietorship over Augustin, Meynardie would "feed, maintain, and provide his education according to his state." The bill of sale also stipulated that the slave would "live free in ten years from this day," an unusual provision that may evince a halfhearted effort to remain in line with laws regulating slavery in France.[66]

On paper, Augustin was an asset to any affluent French household. His new owner attested that "he is a very good wigmaker and he dresses [the hair of] women as well as [that of] men."[67] As a wigmaker and hairdresser, Augustin would have had access to the most personal spaces occupied by his owner's family, and would have come into close contact with their bodies on regular occasion. In a small household—Meynardie and his wife were childless—Augustin's hairdressing duties likely did not occupy him full time. He may have been hired out to friends and neighbors, and he may have taken on other domestic tasks.

However, if Meynardie and his wife hoped that owning a slave would ease their household burden or add to their social cachet, they were sorely mistaken. From the moment Augustin entered Meynardie's household he violated his owners' expectations. Only four years from the date Meynardie bought him, still years away from the decade he had anticipated keeping him, he was at his wit's end. Meynardie wrote to his brother-in-law Pierre Garasché in Cap Français, Saint-Domingue, "the family has given me in him a cruel gift, but one cannot foresee the future. . . . That wretch has treated us to the blackest ingratitude, and his conduct makes me want no less than to skin myself; I draw the curtain over that of which he has been capable and which forces me to address you by the ship that is presently passing by here."[68]

Meynardie's vivid language approaches an inversion of the typical master/slave relationship. While not uncommon for slaves in the Caribbean to suffer flaying for real or imagined infractions, here Meynardie posits that Augustin's deed had a similar effect on his owners. His violation must have been an intimate one indeed for his owner to "draw the curtain over" it. In a small town such as Marennes, where servants spread information about their employers and neighbors knew each other's business as well as their own, Augustin's action must have been committed within the bosom of the household for Meynardie to be able to keep it under wraps, even to close relations. Meynardie's wife added, "he is a rascal who has tricked us . . . we can no longer keep him without running the greatest risks."[69]

While Meynardie and his wife never revealed Augustin's misdeed, considering the possibilities opens up questions about the nature of slavery and resistance in France. The fact that Meynardie made every effort to preserve intense secrecy, and even his choice of language—that he "draw[s] the curtain over that of which he has been capable"—hints at some kind of sexual misconduct, possibly with a member of his owner's family. But Meynardie and his wife had no children, and her own words, that Augustin "is a rascal who has tricked us," hardly imply that she was a victim of his unwelcome attentions, nor were they evocative of extreme violence or attempts on their lives. Surely his dalliance with a servant would not have warranted such secrecy, particularly as men of color did marry white French women, especially servants, including Monréal, Gilles, and Jean Nicolas. Any petty thievery or act of violence on Augustin's part would have prompted Meynardie to turn to authorities or punish him himself. More likely, Augustin engaged in a spot of blackmail, using his easy access to private spaces in the household to do a little snooping, thus violating the trust and confidence of his owners. Whatever he did, it highlights the vulnerability of masters to their household help. Whether purposely or inadvertently, Augustin put Meynardie in a position where he felt, at any rate, as if he had little recourse.

In the end, Augustin's unnamed offenses proved so unbearable that Meynardie and his wife felt they had no option but to send him to her brother in Saint-Domingue, as Meynardie wrote, "so that you might sell him or hire him out for my profit." Meynardie even attached his power of attorney to his request in order to allow his brother-in-law to make all necessary arrangements without delay.[70] This decision came at considerable expense. Not only did Meynardie lose Augustin's labor, he had to pay his passage to Saint-Domingue. As he had already promised to free Augustin he also would eventually be liable for a hefty manumission tax, which slave owners in France usually avoided but colonial emancipators often paid.[71] He begged Garasché, "look out for my interests, my friend, I do not hide from you [that even] when the arrangements that you make on his behalf produce for me 6,000 [livres], they cannot reimburse me for that which this has cost me and will cost me to have him conducted close to you."[72] He added, "I hope that you will make out well for me for the time he has left to serve, moreover that the corrections of America remind him of his work, and he will do by the fear of punishments that which he should have done for me as my due."[73] Although he still intended to free Augustin eventually, as he had promised the Garasché siblings, he expressed the greatest bitterness that "that rascal, in whom I still have an interest, will enjoy without any retribution by me all the fruit of his labor in order for him to put himself in a state to pay all the expenses of his liberty, for which I do not want to make new sacrifice."[74] Whatever Augustin had done, Meynardie expected from him behavior he perceived as his "due," whether because of his identity as a white French male or his status as Augustin's owner. When Augustin failed to meet these expectations, Meynardie turned to what he clearly saw as the ultimate punishment: deportation to Saint-Domingue and "the corrections of America."

Although Augustin too may have considered this the worst fate he could suffer, it is worth considering that he may have had a different perspective from his owner. Life in a small French town probably proved difficult for an enslaved man. His skin color would have made him stand out, and removed from the hustle and bustle occasioned by an Atlantic seaport, he may have been subject to curiosity or derision. Gilles and Jean Nicolas notwithstanding, he may have had difficulty finding peers or sexual partners. Living in close proximity with owners certainly opened up vulnerabilities to abuse, and although the abuse of female slaves has drawn more scholarly attention, men surely were not exempt from it.[75] Augustin, likely a privileged slave even before he arrived in France, may have wanted to return to family or community in Saint-Domingue, and deliberately pursued a strategy that would get him sent back. Such a strategy seems risky, to say the least: in hindsight a multitude of potential perils spring to mind.

Yet it is important not to underestimate Augustin's own knowledge, or disregard the control he had over the situation. He likely knew of Meynardie's family contacts in Cap Français, so could conclude he would be sent there. He certainly realized he was more valuable for his skills as a wigmaker and hairdresser than for his physical labor. Taking these considerations into account, Augustin's unnamed infraction very well could have been a misunderstanding of his owner's expectations but it is equally possible that it was a deliberate rejection of their parameters for his own ends.

Augustin's ultimate legacy to his former owner was his beleaguered self-satisfaction that he had, in spite of his trials, acted in a manner befitting a munificent master. Meynardie did in fact pack Augustin off to Saint-Domingue later that summer; one Jacques Guibert of La Rochelle, a cousin, took charge of placing him on a ship.[76] "Too much indulgence spoiled him," Guibert wrote to Pierre Garasché in the letter that accompanied Augustin back to Saint-Domingue. "He is a bad sort who cost your brother-in-law dearly."[77] Meynardie undoubtedly agreed. "I hope, my friend," he wrote to Garasché, "that you approve of me; you would [even] more if you knew all the griefs I had because of him [Augustin], but I [will] forget them and do not want to dwell on them too much for the purpose of leaving him a slave his whole life; that he be happy one day and I would have the satisfaction of it, there are few Masters, perhaps not a one, who would do for him that which I have done. I hope that he remember my indulgence to the good."[78]

Enslaved men, like free men of color, used the discursive tools at their disposal either to position themselves as free or to rupture expectations for their enslavement. They could go about this in multiple ways. François Gilles blurred the line between slavery and servitude, thus between slavery and freedom. Jean Nicolas called into question exactly what race meant as a category and how it related to slavery. Augustin rejected his owners' expectations of how he should behave. In all these cases, intimate relationships facilitated the blurring of the boundaries of enslavement. Both Gilles and Jean Nicolas married white women and fathered children, thus fulfilling French expectations for masculinity: as *pères de famille*, they did not meet expectations for the social or family position of slaves. Augustin, in contrast, used his intimate position within a household to violate his owner's expectations for how slaves should act, to great effect. All of them exhibited their familiarity with metropolitan expectations for male slaves and French men. Women, on the other hand, particularly enslaved or formerly enslaved women who could not comply with changing understandings of French femininity, had more difficulty manipulating gender ideals to their own benefit.

Women and Community

Women of color, slaves and former slaves alike, had fewer opportunities for self-positioning than men. This difference stemmed in large part from the models of French femininity from which they could choose to potentially accrue some social advantage. Married women such as Neptune's wife Louise possibly benefited most by avoiding encounters with officials, thereby emulating a model of bourgeois femininity removed from the public sphere. Even if Louise's motives for pursuing this tactic stemmed more from self-preservation and fear than a desire to be a good wife and mother, French officials, if they remarked on her choice at all, likely would have seen it as matching their own expectations for women's roles.

Single women and enslaved women for whom sanctified marriage was not always an option did not have this luxury. Nonetheless, they had other models of femininity on which they could draw. In particular, free women of color who supported themselves through their labor could position themselves as "bonnes sujets" by emphasizing their economic self-sufficiency. Moreover, even enslaved women could, by accepting Catholic rites, show their embeddedness in their community. Like men, women of color used their access to French institutions to demonstrate their similarity to their French counterparts, thus working to efface differences based solely on race.

Monsieur Mesnard de Saint Michel brought three slaves named Jean-Baptiste-André Deday, Marie-Catherine Mercier, and Marie-Jeanne Angélique to La Rochelle from his plantation in Saint-Domingue over the course of the 1750s. Taking a close look at these individuals, all slaves of the same owner, offers opportunities to interrogate how gender shaped the choices and experiences of people of color in La Rochelle. Deday, the only man, was born in Cap Français and came to France with his owner around 1752 at the age of about sixteen.[79] He served Mesnard as a domestic slave for eight years, and received his liberty around 1760. He continued working for his former owner as a domestic servant for another fourteen years; in all likelihood his circumstances and the work he performed remained much the same. After working for Mesnard for a total of twenty-two years, Deday eventually left his former owner in 1774 and entered the service of the *curé* of the parish of Sainte-Foy in the Poitou. By 1777 he had switched employers again and was in the service of the Marquis de Miran, an army field marshal.

It is difficult to interpret with certainty the reasons for Deday's long service to a former owner, then his switch of employers in relatively quick succession. On the one hand, it is tempting to view his long service to Mesnard as connoting a kind of loyalty, not to his employer but rather to Mercier and Angélique, who might have been his friends or even relatives. At the very least, they were surely close associates. Similarly, his string of employers in the 1770s opens up a seductive vista of mobility and choice: as a servant, he could change situations as long as he found someone to employ him.[80] Indeed, he found particular success with this strategy, working first for a priest (a helpful ally?) and then for a field marshal, surely an excellent position. In this light, leaving Mesnard's household could be read as a forcible declaration of independence. Such mobility and choice consistently proved more open to male servants than female ones, underscoring that Deday likely had more options and opportunities for employment than did Mercier and Angélique.

The lives of Marie-Catherine Mercier and Marie-Jeanne Angélique, brought to France by the same M. Mesnard, followed a similar path that nonetheless differed in a few essentials.[81] The *mulâtresse* Mercier arrived in France with her owner in 1754 at the age of twenty-three, two years after Deday. The eight-year-old *négresse* Angélique came two years later. They may even have been related: the young Angélique, potentially less reticent than the more experienced Mercier, at one point referred to the older woman as her "relative."[82] Mercier received her freedom shortly after arriving in France, around the time Angélique joined her in La Rochelle. In spite of this, she remained in her former owner's service as a servant for an additional twenty years, until Mesnard's death at the beginning of 1777.

As with Deday, this circumstance offers an occasion to speculate on the opportunities available to Mercier and to try to understand the choices she made. Like Deday, her choice to remain in the employ of her former owner may evince her wish to stay close to Deday and Angélique, although the child may not actually have lived under the same roof. That Mesnard emancipated her relatively soon after her arrival in France could suggest that she was his mistress as well as his slave, and that she had a privileged position in his household. This speculation is borne out by her high level of literacy: she signed her own declaration in a firm and steady hand. Furthermore, in this series of declarations, Mercier and Angélique are the only women and two of just three people of color who are not identified by the epithet "nomé(e)," which by this point connoted enslaved status.[83] This lacuna hints that the Admiralty official accorded Mercier some degree of status. The fact that she stayed with Mesnard also emphasizes the lack of options available to her. After Mesnard's death, she began working as a seamstress.[84] This shift at age forty-six from domestic service in a familiar household to earning her living by piecework may have been terrifying rather than liberating, and Mercier felt some responsibility for Angélique that made her situation all the more weighty.

Angélique's story was a bit more complicated and spotlights the lack of control slaves exercised over their fate and the strength of connections among people of color. Upon her arrival in France Mesnard gave the child Angélique to his sister. The girl served her new mistress for twenty-one years, upon which, according to the official version of the declaration sent to Paris, her mistress emancipated her. However, the first draft of her statement puts forth a different turn of events in a passage that was heavily crossed out.[85] Her mistress had not in fact liberated her, but rather intended to send her back to the colonies to be sold. At that point Mercier intervened: she gave Angélique's owner three hundred livres, and Angélique received her liberty. This circumstance denotes a strong and continuing association between the two women.

From that point on, they worked together as seamstresses, although likely outside the guild system and employed in activity that probably barely enabled them to keep body and soul together.[86] Out of an emotional tie or economic necessity, their fates were linked. The two women went together to make their declarations to the Admiralty, and they were two of only three women of color who did so.[87] Unlike the men of color who emphasized their patriarchal positions in their declarations, Mercier and Angélique had nothing to gain by calling attention to their family situations. As single women they were sexually suspect and a potential economic burden to the community. Instead they took another route. By emphasizing their employment as seamstresses, they highlighted their economic contributions and independence, making clear they had no need for charity.

Comparing the situations of Deday, Mercier, and Angélique emphasizes the role that gender played in determining the options and choices open to freed people of color. While Deday apparently found acceptable conditions of employment outside of his former owner's household, Mercier and Angélique proved less able to do so. This puts the two women in an unusual situation, as few women of color in La Rochelle were unattached to either husbands or masters. Indeed, marriage to men of color offered women of color one possibility besides domestic service, as Neptune's wife Louise found. This option brought a certain level of respectability, and shielded women from interaction with royal authorities. Yet while men of color could position white wives as instruments of integration, women of color who had white men as sexual partners could do no such thing, as marriage between white men and women of color happened rarely, if at all. Unattached women such as Mercier and Angélique had to live by their very poorly paid labor. While some men of color managed to parlay their gender into political and social legitimacy, women of color on their own had more difficulty conforming to contemporary gender ideals, only able to aspire to comparison with white women on the edges of society.

Throughout this chapter, tantalizing glimpses have emerged of a community of people of color in La Rochelle. Gilles and Michel Nicolas attended the burial of the slave Jean-Pierre, called Médor. Neptune, Monréal, and Jean Nicolas made their 1777 Admiralty declarations on the same day and in sequence, conveying that they went together. Gilles and Deday appeared together the next day. Mercier and Angélique had clearly linked their fortunes. People of color in La Rochelle actively sought out community and created their own intimate bonds that were, at least to some extent, based on race. Parish records open a window on this fascinating community.

In the Caribbean, some people of color, slave and free, devoted themselves to Catholicism and played active roles in parish life. Indeed, slaves in
the islands frequently used Catholicism for their own purposes, particularly
as a means through which to assert their own subjectivity in circumstances of
enslavement.[88] Thus, slaves in France arrived with understandings of the flexibility of Catholicism and ways it could potentially ameliorate their lot, even
providing an alternate locus of authority to that of their owners.[89] Particular
significance accrued around the Catholic sacrament of baptism because of
the persistent idea that once slaves received the sacrament, they were free.[90]
Noting the Church's potential to drive a wedge through their owner's hege-
mony, numerous Caribbean slaves, créole and African-born, were receptive
to baptism and to religious education.[91]

A number of people of color in La Rochelle, highly acculturated to French
practices but also familiar with colonial ways, accepted Catholic baptismal,
marriage, and funerary rites.[92] As did whites, they habitually gathered their
closest friends and associates around them to commemorate these life turning points. Because of their circumstances, knowledge, and experiences, the
engagement of slaves and former slaves with the Catholic Church in France
cannot simply be read as imitative of whites.

This point becomes particularly clear when considering who attended the
baptism of infants born to slaves in France. In general, the baptism of French
babies tended to be a masculine affair, conducted while the mother recovered
from the rigors of childbirth.[93] In contrast, for example, the enslaved woman
Catherine took her infant daughter Marianne to receive the sacrament of
baptism in the Saint-Barthélémy parish church herself on 8 January 1726.
Two other slaves, François and Marianne, accompanied her and were named
the baby girl's godparents.[94]

Catherine clearly sought this Catholic rite for her daughter. Her reasons
for doing so may have been complex and multivalent. Whites baptized their
infants out of devotion, a desire to attest to the infant's legitimacy, to guarantee
inheritance, and also because of social pressure; for most families who lived
in France, it was done as a matter of course. Catherine may have possessed
some of the same motives, but given her precarious social position as an enslaved woman, her own actions also indicate deliberate awareness of the ways
Catholicism could create a "social life" for her and her child.[95] Neither legitimacy nor inheritance was at stake: the baby, identified as Catherine's "fille
naturel," was clearly born out of wedlock, and the transmission of property
was an unlikely concern for a woman classified as property herself. Yet she

must have made a huge effort to get herself and her day-old newborn to the parish church. Although Catherine appeared to be outside a traditional nuclear family structure (who was the baby's father? why wasn't he there?), she clearly had a support system. Formalizing baby Marianne's ties to the slaves François and Marianne may not have been her only motivation, although it could have been a strong one. Catherine also may have sought for her daughter the future opportunity to tap into the networks and resources of the Catholic Church, an institution that had the reputation of sometimes interceding between slaves and their owners.

In Catherine's case, her efforts yielded little benefit for her tiny daughter: Marianne died just ten days later, and received a Christian burial.[96] In her burial record Marianne was classified as a slave, revealing that in France slavery sometimes remained a heritable status. Maybe the ritual provided the mother some comfort. The burial record does not divulge if François and Marianne attended the solemnities, but we can imagine that they did, and that Catherine had a network of friends and allies who consoled and supported her.

The experiences of Catherine, Mercier and Angélique, and others make clear that people of color's social connections extended beyond the households in which they lived, and that they sought out equal relationships with others of the same race and status. This is important, for it establishes that even while people of color deliberately blurred racial boundaries and questioned any assumed correlation between race and status, they also searched for others of similar backgrounds for social purposes. Such an association may not have been based on race per se, but rather on common histories, experiences, and social positions in France. From this point of view, this choice is neither surprising nor unusual, as French men and women up and down the social spectrum associated with people of similar rank. However, it does mean that visible associations among people of color could obfuscate their attempts to blur the color line. Seeing people of color together could reinforce the developing notion that race mattered as a social category.

There were multiple ways in which free people of color in La Rochelle could have articulated their roles and positions in the community. Across the board, they deliberately chose to do so in ways whites would understand. This meant emphasizing how they conformed to expectations for French men and women, and using French institutions as forums in which to make claims of belonging. For men, this meant highlighting their patriarchal authority as husbands, fathers, heads of household, and wage earners; even if a man of color did not fit into all of these categories, he often laid claim to at least one. For women, it meant hiding behind their status as wives when they could, or else emphasizing their economic productivity and self-sufficiency. Some individuals could not or would not fit within these parameters. Their violations of French expectations of how slaves should act point to another discursive option available to slaves: outright resistance, a tactic much studied by scholars of the colonies but rarely noted in the metropole.

People of color drew on different ways of portraying themselves to whites as the need arose, but they also made connections and formed relationships with other people of color. Some of these relationships proved long standing, like the marriage between Neptune and Louise, which lasted at least twenty-one years (1756–1777 and beyond). Others presumably were more transitory, as people of color moved on in search of employment or with owners, returned to the colonies, or died. Clearly, though, people of color, slave and free, sought each other out as intimate companions. This did not happen across lines of status; there is no evidence that free people of color, even former slaves, associated with slaves, in spite of the blurry lines between slavery and freedom in France. Furthermore, their association with each other was certainly not to the exclusion of whites: the fact that Monréal, Jean Nicolas, and Gilles all had white wives shows that men of color chose white women as sexual partners. However, the fact that people of color knew each other, probably stopped to chat on the streets of La Rochelle, attended the baptisms of each other's children, and went to make their Admiralty declarations together could have strengthened the impression of a cohesive group based on race.

There was, therefore, an uneasy hovering between resistance and acceptance as race took shape as a social and legal category in the last decades of the Old Regime. People of color used the resources and vocabularies at their disposal to make clear that there was a place for them in Rochelais society. Although they may have employed similar tactics, they made individual claims. Any corporate sense of people of color as a group emerged through their intimate personal relationships with each other.

Race from Colonialism to Revolution

War and revolution curtailed opportunities for forming intimate bonds across lines of race. Beginning with the Seven Years' War, followed by the American, French, and Haitian Revolutions, war disrupted trade, reduced travel opportunities, and led to a decline in personal transatlantic correspondence. Yet personal relationships were not immediately severed, nor did calls for "liberté, egalité, fraternité" instantaneously transform longstanding ways of interaction. While war, revolution, and escalating absenteeism rates meant that even people with colonial ties in France were less able to sustain intimate transatlantic connections, existing connections did not immediately fade away. Similarly, in Saint-Domingue connections across lines of race remained a quotidian fact of life, and old ways of thinking about social status often continued to trump race as a category.

The Haitian Revolution began to change these intimate bonds forged under a system of colonialism and slavery. As race became an increasingly political category, lines of political allegiance more often were perceived to follow lines of race. This led to an oppositional "us versus them" mentality that intensified because as groups shifted and coalesced along political lines, the personal ties that had so long bound them together began to dissolve. Intimate connections across lines of race had been instrumental in producing flexibility and malleability in racial constructs. Once the slowing of trade and the hostilities of revolution began to break down the institutions and practices that had allowed for those intimacies, racial categories quickly solidified as hard and fast binary oppositions. Returning once again to the Belin plantation demonstrates how—and how quickly—this ossification took place, focusing on personal encounters, but ones in which any real intimacy had been lost.

Most slave owners viewed the Haitian Revolution as only a temporary rupture to Saint-Domingue's long eighteenth century of prosperity. Even as Cap Français burned twice, optimism prevailed, and whites confidently anticipated the resumption of the good old days of high profits after the rebellion subsided.[1] Plantation owners continued to see their property as they had always known it: a source of revenue that, like other resources, they intended to pass on to their families in perpetuity. On the Belin des Marais plantation, located in the western province of Saint-Domingue on the Artibonite plain near the town of Saint-Marc, the plantation owners' attitudes illustrate the continuity of this confidence. At the height of the Revolution, just as at the height of the Old Regime, the plantation's owners keenly assumed the profit potential of their property.[2] Yet these hopes for stability were in vain. The Belin plantation did not again reach Old Regime levels of profitability, and soon whites in Saint-Domingue found themselves struggling to hold on to their property, their race-based authority, and indeed their lives.

As the Haitian Revolution began, the Belin plantation was much like any other. It was a well-established piece of property that prospered during the boom years of the 1730s and 1740s, and continued to turn a sizable and reliable profit after Belin's heirs inherited the property on his death in 1769. A generation removed from any personal colonial experience, they read overseers' reports on indigo, cotton, livestock, and slaves from the comfort of their well-appointed drawing rooms back in France. They knew the property and the community in Saint-Marc only through the letters they received from the plantation's procureur St. Macary, who was its manager and the owners' colonial agent.[3] Yet procureurs seldom lived on or even particularly near the plantations under their charge. Based in towns, they had a number of clients whose interests they looked after. They hired an overseer who managed the day-to-day operations, including planting and harvesting crops and managing slaves. The increasing prevalence of absentee landowners made this type of arrangement practical and common. It also meant reports on plantation life were frequently twice removed, at best.

Before and during the French and Haitian Revolutions, St. Macary's letters to the absentee owners focused primarily on business matters: the productivity of the plantation, planting and harvest cycles, and crops. Only rarely did other matters make their way into transatlantic correspondence. This well-established pattern makes any departures from it all the more notable. Once revolution was in the air, however, politics increasingly crept in alongside updates on the weather and projections of crop yields. "Although the colony is a little less agitated at this very moment than it has been for some time, there is nevertheless always fermentation," the agent wrote in 1790, a moment of heightening tension between whites and free people of color. "But," he hastened to add, "that does not carry into the workshops." In this mediated account, constructed for interested parties who had their eyes firmly on the bottom line, politics and labor remained strictly separate. He continued, "As to that which the National Assembly has invariably pronounced on the foundations of our constitution and on the competence of the Colonial Assembly for the establishment of a local regime, opinions always regenerate the spirit of division; in these circumstances all remains pending, and commerce in particular is that which supports the burden. It is desirable that wise and permanent laws come to our aid to make disorder and anarchy cease."[4]

In this letter, written between the outbreak of the French and Haitian Revolutions, the agent for the first time formulated race as a political issue, which he perhaps confronted on the streets of Saint-Marc as the Colonial Assembly explicitly excluded free people of color from exercising rights. He framed it as something to be regulated and contained from above in the halls of government, rather than the concern of ordinary people, whether planters or slaves. Their own proper sphere of interest was commerce, the bulwark of the colony. While political categories rapidly shifted in France and Saint-Domingue, colonial agents and the absentee landowners to whom they wrote remained focused on trade and the wealth generated by colonial goods, which to them seemed reliable and immutable.

In 1790, neither whites nor people of color questioned the necessity of freedom as a precondition for political participation. Yet as free people of color agitated for political rights, recognizing them as one cohesive group marked the first step toward viewing all people of color as one unit. Even the procureur, removed from the action as he was, acknowledged the political coherence of what he called the "olive class," a reference to the generally lighter skin of free people of color of mixed racial origin. The procureur wrote, "for eight months we have been so upset by the rumors of the country . . . we have been obliged to sacrifice everything in favor of what certain people call the common good. . . . We avow that we have had worries about the principles of certain partisans of the rights of man. . . . The olive class is the only one that has presented in favor of the revolution . . . without it the colony would be the most tranquil part of the kingdom."[5] Here, the procureur portrayed free people of color as a unified political group, even though he was surely aware of the social gulfs that group encompassed.

This growing perception, originating with free people of color themselves, consolidated in 1791 when the National Assembly granted free people
of color whose parents had both been free and who met property requirements the same political rights as whites.[6] Upon that occasion, St. Macary
reported that "the colony is still in the midst of lively rumors, more occupied
today with the decrees of the National Assembly of the 15 May [giving free
men of color political rights] concerning the free people of color." The procureur reported whites' uneasiness about this dramatic development: "Opinions that until this point have been divided are all of a sudden reunited to no
longer worry about anything but distancing from themselves the fatal effects
that may result from its [the decree's] execution."[7] This suggests that the decree, which intended to sweep away the distinctions between whites and
qualifying people of color, actually united whites hitherto divided along lines
of social status, against people of color. While social status had sometimes
unified well-to-do whites and free people of color in the past, here, St. Macary
implied, race separated them.

Like most other whites, St. Macary did not view free people of color in the
same category as slaves. While he and other whites might have been gingerly
"distancing themselves" from the decision that gave propertied free people of
color the same rights, they viewed the massive slave rebellion that began unfolding in the north in the summer of 1791 with the liveliest alarm. St. Macary
related that the participants included "about twelve thousand *nègres*, and it is
calculated that their forces will elevate at least to thirty thousand." The insurgents, whom he consistently labeled "brigands have burned everywhere
they've passed, but that which is the most cruel is the frightful ravaging of
whites who were in the aforementioned plantations of which almost not a
one escaped their ferocity. The colony in great danger has promptly opened
its eyes on this unwelcome position, and all the world is reunited to stop
these rebels, and to prevent the contagion from becoming general, we are
reinforcing ourselves whether it be in the plains or in the towns, and we are
taking the most active guard."[8] The insurgents' tactics, he reported, not only
included burning plantation houses and fields of crops, but also destroying
the buildings and implements used to manufacture sugar.[9]

These letters, written in rapid succession in August, September, and October 1791, show how quickly racial alliances shifted. While in August he emphasized the divisions between whites and free people of color, by October he
proclaimed that "all the world is reunited" against the more pressing threat of
the slave uprising. The uprising therefore brought about a quick shift in

concern from the political subjectivity of free people of color to that of slaves. St. Macary still viewed the two groups as distinctly separate, and he expressed no allegiance or personal ties to either.

The National Assembly's decree of 15 May 1791 granting citizenship to free men of color did not efface differences between whites and free people of color in the western province. Indeed, whites in the Artibonite Plain around Saint-Marc generally resisted fulfilling this mandate.[10] The National Assembly gave their resistance legitimacy with legislation of 24 September 1791 which gave colonial assemblies jurisdiction over the political status of citizens of color, thereby dramatically undermining the force of the 15 May decree. In spite of whites' ongoing resistance to extending political equality to free men of color, they came to view "citizens of color" as a cohesive, undifferentiated political group separate from whites in the wake of the decrees.[11] Before the French and Haitian Revolutions began, whites rarely mentioned free people of color in business correspondence; they were isolated individuals, often with whom whites had a business or personal relationship of some sort.[12] As the Haitian Revolution unfolded, the procureur of the Belin plantation began writing about free people of color as a unified political group, sometimes allied with whites and sometimes pitted against them, and an important intermediary between whites and slaves.[13]

St. Macary articulated several facets of this evolving, contradictory view in a single letter in which he fearfully wrote that "the citizens of color become masters of all" on one page, while on another he reported that "the citizens of color have contracted the obligation to work with the whites towards the reestablishment of order and tranquility among the workshops [and] have made many efforts to that effect in spite of the dangers that are almost the same [as] for the whites."[14] These sentiments drew on and hinted at the September and October 1791 Concordats between free people of color and whites in key regions of the west, which promised free people of color recognition of those rights guaranteed by the National Assembly.[15]

At the same time, the insurgent slaves began to recognize a kinship with free people of color based solely on race. In 1790–1791, alliances in the western province were complex and shifting rapidly. After the persecution of free people of color followed by the burning of Port-au-Prince in November 1791, many land-owning free men of color allied themselves with rebelling slaves.[16] When the procureur visited the Belin plantation, he "found the workshop infinitely set against the management of whites, and [the slaves] demanded of me a citizen of color."[17] He accordingly spoke with free colored leaders in the area, and asked them to recommend a "trustworthy man" to oversee the plantation.[18]

As the rebellion spread, in early 1792 the procureur of the Belin plantation tacitly acknowledged its free colored leaders as citizens but also portrayed them in opposition to whites. He wrote, "the town of Port-au-Prince was abandoned in large part to flames, the rest to pillage[.] The citizens of color besieged this capital again against the whites and in consequence [are] masters of the countryside[.] They exercise not only mock battles, but also cruelties by which humanity has suffered much[.] This part of the colony is almost deserted of whites, those who have had the good fortune to escape the fire that pursued them have left the country or have migrated to the [surrounding] quarters."[19] Relations between free people of color and whites continued to deteriorate. Things came to a head in April of 1792, when the residents of the western province feared imminent revolt similar to that in the north. The previously peaceful Belin plantation was drawn into the upheaval when the gérant was captured and killed in a battle that broke out between whites and people of color.[20] Soon slaves joined in the mêlée. The procureur wrote, "your plantation, Messieurs, participates in this loss [due to the insurrection of a great number of workshops], as it was abandoned by twenty-three male *nègres* who were the most bellicose."[21] Although St. Macary still maintained his verbal distinction between "*gens de couleur*," free people of color, and "*nègres*," slaves, the actual groups began to blur in his letters at this point. Perhaps long acceptance of marronage as a slave activity led him to label runaways "*nègres*" while he viewed the rebels who burned Port-au-Prince as "citizens," even though some of the runaway slaves may well have participated in setting the fire.

As the rebellion spread to the Artibonite Plain in March 1792, St. Macary's view of slaves changed rapidly and dramatically. In April he wrote that "one part of this plain has already followed the unhappy example of the insurrection by a large number of workshops that have shaken off the yoke."[22] Another letter elaborated: "our situation becomes more and more critical, disorder is at its limit in our quarter and particularly in the Artibonite plain where there remains not a single white."[23] In the midst of a massive mobilization of slaves by early April, St. Macary could no longer view plantations solely as profitable sites to be managed. Instead, he came to see "workshops" of slaves as political entities, potentially dangerous and ready to rebel.

Although St. Macary persisted in classifying slaves as "bons" and "mauvais sujets," common categories in the Old Regime, these categories took on a new meaning.[24] In the Old Regime, "mauvais sujet" could apply to anyone not considered a good subject to the king or patriarchal order, from rebellious children to hardened criminals to promiscuous wives. In Saint-Domingue the term also applied to recalcitrant slaves who resisted their enslavement by slowing work or exhibiting insolence to the overseer. During the Revolution, the category "sujet" was generally replaced by that of "citoyen." It is significant, therefore, that St. Macary continued to use the Old Regime category to refer to slaves who, after all, were not at this point citizens. When applied to slaves, this category became much more literal; slaves who ran away to join rebels or looted plantation houses could be classified as "bad subjects." It also assumed a political connotation based on alliance with or against the Colonial Assembly. Similarly, "bons sujets" did more than obey orders; they declared their allegiance with whites, thus upholding the racial hierarchy.

This turmoil in categorization did not immediately resolve itself along lines of race. Rather, slave or free status also continued to act as a dividing line. On St. Macary's next visit to the Belin plantation, he thought it prudent to be escorted by a contingent of six free men of color, whom he hired for protection from the rebelling slaves.[25] This demonstrates the tumultuous position of people of color in the colony: St. Macary assumed that slaves had enough solidarity with people of color that they would allow them to pass unfettered, while he himself felt enough fellow feeling with free men of color to trust them to guard his life. Although the tensions he perceived were not straightforwardly racial, they do imply a solidification of race as a defining category. St. Macary, after all, trusted free men of color, not because of personal relationships or common social position but simply because he saw them as intermediaries between whites and slaves, thereby indicating that race, distinct from social status, was becoming the fundamental category that defined life in the colony.

In spite of this unrest, St. Macary assured the Belin heirs that good order continued to reign on their plantation: "Work is observed as much as the circumstance permits," he assured them.[26] His persistent emphasis on products and profits suggests that the Belin heirs expected that their plantation would continue to yield a profit. He told them, "Considering, Messieurs, that in all these misfortunes you should estimate yourselves very happy with the state in which I describe your plantation[.] You are of the number of proprietors of Artibonite who are favored, because the very great part of workshops remain doing nothing, and that the most consequential plantations have not a seed [denceinancié]."[27] In spite of St. Macary's repeated emphasis on their extreme good fortune that they still had a plantation at all, a significant disconnect persisted between the expectations of the owners that the plantation would remain profitable and provide a steady financial resource for their family and the colonial reality of unrest, upheaval, work stoppages, and the difficulties of transatlantic trade in a time of war.[28] Responding to their request for updates on the plantation accounts, the procureur said, "I find myself necessarily running behind this year because of the displacement of my books and papers, which I am only just getting back."[29] This was somewhat of an understatement, as St. Macary had been forced to flee Saint-Marc for his life, leaving his house, business, and all his papers behind.

Given the great contrast between the colonial past and the revolutionary present, both St. Macary's tendency to underplay the changes on the plantation and the heirs' apparent inability to understand that their colonial asset could not provide the financial security it had in the past seem somewhat surprising. They speak, however, to the persistence of Old Regime categories by which people had organized their daily lives: loyalty, social order, and patronage remained strong despite the breakdown in interracial personal relations occasioned by the Revolution. St. Macary's desire to please his employers and to serve them well may have prompted his continual reassurances that "your [plantation], sirs, . . . is the happiest of all the quarter," while their assumption that their plantation would continue to provide revenue speaks to the "unthinkable" quality of the Haitian Revolution.[30]

Even at the height of the slave rebellion, whites' belief in the loyalty of slaves still persisted, and the actions of some slaves reaffirmed this faith. The relations between whites and blacks, former slave owners and former slaves, did not simply dissolve in a wave of revolutionary fervor. The annals of Haitian Revolutionary lore are full of stories of slaves who saved the lives of their former owners, from a letter written by a white colonist who escaped the rebel slaves by living in the woods for three and a half months, sustained by food brought by a "Negro domestic," to three slaves who saved the lives of their former owner and his family, one at the cost of his own life.[31] Other slaves, instead of joining the insurgents, followed their owners into exile in the United States or elsewhere, and some, like most of the Belin slaves and others on the Artibonite Plain, remained on the plantations of their former owners, continuing to work the land. In general, slaves in the western province were less likely to leave plantations or destroy property than those in the north.[32] Although white contemporaries usually read such actions as evidence of the allegiance of "bonnes sujets," Jeremy Popkin points out that slaves and former slaves had complex motivations for their actions, and may have purposefully decided to keep their options open by maintaining ties with former owners.[33]

Like other whites in Saint-Domingue, St. Macary believed that some slaves remained loyal to their absent owners, and it was these, rather than the "mauvais sujets," whom he tended to personalize. Here, personal relationships rested on what the procureur understood as firm racial hierarchy. He particularly mentioned the slave driver Bastien and his son Augustin, both of whom he classified as "excellent subjects; they have made proof on this occasion of their attachment in favor of their masters and the first [that is, Bastien] appeared in the workshop to preach them a sermon of good."[34] Bastien's dedication extended even farther; he also visited St. Macary in town to update him on the work taking place on the plantation.[35] From the "great slackening" in the work that Bastien reported, St. Macary concluded that "it is not surprising as there is no white to supervise them."[36] Bastien, likely knowing what St. Macary wanted to hear, "informed me with pleasure that the whole workshop asked to be commanded by a white and that he wanted very much to have an overseer."[37]

Yet Bastien's fidelity perhaps was not as disingenuous as the procureur perceived it. The slave also benefited from being perceived as a "bon sujet." In fact, the slave driver hedged his bets by representing himself as a faithful slave in order to obtain permission to act with greater independence. "In order to disapprove of their [the other slaves'] conduct it was necessary [for him] to remove himself from the plantation," Macary wrote. "I have given his outing my permission."[38] Slave drivers such as Bastien had more opportunities to form personal relationships with whites because of their positions of responsibility. Like Bastien, they also had the wherewithal and the permission to travel off the plantation. Consequently, slave drivers frequently were the ringleaders in rebellion as evidenced by the uprising in the north. By representing himself as a "good subject," a loyal slave, Bastien obtained permission to journey away from the plantation. By failing to realize that the old categories of "bon" and "mauvais sujet" were too narrow to hold the current events, St. Macary essentially sanctioned Bastien's freedom of movement, exactly what he would need to take the lead in planning a rebellion.

Moreover, the slaves who remained on the plantation proved less compliant than St. Macary led the heirs to believe, possibly even less than he himself thought. Several months later, he reported that he had appointed a man of color to run the plantation "following the refusal that the workshop made to initially trust in the white that I wanted to give them to succeed the late M. Trastous," the overseer whom the slaves had killed.[39] Again, St. Macary understated the conflict: the white man he had chosen "had been obliged to flee."[40] Eventually the workshop did accept a white overseer, one M. Bergé, who, St. Macary congratulated himself, had "a love for his station," a desperate nod to social order at a moment of intense turmoil.[41]

In spite of the procureur's evident desire to assure his employers that all was well on the plantation and that any disruption in their revenues was minor and temporary, unrest among slaves grew, and they took advantage of the general upheaval to engage in old forms of resistance as well as new. Although the Belin plantation, according to St. Macary, never reached a state of out-and-out rebellion, slaves pillaged the plantation house, stopped work, and avoided punishment.[42] Even though the procureur threatened the overseers with retribution because of the "slacking off that shows itself among all parties, . . . the sick [slaves] remain at the hospital, the lazy [slaves] go there in a crowd under the weakest reasons of indisposition."[43] Rebellion during the Haitian Revolution took various forms and existed on a continuity, as it always had.

By 1794, the British occupied much of the western province of Saint-Domingue, including the area around Saint-Marc where the Belin plantation was located. In Saint-Marc, leading free people of color agreed to accept occupation as long as the British maintained racial equality, but in the face of the betrayal of this promise they joined the forces of Louverture.[44] In the fall of that year, Louverture's forces repeatedly attacked and burned Saint-Marc.[45] Sometime between 1793 and 1798 St. Macary fled, like so many whites who had made their homes in Saint-Domingue, although it is unclear if he sought to escape the British, the rebelling slaves, or the dominance of free people of color in Saint-Marc.[46] He joined the flood of nearly 45,000 refugees, white and people of color, free and slave, who had left the colony, and made his way to the slavery-friendly city of Baltimore.[47] His penultimate letter to the Belin heirs, dated 24 March 1798, resigned his position as procureur of the plantation. He had not been able to communicate or give any orders regarding it for four years, although a person of his acquaintance had recently passed by and sent him a report that he passed along to his employers.[48]

Of more than two hundred slaves at the height of the plantation's productivity, one hundred twenty-four reputedly still remained, a vivid testament to the few options available to formerly enslaved people in Saint-Domingue, and to the success of the British in restoring slavery under their occupation.[49] Although St. Macary offered "to have a person in whom I have confidence pass by the place" if the heirs sent him a new power of attorney, he expressed the view that "it will be impossible to ever retake the colony."[50] St. Macary's final letter, written two months later, strikes a much more hopeful note: the French forces were pushing back the British at last, and with the proper documentation loyal citizens of the Republic might reclaim their property. He urged the Belin heirs to send him the necessary paperwork with due haste as "my project is to get myself there promptly as I can so I can take up my affairs again."[51]

In the end, after all the changes St. Macary witnessed and even after acknowledging the political subjectivity of free people of color, some of whom had been slaves, he still conceived Saint-Domingue as a profit center, a place where whites benefited from the labor of people of color. The French government also continued to treat Saint-Domingue as a resource and, as with slaves in France, prioritized private property over liberty when it offered reparations to former plantation owners in 1825 once it finally acknowledged the loss of the colony. The Belin heirs cashed in on this opportunity: their plantation was valued at 54,818.23 francs, the costliest in the entire parish of Saint-Marc.[52] Belin's heirs remained among the wealthiest citizens of La Rochelle, while the reparations that bolstered their affluence crippled Haiti's economy.

Although Belin's heirs continued to prosper in La Rochelle, the French and Haitian Revolutions severely disrupted transatlantic commerce and brought economic hardship. By 1792, trade with the Antilles had basically stopped. In the wake of this economic shutdown, several of the city's most important and wealthiest families declared bankruptcy, including the mayor Daniel Garasché, whose family had major merchant houses in Le Cap and Port-au-Prince. Things went from bad to worse when England, Holland, Spain, and Portugal entered the war against France, disrupting La Rochelle's trade with Northern Europe as well. By the time Napoleon took power in 1799, Rochelais commerce was basically dead.[53]

Yet in spite of the rupturing of long-held transatlantic ties, prominent residents of the port continued to support slavery. As soon as the French Revolution began, Rochelais with connections to Saint-Domingue founded the pro-slavery Franco-American Society and began correspondence with the Club Massiac in Paris.[54] The La Rochelle society soon became the club's most ardent affiliate.[55] This nationwide bloc of slave owners did not always present a united front, though, and the Franco-American Society continued the nuanced approach to race born of personal experience that had long been characteristic in La Rochelle. They broke with the Club Massiac in urging that free people of color be accorded representation in colonial assemblies.[56] "You do not know," said a letter from the Franco-American Society to the Club Massiac, "that free people of color are the strength of the colony. It is good politics to attach them to it."[57] Aimé-Paul Fleuriau de Touchelonge, elder legitimate son of Rochelais merchant Aimé-Benjamin Fleuriau, elaborated on this sentiment. He wrote, "We are no longer able to refuse [to give free people of color rights]; the request seems perfectly just. In the eyes of reason, of humanity, and of every créole whose own interest does not absolutely blind him, it is an absolute necessity to have all the class of people of color on our side if we do not want to see them the leaders of the rebellion of the blacks [*noirs*]."[58] This point of view makes clear the prevalence of economic self-interest above a commitment to racial equality, yet it does affirm that personal knowledge of and experience with colonial life shaped the approach of the Rochelais in contrast to other pro-slavery merchants. After all, Fleuriau de Touchelonge had long maintained a relationship with his mixed-race half-siblings, children of his father and his father's onetime slave.[59]

In breaking with Paris, the Rochelais members of the Franco-American Society agreed with colonists that Parisian-based deputies to the National Assembly knew nothing "of the climate or the regime of the colonies."[60] The decades-old relationships that bound port town and colony were severely shaken, however, when colonial secession came to seem possible, particularly with the creation of a separate Colonial Assembly. Rochelais finally began to realize that their own interests did not necessarily align with those of the residents of Saint-Domingue.

With the National Assembly's decision to open ports in Saint-Domingue to foreign ships on 20 July 1790, the welfare of colonists and Rochelais traders definitively split. The lifeblood of La Rochelle depended on protected trade with the colonies, while colonists eagerly sought opportunities to trade with ships flying any flag, not just French colors. The Rochelais merchants sought frantically to protect their livelihood by endorsing a mercantilist approach to the National Assembly decades after such a trade-based strategy had fallen out of favor. Commerce, the merchants desperately emphasized in a petition, made nations great: "[commerce] will always be great, always useful. It will constantly be the origin of good fortune, glory and the force of nations that welcome and encourage it." Colonial commerce had a particularly indispens-able role, for many Frenchmen "[do] not subsist except on colonial com-merce."[61] Certainly many Rochelais did not subsist except on colonial commerce, and the virtual cessation of transatlantic trade during the Revolu-tion, coupled with the subsequent independence of Haiti and the loss of cap-ital and income entailed for plantation owners, crippled the city.[62] In the confusion of the Revolutions, ships were lost, papers burned, and debts, es-pecially those incurred an ocean away, were increasingly difficult to collect. People of color continued to live and work in La Rochelle. But with the rup-ture of its residents' personal and commercial bonds with Saint-Domingue, whites had little reason to argue for their inclusion in a new France where all citizens were assumed to be white.

The final episode in this French Atlantic story reveals the continuities and changes in race as a social and legal category during and after the Haitian Revolution. On 20 May 1802, Napoleon reestablished slavery in France's col-onies. This had deep consequences for people of color in the metropole and for emerging understandings of what it meant to be French. Subsequent leg-islation also delineated people of color as a separate, legally bounded cate-gory. That July, a law barred people of color from entering France.[63] The next year, a ministerial decree banned marriage between whites and people of color.[64] In 1807, another decree mandated the registration of all people of color in France, a measure redolent of the 1777 Police des Noirs.[65]

Yet numerous people of color continued to live in France. Some, of course, had been there for years. During the Revolution, some made their way as refugees alone or in the company of whites. A number of free colored soldiers who had fought in Saint-Domingue also found themselves in the metropole, some prisoners of war released by the English, others ordered to France by Napoleon, who wanted to keep a close eye on "all who would be capable of resisting the establishment of a uniform regime."[66] Not wanting this thousand-strong contingent of free men of color with military experi-ence running freely about France, the emperor ordered them to depots estab-lished on coastal islands: close enough to keep an eye on them, isolated enough to contain them. Notably, these men of color were held on the Île d'Aix and the Île d'Oléron, sandy barrier islands off the coast of La Rochelle.[67]

Three of these men, Gautras, Letellier, and Garnard, all had fought under André Rigaud in Saint-Domingue. By the end of 1798, all three were interned on the Île d'Oléron, without money or pay, unable to return home. They wrote a letter to the Minister of War protesting their treatment. Their appeal relied not on personal connections, but rather on their service as soldiers and citizens:

> Men of color, we have constantly served the French Republic and the government with zeal, courage, and, we dare to say, with distinction. . . . The immense sacrifices we have made for the triumph of the French Republic, the blood we have so often spilled in combat for her, and the unfortunate position in which we now find ourselves gives us some rights to justice and to the benevolence of those who, like you, have served with so much success and glory, and allows us to hope that you will give prompt orders to allow us to be paid that which is due to us until the present time.

In this, they positioned themselves as equal to other citizens, yet they also painted a picture of pathos: "You will feel with us, Citizen Minister, how terrible our position must be, in a country where we are deprived of all acquaintance and means of existence."[68] Their status as citizen-soldiers prompted their imprisonment and shaped their plea for release. This early example suggests how "citizen of color" became a contradiction in terms in the nineteenth century, as France increasingly became defined as white. It also shows that revolution created new, gendered ways for men of color to define themselves as citizens.[69] Intimacy was no longer a fundamental method for defining or changing an individual's position, as it had been in the Old Regime.

Intimate relationships are part of the history of race in France. Close contact of multiple sorts between whites and people of color, while shaped by domination, brought broad understanding of the range of roles and positions of individuals of different racial backgrounds in the French empire. "Race" had contested, constructed, and shifting meanings, and examining intimacies reveals how individuals and families understood and experienced it as a social, cultural, and legal construct. Even in an era of growing racial stratification, people creatively adapted to and resisted the barriers being erected around them. Gendered notions of the patriarchal family were at the heart of justifications for slavery, and also formed the core of resistance to racial ideologies. This meant that common masculinity facilitated bonds across race, as mixed race children demanded that white fathers live up to patriarchal ideals, and men of color held up their own status as husbands and fathers to demonstrate their independence and belonging.

Within this discourse women of color had less recourse to claim independence, yet they could still appeal to gendered ideals of femininity in efforts to create room for themselves in the face of heightened legal restrictions. Colonialism could even, on occasion, open up opportunities for white women's economic participation. Concentrating on families and households reorients thinking about race in the French Atlantic and illuminates the process by which race ultimately did—or did not—become a constitutive category.

NOTES

Introduction. Interracial Intimacy in the French Atlantic

1. Dominique Rogers puts the population of Saint-Domingue in 1771 at 18,418 whites, 6,180 free people of color, and 219,698 slaves. Dominique Rogers, "Les libres de couleur dans les capitales de Saint-Domingue: Fortune, mentalités et intégration à la fin de l'Ancien Régime" (dissertation, Université Michel de Montaigne, Bordeaux III, 1999), 66; she references G1/509/30, ANOM. Historians generally agree that in the eighteenth century there were 4,000–5,000 slaves in France, based on estimates published by the *Causes célèbres*, which put the number at 4,000 in 1738. François Gayot de Pitaval, *Causes célèbres et intéressantes avec les jugemens qui les ont décidées*, 20 vols. (Paris: G. Cavelier, 1734–1754), 13: 537. See Shelby Thomas McCloy, *The Negro in France* (Lexington: University of Kentucky Press, 1961), 5; Léo Elisabeth, "The French Antilles," in *Neither Slave Nor Free: The Freedman of African Descent in the Slave Societies of the New World*, ed. David W. Cohen and Jack P. Greene (Baltimore: Johns Hopkins University Press, 1972), 134–71, 158–59; Pierre Pluchon, *Nègres et juifs au XVIIIe siècle: Le racisme au siècle des Lumières* (Paris: Tallandier, 1984), 148; Sue Peabody, *"There Are No Slaves in France: The Political Culture of Race and Slavery in the Ancien Régime* (New York: Oxford University Press, 1996), 5. Pierre Boulle has identified 2,329 people of color, slaves and free, who were living in France and were counted in the 1777 Police des Noirs survey, but he acknowledges that this number is incomplete and accepts 5,000 as the estimated population. He also says that people of color in Paris, especially those belonging to members of the aristocracy, were likely to have been undercounted. Pierre H. Boulle, *Race et esclavage dans la France de l'Ancien Régime* (Paris: Perrin, 2007), 109, 126. Relying on official slave registers, Noël identifies 4,284 individuals who were registered as slaves in Paris, Nantes, La Rochelle, and Bordeaux from 1717 to 1791, 680 of whom appeared in records in La Rochelle; this figure does not include free people of color. Erick Noël, *Être noir en France au XVIIIe siècle* (Paris: Tallandier, 2006), Document 11, 281. Dwain Pruitt argues that the number of slaves in France was actually much higher than these registers show. Dwain Pruitt, "'The Opposition of the Law to the Law': Race, Slavery, and the Law in Nantes, 1715–1778," *French Historical Studies* 30, 2 (2007), especially 169–74. Brett Rushforth says that parish registers are the most reliable source for actual numbers of slaves in New France, although the slave population was in fact much higher than registers implied. Brett Rushforth, *Bonds of Alliance: Indigenous and Atlantic Slaveries in New France* (Chapel Hill: University of North Carolina Press, 2012), 291–92. My own research accords with the idea that slaves and free people of color were undercounted in official documents.

2. 2 August 1755, "Registre de la Majesté commencé le 23 mars 1753 et fini le 14 avril 1757," B 6086, ADCM. The declaration recording his arrival classified him as "of the Banguia nation," a

rare ethnic attribution among slaves in Saint-Domingue. See David Geggus, "Sugar and Coffee Cultivation in Saint-Domingue and the Shaping of the Slave Labor Force," in *Cultivation and Culture: Labor and the Shaping of Slave Life in the Americas*, ed. Ira Berlin and Philip Morgan (Charlottesville: University of Virginia Press, 1993) 73–98, 81.

3. Paul Lovejoy, *Transformations in Slavery: A History of Slavery in Africa* (Cambridge: Cambridge University Press, 1983), 6–8.

4. Suzanne Miers and Igor Kopytoff, eds., *Slavery in Africa: Historical and Anthropological Perspectives* (Madison: University of Wisconsin Press, 1977), 17–19.

5. By 1777, the earliest year for which figures are available, Hardy's owner Aimé-Benjamin Fleuriau owned 244 slaves on his plantation. Jacques de Cauna, *Au temps des isles à sucre: Histoire d'une plantation de Saint-Domingue au XVIIIe siècle* (Paris: Karthala, 2003), 97.

6. 6 August 1755, "Registre de la Majesté commencé le 23 mars 1753 et fini le 14 avril 1757," B 6086, ADCM.

7. Jean Marie Renaud, 11 December 1753, parish records, Sainte-Rose, Léogane, 85MIOM/83, ANOM; Marie-Severin-Augustin Regnaud, 25 October 1755, parish records, Saint-Barthélémy, GG 276, AMLR.

8. Hardy, 19 August 1771, parish records, Saint-Barthélémy, GG 309, AMLR.

9. 16 September 1751, "Registre de la Majesté commencé le 22 janvier 1751 et fini le 21 mars 1753," B229, ADCM; "Passagers embarqués en France," 1753, Colonies F 5B 57, ANOM.

10. John Garrigus, *Before Haiti: Race and Citizenship in French Saint-Domingue* (New York: Palgrave Macmillan, 2006), 40.

11. Clare Robertson and Martin Klein, "Women's Importance in African Slave Systems," in Robertson and Klein, eds., *Women and Slavery in Africa* (Madison: University of Wisconsin Press, 1983), 3–25, 8–11.

12. On Champlain's baptism, see Thomas Brosset, "Samuel Champlain, le fondateur de Québec, avait été baptisé à La Rochelle," *Sud-Ouest*, April 13, 2012.

13. John Clark, *La Rochelle and the Atlantic Economy During the Eighteenth Century* (Baltimore: Johns Hopkins University Press, 1981), 21.

14. Ibid., chap. 2.

15. On the Parlement of Paris' jurisdiction in the eighteenth century, see J. H. Shennan, *The Parlement of Paris* (Ithaca, N.Y.: Cornell University Press, 1968), 78. This text also provides excellent background on the Parlement of Paris and information on its changing structure and function. On the Parlements generally, also see James D. Hardy, *Judicial Politics in the Old Regime: The Parlement of Paris During the Regency* (Baton Rouge: Louisiana State University Press, 1967); Bailey Stone, *The Parlement of Paris, 1774–1789* (Chapel Hill: University of North Carolina Press, 1981); Bailey Stone, *The French Parlements and the Crisis of the Old Regime* (Chapel Hill: University of North Carolina Press, 1986).

16. Peabody, *"There Are No Slaves in France"*, 49. Several other Parlements also failed to register these laws, including the Parlements of Toulouse, Pau, and Douai. Isambert, Decrusy, and Taillandier, *Recueil général des anciennes lois françaises, depuis l'an 420 jusqu'à la Révolution de 1789*, 29 vols. (Paris: Belin-Leprieur, 1830), 21: 122.

17. Bertrand Van Ruymbeke, "Introduction," in *Memory and Identity: The Huguenots in France and the Atlantic Diaspora*, ed. Bertrand Van Ruymbeke and Randy Sparks (Columbia: University of South Carolina Press, 2003), 1–25, 6. Van Ruymbeke also points to La Rochelle's particular prominence in this diaspora because of the predominance of Protestant merchants in the city, 13.

18. Carolyn Chappell Lougee, "Cross Purposes: The Intendant of La Rochelle and Protestant Policy at the Revocation," in *Tocqueville and Beyond: Essays on the Old Regime in Honor of David D. Bien*, ed. Robert M. Schwartz and Robert A. Schneider (Newark: University of Delaware Press, 2003). Nicole Vray calculates that about 550 members of merchant families left La Rochelle during the Refuge. Nicole Vray, *La Rochelle et les protestants du XVIe au XXe siècle* (La Crèche: Geste, 1999), 161.

19. Gérard Lafleur and Lucien Abénon, "The Protestants and the Colonization of the French West Indies," in *Memory and Identity*, 267–84, 268–69, table 1, 284; Jacques de Cauna, *L'Eldorado des Aquitains: Gascons, Basques et Béarnais aux Îles d'Amérique (XVIIe–XVIIIe siècles)* (Biarritz: Atlantica, 1998), 97, 34–38.

20. Nicole Vray identified thirty-eight Protestant groups in La Rochelle that met regularly by 1764, some with more than fifty participants, in spite of the fact that such groups were made expressly illegal by Article II of the Revocation of the Edict of Nantes, 22 October 1685. Vray, *La Rochelle et les protestants*, 171.

21. Clark, *La Rochelle and the Atlantic Economy*, 50.

22. Lafleur and Abénon, "The Protestants and the Colonization of the French West Indies," 272.

23. Cauna, *Eldorado des Aquitains*, 110. According to Cauna, more than six hundred ships departed La Rochelle for the Antilles between 1673 and 1695.

24. Sugar consumption during the eighteenth century increased from twenty-five million pounds per year in 1730 to eighty-four million pounds per year in 1770. After 1770 consumption fell because of the economic crisis in France. Robert Louis Stein, *The French Sugar Business in the Eighteenth Century* (Baton Rouge: Louisiana State University Press, 1988), 101.

25. Claude Laveau, *Le monde rochelais des Bourbons à Bonaparte* (La Rochelle: Rumeur des Ages, 1988), 87.

26. Cauna, *Eldorado des Aquitains*, 13. Also see Gabriel Debien, *Le peuplement des Antilles françaises au XVIIe siècle: Les engagés partis de La Rochelle* (Cairo: Institut Français d'Archéologie Orientale du Caire, 1942).

27. On Saint-Marc, Port-au-Prince, and Léogane as centers for people from the southwest of France, see Cauna, *Eldorado des Aquitains*, 323–24, 326–27, 327.

28. The Garasché family had a merchant house in Cap Français; the Roderigue family had property in New Orleans; closer to the end of the eighteenth century the Van Hoogwerff family owned a plantation in Cayenne. On the quartier Morin, near Cap Français, as an enclave of migrants from the southwest of France, see Cauna, *Eldorado des Aquitains*, 295–98. There was also a canton named Rochelais near Fond des Nègres in the South Province that presumably was a Rochelais enclave.

29. Cauna's sample focuses on indentured servants. On the possible religious nature of migration at the end of the seventeenth century, see Debien, *Les engagés partis de La Rochelle*, 53–58.

30. Cauna, *Eldorado des aquitains*, 126–27.

31. Ibid., 130–31.

32. Gabriel Debien, *Études antillaises (XVIIIe siècle)* (Paris: Librairie Armand Colin, 1956), 34.

33. Rogers, "Les libres de couleur," 53; Médéric-Louis-Elie Moreau de Saint-Méry, *La description topographique, physique, civile, politique et historique de la partie française de Saint-Domingue*, 3rd ed., 3 vols. (Saint-Denis: Société Française d'Histoire d'Outre-mer, 2004), 2: 1053.

34. Moreau de Saint-Méry, *La description . . .*, 2: 787–902, esp. 811–19, 74–885, 91.

35. Ibid., 885.

36. Ibid., 1096, 1096–1106.

37. Moreau de Saint-Méry, *La description* . . . , 2: 958, 969. Also see Stewart King, *Blue Coat or Powdered Wig: Free People of Color in Pre-Revolutionary Saint-Domingue* (Athens: University of Georgia Press, 2001), esp. 276.

38. King, *Blue Coat or Powdered Wig*, 37.

39. Rogers, "Les libres de couleur," 9.

40. Moreau de Saint-Méry, *La description* . . . , 2: 722–23.

41. Garrigus, *Before Haiti*, 32.

42. David Geggus, "Urban Development in Eighteenth-Century Saint-Domingue," *Bulletin du Centre d'Histoire des Espaces Atlantiques* 5 (1990), 197–228, 211.

43. "Intime," in *Encyclopédie: ou dictionnaire raisonné des arts et des métiers, etc.*, ed. Denis Diderot and Jean le Rond d'Alembert (Paris: Chez Briasson, David, le Breton, Durand, 1751–1765), 8: 842.

44. Roger Chartier, *A History of Private Life*, building on histories of *mentalités* by Philippe Ariès and others, laid out a broadly conceived private sphere as a topic worthy of historical investigation. In doing so, the volume frequently equated privacy with interiority and suggested a growing divide between public and private. Roger Chartier, ed., *History of Private Life*, vol. 3, *Passions of the Renaissance*, trans. Arthur Goldhammer (Cambridge, Mass.: Belknap Press of Harvard University Press, 1989). In the Introduction, Philippe Ariès draws a clean line between the "precarious intimacy" of the medieval period and the "privacy" that emerged during the nineteenth century, where "work, leisure, and home life are separate, compartmentalized activities" (1–2). Also see, for example, Annik Pardailhé-Galabrun, *The Birth of Intimacy: Privacy and Domestic Life in Early Modern Paris* (Philadelphia: University of Pennsylvania Press, 1991).

45. Sarah Hanley, "Engendering the State: Family Formation and State Building in Early Modern France," *French Historical Studies* 16, 1 (1989); Lynn Avery Hunt, *The Family Romance of the French Revolution* (Berkeley: University of California Press, 1992); Sarah Maza, *Private Lives and Public Affairs: The Causes Célèbres of Prerevolutionary France* (Berkeley: University of California Press, 1993); Jennifer Ngaire Heuer, *The Family and the Nation: Gender and Citizenship in Revolutionary France, 1789–1830* (Ithaca, N.Y.: Cornell University Press, 2005).

46. See, for example, Ann Stoler, *Carnal Knowledge and Imperial Power: Race and the Intimate in Colonial Rule* (Berkeley: University of California Press, 2002); Elisa Camiscioli, *Reproducing the French Race: Immigration, Intimacy, and Embodiment in the Early Twentieth Century* (Durham, N.C.: Duke University Press, 2009), 2–4; Eliza Ferguson, *Violence, Intimacy, and Community in Fin-de-Siècle Paris* (Baltimore: Johns Hopkins University Press, 2009). Emma Rothschild insists on the continuity between public and private in *The Inner Life of Empires: An Eighteenth-Century History* (Princeton, N.J.: Princeton University Press, 2011), 2.

47. Maza, *Private Lives and Public Affairs*, 89–92, 187; Norbert Elias, *The Court Society*, trans. Edmund Jephcott (Oxford: Blackwell, 1983), 117.

48. Sarah Maza, *Servants and Masters in Eighteenth-Century France: The Uses of Loyalty* (Princeton, N.J.: Princeton University Press, 1983), 71.

49. See Daryl Hafter and Nina Kushner, eds., *Women and Work in Eighteenth-Century France*, (Baton Rouge: Louisiana State University Press, 2015); Hannah Williams, "Academic Intimacies: Portraits of Family, Friendship, and Rivalry at the Académie Royale," *Art History* 36, 2 (April 2013): 338–65.

50. Dena Goodman, *The Republic of Letters: A Cultural History of the French Enlightenment*

(Ithaca, N.Y.: Cornell University Press, 1994); Bruce Redford, *The Converse of the Pen: Acts of Intimacy in the Eighteenth-Century Familiar Letter* (Chicago: University of Chicago Press, 1986); Heidi Bostic, "Graffigny's Self, Graffigny's Friend: Intimate Sharing in the *Correspondence* 1750–1752, *Studies in Eighteenth-Century Culture* 42 (2014): 215–36.

51. Clark, *La Rochelle and the Atlantic Economy*, 79. An example of this practice of combining household and business accounts are the "Comptes domestiques de les familles Charruyer, Dupont," MS 1921 and MS 1922, Médiathèque de La Rochelle.

52. Jennifer Morgan, *Laboring Women: Reproduction and Gender in New World Slavery* (Philadelphia: University of Pennsylvania Press, 2004), esp. chap. 3.

53. Philippe Ariès, *Centuries of Childhood: A Social History of Family Life*, trans. Robert Baldick (New York: Vintage, 1962); Edward Shorter, "Illegitimacy, Sexual Revolution, and Social Change in Modern Europe," *Journal of Interdisciplinary History* 2, 2 (1971); Lawrence Stone, *The Family, Sex, and Marriage in England, 1500–1800* (New York: Harper and Row, 1979). On affection within the family, see François Lebrun, *La vie conjugale sous l'ancien régime* (Paris: Librarie Armand Colin, 1975); James F. Traer, *Marriage and the Family in Eighteenth-Century France* (Ithaca, N.Y.: Cornell University Press, 1980); Robert Wheaton and Tamara K. Hareven, eds., *Family and Sexuality in French History* (Philadelphia: University of Pennsylvania Press, 1980).

54. Ann Laura Stoler, "Tense and Tender Ties: The Politics of Comparison in North American History and (Post) Colonial Studies," *Journal of American History* 88, 3 (December 2001): 829–65. Also see Stoler, *Carnal Knowledge and Imperial Power*.

55. See, for example, Nancy van Deusen, "The Intimacies of Bondage: Female Indigenous Servants and Slaves and Their Spanish Masters, 1492–1555," *Journal of Women's History* 24, 1 (Spring 2012): 13–43; Catherine Linton and Michele Gillespie, eds., *The Devil's Lane: Sex and Race in the Early South* (New York: Oxford University Press, 1997); Martha Hodes, ed., *Sex, Love, Race: Crossing Boundaries in North American History* (New York: New York University Press, 1999).

56. See the special issue of *Critical Inquiry* on "Intimacy," 24, 2 (Winter 1998), esp. Lauren Berlant, "Intimacy: A Special Issue," 281–88.

57. Lara Putnam, "To Study the Fragments/Whole: Microhistory and the Atlantic World," *Journal of Social History* 33, 3 (Spring 2006): 615–30, 616. Also see Rebecca Scott and Jean Hébrard, *Freedom Papers: An Atlantic Odyssey in the Age of Emancipation* (Cambridge, Mass.: Harvard University Press, 2012); Linda Colley, *The Ordeal of Elizabeth Marsh: A Woman in World History* (Now York: Pantheon, 2007); Robert Harms, *The Diligent: A Voyage Through the Worlds of the Slave Trade* (New York: Basic, 2002).

58. Doris Garraway, *The Libertine Colony: Creolization in the Early French Caribbean* (Durham, N.C.: Duke University Press, 2005), 260–75, esp. 261; Joan Dayan, *Haiti, History, and the Gods* (Berkeley: University of California Press, 1995), 229–37. For Moreau's taxonomy, see *La description . . .* , 1: 86–100. Moreau elaborates on a taxonomy laid out by Michel René Hilliard d'Aubertenil, *Considérations sur l'état présent de la colonie française de Saint-Domingue* (Paris: Chez Grangé, 1776), 2: 83.

59. Moreau de Saint-Méry, *La description . . .* , 1: 83.

60. As excellent examples of how these categories have shaped boundaries of scholarship, see recent scholarship on the social history of free people of color in Saint-Domingue: King, *Blue Coat or Powdered Wig*; Garrigus, *Before Haiti*; Rogers, "Les libres de couleur," 443–53.

61. Moreau de Saint-Méry, *La description . . .* , 1: 29.

62. William Cohen, *The French Encounter with Africans: White Response to Blacks,*

1530–1880 (Bloomington: Indiana University Press, 1980), esp. chap. 1; Yvan Debbasch, *Couleur et liberté: Le jeu du critère ethnique dans un ordre juridique esclavagiste* (Paris: Dalloz, 1967). Also see Sue Peabody, "'A Nation Born to Slavery': Missionaries and Racial Discourse in Seventeenth-Century French Antilles." *Journal of Social History* 38, 1 (2004), 113–26, esp. 113–14; Pierre H. Boulle, "François Bernier and the Origins of the Modern Concept of Race," in *The Color of Liberty: Histories of Race in France*, ed. Sue Peabody and Tyler Stovall (Durham, N.C.: Duke University Press, 2003), 11–27, 12; Guillaume Aubert, "'The Blood of France': Race and Purity of Blood in the French Atlantic World," *William and Mary Quarterly* 61, 3 (2004): 439–78, esp. 441–42; Pierre H. Boulle, *Race et esclavage*, chaps. 1–3; and Pierre H. Boulle, "'In Defense of Slavery': Eighteenth-Century Opposition to Abolition and the Origins of Racist Ideology in France," in *History from Below: Studies in Popular Protest and Popular Ideology*, ed. Frederick Krantz (Montreal: Concordia University, 1985), 221–41. A special issue of *William and Mary Quarterly* on "Constructing Race: Differentiating Peoples in the Early Modern World" also focused on pre-eighteenth-century racial ideas, although it did not include any articles on France or its empire. *William and Mary Quarterly* 3rd ser. 14, 1 (January 1997).

63. See, for example, Gwendolyn Midlo Hall, *Social Control in Slave Plantation Societies: A Comparison of St. Domingue and Cuba* (Baltimore: Johns Hopkins University Press, 1971). John Garrigus adheres to this chronology, although he attributes the shift to a switch from viewing race as a social category to a biological one, brought about by the restructuring of empire in the wake of the Seven Years' War. Garrigus, *Before Haiti*, 8. This chronology has been widely accepted beyond the French context as well, and historians generally identify the 1760s as marking a shift toward scientific racism. One recent summary is George Frederickson, *Racism: A Short History* (Princeton, N.J.: Princeton University Press, 2002); Frederickson differentiates between "implicit racism," which he dates to the seventeenth century, and "explicit racism," which he claims emerged in the eighteenth and nineteenth centuries. Also see George Frederickson, "Toward a Social Interpretation of the Development of American Racism," in, *Key Issues in the Afro-American Experience*, ed. Nathan Huggins, Martin Kilson, and Daniel Fox, 2 vols. (Harcourt Brace Jovanovich: New York, 1971), 1: 240–54. This chronology has become so entrenched that Sue Peabody critiques it as a "truism," Peabody, "'A Nation Born to Slavery,'" 113. In France, Pierre Boulle dates the hardening of racial policies to the mid-eighteenth century, and claims they were driven by the metropolitan influence of colonial planters. Boulle, *Race et esclavage*, 73–79. Erick Noël pushes the change to even later, claiming that in the writings of the philosophes "the concept of racism had not yet really emerged." Noël, *Être noir en France au XVIIIe siècle*, chap. 2, 29, 34, 25, 27. For a countervailing view on the racism of the philosophes, see Emmanuel Chukwudi Eze, *Race and the Enlightenment: A Reader* (Cambridge, Mass.: Blackwell, 1997). Christopher Miller concisely summarizes the reluctance of the French to come to terms with histories of racism and slavery in the Preface to *The French Atlantic Triangle: Literature and Culture of the Slave Trade* (Durham, N.C.: Duke University Press, 2008).

64. Rogers, "Les libres de couleur," chap. 4; see also Robert Taber, "The Issue of Their Union: Family, Law, and Politics in Western Saint-Domingue, 1777 to 1789" (dissertation, University of Florida, 2015).

65. Foundational texts that claim that racism predates slavery include Winthrop Jordan, *White over Black: American Attitudes Toward the Negro, 1550–1812* (Chapel Hill: University of North Carolina Press: 1968); William Cohen, *The French Encounter with Africans*. The opposite point of view is expressed by Edmund Morgan, *American Slavery, American Freedom: The Ordeal of Colonial Virginia* (New York: Norton, 1975).

Chapter 1. Proximity and Distance in Plantation Society

1. "Testament, M. Belin des Marais," 25 January 1769, E 294, ADCM. On servants' salaries, see Sarah Maza, *Servants and Masters in Eighteenth-Century France: The Uses of Loyalty* (Princeton, N.J.: Princeton University Press, 1983), 79–81.

2. On patron-client relationships, see Roland Mousnier, *Les institutions de la France sous la monarchie absolue*, 2 vols. (Paris: Presses Universitaires de France, 1974). Later Lawrence Stone, Sharon Kettering, and William Beik all argued that in the seventeenth century, in particular, relationships of patronage and clientage were based primarily on self-interest. Lawrence Stone, *The Family, Sex, and Marriage in England, 1500–1800* (New York: Harper and Row, 1979); Sharon Kettering, *Patrons, Brokers, and Clients in Seventeenth-Century France* (New York: Oxford University Press, 1986); and William Beik, *Absolutism and Society in Seventeenth-Century France: State Power and Provincial Aristocracy in Languedoc* (New York: Cambridge University Press, 1985). Jonathan Dewald, on the other hand, places affective ties firmly at the center of such patron-client relationships. Jonathan Dewald, *Aristocratic Experience and the Origins of Modern Culture: France, 1570–1715* (Berkeley: University of California Press, 1993), esp. chap. 4.

3. On the plantation synthesis of "field" and "factory," see Sidney Mintz, *Sweetness and Power: The Place of Sugar in Modern History* (New York: Viking, 1985); also David Geggus, "Sugar and Coffee Cultivation in Saint-Domingue and the Shaping of the Slave Labor Force," in *Cultivation and Culture: Labor and the Shaping of Slave Life in the Americas*, ed. Ira Berlin and Philip Morgan (Charlottesville: University of Virginia Press, 1993), 73–98. On movements toward industrialization in France, see William Sewell, "The Empire of Fashion and the Rise of Capitalism in Eighteenth-Century France," *Past & Present* 206 (2010): 81–120. On how commercial capitalism challenged the social order, see Sewell, "Connecting Capitalism to the French Revolution: The Parisian Promenade and the Origins of Civic Equality in Eighteenth-Century France," *Critical Historical Studies* 1, 1 (2014): 5–46.

4. Michelle Miller has argued for the importance of hierarchical friendship as emblematic of a growing appreciation of difference. Michelle L. Miller, "Material Friendship: Service and Amity in Early Modern French Literature" (dissertation, University of Michigan, 2008).

5. Dominique Rogers, "Les libres de couleur dans les capitales de Saint-Domingue: Fortune, mentalités et intégration à la fin de l'ancien régime" (dissertation, Université Michel de Montaigne, Bordeaux III, 1999), 443–53.

6. There are no reliable figures for absenteeism in the French Caribbean in the eighteenth century, although historians agree that absenteeism was very high in Saint-Domingue and was on the rise by the end of the eighteenth century. In the seventeenth century, about 50 percent of those who set out for the colonies from France remained there; the rest either returned to France or died. Philip P. Boucher, *France and the American Tropics to 1700: Tropics of Discontent?* (Baltimore: Johns Hopkins University Press, 2008), 10. Also see David Eltis, *The Rise of African Slavery in the Americas* (Cambridge: Cambridge University Press, 2000), 9, table 1–1. Carolyn Fick agrees that at the end of the eighteenth century most colonists envisioned themselves returning to France, and suggests that more than 50 percent of landowners did not live in the colony. Carolyn Fick, *The Making of Haiti: The Saint Domingue Revolution from Below* (Knoxville: University of Tennessee Press, 1990), 16. Pierre de Vaissière makes the same argument, drawing from published primary sources that express colonists' deep desires to return to France. He claims that in 1752, only ten of the thirty-nine sugar plantations in Léogane were overseen by the owners themselves, and that the proportion was similar in Cul-de-Sac and

Petit-Goave. Pierre de Vaissière, *Saint-Domingue: La société et la vie créoles sous l'ancien régime (1629–1789)* (Paris: Perrin et Cie, 1909), 298–301. Malick Ghachem gives a good overview of available literature, and accepts that Saint-Domingue had "an unusually high rate of absentee plantation ownership." Malick Ghachem, *The Old Regime and the Haitian Revolution* (New York: Cambridge University Press, 2012), 157n103. Robin Blackburn says that absenteeism was "a little less extensive" in Saint-Domingue than in Jamaica, where he puts the rate at about 33 percent. Robin Blackburn, *The Making of New World Slavery: From the Baroque to the Modern, 1492–1800* (Stanford, Calif.: Stanford University Press, 1997), 431.

7. For the lettres-patentes of the Compagnie Royale de Saint-Domingue, see "Édit en forme de Lettres-Patentes pour l'établissement de la Compagnie Royale de Saint-Domingue," September 1698, in Médéric-Louis-Élie Moreau de Saint-Méry, *Loix et constitutions des colonies françaises de l'Amérique sous le vent*, 5 vols. (Paris, 1784–1790), 1: 610–18. Henri Teychenié mentions Ozée Belin's role as a director, Henri Teychenié, "L'habitation des Belin (membres de la famille Charruyer, armateurs rochelais) à Saint-Domingue, dans la deuxième moitié du XVIIIe siècle" (master's thesis, Université de Paris I, 1959), 5.

8. On the Huguenot Diaspora, see Jon Butler, *The Huguenots in America: A Refugee People in New World Society* (Cambridge, Mass.: Harvard University Press, 1983); Bertrand Van Ruymbeke, *From New Babylon to Eden: The Huguenots and Their Migration to Colonial South Carolina* (Columbia: University of South Carolina Press, 2006); Carolyn Lougee Chapell, "Family Bonds Across the Refuge," in *Memory and Identity: The Huguenots in France and the Atlantic Diaspora*, ed. Bertrand Van Ruymbeke and Randy J. Sparks (Columbia: University of South Carolina Press, 2003), 172–93.

9. Gérard LaFleur, *Les protestants aux Antilles françaises du vent sous l'ancien régime* (Basse-Terre: Société d'Histoire de la Guadeloupe, 1988), 84.

10. On Saint-Malo's role in the slave trade, see Alain Roman, *Saint-Malo au temps des négriers* (Paris: Karthala, 2001), 37–41.

11. "Billet d'Intérêts cédé à Monsieur Guillemaut de Beauleau le 12e Aoust 1722," E 297, ADCM.

12. Mutual Testament, Paul Belin and Françoise Guillemaut, 1722, E 294, ADCM.

13. G. Rouzier, 13 July 1728, E 297, ADCM. In a note signed by G. Rouzier, he refers to Demoiselle Françoise Guillemaut as the "femme procuratrice de Paul Belin Sieur de Marais." Also see Teychenié, "L'habitation des Belin," 13.

14. Henri Teychenié, "Les esclaves de l'indigoterie Belin à Saint-Domingue (1762–1793)," *Revista de Ciencias Sociales* 4, 1 (1960): 238–66, 237.

15. Étienne Belin received four *futailles* of indigo worth 7,012 livres 15 sols. Paul Belin des Marais to M.M.E. de la Vincendière and Gel. Bernard, merchants in Saint-Marc, 12 July 1768, E 298, ADCM. Later he received ten barrels of indigo. De la Vincendière and Gel. Berand to Belin des Marais, 15 October 1768, E 298, ADCM.

16. Bossinot de Bellissur to Belin des Marais, 19 May 1764, E 298, ADCM. Bossinot was married to Belin's niece.

17. These statistics apply to 1730–1731. Sue Peabody, "'A Dangerous Zeal': Catholic Missions to Slaves in the French Antilles, 1635–1800." *French Historical Studies* 25, 1 (2002): 53–90, table 3, 75. Allard Belin, Paul Belin's cousin, owned slaves in La Rochelle. The slaves Jean Naicré and Louis Mauré "belonging to Allard Belin, banker" were baptized in La Rochelle, 9 May 1719 and 1 September 1721, parish records, Saint-Barthélémy, GG 239 and GG 241, AMLR.

18. Association between Paul Belin des Marais and Pierre Paumier, Notary Compatris, 8

July 1734, ADCM. Paumier's will was made in his room on Belin's plantation and it dispenses Belin from having to pay him additional wages, implying he may have worked as Belin's overseer. "Testament de feu Pierre Paumier," 28 September 1733, E 295, ADCM.

19. On his death a few years later, the inventory of his estate shows that Paumier had very few assets. "Inventaire des Biens de défunt Pierre Paumier," 6 October 1735, E 295 ADCM.

20. When Paumier made his will in 1733, a year *before* he initially formed the partnership with Belin, he was already "possessed of bodily illness," although he considered himself "sound of spirit and judgment" and he knew exactly what he was doing when he made Paul Belin des Marais his universal legatee. This makes it likely that he made their later agreement knowing full well he was unwell, and anticipating the necessity of transferring his meager assets across the Atlantic. "Testament de feu Pierre Paumier," 28 September 1733, E 295, ADCM.

21. "Quittance consentie à Madame des Marais Belin par Anne Vincent légataire de Pierre Paumier son fils de la somme de 2000#," 3 October 1736, E 295, ADCM.

22. Belin des Marais to de la Vincendière, 6 February 1767, E 298, ADCM.

23. Paul Butel, *Histoire des Antilles françaises: XVIIe–XXe siècle* (Paris: Perrin, 2002), 91.

24. John Garrigus, *Before Haiti: Race and Citizenship in French Saint-Domingue* (New York: Palgrave Macmillan, 2006), 47–48.

25. On urban racial integration and the diversity of economic contributions of free people of color, see Rogers, "Les libres de couleur," 430–38 and 169–233.

26. "Code Noir," March 1685, Articles LV, LVII, and LIX, Moreau de Saint-Méry, *Loix et constitutions*, 1: 423–24.

27. Aubert, Guillaume. "'The Blood of France': Race and Purity of Blood in the French Atlantic World," *William and Mary Quarterly* 61, 3 (2004): 439–78, especially 460–66.

28. Peabody, "'A Dangerous Zeal,'" table 3, 75.

29. Garrigus, *Before Haiti*, 8.

30. "Ordonnances du Roi, concernant le Gouvernement Civil des Isles sous le Vent," 1 February 1766, Articles XXVII and XXXVII, reiterate that permission to free slaves must be received from the colonial Governor and the Intendant, 13–27; "Arrêt du Conseil du Cap, touchant l'Affranchissement des Esclaves," 28 January 1768, stipulates that owners must publish their intention to free slaves and provides for record keeping of all manumissions, 152–53; "Ordonnance du Roi, touchant le Gourvernement Civil," 22 May 1775 sets fees for manumission, Article XI, 577–587; "Ordonnance des Administrateurs, concernant les Libertés," 23 October 1775 again tries to regulate manumission, 610–13; all in Moreau de Saint-Méry, *Loix et constitutions*, vol. 5. Ghachem places this legislation in the context of a struggle between slave owners and royal officials over who had authority over the institution of slavery. Ghachem, *The Old Regime and the Haitian Revolution*, 82–96.

31. The "Liste des nègres, négresses, négrillons et négrittes mentionnés dans le procès verbale," written by Fougerais, 26 January 1762, E 295, ADCM, lists Alexis as a "commandeur de nation cotocoly, agé d'environ 55 ans." Although this is the first time Alexis appears in the archival record, this is also the first plantation report available for the Belin estate.

32. Belin des Marais to M. Payen, 14 June 1768, E 298, ADCM.

33. Belin des Marais to MM. de la Vincendière and Gel. Berard, 14 June 1768, E 298, ADCM.

34. Belin des Marais to M. Payen, 14 June 1768, E 298, ADCM.

35. Ibid.; Belin des Marais to MM. de la Vincendière and Gel. Berard, 14 June 1768, E 298, ADCM.

36. In 1762 Belin owned 159 slaves. "Liste des nègres, négresses, négrillons et négrittes," 1762,

E 295 ADCM. By 1790, the number of slaves attached to the plantation had grown to 205, and they were valued at 433,795 livres. "Inventaire général du mobilier composant l'habitation de messieurs les héritiers Belin des Marais," 2 June 1790, 4 J 2915, ADCM.

37. Belin des Marais to MM. de la Vincendière and Gel. Berard, 12 July 1768, E 298, ADCM.

38. Belin des Marais to MM. de la Vincendière and Gel. Berard, 16 August 1768, E 298, ADCM.

39. Cynthia Bouton, "Famine Within, Foodstuffs Without: The Politics of Provisioning in Revolutionary Saint-Domingue," paper presented at conference of the Association of Caribbean Historians, Fort-de-France, Martinique, 2014, cited with the permission of the author.

40. "Code Noir," March 1685, Articles XXII, XXIII, and XXIV, Moreau de Saint-Méry, *Loix et constitutions*, 1: 418.

41. Ibid., Article XXVI, 418–19.

42. Jean-Baptiste du Tertre, *Histoire générale des Antilles habitées par les François, devisée en deux tomes, et enrichi de Cartes & de Figures*, 4 vols. (Paris: Thomas Jolly, 1667), 2: 513.

43. Jean-Baptiste Labat, *Nouveau voyage aux isles de l'Amérique: contenant l'histoire naturelle de ces pays, l'origine, les mœurs, la religion & le gouvernement des habitans anciens & modernes. Les guerres & les évènemens singuliers que y sont arrivés pendant le long sejour que l'auteur y a fait: L commerce & les manufactures qui y sont établies, & les moyens de les augmenter: Avec une description exacte & curieuse de toutes ces isles. Ouvrage enrichi de plus de cent cartes, plans, figures en tailles-douces*, 6 vols. (Paris: P.F. Giffart, 1722), 5: 189.

44. Du Tertre, *Histoire générale des Antilles*, 2: 519. Moreau de Saint-Méry, writing at the end of the eighteenth century, does not mention this practice, although he does state the popularity of hunting wild boar. This is not unexpected, as Moreau offers very few observations of the daily life of slaves, focusing instead on the delineation of racial characteristics and descriptions of African-influenced celebrations. Moreau de Saint-Méry, *La description . . .* , 3: 1403. On festivals, particularly dancing and music, see 1: 63–70.

45. Belin des Marais to de la Vincendière, 22 November 1768, E 298, ADCM.

46. Bernard Moitt and Gabriel Debien both say that the slave driver, or commandeur, was the most valuable slave on the plantation, one who had a "stake in the system" because of his comparatively high status among slaves and his close working relationship with whites. Bernard Moitt, *Women and Slavery in the French Antilles, 1635–1848* (Bloomington: Indiana University Press, 2001), 40; Gabriel Debien, *Les esclaves aux Antilles françaises (XVIIe–XVIIIe siècles)* (Basse-Terre: Société d'Histoire de la Guadeloupe, 1974), 124.

47. De la Vincendiére and Gel. Berard to Belin des Marais, 15 October 1768, E 298, ADCM.

48. Ibid.

49. Ibid. In this circumstance, a levee refers to a raised ridge surrounding a field that is to be irrigated. These ridges would not normally be cultivated, and would be considered "waste land."

50. De la Vincendière and Gel. Berard to Belin des Marais, 21 November 1768, E 298 ADCM.

51. De la Vincendière and Gel. Berard to Belin des Marais, 15 October 1768, E 298 ADCM.

52. William E. Wiethoff, *Crafting the Overseer's Image* (Columbia: University of South Carolina Press, 2006), especially chaps. 2 and 4. Also see Michael Wayne, *Death of an Overseer: Reopening a Murder Investigation from the Plantation South* (New York: Oxford University Press, 2001); John Spencer Bassett, *The Southern Plantation Overseer as Revealed in His Letters* (Northhampton, Mass.: Smith College, 1925); William Scarbourough, *The Overseer: Plantation Management in the Old South* (Baton Rouge: Louisiana State University Press, 1966).

53. Belin des Marais to MM. de la Vincendière and Gel. Berard, 24 January 1769, E 298, ADCM.

54. Such measures included plans to require all free men of color to serve in the militia, the denial of honorific titles to free people of color while according them even to poor whites, a growing correlation between citizenship and whiteness, and a series of new racial laws starting in the 1770s. Garrigus, *Before Haiti*, 142, 47–48, 149–50, and chaps. 4 and 5.

55. Ghachem, *The Old Regime and the Haitian Revolution*, 139.

56. The term "renegade planters" is Ghachem's, introduced on 124.

57. "Succession Paul Belin, 8 aoust 1769," E 299, ADCM.

58. The plantation was valued at 54,818.23 francs. "Ministère des Finances-État Détaillé des Liquidations opérées à l'époque du 1er janvier 1830 par la commission chargée de répartir l'Indemnité attribuée aux anciens Colons de Saint-Domingue, en exécution de la Loi du 30 avril 1826 et conformément aux dispositions de l'Ordonnance du 9 mai suivant," 1829, Bibliothèque SOM D 64 1829, ANOM.

59. Pierre-Henry Seignette to Alexandre Ozée Quentin Hallays, 22 June 1769, in "Copie de lettres écrites de Paris relativement à la succession de M. Belin Desmarais," E 299, ADCM. Although this book of letters does not actually identify Pierre-Henry Seignette as the writer, contextual clues make him the only choice. He refers to his brother Paul-Louis Seignette Desmarais, who inherited their uncle's house; Pierre is the only other possible heir. In this I follow Teychenié, who also refers to a letter from "P.H. Seignette" to Hallays in this same series; this letter, dated June 1796, appears in this same book of letters. Teychenié, "L'habitation des Belin," 157. The document prepared by the notary Delavergne for Belin's heirs states that Hallays lived in "Cul [de Sac], on the Island and Coast of Saint-Domingue," 13 January 1772, E 299, ADCM.

60. Ghachem, *The Old Regime and the Haitian Revolution*, 156. Ghachem cites Gabriel Debien, *Les colons de Saint-Domingue et la Révolution: Essai sur le club Massiac (août 1789–août 1792)* (Paris: Librairie Armand Colin, 1953), 30–32.

61. Colonel Malenfant, *Des colonies, et particulièrement de celle de Saint-Domingue* (Paris: Chez Audibert, 1814), 206–207. Also see Debien, *Les esclaves aux Antilles*, 159.

62. *Le Veillon*, 29 January 1776, Passenger lists, Colonies F 5B 57, ANOM.

63. Pierre-Henry Seignette to Alexandre Ozée Quentin Hallays, 22 June 1769, in "Copie des lettres écrites de Paris relativement à la succession de M. Belin Desmarais," E 299, ADCM.

64. De la Vincendière and Berard to widow of Paul Belin des Marais, 22 September 1769, E 298, ADCM.

65. Procuration of coheirs, prepared by Notary Delavergne in La Rochelle, 13 January 1772, E 299, ADCM.

66. David Geggus, "Slave and Free Colored Women in Saint Domingue," in *More Than Chattel: Black Women and Slavery in the Americas*, ed., David Barry Gaspar and Darlene Clark Hine (Bloomington: Indiana University Press, 1996), 68.

67. Garrigus, *Before Haiti*, chap. 3.

68. De la Vincendière and Gel. Berard to Madame the widow Belin des Marais, 22 September 1769, E 298, ADCM.

69. According to Julie Hardwick, husbands and heads of household were supposed to show that they worked hard, kept good company, and showed astuteness in their financial affairs as a way to demonstrate their masculinity. Julie Hardwick, *The Practice of Patriarchy: Gender and the Politics of Household Authority in Early Modern France* (University Park: Pennsylvania State University Press, 1998), 91. Robert Nye similarly identifies a masculine "bourgeois honor"

rooted in virtue, which in part meant hard work. Robert Nye, *Masculinity and Male Codes of Honor in Modern France* (Berkeley: University of California Press, 1993), 32 and chap. 3. Also see Gayle Rubin, "The Traffic in Women: Notes on the 'Political Economy' of Sex," in *Toward an Anthropology of Women*, ed. Rayna Reiter (New York: Monthly Review Press, 1975), 157–210; Eve Sedgwick, *Between Men: English Literature and Male Homosocial Desire* (New York: Columbia University Press, 1995).

70. The Code Noir provided that owners could manumit slaves either by deed or in their wills, and placed no restrictions on manumission, but this liberal policy soon began to be rolled back. A 1713 ordinance provided that owners needed written permission from colonial authorities to manumit their slaves. An ordinance in 1736 specified that baptism did not connote manumission, reiterated the necessity of obtaining official permission, levied a fine against slave owners who did not follow the procedure, and specified that improperly freed slaves would be confiscated and sold at the king's profit. By 1768, owners could not free slaves without publishing their permission at their Siège Royal during three consecutive sessions. Code Noir, March 1685, Article LV, Moreau de Saint-Méry, *Loix et constitutions*, 1: 423; "Ordonnance du Roi, concernant l'Affranchissement des Esclaves," 24 October 1713, ibid., 2: 398–99; "Ordonnance du Roi, concernant l'Affranchissement des Esclaves des Isles; et Ordonnance des Administrateurs en conséquence, " 15 June 1736, ibid., 3: 452–54; "Arrét du Conseil du Cap, touchant l'Affranchissement des Esclaves," 28 January 1768, ibid., 5: 152–53.

71. On the process of manumission, see Stewart R. King, *Blue Coat or Powdered Wig: Free People of Color in Pre-Revolutionary Saint Domingue* (Athens: University of Georgia Press, 2001), 108–9. King specifies that many owners successfully had these taxes waived or reduced. This would have required additional paperwork, and made manumission a longer process. Also see Garrigus, *Before Haiti*, 86; "Lettres-Patent du Roi," 22 April 1775; and "Ordonnance des Administrateurs concernant les Libertés," 23 October 1775, both in Moreau de Saint-Méry, *Loix et constitutions*, 5: 587 and 610–13 respectively.

72. A number of slave owners did go through with this process. A certain Boisdenier, a planter client of Port-au-Prince procureur Pierre Garasché, wrote to his agent asking him to see to the enregistration of the manumission of one of his slaves. He did not hesitate at the one thousand livre price, or the various other small fees associated with the manumission process. Boisdernier to Garasché, 30 June 1780, 4 J 1610, ADCM. On the continuum of slavery and freedom, see Rebecca J. Scott, *Degrees of Freedom: Louisiana and Cuba After Slavery* (Cambridge, Mass.: Belknap Press of Harvard University Press, 2005); on "libertés de savane," see Debien, *Les esclaves aux Antilles françaises*, 380–87.

73. De la Vincendière to E. Belin and Seignette l'ainé, 12 October 1770, E 300, ADCM.

74. Seignette to Dulary, 10 November 1771, E301, ADCM.

75. Gabriel Debien, "Une indigoterie à Saint-Domingue à la fin du XVIIIe siècle," *Revue d'Histoire des Colonies* 23 (1940–1946), 34; Garrigus also cites Debien, *Before Haiti*, 40.

76. The record classifies him as "*Asmatique* and big feet." "État des nègres et négresses & l'habitation de Mons. Belin Desmarais," 1765, E 295, ADCM.

77. Seignette to Dulary, 10 November 1771, E301, ADCM.

78. François Quesnay's *Tableau économique*, originally published in 1759, is considered a founding Physiocratic text. François Quesnay, *Tableau oeconomique* (Versailles?: none, 1759). On maximizing profit through rational land management, see Judith Miller, "Economic Ideologies, 1750–1800: The Creation of Modern Political Economy?," *French Historical Studies* 23, 3 (2000): 509–10. Other works on the Physiocrats include Elizabeth Fox-Genovese, *The Origins of*

Physiocracy: Economic Revolution and Social Order in Eighteenth-Century France (Ithaca, N.Y.: Cornell University Press, 1976); Georges Weulersse, *Le mouvement physiocratique en France (de 1756 à 1770)*, 2 vols. (Paris: F. Alcan, 1910); Georges Weulersse, *La physiocratie à la fin du règne de Louis XV, 1770–1774* (Paris: Presses Universitaires de France, 1959); Georges Weulersse, *La physiocratie sous les ministères de Turgot et de Necker (1774–1781)* (Paris: Presses Universitaires de France, 1950); Georges Weulersse and Corinne Beutler, eds., *La physiocratie à l'aube de la Révolution, 1781–1792* (Paris: École des Hautes Études en Sciences Sociales, 1985). Although some scholars have argued for a connection between Physiocracy and the emergence of natural rights philosophy and abolition, in this case the outcome of such philosophy is rationalized plantation management, keeping slavery intact. See Miller, "Economic Ideologies," 509–10, and Florence Gauthier, *Triomphe et mort du droit naturel en Révolution: 1789–1795–1802* (Paris: Presses Universitaires de France, 1992).

79. See Ghachem, *The Old Regime and the Haitian Revolution*, 156–62 for an overview of this legislation. The full text of the laws can be found in "Ordonnance du Roi concernant les Procureurs et Économes-gérans des Habitations situées aux Isles sous le vent," 3 December 1784, Moreau de Saint-Méry, *Loix et constitutions*, 6: 655–67.

80. Ghachem, *The Old Regime and the Haitian Revolution*, 160.

81. "Ordonnance du Roi concernant les Procureurs et Économes-gérans des Habitations situées aux Isles sous le vent," 23 December 1785, Moreau de Saint-Méry, *Loix et constitutions*, 6: 918–28, particularly Titre VI, Art. XXI, 927.

82. "Ordonnance du Roi concernant les Procureurs et Économes-gérans des Habitations situées aux Isles sous le vent," 3 December 1784, Moreau de Saint-Méry, *Loix et constitutions*, 6: 657.

83. On the British Caribbean, see Barbara Bush, "Hard Labor: Women, Childbirth, and Resistance in British Caribbean Slave Societies," in *More Than Chattel*, ed. Gaspar and Hine, 193–217; and Katherine Paugh, "The Politics of Childbearing in the British Caribbean and the Atlantic World during the Age of Abolition, 1776–1838," *Past & Present* 221, 1 (2013): 119–60, especially 137–38 and 158–59. These two authors date amelioration policies to the 1790s. Also see Arlette Gautier, *Les Sœurs de solitude: La condition féminine dans l'esclavage aux Antilles du XVIIe au XIX siècles* (Paris: Éditions Caribéens, 2010), 90–92.

84. "Compte que moy Vizeux Gérant l'haon [habitation] Belin Desmarais rendu à Messieurs St. Macary Baucamp et Poujés Fréres negts. [négociants] St. Marc et charges de la Procuration," 23 July 1786, 4 J 2915, ADCM.

85. Ibid.

86. For a good description of how indigo was made, see G. Terry Sharrer, "The Indigo Bonanza in South Carolina, 1740–90," *Technology and Culture* 12, 3 (1971), especially 250–52. Contemporary sources also describe the making of indigo. See, for example, Du Tertre, *Histoire Generale des Antilles*, 2: 107–10. John Garrigus describes the increasing importance of indigo production to the economic prosperity of Saint-Domingue in John Garrigus, "Blue and Brown: Contraband Indigo and the Rise of a Free Colored Planter Class in French Saint-Domingue," *Americas* 50, 2 (1993). One recent study suggests that the divisions between skilled and unskilled slave labor were not as sharp as historians have interpreted them. Justin Roberts, *Slavery and the Enlightenment in the British Atlantic, 1750–1807* (New York: Cambridge University Press, 2013).

87. "Inventaire Général du mobilier composant l'habitation de Messieurs les héritiers Belin Desmarais à la mort de M. Vizeux Gérant remplacé par le Sieur Trastous ce jour 2 Juin 1790: aux

appointements de 6000 [Livres] par an Compris les soins de l'hôpital," 2 June 1790, 4 J 2915, ADCM.

88. Dominique Rogers and Stewart King show that the labor of women of color who worked as housekeepers was highly valued, but in this case I did not find instances of enslaved housekeepers given cash payment for their services. Dominique Rogers and Stewart King, "Housekeepers, Merchants, Rentières: Free Women of Color in the Port Cities of Colonial Saint-Domingue, 1750–1790," in *Women in Port: Gendering Communities, Economies, and Social Networks in Atlantic Port Cities, 1500–1800*, ed. Douglas Catterall and Jodi Campbell (Boston: Brill, 2012), 360–65.

89. During the Seven Years' War, about 2,000 Africans a year were brought to the colony, compared to 14,000 a year in the ten subsequent years, 20,000 a year after 1783, and more than 30,000 a year in the late 1780s. Garrigus, *Before Haiti*, 173. Also see David Eltis et al., *The Transatlantic Slave Database*. Raynal wrote, "We compel the *Négresses* to work so hard, before and after their pregnancy, that their fruit does not reach term, or survives only a short time after the birth." Abbé Guillaume-Thomas-François Raynal, *Histoire philosophique et politique des etablissemens et du commerce des Européens dans les deux Indes*, 7 vols. (Paris: Lacombe, 1778), 4: 212. A substantial literature exists on changing ideas about women and femininity, and women's responses. These works include Joan B. Landes, *Women and the Public Sphere in the Age of the French Revolution* (Ithaca, N.Y.: Cornell University Press, 1988), especially chap. 3; Sarah Maza, *Private Lives and Public Affairs: The Causes Célèbres of Prerevolutionary France* (Berkeley: University of California Press, 1993); Lieselotte Steinbrügge, *The Moral Sex: Woman's Nature in the French Enlightenment*, trans. Pamela E. Selwyn (New York: Oxford University Press, 1995); and Dominique Godineau, *The Women of Paris and Their French Revolution* (Berkeley: University of California Press, 1998).

90. Ghachem attributes revisions to "anxiety about planter brutality and its potential to incite a slave revolution." Ghachem, *The Old Regime and the Haitian Revolution*, 157; see also 156–62. Gautier, on the other hand, attributes them to anxiety about the slave population. Gautier, *Les Sœurs de Solitude*, 97–102.

91. Titre II, Article VII and Article VIII, "Ordonnance du Roi concernant les Procureurs et Économes-gérans des Habitations situées aux Isles sous le Vent," 3 December 1784, Moreau de Saint-Méry, *Loix et constitutions*, 6: 659.

92. Raynal, *Histoire philosophique et politique des . . . deux Indes*, 212–13.

93. Gautier, *Les Sœurs de Solitude*, 97–100.

94. Seignette to Dulary, 8 April 1774, E 301 ADCM.

95. In a 1786 report, for example, the overseer recorded payments of thirty livres each made to Zabeau, Rozette, Julienne, and Olive, the only payments made to female slaves. Each of these women had recently given birth, and was listed as a "nourrice." Rozette gave birth to Scipion 10 August 1785; Zabeau gave birth to Brigitte 29 July; Julienne delivered Petite Roze 31 July; and Fanchette was born to Olive 14 March 1786. Lison gave birth to Savotte 31 June 1785, but did not receive a payment, possibly because either mother or child died. "Compte que moy Vizeux Gérant l'haon [habitation] Belin Desmarais rendu à Messieurs St. Macary Baucamp et Poujés Fréres negts. [négociants] St. Marc et charges de la Procuration," 23 July 1786, 4 J 2915, ADCM.

96. Françoise had twins, a son named Febre and a daughter named Celeste, 13 January 1788; Heleine gave birth to St. Philipe 24 February 1788; Monique delivered her daughter Charlotte 24 February 1788; and Camille gave birth to Hortense 10 March 1788. This list appears in the accounts of 1788, which lists payments of thirty livres to "une négresse nommée Françoise pour

avoir conservé son enfant," the same amount for the same "service" to Monique, Heleine, and Camille. "Compte que moi Robert Vizeux Gérant l'habitation de M. Led[it] héritiers Belin Desmarais rend à MM. St. Macary Baucamp et Poujés frères charges de la procuration," 13 July 1788, 4 J 2915, ADCM. A slave woman named Heleine, possibly the same one, died 29 November that same year. Françoise did not receive a double payment for having delivered twins. "État des Naissances & Mortalités des Nagres [Nègres] & animaux dépendants de l'habitation de Messieurs les héritiers Belin située à l'Artibonite depuis le 31 juillet 1788," 4 J 2915, ADCM.

97. St. Macary to Messieurs les Héritiers Belin des Marais, 14 May 1791, 4 J 2915, ADCM. See also "Inventaire Général du mobilier composant l'habitation de Messieurs les Héritiers Belin Desmarais à la mort de M. Vizeux Gérant," 2 June 1790, 4 J 2915, ADCM. St. Macary gives another accounting of recent births and pregnancies in his letter to the same of 29 June 1791.

Chapter 2. Legitimating Authority

1. Sue Peabody, "An Alternative Genealogy of the Origins of French Free Soil: Medieval Toulouse," *Slavery & Abolition* 32, 3 (September 2011): 341–62.

2. The Code Noir classified slaves as meubles. An *Arrêt* of August 1687 reiterated this provision, but elaborated that it should not be enforced retroactively; if earlier testaments had treated slaves as inseparable from the estate they worked, for example, they would not be overturned. In 1705 a court case again challenged this classification, claiming that slaves were to a plantation "as the pigeons to the dovecotes and the fish to the ponds." By 1718, although officials never formally reclassified slaves as *immeubles*, policy stated that "they [slaves] are attached to that estate [where they work], in a manner in which they contribute to its nature and become *immobiliers* with it." Médéric-Louis-Élie Moreau de Saint-Méry, *Loix et constitutions des colonies françaises de l'Amérique sous le vent*, 5 vols. (Paris: Moreau de Saint-Méry, 1784–1790); "Code Noir ou Édit servant de Règlement pour le Gouvernement et l'Administration de la Justice et de la Police des Isles Françoises de l'Amérique, et pour la Discipline et le Commerce des Nègres et Esclaves dans ledit Pays," March 1685, 1: 414–24, Article XLIV, 421; "Arrêt du Conseil d'État, sur l'exécution de l'Article quarante-quatrième de la Déclaration du mois de Mars 1685, touchant les Esclaves des Isles de l'Amérique, qui déclare les Nègres meubles," August 1687, 1: 460; "Acte de Notoriété du Châtelet de Paris, portant que les Nègres attachés à la Culture à Saint-Domingue sont Meubles," 13 November 1705, 2: 41–42; "Mémoire et Lettre du Conseil de Marine, au sujet du Droit d'Aubaine, et de la nature mobilière ou immobilière des Esclaves, et Ordonnance des Administrateurs sur le même sujet," 20 October 1717 and 6 April 1719, 2: 597–600, 600. On the difference between meubles and immeubles, see Ralph E. Giesey, "Rules of Inheritance and Strategies of Mobility in Prerevolutionary France," *American Historical Review* 82, 2 (1977): 271–89.

3. Jennifer Heuer found that "officials in general tended to view blacks and people of color as colonial subjects, and not as foreigners or French citizens," and that this tendency continued in the Napoleonic and Restoration periods. Jennifer Heuer, "The One-Drop Rule in Reverse? Interracial Marriages in Napoleonic and Restoration France," *Law and History Review* 27, 3 (2009): 515–48, 534.

4. "Code Noir," March 1685, in Moreau de Saint-Méry, *Loix et constitutions*, 1: 414–424, Articles XLII–XLIII.

5. Malick Ghachem, *The Old Regime and the Haitian Revolution* (New York: Cambridge University Press, 2012), 172, 167–74. Also see Malick Ghachem, "Prosecuting Torture: The Strategic Ethics of Slavery in Pre-Revolutionary Saint-Domingue (Haiti)," *Law and History Review* 29, 4 (2011): 985–1029.

6. Bernard Moitt, *Women and Slavery in the French Antilles, 1635–1848* (Bloomington: Indiana University Press, 2001), chap. 6, esp. 104–10. Pierre de Vaissière relates the story of a slave owner who shot a slave and was fined a mere hundred livres, and another colonist who killed an eleven-year-old girl and was fined six hundred livres. Pierre de Vaissière, *Saint-Domingue: La société et la vie créoles sous l'ancien régime (1629–1789)* (Paris: Perrin, 1909), 86.

7. The best-known example of the philosophes' criticism of torture is Voltaire's *Treatise on Tolerance*, trans. Brian Masters (Cambridge: Cambridge University Press, 2000).

8. For examples of how slaves generated their own understandings of contested discourses, see Laurent Dubois, *A Colony of Citizens: Revolution and Slave Emancipation in the French Caribbean, 1787–1804* (Chapel Hill: University of North Carolina Press, 2004); Steven Hahn, *A Nation Under our Feet: Black Political Struggles in the Rural South, from Slavery to the Great Migration* (Cambridge, Mass.: Harvard University Press, 2003).

9. Robert Harms, *The Diligent: A Voyage Through the Worlds of the Slave Trade* (New York: Basic, 2002), 6–11; Sue Peabody, *"There Are No Slaves in France": The Political Culture of Race and Slavery in the Ancien Régime* (New York: Oxford University Press, 1996), 24–37, esp. 24–25.

10. On the freedom suit of Pauline Villeneuve and the subsequent crusade by Gérard Mellier, a Nantais official, to have slaves classified as moveable property, see Harms, *The Diligent*, 6–11 and 13–24.

11. Isambert, Decrusy, and Taillandier, *Recueil général des anciennes lois françaises, depuis l'an 420 jusqu'à la Révolution de 1789*, 29 vols. (Paris: Belin-Leprieur, 1830), 21: 122–26. For additional contextualization of the constitutional crisis following the death of Louis XIV, during which the law was drafted, see Peabody, *"There Are No Slaves in France"*, 16.

12. Isambert et al., *Recueil général des anciennes lois françaises*, 21: 125–26, Article 15. As of yet, no evidence has been found that slaves or their allies used this provision of the law to obtain freedom. Peabody finds that the first legal challenges to slavery in France came in 1738. Peabody, *"There Are No Slaves in France"*, 23. She discusses the case of *Jean Boucaux v. Verdelin* in depth, 23–37.

13. The Parisian Admiralty first accepted a slave declaration in 1736. Slaves were technically supposed to be declared at their port of entry, not in Paris. Erick Noël, *Être noir en France au XVIIIe siècle* (Paris: Tallandier, 2006), 71; Peabody, *"There Are No Slaves in France"*, 23.

14. On law as a site for conflict and negotiation, see Hendrick Hartog, "Pigs and Positivism," *Wisconsin Law Review* 4 (1985): 899–935.

15. "Registre de sa Majesté du siège de l'amirauté commencé le 17 septembre 1719 et fini le 7 mai 1729," B 224, ADCM.

16. 129 had not presented a letter, while there is no indication for five. "Registre de sa Majesté Commencé le 11e mai 1729 et fini le 16 octobre 1737," B 225, ADCM.

17. "Registre de sa Majesté du siège de l'amirauté commencé le 17 septembre 1719 et fini le 7 mai 1729," B 224, ADCM.

18. "Registre de sa Majesté Commencé le 11e May 1729 et fini le 16 octobre 1737," B 225, ADCM.

19. Peabody, *"There Are No Slaves in France"*, 23.

20. Noël, *Être noir en France au XVIIIe siècle*, puts the exact number at 247, Document 11, 281. Noël bases his figures on "Mémoires et pièces concernant les Noirs et gens de couleur," 1694–1789, B 5592, ADCM.

21. 11 January 1725, in "Registre de sa Majesté du siège de l'amirauté commencé le 17 septembre 1719 et fini le 7 mai 1729," B 224, ADCM.

22. 30 March 1756, "Registre de sa Majesté commencé le 23 mars 1753 et fini le 14 avril 1757," B 6086, ADCM.

23. Faure sent his power of attorney to Michel Prevost of Port Margot in Saint-Domingue, who obtained the necessary permission. 4 December 1724, in "Registre de sa Majesté du siège de l'amirauté commencé le 17 septembre 1719 et fini le 7 mai 1729," B 224, ADCM.

24. 11 January 1725, "Registre de sa Majesté du siège de l'amirauté commencé le 17 septembre 1719 et fini le 7 mai 1729," B 224, ADCM.

25. "Registre de sa Majesté du siège de l'amirauté de La Rochelle commencé le dix-septième 7 [septembre], mil sept cent dix-neuf et fini le 7 mai 1729," B 224, ADCM.

26. "Registre de sa Majesté commencé le 11e mai 1729 et fini le 16 octobre 1737," B 225, ADCM. Specifically, Jean Gilbert made declarations regarding slaves on 5 August 1730, 15, 16, and 17 July 1732, 15 January 1733, 13 May 1733, 22 and 23 October 1734, and 24 January 1735.

27. Jean-Jacques Mithon de Senneville, a colonial official and acting intendant of Saint-Domingue in 1720. 7 August 1720, "Registre de sa Majesté du siège de l'amirauté commencé le 17 septembre 1719 et fini le 7 mai 1729," B 224, ADCM.

28. "Registre de sa Majesté commencé le 11e mai 1729 et fini le 16 octobre 1737," B 225, ADCM. Rasteau made declarations 1 July 1730, 28 June 1731, 6 July 1731, 19 August 1732, 23 August 1732, 4 November 1732, 28 March and 31 August 1737.

29. Isambert et al., Recueil général des anciennes lois françaises, 22: 112.

30. Ibid. Also see Peabody, "There Are No Slaves in France", 37–38.

31. Isambert et al., Recueil général des anciennes lois françaises, 22: 113.

32. Peabody, "There Are No Slaves in France", chap. 2, esp. 23–37, and Noël, Être noir en France au XVIIIe siècle, 71–72.

33. Peabody, "There Are No Slaves in France", 24–25.

34. Ibid., 37.

35. Unregistered laws received little publicity, the courts could refuse to prosecute pertinent cases, and such laws might not be enforced. Peabody, "There Are No Slaves in France", 18–19. Also see J. H. Shennan, The Parlement of Paris (Ithaca, N.Y.: Cornell University Press, 1968), 285–325.

36. Referenced in Barentin to Maurepas, 22 September 1741, Marine B3 405, AN.

37. Although copies of such declarations usually were sent to all cities to which they pertained, the Declaration of 1738 apparently never reached La Rochelle. Laws pertaining to the Admiralty generally were copied into the Admiralty registers; the Declaration of 1738 does not appear in the "Registre de sa Majesté commencé le 19 octobre 1737 et fini le 27 juin 1744," B 226, ADCM. Furthermore, Barentin, the intendant of La Rochelle, wrote to the Count of Maurepas, the Minister of the Marine, that La Rochelle had never received a copy of the declaration. Barentin to Maurepas, 22 September 1741, fol. 267, Marine B3 405, AN, cited in Peabody, "There Are No Slaves in France", 156n25.

38. Nicollas Chasseau said his two female slaves would learn how to sew (27 July 1739); Louis Cassou and Pierre Barbier said their slaves would learn how to cook (22 June 1742, 11 February 1743); and Catherine Corlu said her slave François would learn to be a cooper (15 June 1743). "Registre de sa Majesté commencé le 19 octobre 1737 et fini le 27 juin 1744," B 226, ADCM, and "Registre de sa Majesté commencé le 27 juin 1744 et fini le 3 novembre 1747," B 227, ADCM. Beginning in 1741, many slave owners explicitly promised to comply with the Declaration of 1738. For example, Sieur Germain Michel Philiponas of Léogane promised to pay the fine demanded by the Declaration if he did not follow its conditions, 21 July 1741, "Registre de sa Majesté commencé le 19 octobre 1737 et fini le 27 juin 1744," B 226, ADCM.

39. Slave owners in Nantes did not provide the name of the trade or master who would train their slaves before the Declaration of 1738. Their change in behavior implies compliance with the law. See B 4512 and B 4520 for examples of declarations of slaves which provide information about their métiers after 1738, Archives Départmentales de la Loire Atlantique. Owners said slaves would learn to be blacksmiths, tailors, lacemakers, cooks, wigmakers, laundresses, and seamstresses. For declarations before 1738, see, for example, B 4491.

40. "Reiteration de Nègre, Made. Gallifat," 10 March 1755, "Registre de sa Majesté commencé le 23 mars 1753 et fini le 14 avril 1757," B 6086, ADCM.

41. Isambert et al., *Recueil général des anciennes lois françaises*, 22, Declaration of 1738, Article 11, 115.

42. The slaves who received their freedom were Henriette, 5 February 1739, Pierre, 21 February 1742, Lepré, 28 February 1742, "Registre de sa Majesté commencé le 19 octobre 1737 et fini le 27 juin 1744," B 226, ADCM; and Jean-Baptiste, 19 August 1745, "Registre de sa Majesté Commencé le 27 juin 1744 et fini le 3 novembre 1747," B 227, ADCM. The first recorded manumission in the Rochelais Admiralty records took place 4 October 1721. A white man manumitted a *mulâtre* boy who may have been his son. "Registre de sa Majesté du siège de l'amirauté commencé le 17 septembre 1719 et fini le 7 mai 1729," B 224, ADCM.

43. Barentin to Maurepas, 22 September 1741, fol. 267, Marine B3 405, AN. Similarly, Ira Berlin notes that former French colonists who emigrated to Philadelphia in the 1790s freed their slaves under Pennsylvania law, but "quickly turned around and bound them into long-term indentures." Nearly five hundred slaves were indentured. Ira Berlin, *Many Thousands Gone: The First Two Centuries of Slavery in North America* (Cambridge, Mass.: Belknap Press of Harvard University Press, 1998), 450n35.

44. Barentin to Maurepas, 22 September 1741, Marine B3 405, AN.

45. Barentin to Maurepas, two letters, both written on 22 September 1741, Marine B3 405, AN.

46. "Registre de sa Majesté commencé le 19 octobre 1737 et fini le 27 juin 1744," B 226, ADCM. Henriette's owner, whose name is unclear, originally registered his intention at Rochefort, 11 November 1738.

47. Barentin to Maurepas, 19 December 1741, Marine B3 405, AN.

48. "Extrait du testament du feu Sr. Nicolas Rigault, 28 8bre 1730," enclosed in Barentin to Maurepas, 19 December 1741, Marine B3 405, AN.

49. 21 February 1742, "Registre de sa Majesté commencé le 19 octobre 1737 et fini le 27 juin 1744," B 226, ADCM.

50. See entries for 16 February 1735 and 31 July 1731, "Registre de sa Majesté Commencé le 11e mai 1729 et fini le 16 octobre 1737," B 225, ADCM. When he had to go back to sea, the ship's captain Paul Seignette left his slave Jean-Baptiste in the care of Jean Vivier. 19 October 1737, "Registre de sa Majesté commencé le 19 octobre 1737 et fini le 27 juin 1744," B 226, ADCM.

51. 16 April 1742, "Registre de sa Majesté commencé le 19 octobre 1737 et fini le 27 juin 1744," B 226, ADCM.

52. "Code Noir," March 1685, Moreau de Saint-Méry, *Loix et constitutions*, 414–24, Article II. The Code Noir was initially promulgated in the context of intense controversy and conflict over religion in France, which culminated in the Revocation of the Edict of Nantes in the same year.

53. Gabriel Debien, *Les esclaves aux Antilles françaises (XVIIe–XVIIIe siècles)* (Basse-Terre: Société d'Histoire de la Guadeloupe, 1974), 252.

54. Papiers Desmé de Chavigny, microfilm at ANOM, M1 B 23, cited in Debien, *Les esclaves aux Antilles françaises*, 277.

55. The Declaration of May 1724 summed up laws against Protestants, stipulating that the Roman Catholic religion was the only one in France and that all marriages had to be conducted by Catholic priests. Any marriages by a Protestant pastor did not count as marriages at all, and the children born of these unions were considered illegitimate. Isambert et al., *Recueil général des anciennes lois françaises* 21: 261–70. David Bien argues that Catholic judges, long considered conservatives, absorbed ideas of natural law and applied them to Protestant marriage beginning after the conclusion of the Seven Years' War in 1763. Protestants won de facto rights to marriage and inheritance in the courts from the mid-1760s onward. This has broad implications for La Rochelle, where Protestants made up the wealthiest portion of the population; they were extremely concerned about inheritance rights, and took precautions to secure them. David D. Bien, "Catholic Magistrates and Protestant Marriage in the French Enlightenment," *French Historical Studies* 2, 4 (1962): 409–29.

56. Margaret Maxwell, "The Division in the Ranks of the Protestants in Eighteenth-Century France," *Church History* 27, 2 (1958): 107–23, 107. On Protestants in Bordeaux who baptized their children in Catholic churches, see Alfred Leroux, *Les religionnaires de Bordeaux de 1685 à 1802* (Bordeaux: Feret & Fils, 1920), 175–184.

57. Nicole Vray, *La Rochelle et les protestants du XVIe au XXe siècle* (La Crèche: Geste Éditions, 1999), 178.

58. On relations of godparentage as a source of patronage, see Maurice Aymard, "Friends and Neighbors," in *A History of Private Life: Passions of the Renaissance*, ed. Rogier Chartier, 5 vols. (Cambridge, Mass.: Harvard University Press, 1989), 3: 447–92, 452; Christine Adams, *A Taste for Comfort and Status: A Bourgeois Family in Eighteenth-Century France* (University Park: Pennsylvania State University Press, 2000), 89; Robert Wheaton, "Affinity and Descent in Seventeenth-Century Bordeaux," in *Family and Sexuality in French History*, ed. Robert Wheaton and Tamara K. Hareven (Philadelphia: University of Pennsylvania Press, 1980), 117; Jean-Louis Flandrin, *Families in Former Times: Kinship, Household, and Sexuality in Early Modern France*, ed. and trans. Richard Southern (Cambridge: Cambridge University Press, 1979), 30; Margaret H. Darrow, *Revolution in the House: Family, Class, and Inheritance in Southern France, 1775–1825* (Princeton, N.J.: Princeton University Press, 1989), 102–103.

59. Parish records, Saint-Barthélémy, 1760, GG 286, and 1761, GG 288, AMLR.

60. Parish records, Saint-Barthélémy, 1785, GG 336, AMLR.

61. Parish records, Saint-Barthélémy, 1766, GG 298, AMLR.

62. Parish records, Saint-Barthélémy, 1786, GG 338, AMLR.

63. Seymour Drescher, "Manumission in a Society Without Slave Law: Eighteenth-Century England," *Slavery & Abolition* 3, 10 (1989): 85–101, 94–96.

64. Sue Peabody, " 'A Dangerous Zeal': Catholic Missions to Slaves in the French Antilles, 1635–1800." *French Historical Studies* 25, 1 (2002): 53–90, 68–69, and 78–79.

65. For example, the slave Catherine Morgan sought help from a lawyer who also was godfather to one of her children. Peabody, *"There Are No Slaves in France"*, 45.

66. Le Pers quoted in Pierre-François-Xavier de Charlevoix, *Histoire de l'Isle Espagnole ou de S. Domingue: Ecrite particulierement sur des Memoires Manuscrits du P. Jean-Baptiste de Pers, Jesuite, Missionnaire à Saint Domingue, & sur les Pieces Originales, qui se conservent au Dépôt de la Marine*. 2 vols. (Paris: Jacques Guerin, 1730), 2: 504–5. Peabody quotes a similar excerpt, Peabody, "'A Dangerous Zeal,'" 75.

67. Charlevoix, *Histoire de l'Isle Espagnole*, 502, also cited in Peabody, "'A Dangerous Zeal," 76.

68. 2 December 1727, parish records, Notre Dame, GG 78, AMLR.

69. Parish records, Saint-Barthélémy, 1724, GG 244, AMLR.

70. Parish records, Saint-Barthélémy, 1727, GG 78, AMLR.

71. Parish records, Saint-Barthélémy, 1753, GG 272, AMLR.

72. Jules Mathorez gives the only example I know of a Protestant baptism for a slave, which took place in Ablon in 1604. Jules Mathorez, *Les étrangers en France sous l'ancien régime*, 2 vols. (Paris: Édouard Champion, 1919), 2: 367. Jacques Pannier, from whom Mathorez draws the example, elaborates that the slave was actually a Turk, forty years old, owned by one M. de Rosni, who named his charge Maximilien. He also states that an Indian professed his Protestant faith in Ablon in 1603, and that a "Moor and a Mooress" were married as Protestants in Paris in 1604. Jacques Pannier, *L'Église réformée à Paris sous Henri IV* (Paris: H. Champion, 1911), 188.

73. On the commodification of slaves, see Stephanie E. Smallwood, *Saltwater Slavery: A Middle Passage from Africa to American Diaspora* (Cambridge, Mass.: Harvard University Press, 2007), esp. 35–36.

74. 12 November 1739, parish records, Notre Dame, GG 90, AMLR.

75. Jean-Baptiste Du Tertre, *Histoire générale des Antilles habitées par les François, devisée en deux tomes, et enrichi de Cartes & de Figures*, 4 vols. (Paris: Thomas Jolly, 1667), 2: 528.

76. Jean-Baptiste Labat, *Nouveau voyage aux isles de l'Amerique: contenant l'histoire naturelle de ces pays, l'origine, les moeurs, la religion & le gouvernement des habitans anciens & modernes: les guerres & les evenement singuliers que y sont arrives pendant le long sejour que l'auteur y a fait: le commerce & les manufactures qui y sont établies, & les moyens de les augmenter: avec une description exacte & curieuse de toutes ces isles: ouvrage enrichi de plus de cent cartes, plans & figures en tailles-douces . . . ,* 6 vols. (Paris: P.F. Giffart, 1722), 4: 145–46.

77. Michel-René Hilliard d'Auberteuil, *Considérations sur l'état présent de la colonie française de Saint-Domingue*, 2 vols. (Paris: Grangé, 1776–1777), 2: 77.

78. Médéric-Louis-Élie Moreau de Saint-Méry, *La description topographique, physique, civile, politique et historique de la partie française de Saint-Domingue*, 3rd ed., 3 vols. (Saint-Denis: Société Français d'Histoire d'Outre-mer, 2004), 1: 55.

Chapter 3. Navigating Transatlantic Separations

1. Of 6,200 indentured servants who departed from La Rochelle from 1635 to 1715, only forty were women. Gabriel Debien, "Les engagés pour les Antilles (1634–1715)," (dissertation, Université de Paris, 1951), 83–85. In Saint-Domingue in 1700, there were twenty white men for every white woman. Throughout the eighteenth century, there continued to be two white men for every white woman, and four to five white men born in the metropole for every one metropolitan-born woman. Arlette Gautier, *Les Sœurs de solitude: Femmes et esclavage aux Antilles du XVIIe au XIXe siècle* (Rennes: Presses Universitaires de Rennes, 2010), 32; Gautier cites ANSON, G1, 509. In the eighteenth century 41.6 percent of migrants to New England from the British Isles traveled in families, compared to 14.0 percent of those who traveled to the British West Indies. Bernard Bailyn, *Voyagers to the West: A Passage in the Peopling of America on the Eve of the Revolution* (New York: Knopf, 1986), table 6.2, 210–11. Also see Alison Games, *Migration and the Origins of the English Atlantic World* (Cambridge, Mass.: Harvard University Press, 1999). Games contrasts the family- and kin-dominated migration to New England with migrations to Virginia and Providence Island, which tended to include a preponderance of young

single men, usually servants (chap. 1). She also points out that once in the colonies, migrants tended to keep moving among locales (chapter 7).

2. Bernard Moitt, *Women and Slavery in the French Antilles, 1635–1848* (Bloomington: Indiana University Press, 2001), 12.

3. London merchants also tended to travel alone to the British Atlantic colonies, with the intention of returning to England. Games, *Migration and the Origins of the Atlantic World*, 42–45.

4. John Garrigus, *Before Haiti: Race and Citizenship in French Saint-Domingue* (New York: Palgrave Macmillan, 2006), 5.

5. Douglas Catterall and Jodi Campbell, eds., *Women in Port: Gendering Communities, Economies, and Social Networks in Atlantic Port Cities, 1500–1800* (Boston: Brill, 2012), especially Introduction, 3–9 on gender as a category in the Atlantic world, and Section One, "Metropolitan Frameworks," 37–150.

6. Jean-Claude Perrot notes the variations in legal traditions; under the customary law of Normandy, marriage contracts and testaments had little legal force, and customary law disadvantaged women. Jean-Claude Perrot, "Note sur les contrats de mariage normands," in *Structures et relations sociales à Paris au XVIIIe siècle*, ed. Adeline Daumard and François Furet (Paris: A. Colin, 1961), 95–97.

7. In general, provisions of the Coutume de Paris regarding the disposition of property did not work well with the colonial plantation system. Edith Géraud-Llorca, "La Coutume de Paris outre-mer: L'habitation antillaise sous l'ancien régime," *Revue Historique de Droit Français et Éranger* 60, 2 (1982): 207–59, 208.

8. 24 April 1714, Parish records, Saint-Barthélémy, La Rochelle, GG 234, AMLR. Médéric-Louis-Élie Moreau de Saint-Méry, *La description topographique, physique, civile, politique et historique de la partie française de Saint-Domingue* (Saint-Denis: Société Français d'Histoire d'Outre-mer, 2004), 2: 936–53.

9. Stewart King, *Blue Coat or Powdered Wig: Free People of Color in Pre-Revolutionary Saint-Domingue* (Athens: University of Georgia Press, 2001), 133.

10. Although Aimé-Benjamin Fleuriau's plantation was in Croix-des-Bouquets, about thirty miles away, the Veuve Royer clearly knew him. She wrote to her daughter, explaining, "I was obliged to send it [a letter] at the expense of Monsieur Fleuriau at Léogane." Veuve Royer to Marie-Magdelaine Royer Regnaud, 4 August 1735, E 513, ADCM. On connections based on geography that persisted as colonists and former colonists moved around the Atlantic basin, see R. Darrell Meadows, "Engineering Exile: Social Networks and the French Atlantic Community, 1789–1799," *French Historical Studies* 23, 1 (2000): 67–102.

11. "Extrait des minutes du Greffe du Siège Royale de Léogane, Coste Saint-Domingue," 22 December 1718, E 516, ADCM.

12. Siblings in particular were usually vocal on their views toward a proposed marriage. Julie Hardwick, *The Practice of Patriarchy: Gender and the Politics of Household Authority in Early Modern France* (University Park: Pennsylvania State University Press, 1998), 58.

13. "Procuration," between Marie Douteau, veuve Royer, and Demoiselle Ester Douteau, 10 November 1734, E 516, ADCM. The Edict of 1556 aimed to discourage clandestine marriage by raising the age of majority to twenty-five for women and thirty for men. Paul Ourliac and Jehan de Malafosse, *Le Droit familial*, vol. 3, *Histoire du droit privé* (Paris: Presses Universitaires de France, 1968), 204–5. By the eighteenth century, marriage was considered a contractual relationship more than a sacramental one. James Traer, *Marriage and the Family in Eighteenth-Century*

France (Ithaca, N.Y.: Cornell University Press, 1980), 31–47, esp. 33; on the philosophes and their use of contract theory to challenge the indissolubility of the marriage bond, see 52.

14. The marriage record of Marie-Magdelaine Royer's parents indicates that her mother was born in La Rochelle and her father born in Toulouse. Mariage de Jean-Jacques et Marie Douteau, 15 June 1709, Saint-Barthélémy, BMS, GG 231, AMLR.

15. On marriage contracts see Hardwick, *The Practice of Patriarchy*, 60–66. In Saint-Domingue even freed men and women had marriage contracts made, demonstrating the importance and the ubiquity of the process. For example, Pierre Paysan and Marie-Louise Agathe, both classified as "Arada," suggesting that they had been brought to Saint-Domingue as slaves, entered into a marriage contract. Like Marie-Magdelaine Royer and Jean-Severin Regnaud de Beaumont, they specified that their marriage would be governed by the Coutume de Paris. "Contrat de marriage," prepared by Notary Lambert in Léogane, 30 January 1778, DPPC NOT SDOM 1181, ANOM.

16. John Clark, *La Rochelle and the Atlantic Economy During the Eighteenth Century* (Baltimore: Johns Hopkins University Press, 1981), 98–99.

17. "Contrat de mariage," 29 March 1735, E 513, ADCM. I have not found their actual marriage record in the parish records for any of the five parishes of La Rochelle for 1735 or 1736. They may have married outside La Rochelle, although it seems unlikely that they would marry in a parish other than the one where they lived at the time their marriage contract was signed, and in which they were both baptized. They could have been Protestant; often Protestants tried to avoid getting married in the Catholic Church (see Chapter 2), although they were baptized Catholic, all their children were baptized Catholic, and Marie-Magdelaine's parents were married in Saint-Barthélémy parish. They could not have been married too far away, as their first child was born in La Rochelle almost exactly nine months after their marriage contract was signed.

18. On the Coutume de Paris, see Simon François Langloix, *Principes généraux de la Coutume de Paris, où les articles du texte, & les ordonnances qui y ont rapport, sont rangés dans un ordre méthodique, pour en faciliter l'usage*, 3rd ed. (Paris: Prault Père, Imprimeur du Roi, 1746), 188–89. On the Coutume de La Rochelle, see René-Josué Valin, *Nouveau commentaire sur la Coutume de La Rochelle et du pays d'Aunis* (La Rochelle: René-Jacob Desbordes, 1756), 1: 484–500.

19. Langloix, *Principes généraux de la Coutume de Paris*, 189–91; Valin, *Nouveau commentaire sur la Coutume de La Rochelle*, 491.

20. Langloix, *Principes généraux de la Coutume de Paris*, 143.

21. "Contrat de mariage," 29 March 1735, E 513, ADCM. Five thousand livres of the groom's individual estate, just less than one-third of his total liquid assets, were to enter the couple's joint estate to be used to buy furniture. The bride received a dowry of thirty thousand livres from her mother, an advance on her inheritance. Again, about one-third of her total assets entered their joint estate, to be used to purchase personal property, while the remainder was reserved as part of Marie-Magdelaine's personal estate. Julie Hardwick found that among notaries' families about 40 percent of individual property entered the marital community. Hardwick, *The Practice of Patriarchy*, 62.

22. Clark, *La Rochelle and the Atlantic Economy*, 59–61. For example, the dowries of merchant Allard Belin's daughters came to about thirty thousand livres each, comprising twenty thousand livres in cash and also household items. Elizabeth Belin, daughter of one of the most important Rochelais merchants, brought a dowry of forty-five thousand livres to her marriage

to Rochelais merchant Pierre-Jean Van Hoogwerff. Jean-Marie Deveau, "Les affaires Van Hoogwerf à Saint-Domingue de 1773 à 1791," in *Actes du Colloque de Bordeaux des 15 et 16 mars 1991*, ed. Paul Butel (Bordeaux: Maison des Pays Ibériques, 1992). In general, by the end of the eighteenth century 43 percent of marriage contracts showed dowries of one thousand six hundred to forty thousand livres, and only 7 percent above forty thousand livres. Jacques Lelièvre, *La pratique des contrats de mariage chez les notaires de Paris de 1769 à 1804* (Paris: Éditions Cujas, 1959).

23. Valin, *Nouveau commentaire sur la Coutume de La Rochelle*, 483–84; Charles A. Bourdot de Richebourg, *Nouveau Coutumier Général, ou corps des coutumes générales et particulières de France, et des provinces*, 4 vols. (Paris: Robustel, 1724), 4: 856, Chapter IX, Article XXII. Also see Jean Yver, *Égalité entre héritiers et exclusion des enfants dotés: Essai de géographie coutumière* (Paris: Sirey, 1966), and Emmanuel Le Roy Ladurie, "Family Structures and Inheritance Customs in Sixteenth-Century France," in *Family and Inheritance: Rural Society in Western Europe, 1200–1800*, ed. Jack Goody, Joan Thirsk, and E. P. Thompson (Cambridge: Cambridge University Press, 1976), 37–70. Under Parisian common law, if all the children died after inheriting the dowry but before having children themselves, the money would remain in the husband's family. Langloix, *Principes généraux de la Coutume de Paris*, 150. Under the common law of La Rochelle, it would pass back to the wife's. Richebourg, *Nouveau Coutumier General*, 859, Ch. XVIII.

24. Langloix, *Principes généraux de la Coutume de Paris*, 71. For an overview of the transmission of property in different parts of France, see François Lebrun, *La vie conjugale sous l'ancien régime* (Paris: Armand Colin, 1975), 74–78.

25. The Parisian law stipulated that "the dowry, either customary or predetermined, is only for a life interest with regard to the wife, after the death of which the holdings lawfully return to the heirs of the husband, if there is not a stipulation to the contrary in the marriage contract." Langloix, *Principes généraux de la Coutume de Paris*, 148. If the couple had children, eventually the dowry would belong to the children.

26. Richebourg, *Nouveau Coutumier Général*, 859, Chapter XVI, Article XLVII; Chapter XVIII, Article L.

27. The widow of Issac Garasché, a négociant in La Rochelle, went into partnership with her sons and continued running his business after his death with the help of her extensive and well-connected family in the 1720s and 1730s. 5 J 21, ADCM. On widows in partnership with their sons in early modern Rouen, see Brunelle, "The Price of Assimilation," 166–67.

28. The financial ties between two families built by marriage lasted only as long as the union itself; they thus needed to be constantly renewed, and indeed families who had long-standing trade alliances also had similarly long histories of intermarriage. One example of this practice is the Belin and Seignette families, who intermarried frequently from the 1720s through the 1740s. Parish records, FF 243, GG 250, GG 254, GG 256, GG 261, all in AMLR.

29. Martha Howell, *The Marriage Exchange: Property, Social Place, and Gender in Cities of the Low Countries, 1300–1550* (Chicago: University of Chicago Press, 1998), 140–43.

30. For example, Aimé-Benjamin Fleuriau divided the bulk of his estate into three equal portions which were inherited by his children. His eldest son inherited the family hôtel particulier in La Rochelle, his younger son inherited other various properties, while his daughter primarily inherited liquid assets. "Dépôt du testament olographe de M. Aimé-Benjamin Fleuriau," 21 August 1787, Notary Delavergne fils, 3 E 1698, ADCM.

31. "Contrat de Mariage," 29 March 1735, E 513, ADCM.

32. Valin, *Nouveau commentaire sur la Coutume de La Rochelle*, 596.

33. As both Barbara Diefendorf and Martha Howell point out, the option of renouncing estates also enabled women to purposely avoid financial obligations, sometimes at the expense of other family members. Barbara B. Diefendorf, "Women and Property in *Ancien Régime* France: Theory and Practice in Dauphiné and Paris," in *Early Modern Conceptions of Property*, ed. John Brewer and Susan Staves (New York: Routledge, 1995), 170–93, 177; Howell, *Marriage Exchange*, 120.

34. For example, her mother refers to the "indigo that I must send to my daughter." Veuve Royer, no name of recipient, 4 August 1735, E 515, ADCM. Such a situation also arose in the marriage between Paul Belin and Françoise Guillemaut, discussed in Chapter 1. Françoise and her widowed mother remained integrally involved in transatlantic trade. Belin's mother-in-law contributed to the outfitting of his ships, and Françoise herself held Belin's procuration and made a number of transactions in her husband's name. The file "Comptes particulières de Paul Belin des Marais" includes receipts and contracts made by Françoise Guillemaut, E 296, ADCM. She is also referred to as Belin's "Procuratrice" in G. Rouzier to Belin, 13 July 1728, E 297, ADCM.

35. "Contrat de mariage," 29 March 1735, E 513, ADCM.

36. Madame Regnaud de Beaumont had evidently enquired about the application of the Coutume de Paris in Saint-Domingue, for her agent Prevost wrote to her, "As for what you ask me about the Coutume de Paris, it is true that in Saint-Domingue the wife is privileged above the other debtors." Prevost in Léogane to Madame Regnaud de Beaumont in La Rochelle, 25 March 1773, E 514, ADCM.

37. The marriage of Paul Belin and Françoise Guillemaut, discussed in Chapter 1, also prepared the couple for a long transatlantic separation. They made a mutual will in 1722, soon after their marriage, in which they each named the other as the universal legatee. Mutual Testament, Paul Belin and Françoise Guillemaut, 1722, E 294, ADCM.

38. Valin, *Nouveau commentaire sur la Coutume de La Rochelle*, 491.

39. See Natalie Zemon Davis, *The Return of Martin Guerre* (Cambridge, Mass.: Harvard University Press, 1983).

40. Clare Crowston, *Credit, Fashion, Sex: Economies of Regard in Old Regime France* (Durham, N.C.: Duke University Press, 2013).

41. "Procuration le Sieur Bidet à Dmlle Delissart son Épouse," [date illegible] 1777, 3 E 1688; "Procuration M Pre [Pierre] Neau à son épouse," 28 April 1763, 3 E 1674; "Procuration Jean Margoteau marinier à son épouse," 25 June 1743, 3 E 2105, all in ADCM.

42. For example, "Procuration le Sieur Bidet à Dmlle Delissart son Épouse."

43. Women in French port cities had long engaged in commerce as wives, widows, and single women. Gayle Brunelle, "The Prince of Assimilation: Spanish and Portuguese Women in French Cities, 1500–1650," in *Women in Port*, ed. Catterall and Campbell, 155–82, esp. 158–59.

44. He was listed as "absent" at the baptism of their first child. Jean-Severin-Nicolas Regnaud, 22 December 1735, Parish records, Saint-Barthélémy parish, GG 251, AMLR.

45. Jean-Severin Regnaud, 21 November 1743, Parish records, Saint-Barthélémy, GG 259, AMLR.

46. In 1739, Regnaud de Beaumont sold a plantation he owned in the South Province, thus consolidating family holdings. It is possible that he also sold the Royer plantation. Gabriel Debien, "À Saint-Domingue avec deux jeunes économes de plantation (1774–1788)," *Revue de la Société d'Histoire et de Géographe d'Haïti*, 16, 58 (1945): 1–60, 5.

47. Bechade to Madame Regnaud de Beaumont, 21 December 1751, E 514, ADCM.

48. Baptism, Sainte-Rose Parish in Léogane, Saint-Domingue, Jean-Marie Renaud, 11 December 1753, 85MIOM/83, ANOM; also "Extrait des Registres de la paroisse de Sainte-Rose de Léogane Isle et Coste de Saint-Domingue," copy made 5 July 1766, E 514, ADCM. She and her son left Saint-Domingue about 15 or 20 May 1755. Bechade to Madame Veuve Royer, 4 July 1755, E 514, ADCM. The passenger lists for La Rochelle for this period are no longer extant.

49. Marie-Severin-Augustin Regnaud, 25 October 1755, Parish records, Saint-Barthélémy GG 276, AMLR. The child's mother was said to have "recently arrived" from Léogane, where the child's father was a planter. Madame Regnaud de Beaumont's registration of her slave Lizette specified that she arrived in La Rochelle on 31 July 1755. 6 August 1755, "Registre de sa Majesté commencé le 23 mars 1753 et fini le 14 avril 1757," B 6086, ADCM.

50. Power of attorney, Notaire Gariteau Fils, 26 March 1743, 3 E 2105, ADCM. A copy was prepared just a few days later; copy of power of attorney, prepared by Notaire Delavergne, 5 April 1743. It was later affixed to a contract for a piece of property she bought on 9 April 1771, E 513, ADCM. Jean-Severin sent his wife a renewal of the power of attorney, 2 December 1772, E 516, ADCM.

51. Receipt from Girard, captain of the ship the *Phaeton* bound for La Rochelle from Léogane, for sugar, cocoa, and coffee received from Jean-Severin Regnaud de Beaumont, to be delivered to Madame Regnaud de Beaumont, 14 July 1750, E 512, ADCM. Gayle Brunelle shows that female cloth merchants in Rouen had dealings with merchants in Europe, the Americas, and Africa. Gayle Brunelle, *The New World Merchants of Rouen, 1559–1630* (Kirksville, Mo.: Sixteenth Century Journal, 1991), 88ff.

52. On the process of outfitting a ship, see Robert Harms, *The Diligent: A Voyage Through the Worlds of the Slave Trade* (New York: Basic, 2002), 76. On the *Bellonne* in particular, see Jean Mettas, ed., *Répertoire des expéditions négrières françaises au XVIIIe siècle*, vol. 2, *Ports autres que Nantes* (Paris: Société Française d'Histoire d'Outre-Mer, 1984), 260, 275–76.

53. For example, one voyage brought in 246,800 livres from the trade in slaves, with a total profit of 163,703 livres 8 sols. Summary of profits, no date, E 512, ADCM. Another voyage brought a net profit of 19,379 l. 8 s. 6 d. "Expenses from the disarmament of the ship the *Bellonne*," Camaud, 1 April 1743, E 512, ADCM.

54. Account and repartition, 25 May 1751, E 512, ADCM.

55. The Regnaud de Beaumonts owned a share in the ship from at least as early as 1741. E 512, ADCM.

56. Paul Butel, *Histoire des Antilles françaises, XVIIe–XXe siècle* (Paris: Perrin, 2002), 165.

57. Mettas, ed., *Répertoire des expéditions négrières françaises*, 2: 260, 275–276.

58. David Geggus, "The French Slave Trade: An Overview," *William and Mary Quarterly* 58, 1 (January 2001): 119–38, 123.

59. David Eltis et al., Voyages Database, 2009, *Voyages: The Trans-Atlantic Slave Trade Database*, http://www.slavevoyages.org, accessed 15 October 2014.

60. Geggus, "The French Slave Trade: An Overview," 122.

61. David Geggus, "The Slaves and Free People of Color in Cap Français," in *The Black Urban Atlantic in the Age of the Slave Trade*, ed. Jorge Cañizares-Esguerra, Matt Childs, and James Sidbury (Philadelphia: University of Pennsylvania Press, 2013), 101–21, 113.

62. On the extent to which the Seven Years' War affected colonial trade, see Pierre H.

Boulle, "Patterns of French Colonial Trade and the Seven Years' War," *Histoire Sociale— Social History* 7, 3 (1974): 48–86. Boulle charts a 70 percent decline in colonial trade, 50–52.

63. Jacob de Griselles to Madame Regnaud de Beaumont, 22 October 1768, E 514, ADCM.

64. For example, she purchased a piece of property for fifteen thousand livres. Notary contract for purchase of property from Sieur Simon Lazard Didier Boucheron of Niort, 12 May 1770, E 512, ADCM.

65. Francs were an administrative unit of currency equal to livres.

66. Jacob de Griselles to Madame Regnaud de Beaumont, 30 December 1769, E 514, ADCM.

67. Jacob de Griselles to Madame Regnaud de Beaumont, 27 April 1770, E 514, ADCM.

68. Jacob de Griselles to Madame Regnaud de Beaumont, 15 April 1770, E 514, ADCM.

69. For a similar look at women's anxiety about bankruptcy and their inability to recoup lost dowries, see *The Memoirs of Glückel of Hameln*, trans. Marvin Lowenthal (New York: Schocken, 1977), 227–30, 255–57, 64.

70. Jacob de Griselles to Madame Regnaud de Beaumont, 4 May 1770, E 514, ADCM.

71. Her copy of Madame Regnaud de Beaumont to Jacob de Griselles, 21 July 1770, E 514, ADCM.

72. Jacob de Griselles to Madame Regnaud de Beaumont, 3 August 1770, E 514, ADCM.

73. Her copy of Madame Regnaud de Beaumont to Jacob de Griselles, 7 August 1770, E 514, ADCM.

74. Jacob de Griselles to Madame Regnaud de Beaumont, 18 May 1771, E 514, ADCM.

75. Gautier, *Les Sœurs de Solitude*, 34.

76. For examples of white men who transferred assets to children of color and the tactics they used, see Garrigus, *Before Haiti*, 60–66. Matthew Gerber finds that in France fathers sometimes made provisions for their illegitimate children as well. Matthew Gerber, *Bastards: Politics, Family, and Law in Early Modern France* (New York: Oxford University Press, 2012), 55–62.

77. Similarly, in Brazilian as in French law, illegitimate children could not inherit their parents' estates, although parents could leave them legacies. Linda Lewin, *Surprise Heirs: Illegitimacy, Patrimonial Rights, and Legal Nationalism in Luso-Brazilian Inheritance, 1750–1821* (Stanford, Calif.: Stanford University Press, 2003), 1: 71, 75–76. Guillaume Aubert's work linking claims of race, family, and succession in Gorée and Saint-Louis de Sénégal demonstrates that these questions were also being debated in other parts of the French empire. Guillaume Aubert, "'Nègres ou mulâtres nous sommes tous Français': Race, genre et nation à Gorée et à Saint-Louis du Sénégal, fin XVIIe–fin XVIIIe siècle," in Cécile Vidal, ed., *Français? La nation en débat entre colonies et métropole, XVIe–XIXe siècle* (Paris: École des Hautes Études en Sciences Sociales, 2014), 125–47.

78. Gerber, *Bastards*, 56.

79. The Code Noir accepted mixed-race children as legitimate if their parents married in the Catholic Church; in that case, it provided that both mother and child were free. Article IX, "Code Noir," March 1685, in Médéric-Louis-Élie Moreau de Saint-Méry, *Loix et constitutions des colonies françaises de l'Amérique sous le vent*, 5 vols. (Paris, 1784–1790), 1: 414–24. John Garrigus shows that some white men did in fact marry women of color. *Before Haiti*, 41, 47–48.

80. On property that could be allocated via testament versus lineage property (*acquets* vs. *propres*), see Ralph E. Giesey, "Rules of Inheritance and Strategies of Mobility in Prerevolutionary France," *American Historical Review* 82, 2 (1977): 271–89.

81. King, *Blue Coat or Powdered Wig*, 215. Garrigus, *Before Haiti*, 45–49 and 65–66. Also see,

for example, "donation of Sieur Jean-Jacques Renard to Jacques Dominique, free *quateroon*, aged about one year, and to the children to be born to Catherine called Deda, free *mulâtresse*," Notary Beaudould, Port-au-Prince, 26 September 1785, DPPC NOT SDOM 85, ANOM.

82. On Regnaud de Beaumont's debts, see the correspondence between J. LeDuc and Madame Regnaud de Beaumont from 8 May 1771 to 22 February 1772, E 514, ADCM; and E.L. Seignette to Garesché and Billotteau, in which he lists Regnaud's debts to him as 13,746 l. 3 s. 4 d., 22 August 1780, 4 J 1610, ADCM.

83. Jean-Marie-Olive Regnaud de Beaumont to Marie-Magdelaine Royer Regnaud de Beaumont, 7 May 1774, E 514, ADCM.

84. Jean-Marie-Olive Regnaud de Beaumont to Marie-Magdelaine Royer Regnaud de Beaumont, 18 May 1782, E 514, ADCM.

85. In a similar case a few years later, *Raymond v. Casse* (1779), the Parlement of Paris upheld the right of Antoine Casse to leave legacies that comprised his entire estate to a natural (white) son and substantial annual pensions to his three mixed-race children. Gerber, *Bastards*, 153–54, 166–68; Matthew Gerber, "Bastardy, Race, and Law in the Eighteenth-Century French Atlantic: The Evidence of Litigation," *French Historical Studies* 36, 4 (2013), 571–600, 593–98.

86. "Testament du Sr. Regnaud de Beaumont homologué le 28 Juin 1775," E 513, ADCM. Hervé de Halgouet refers to a similar case, where a man in Saint-Domingue showed "exorbitant" generosity to his *ménagère*, who might have been his natural daughter, at the expense of his wife and daughter in France. Hervé du Halgouet, "Inventaire d'une habitation à Saint-Domingue," *Revue d'Histoire des Colonies* 21, 4–5 (1933): 236. According to the Coutume de Paris fathers could only leave illegitimate children property, including annuities, in usufruct; they could not transmit immeubles to illegitimate offspring. Langloix, *Principes généraux de la Coutume de Paris*, 237.

87. For a similar case in which a father left legacies comprising the bulk of his wealth to his illegitimate children, both mixed-race and white, see Gerber, "Bastardy, Race, and Law," on *Raymond v. Casse*, 593–98.

88. Jean-Severin Regnaud, 27 July, 1775, Parish records, Sainte-Rose, Léogane, Saint-Domingue, 85MIOM/64, ANOM.

89. Also see Sandra Lauderdale Graham, *Caetana Says No: Women's Stories from a Brazilian Slave Society* (New York: Cambridge University Press, 2002), "The Second Story," 83–169.

90. Michel Samuel DeColon to the widow Royer Regnaud de Beaumont, 3 February 1777 and 15 July 1776, E 514, ADCM.

91. Michel Samuel DeColon to the widow Royer Regnaud de Beaumont, 15 July 1776, E 514, ADCM. The Code Noir defined slaves as meubles, and as such they were not attached to the plantation, as were serfs, and could only be sold separately from it. Although DeColon's language is ambiguous, he likely sold the plantation and the slaves separately. On defining slaves as property, see Articles XLIV–LIV, "Code Noir," March 1685, in Moreau de Saint-Méry, *Loix et constitutions*, 1: 414–24. Subsequent laws affirmed the classification of slaves as *meubles*. See 215n2 of this book.

92. Colonial legal practices made it virtually impossible for a creditor to obtain the property of a debtor. Géraud-Llorca, "La Coutume de Paris Outre-mer," 244–57. At least 10 percent of colonists' debts for slaves alone regularly went unpaid. Carolyn Fick, *The Making of Haiti: The Saint Domingue Revolution from Below* (Knoxville: University of Tennessee Press, 1990), 24.

93. Michel Samuel DeColon to the widow Royer Regnaud de Beaumont, 15 July 1776 E 514, ADCM.

94. Dominique Rogers, "Les libres de couleur dans les capitales de Saint-Domingue: Fortune, mentalités et intégration à la fin de l'Ancien Régime" (dissertation, Université Michel de Montaigne, Bordeaux III, 1999), 173. Of her sample of a total of 281 free women of color in Cap Français and Port-au-Prince, about 20 percent were employed as domestics and about 15 percent as shopkeepers. The preponderance of shopkeepers lived in Cap Français, most of the domestics in Port-au-Prince.

95. Ibid., 453–55.

96. Michel Samuel DeColon to the widow Royer Regnaud de Beaumont, 15 July 1776, E 514, ADCM.

97. In France, lawyers had successfully used illegitimacy as a means of challenging inheritance from 1656. Gerber, "Bastardy, Race, and Law," 582.

98. For an elaboration on the laws surrounding the paying of debts before the division of the estate, see Gabriel Lepointe, *Droit Romain et ancien droit français: Régimes matrimoniaux, libéralités, successions* (Paris: Montchrestien, 1958), 394–95.

99. Renunciation of Common Goods, 4 November, 1775, E 513, ADCM.

100. "Vente d'un négrillon et une négritte par Sieur DeColon," 24 February 1777, DPPC NOT SDOM 1527, ANOM. This contract of sale names DeColon as the procureur of Madame Regnaud de Beaumont.

101. "Procuration par Sieur DeColon à M.M. Paul Nairac et fils ainé négociants à Bordeaux," 26 June 1778, DPPC NOT SDOM 1527, ANOM.

102. "Entre les héritiers Regnaud de Beaumont contre le nègre nommé L'Amoureux," 4 April 1778, DPPC Greffes 1, ANOM. "DeColon à Dlle de Beaumont," 13 April 1785, DPPC Greffes 2, ANOM.

103. Jean-Marie-Olive to Marie-Magdelaine Royer Regnaud de Beaumont, 6 August 1786, E 514, ADCM. Also see Debien, "À Saint-Domingue," 2.

104. Marie-Magdelaine Regnaud de Beaumont wrote a frantic letter to the priest in Saint-Marc on 28 July, 1789, asking for news of her son. She says that her last letter from him was dated 6 August 1786, and she did not know if he was alive or dead. Also see Regnaud de Beaumont sisters to Buchiére, 19 June 1797, both E 515, ADCM.

Chapter 4. Economies of Race and Gender

1. Arlette Gautier, *Les Sœurs de solitude: Femmes et esclavage aux Antilles du XVIIe au XIXe siècle* (Rennes: Presses Universitaires de Rennes, 2010), 32.

2. Yvonne Fabella, "Inventing the Créole Citizen: Race, Sexuality and the Colonial Order in Pre-Revolutionary Saint Domingue" (dissertation, Stony Brook University, 2008), 191–93.

3. Michel-René Hilliard d'Auberteuil, *Considérations sur l'état présent de la colonie française de Saint-Domingue*, 2 vols. (Paris: Chez Grangé, 1776), 2: 31–32. Scholars have generally followed this interpretation. See Joan Dayan, *Haiti, History, and the Gods* (Berkeley: University of California Press, 1995), 175–180; Barbara Bush, *Slave Women in Caribbean Society, 1650–1838* (Bloomington: Indiana University Press, 1990), 114, 134; Marietta Morrissey, *Slave Women in the New World: Gender Stratification in the Caribbean* (Lawrence: University Press of Kansas, 1989), 149–150.

4. Yvonne Fabella, "Redeeming the 'Character of the Créoles': Whiteness, Gender and Creolization in Pre-Revolutionary Saint Domingue," *Journal of Historical Sociology* 23, 1 (2010): 40–72, 52–64.

5. Médéric-Louis-Élie Moreau de Saint-Méry, *La description topographique, physique, civile,*

politique et historique de la partie française de Saint-Domingue, 3 vols. (Saint-Denis: Société Française d'Histoire d'Outre-mer, 2004), 1: 39–40. Also see Fabella, "Redeeming the 'Character of the Créoles,'" 56–58. Scholars who have emphasized the importance of white femininity in reproducing white power include Barbara Bush, "White 'Ladies', Coloured 'Favourites' and Black 'Wenches': Some Considerations on Sex, Race and Class Factors in Social Relations in White Créole Society in the British Caribbean," *Slavery and Abolition* 2, 3 (1981): 245–62; Ann Laura Stoler, "Carnal Knowledge and Imperial Power: Gender, Race and Morality in Colonial Asia," in *Gender at the Crossroads of Knowledge: Feminist Anthropology in the Postmodern Era*, ed. Micaela di Leonardo (Berkeley: University of California Press, 1991), 51–101; Kathleen Wilson, *The Island Race: Englishness, Empire and Gender in the Eighteenth Century* (London: Routledge, 2003), chap. 4.

6. John Garrigus, *Before Haiti: Race and Citizenship in French Saint-Domingue* (New York: Palgrave, 2006), 154–56. Contemporary sources discussed by Garrigus include Brueys d'Aigailliers, Girod de Chantrans, and, most notably, Moreau de Saint-Méry.

7. Recent scholarship has begun to disrupt these assumptions about women of color. Scholarship specifically on women in the French Antilles has focused primarily on enslaved women. Gautier, *Les Sœurs de solitude*; Bernard Moitt, *Women and Slavery in the French Antilles, 1635–1848* (Bloomington: Indiana University Press, 2001). On free people of color more generally, see Garrigus, *Before Haiti*; Stewart King, *Blue Coat or Powdered Wig: Free People of Color in Pre-Revolutionary Saint Domingue* (Athens: University of Georgia Press, 2001); Dominique Rogers, "Les libres de couleur dans les capitales de Saint-Domingue: Fortune, mentalités et intégration à la fin de l'Ancien Régime" (dissertation, Université Michel de Montaigne, Bordeaux III, 1999). Little attention has been paid so far to white women; an exception is the scholarship of Yvonne Fabella, cited above.

8. Hilliard d'Auberteuil, *Considérations sur . . . Saint-Domingue*, 32.

9. Bernard Moitt claims that male and female slave owners treated slaves in similarly brutal ways, *Women and Slavery*, xvi. In this he follows other scholars of the Caribbean, including Morrissey, *Slave Women in the New World*, 4; Bush, *Slave Women in Caribbean Society*, 114.

10. Thavolia Glymph, *Out of the House of Bondage: The Transformation of the Plantation Household* (New York: Cambridge University Press, 2008).

11. Hilary McD. Beckles, *Centering Women: Gender Discourses in Caribbean Slave Society* (Kingston: Ian Randle, 1999), 69; Morrissey, *Slave Women in the New World*, 150–51.

12. Rogers, "Les libres de couleur," chap. 7.

13. Ibid., 438–50.

14. Carolyn Fick, *The Making of Haiti: The Saint-Domingue Revolution from Below* (Knoxville: University of Tennessee Press, 1990), 18; Pierre Pluchon, *Histoire des Antilles et de la Guyane* (Toulouse: Privat, 1982), 163; David Geggus, "The Major Port Towns of Saint Domingue in the Later Eighteenth Century," in *Atlantic Port Cities*, ed. Franklin Knight and Peggy Liss (Knoxville: University of Tennessee Press, 1991), 87–116, 108. Although Debien agrees that owners often freed their ménagères, he considers it "a great exaggeration" that most emancipations were of owners' mistresses and children. Gabriel Debien, *Les esclaves aux Antilles françaises* (Basse-Terre: Société d'Histoire de la Guadeloupe, 1974), 376–77. Garrigus begins to qualify this assumption by emphasizing the complexity and variety of relationships between white men and women of color. Garrigus, *Before Haiti*, 56–60. Dominique Rogers has begun to revise this assumption altogether by demonstrating that whites freed slaves identified as "nègres" almost as frequently as they freed slaves of mixed race. Rogers, "Les libres de couleur," 68–75.

15. This revises the usual figure of two-thirds slightly upward. Rogers, "Les libres de couleur," 69. Rogers has also found that people of color who were not of mixed racial origin comprised nearly half of those emancipated, and of these, slaves from Africa were a substantial proportion. In Port-au-Prince 45.3 percent and in Cap Français 48.6 percent of emancipated slaves were classified as "*nègres*"; 14.3 percent of emancipated slaves in Port-au-Prince were born in Africa, and 12.6 percent in Cap Français. Rogers, "Les libres de couleur," 71.

16. This high proportion of children among emancipated slaves accords with what other scholars have found. In his sample, Garrigus found that in 1760 children or women with children comprised 55 percent of emancipations. Garrigus, *Before Haiti*, 60. Arlette Gautier, looking at notary records in Nippes from 1721–1770, found that only twenty-two men were emancipated, compared to eighty-three women and one hundred thirty-three children. Gautier, *Les Sœurs de solitude*, 153.

17. Susan Socolow, "Economic Roles of the Free Women of Color," in *More Than Chattel: Black Women and Slavery in the Americas*, ed. David Barry Gaspar and Darlene Clark Hine (Indianapolis: Indiana University Press, 1996), 279–97; 281.

18. Ibid., 286–87.

19. "Liberté par Dame Ve. Demarles à Manite Mss," 30 January 1784, Notary Razond, DPPC NOT SDOM 1530. Rogers points out the difference between acts that gave liberty and acts that ratified liberty. Of the 1,630 liberty acts she studied, 151 were ratifications. Rogers, "Les libres de couleur," 72.

20. The Ordinance of 10 July 1768 specified that owners who wanted to emancipate their slaves had to publish their intention to do so in advance, and it tightened regulations for keeping records on emancipated slaves. "Ordonnance du Roi, sur la forme des affranchissements des Esclaves," 10 July 1768, Médéric-Louis-Élie Moreau de Saint-Méry, *Loix et constitutions des colonies françaises de l'Amérique sous le vent*, 5 vols. (Paris: Moreau de Saint-Méry, 1784–1790), 5: 190–92.

21. The Ordinance of 23 October 1775 allowed the king to tax emancipations. "Ordonnance des Administrateurs, concernant les Libertés," 23 October 1775, in ibid., 5: 610–13. Officials sometimes waived these fees, but I found no evidence they had done so in any of the emancipation documents I examined.

22. Malick Ghachem, *The Old Regime and the French Revolution* (New York: Cambridge University Press, 2012), 95, ff 63; Garrigus, *Before Haiti*, 177; Debien, *Les esclaves aux Antilles françaises*, 374; Lucien Peytraud, *L'Esclavage aux Antilles françaises avant 1789, d'après des documents inédits des Archives coloniales* (Paris: Hachette, 1897), 413.

23. "Règlement des Administrateurs concernant les Gens de couleur libres," 24 June and 16 July 1773, Moreau de Saint-Méry, *Loix et constitutions des colonies françaises*, 5: 448–50.

24. One classic example here is Equiano, who amasses the capital necessary to purchase himself and at the injunction of his owner gets the necessary paperwork drawn up by a notary. Olaudah Equiano, *The Interesting Narrative of the Life of Olaudah Equiano or, Gustavus Vassa, the African* (New York: Modern Library, 2004), 134–36.

25. "Liberté," 24 November 1779, Notary Degrandpré, DPPC NOT SDOM 436, ANOM.

26. "Liberté pour Marie Lomie ditte Louise," 3 January 1777, Notary Degrandpré, DPPC NOT SDOM 435, ANOM.

27. Debien, *Les esclaves aux Antilles françaises*, 380–87; Garrigus, *Before Haiti*, 43–44; Ghachem, *The Old Regime and the Haitian Revolution*, 87–89.

28. Ghachem, *The Old Regime and the Haitian Revolution*, 87.

29. Ibid., 88; Debien, *Les esclaves aux Antilles françaises*, 386–87.

30. Ghachem, *The Old Regime and the Haitian Revolution*, 88.

31. "Testament de la Dame Veuve de Labruyere," 13 March 1779, Notary Grasset, DPPC NOT SDOM 811, ANOM.

32. Legacies to ménagères ranged from as little as 300 to more than 5,000 livres. Rogers, "Les libres de couleur," 569–71. Legacies to servants similarly varied, but often were a one-time sum equivalent to about a year's wages. Sarah Maza, *Servants and Masters in Eighteenth-Century France: The Uses of Loyalty* (Princeton, N.J.: Princeton University Press, 1983), 170–71.

33. "Liberté," 10 April 1778, Notary Degrandpré, DPPC NOT SDOM 435, ANOM.

34. Guy-Pierre Coustard, a colonel of the infantry in Port-au-Prince, represented Madame DuVivier. He also represented Madame Veuve Bourgogne, discussed above. In spite of the similarity of the women's names, they seem to be two different (although possibly related) women and these emancipations are in two separate acts. In this case, Toinette received her liberty "in consideration of her great age and of services that she rendered and continues to render her mistress." "Liberté," 10 April 1778. Other women also were represented by men, such as the Dame Veuve Perdereau, who gave authority to one M. Salaignac to represent her before the notary in the process of freeing her slave Marie-Rose. "Liberté," 14 November 1770, Notary De-grandpré, DPPC NOT SDOM 436, ANOM.

35. "Liberté," 6 May 1779, Notary Dugrandpré, DPPC NOT SDOM 436, ANOM. This was apparently the same Jeanne Mathurine Drouillard de Volunbrun whose removal of twenty people she claimed as slaves from Saint-Domingue to New York and finally to Baltimore caused controversy in the late 1790s. Martha S. Jones, "Time, Space, and Jurisdiction in Atlantic World Slavery: The Volunbrun Household in Gradual Emancipation New York," *Law and History Review* 29, 4 (November 2011): 1031–60.

36. "Liberté," 14 August 1781, Notarty Dugrandpré, DPPC NOT SDOM 437, ANOM.

37. "Donation d'une négresse et son enfant. Madame Ve. Guillier aux enfants mulâtres de Madeleine Negsse. L.," 30 August 1781, Notary Pard-Grandmaison, DPPC NOT SDOM 1518, ANOM. For another example of a white woman giving a slave to a woman of color and her children, see "Donation d'une négresse par la veuve Dupin à N[ome]és Ourant et femme et à leurs enfants," 21 February 1779, DPPC NOT SDOM 1518, ANOM.

38. The deed of gift refers to this emancipation contract, although I have not found the emancipation itself. There is a gap in the notary's records from 1772 to 1775, during which emancipation paperwork would have been processed.

39. Literature tends to highlight divisions and rivalries between petits blancs and free people of color, emphasizing instead alliances between free people of color and planters. Fick, *The Making of Haiti*, 18.

40. "Testament, Dame Ve. Chefehier," 1 October, 1782, Notary Razond, Léogane, DPPC NOT SDOM/1529, ANOM.

41. She was born on 14 June 1700 and baptized in Saint-Barthélémy parish in La Rochelle two days later. Her parents were Estienne Millet and Elizabeth Thomade. Her father was a tailor of men's suits. Her godfather, Pierre Chaigneau, was a button maker. Jeanne Millet, 16 June 1700, parish records, Saint-Barthélémy, GG221, ADCM.

42. Rogers notes that owners sometimes left similar legacies to slaves. Rogers, "Les libres de couleur," 62.

43. Martha Howell, *The Marriage Exchange: Property, Social Place, and Gender in Cities of the Low Countries, 1300–1550* (Chicago: University of Chicago Press, 1998), 136–37. On the

importance of exchanging objects, see Orest Ranum, "Refuges of Intimacy," in *A History of Private Life*, vol. 3, *Passions of the Renaissance*, ed. Roger Chartier, trans. Arthur Goldhammer (Cambridge, Mass.: Harvard University Press, 1989), esp. 246–52.

44. Ibid., 166.

45. Garrigus, *Before Haiti*, 162–69.

46. Rogers, "Les libres de couleur," Chapter 5.

47. Parish Register, Léogane, 1782, ANOM.

48. Fabella, "Redeeming the 'Character of the Créoles,'" 49–50, 51.

49. Ibid., esp. 56–57.

50. On white women as economic agents in the British Caribbean, see Beckles, *Centering Women*, chap. 4.

51. Garrigus, *Before Haiti*, 176.

52. Ibid.

53. Rogers, "Les libres de couleur," 105, 111.

54. "Vente par Sr. Bion à De. Ve. Gaston Prou," 30 June 1783, Notary Razond, DPPC NOT SDOM 1529, ANOM. Although I did not find the original lending contract, other contracts she made with notary Lambert refer to this loan and to her impending journey to France, for which she was getting her affairs in order. "Procuration de Ve. Gaston Prou," 5 March 1779, Notary Lambert, DPPC NOT SDOM 1181, ANOM. Also see contracts of 1 and 19 April 1779.

55. "Procuration de Ve. Gaston Prou," 5 March 1779, Notary Lambert, DPPC NOT SDOM 1181, ANOM.

56. Rogers, "Les libres de couleur," 438–39.

57. "Renonciation," 19 April 1779, Notary Lambert, DPPC NOT SDOM 1181, ANOM.

58. Rogers, "Les libres de couleur." Beckles, *Centering Women*, says that most white female slave owners in the British Caribbean were "generally urban, in possession of less than ten slaves, the majority of whom were female" (63).

59. "Bail de 2 chambres et cabinet, par Sr Pre. Thenet à Ve. Coquillau," 15 June 1777, Notary Plaird-Grandmaison, DPPC NOT SDOM 1517, ANOM. I have translated "cabinet" as "office." It could refer to a surgery as she rented from a surgeon.

60. "Bail a ferme," 3 December 1777, Notary Degrandpré, DPPC NOT SDOM 435, ANOM.

61. "Bail de terrain par Veuve Neker à Jean-Pierre dit Morin," 22 April 1781, DPPC NOT SDOM 1518, ANOM.

62. "Bail à ferme par Étienette-Louise Montare Veuve Rondeau et Jean-Jacques Poissan . . . à Catherine Rondeau Ve. Montas," 6 Mars 1778, Notary Grasset, DPPC NOT SDOM 810, ANOM.

63. "Reglement de compte entre Sr Jeanton et la Ve. Jeanton son mère," 11 April 1778, Notary Plard Grandmaison, DPPC NOT SDOM 1517, ANOM.

64. "Bail de 5 Esclaves par la Veuve Jeanton à Joseph Jeanton son fils," 2 December 1779, Notary Plard Grandmaison, DPPC NOT SDOM 1518, ANOM.

65. "Règlement de comptes et affaires entre S. Joseph Jeanton et Veuve Jeanton," 7 May 1781, DPPC NOT SDOM 1518, ANOM.

66. White women occasionally also entered into partnerships with white women. Although surely they sometimes went into business with people of color as well, I found no instances of this.

67. "Société entre Srs. Cruzeau et Méance, et Dlle Méance," 9 June 1784, Notary Razond, DPPC NOT SDOM 1530, ANOM.

68. "Société entre Marie Louise Haurein Ve. White avec S. Jacob St. Macary,"3 April and 1 May 1778, Notary Grasset, DPPC NOT SDOM 810, ANOM. St. Macary was also a procureur for the Belin plantation, discussed in Chapter 1 and the Epilogue.

69. "Société S. G. Audebert et Dlle. F. Chabert Beaulieu," 21 September 1777, Notary Collinet, DPPC NOT SDOM 395, ANOM.

70. "Société," 16 May 1777, Notary Degrandpré, DPPC NOT SDOM 435, ANOM.

71. "Dissolution de société et conventions," 6 June 1781, Notary Collinet, DPPC NOT SDOM 395, ANOM.

72. "Société," 8 May 1783, Notary Collinet, DPPC NOT SDOM 395, ANOM.

73. Similarly, Martha Howell points out how widows could use their gender to avoid responsibility for their late husbands' debts. Martha Howell, *The Marriage Exchange: Property, Social Place, and Gender in Cities of the Low Countries, 1300–1550* (Chicago: University of Chicago Press, 1998), 151.

74. One widow, Marguerite Suzanne Huet, made three declarations, all of them renewing the registration of a single slave. 24 August 1748, "Registre de sa Majesté commencé le 9 novembre 1747 et fini le 16 janvier 1751," B 228, ADCM; 13 August 1751, "Registre de sa Majesté commencé le 22 janvier 1751 et fini le 21 mars 1753," B 229, ADCM; 10 March 1755, "Registre de sa Majesté commencé le 23 mars 1753 et fini le 14 avril 1757," B 6086, ADCM.

75. 16 September 1751, "Registre de sa Majesté commencé le 22 janvier 1751 et fini le 21 mars 1753," B229, ADCM.

76. Ibid.

77. Isambert, Decrusy, and Taillandier, *Recueil général des anciennes lois françaises, depuis l'an 420 jusqu'à la Révolution de 1789* (Paris: Belin-Leprieur, 1830), 12: 113.

78. For example, slave owner Madame de Volunbrun apprenticed a twelve-year-old slave named Ali to the free *mulâtre* Laurent to have him trained as a goldsmith. 16 May 1781, Notary Degrandpré in Port-au-Prince, DPPC NOT SDOM 437, ANOM.

79. "Apprentissage du nommé Tranchemontagne, nègre de Made. Regnaud avec La Veuve St. Marc," 6 November 1752, prepared by Notaries Delavergne and Solleau, E 512, ADCM. Tranchemontagne's apprenticeship contract was the only one I found for a slave in La Rochelle; I would like to thank Robert DuPlessis for bringing it to my attention. According to the king's Edict of 1704, which mandated registration of apprenticeship contracts, certification of master status, and other documents related to the guilds, each apprenticeship in every town where guilds were active should have been registered with a royal clerk. René de Lespinasse, *Histoire général de Paris: Les métiers et corporations de la ville de Paris*, 3 vols. (Paris, 1886–1887), 1: 136–37. *Édit du Roi portent création d'offices de greffiers pour l'enregistrement des brevets d'apprentissage, lettres de maîtresse, élections des jurés et redditions des comptes*, August, 1704. According to Lespinasse, another edict with the same goal was issued 10 February 1705: "Déclaration du Roi réglant à nouveau les fonctions des greffiers susdits, en raison des oppositions qu'ils rencontraient parmi les maîtres des communautés dans l'exercice de leurs fonctions," 137n1. He cites Coll. Lamoignon, vol. XXII, fol. 336. I found no suggestion that Tranchemontagne's apprenticeship was so registered; instead, his contract was made more privately, before a notary. Terms of apprenticeship usually lasted between four and five years, the time deemed necessary by the guild to gain proficiency in the craft. In his study of apprenticeships in Paris, Steven Kaplan found that on average, they lasted for four years and ten months. Steven Kaplan, "L'apprentissage au XVIIIe siècle: Le cas de Paris," *Revue d'Histoire Moderne et Contemporaine* 40, 3 (1993): 436–79, 450.

80. Contract of indenture of Jean Mesele, 2 July 1733, Notary archives of René Rivière, 1733–1734, 2 Mi 1790–R 17 (3 E 1805), ADCM. In the same file, also see the contract of indenture of François Coiudreau Carron, 7 July 1733. Carron promised to teach his trade of blacksmith to two slaves. Both young men contracted themselves for two years and received their passage, room and board, and a small salary. Such contracts of indenture are relatively common in the La Rochelle notary archives. Also see Gabriel Debien, "Les engagés pour les Antilles, 1634–1715," *Revue d'Histoire des Colonies* 37 (1951): 2–277. Garrigus claims that free people of color in the south province of Saint-Domingue worked as artisans, merchants, or farmers. John Garrigus, *Before Haiti*, 72–81.

81. Steven Kaplan found that only 41 percent of apprentices paid fees to their masters, and that the percentage of those who paid fees varied according to trade. Fees themselves also depended on trade, and ranged up to 1,200 livres for prestigious *métiers* such as merciers. The average price paid by apprentice rope makers was 136 livres, 542 livres for épicers, 763 for merciers, 700 for watchmakers, 520 for carpet makers, 150 for locksmiths, 114 for joiners, 128 for sculptors, 160 for pastry makers, 100 for cork makers, 125 for glaziers, and 150 for brush makers. Kaplan, "L'apprentissage au XVIIIe siècle," 448–50. Clare Crowston found that among seamstresses in Paris in the 1750s, the average price paid to a master was 155 livres, with an average of 206 livres among the 75 percent of paying contracts. Clare Haru Crowston, *Fabricating Women: The Seamstresses of Old Regime France, 1675–1791* (Durham, N.C.: Duke University Press, 2001), 213, Table 7.3. On the price of apprenticeship in the provinces, see Maurice Garden, *Lyon et les Lyonnais au XVIIIe siècle* (Paris: Flammarion, 1975), esp. 330.

82. Like slaves, apprentices rarely received wages. Of Steven Kaplan's sample of three hundred sixteen apprenticeship contracts, only six offered wages to their apprentices. An interesting exception to this general rule was master sculptor Geneviève Seigneur, who paid her twelve-year-old apprentice three livres per week from his third year of apprenticeship. Kaplan concludes that as a widow, "doubtless she was going to rely on him enormously." Kaplan, "L'apprentissage au XVIIIe siècle," esp. 440.

83. For example, widows of master tailors could only engage one journeyman per year, who had to be approved by guild leaders. Crowston, *Fabricating Women*, 84.

84. Ibid., 183–84, 228; 40 percent of artisans chose a wife whose father had the same profession in the first half of the eighteenth century; this number rose to 54 percent in the second half of the century. The Widow Vinet, proprietress of her own workshop, therefore would have been an attractive marriage prospect for unmarried coopers in La Rochelle. François Lebrun, *La Vie conjugale sous l'ancien régime* (Paris: Librairie Armand Colin, 1975), 26.

85. Marie-Magdelaine Regnaud, 17 April 1737, parish records, Saint-Barthélémy, GG 253, ADCM.

86. "Apprentissage du nommé Tranchemontagne, nègre de Made. Regnaud avec La Veuve St. Marc," 6 November 1752, prepared by Notaries Delavergne and Solleau, E 512, ADCM.

87. Ibid. This phrasing accords with the phrasing Crowston found in apprenticeship contracts prepared by nonguild notaries. Crowston, *Fabricating Women*, 304.

88. "Apprentissage du nommé Tranchemontagne, nègre de Made. Regnaud avec La Veuve St. Marc," 6 November 1752, prepared by Notaries Delavergne and Solleau, E 512, ADCM.

89. Ibid.

90. S. R. Epstein, "Craft Guilds, Apprenticeship, and Technological Change in Preindustrial Europe," *Journal of Economic History* 58, 3 (1998), 684–713, 691. Also see Robert J. Steinfeld, *The Invention of Free Labor: The Employment Relation in English and American Law and Culture,*

1350–1870 (Chapel Hill: University of North Carolina Press, 1991), and E. Lipson, *The Economic History of England*, 5th ed., 3 vols. (London: A& C. Black, 1945–48), 3: 312–13.

91. Clare Crowston argues that members of the tailors' guild "saw their status as guild masters as imbricated with their role as male heads of household. As masters, they believed, they were entitled to offer employment to their family members and to endow them with the benefits of mastership, including the right of their widows and daughters to work in the trade as long as they did not marry outside it." In direct contrast, she finds that members of the seamstresses' guild viewed their trade as a means of financial independence and freedom from patriarchal authority. Clare Crowston, "Engendering the Guilds: Seamstresses, Tailors, and the Clash of Corporate Identities in Old Regime France," *French Historical Studies* 23, 2 (2000): 339–71, 341.

92. Historians have disagreed about how women's guilds fit into the guild structure overall. Martha Howell argues in *Women, Production, and Patriarchy* that women's guilds were restricted because of the gender of their members. On the other hand, Daryl Hafter argues that women were not restricted in guilds because of their gender. They had opportunities to join guilds, become mistresses, and engage in lawsuits on behalf of their guild. Daryl Hafter, "Female Masters in the Ribbonmaking Guild of Eighteenth-Century Rouen," *French Historical Studies* 20, 1 (1997): 1–14.

93. "Apprentissage du nommé Tranchemontagne, nègre de Made. Regnaud avec La Veuve St. Marc," 6 November 1752, prepared by Notaries Delavergne and Solleau, E 512, ADCM. Note signed "Veuve St Marcq" appended to Apprenticeship contract.

94. Tranchemontagne, 9? June 1753, parish records, Saint-Barthélémy, 1753, GG 272, AMLR.

95. 6 August 1755, "Registre de sa Majesté commencé le 23 mars 1753 et fini le 14 avril 1757," B 6086, ADCM. Fleuriau's slave Hardy arrived by the same ship.

96. "Passagers embarqués en France," 1753, Colonies F 5B 57, ANOM.

97. Justin Girod de Chantras, *Voyage d'un Suisse dans différentes colonies d'Amérique*, ed. Pierre Pluchon (Paris: Librairie Jules Tallandier, 1980), 188.

Chapter 5. What's in a Name?

1. "Registre pour recevoir les déclarations des Nègres, Négresses, Mulâtres et Mulâtresses qui sont dans cette ville de La Rochelle, suivant les lettres de M. L'Intendant," 1763, 352–19, AMLR. Existing passenger lists for ships arriving in and departing from La Rochelle are extremely spotty. Fleuriau's date of arrival in France can be established by his Admiralty declaration of his slave Hardy, but neither Fleuriau, Hardy, nor the Mandron children appear on surviving lists of arriving passengers. The first official evidence of the children's presence in France is Fleuriau's 1763 declaration, and he does not specify when they arrived. They likely traveled to France with their father in 1755, although they certainly could have arrived later.

2. Pierre Boulle, "'In Defense of Slavery': Eighteenth-Century Opposition to Abolition and the Origins of Racist Ideology in France," in *History from Below: Studies in Popular Protest and Popular Ideology*, ed. Frederick Krantz (Montreal: Concordia University Press, 1985), 221–4; Carolyn Fick, *The Making of Haiti: The Saint Domingue Revolution from Below* (Knoxville: University of Tennessee Press, 1990), chap. 3; John Garrigus, *Before Haiti: Race and Citizenship in French Saint-Domingue* (New York: Palgrave Macmillan, 2006), chap. 8.

3. Most French families in the seventeenth and eighteenth centuries lived in nuclear units. Jean-Louis Flandrin, *Families in Former Times: Kinship, Household, and Sexuality in Early Modern France*, ed. and trans. Richard Southern (Cambridge: Cambridge University Press, 1979), 53–92.

4. Matthew Gerber, "Bastardy, Race, and Law in the Eighteenth-Century French Atlantic: The Evidence of Litigation," *French Historical Studies* 36, 4 (2013): 571–600, 571–72.

5. James Traer, *Marriage and the Family in Eighteenth-Century France* (Ithaca, N.Y.: Cornell University Press, 1980), especially chap. 1, 22–47, 41.

6. Fleuriau had two siblings and seven half-siblings, children of his father and a previous wife. Jacques de Cauna, *Au temps des isles à sucre: Histoire d'une plantation de Saint-Domingue au XVIIIe siècle* (Paris: Karthala, 1987), 254. Given the number of siblings and the modest nature of his father's work, he was unlikely to inherit much. On sugar refining in France see Robert Louis Stein, *The French Sugar Business in the Eighteenth Century* (Baton Rouge: Louisiana State University Press, 1988), chaps. 7 and 8. Many sugar refiners in La Rochelle were Protestant, a fact that did not escape the notice of the Intendant. Begon (Intendant of La Rochelle) to the Minister of the Marine Jérôme Phelypeaux, comte de Pontchartrain, 13 February 1700, G7 339, AN.

7. Jacques de Cauna, *L'eldorado des Aquitains: Gascons, Basques et Bérnais aux Îles d'Amérique (XVIIe–XVIIIe siècles)* (Biarritz: Atlantica, 1998), 13.

8. For an overview of Fleuriau's early life, see Cauna, *Au temps des isles à sucre*, 21–34, 28.

9. Cissie Fairchilds, "The Production and Marketing of Populuxe Goods in Eighteenth-Century Paris," in *Consumption and the World of Goods*, ed. John Brewer and Roy Porter (New York: Routledge, 1993), 228–48. Although Fairchilds does not explicitly classify sugar as a "populuxe" good, the expanding popularity and availability of this good bring it under her rubric.

10. Land prices in Croix-des-Bouquets were unusually high. Stewart King puts the colony-wide average in the eighteenth century at 23,970 livres, less than half the 65,636-livre average for Croix-des-Bouquets. He does not specify if the plantations in and around Croix-des-Bouquets were larger than those elsewhere, although he suggests earlier that they were. Stewart King, *Blue Coat or Powdered Wig: Free People of Color in Pre-Revolutionary Saint Domingue* (Athens: University of Georgia Press, 2001), 138.

11. A much later document refers to "Jeanneton ancienne esclave de M. Fleuriau." "Livre des comptes," 1777, 1 Mi 255, ADCM. Cauna assumes this refers to Jeanne, and hypothesizes Jeanne belonged to another Rochelais colonist before Fleuriau bought her, because the name Guimbelot was very common in the port town. Perhaps she had belonged to Jacques Guimbelot, who was married in Croix-des-Bouquets in 1729. Cauna, *Au temps des isles à sucre*, 30. She was certainly free well before Fleuriau returned to France. Police des Noirs survey, 1763, 352, AMLR.

12. Parish records, Croix-des-Bouquets, Saint-Domingue, 85 MIOM 46 and 85 MIOM 47, ANOM. Although I did not find the baptism record of Jean-Baptiste in this collection, he certainly was Fleuriau's son. Fleuriau left Jean-Baptiste's heirs a legacy in his will equal to that left to his other Saint-Domingue children who were still alive, and Marie-Jeanne referred to Jean-Baptiste as her brother in her own will.

13. To be precise, she was identified as "Marie-Jeanne *négresse libre*" in Marie-Jeanne's baptism; "Jeanne *dite* Guimbelot *négresse libre*" in Marie-Charlotte's; "Jeanne *négresse libre*" in Joseph-Benjamin's and Toinette's; and "Jeanne Guimbelot *négresse libre*" in Pierre-Paul's, Jean's, and Marie-Magdeline's. Parish records, Croix-des-Bouquets, Saint-Domingue, 85 MIOM 46 and 85 MIOM 47, ANOM.

14. "Livre des comptes," 1743, 1 Mi 255, ADCM. Fleuriau's accounts of 1743 record his disbursal of first 397 livres, then 127 livres "au profit de sa petite." This sum suggests, although does not prove, that Jeanne had received her freedom, and perhaps that her former owner was helping her set up house.

15. "Livre des comptes," 1777, 1 Mi 255, ADCM. Cauna points out that this reference to her as a personal slave, not a slave belonging to the plantation, strongly implies a sexual relationship. Jacques de Cauna, "Une famille transatlantique: les Fleuriau," *Cahiers de Framespa* 9 (2012), http://framespa.revues.org/978; accessed 11 November 2014.

16. Patricia Hill Collins, *Black Feminist Thought: Knowledge, Consciousness, and the Politics of Empowerment*, 2nd ed. (New York: Routledge, 2000); Elsa Barkley Brown, "'What Has Happened Here': The Politics of Difference in Women's History and Feminist Politics," *Feminist Studies* 18, 2 (1992); Annette Gordon-Reed, *The Hemingses of Monticello: An American Family*, (New York: Norton, 2008); Saidiya V. Hartman, *Scenes of Subjection: Terror, Slavery, and Self-Making in Nineteenth-Century America* (New York: Oxford University Press, 1997). Hartman calls such lack of options "the extremity of constraint," 85. Female servants in France also were more vulnerable to sexual abuse. Sarah Maza, *Servants and Masters in Eighteenth-Century France: The Uses of Loyalty* (Princeton, N.J.: Princeton University Press, 1983), 89.

17. Jean-Baptiste Du Tertre, *Histoire générale des Antilles habitées par les françois, devisée en deux tomes, et enrichi de Cartes et de Figures*, 4 vols. (Paris: Thomas Jolly, 1667), 2: 511–12.

18. A number of historians, including Hilary Beckles, Bernard Moitt, and David Geggus, say that enslaved women could pursue sexual relationships with white men for their own advancement. Hilary Beckles, "Black Female Slaves and White Households in Barbados," 111–25, 117–19; Bernard Moitt, "Slave Women and Resistance in the French Caribbean," 239–58, 245; and Geggus, "Slave and Free Colored Women in Saint Domingue," 259–78, 265; all in *More Than Chattel: Black Women and Slavery in the Americas*, ed. David Barry Gaspar and Darlene Clark Hine (Bloomington: Indiana University Press, 1996). More recently historians have challenged the formulation of sexual service as a kind of agency. Hartman, *Scenes of Subjection*, 85.

19. Arlette Gautier, *Les Sœurs de solitude: Femmes et esclavage aux Antilles du XVIIe au XIXe siècle* (Rennes: Presses Universitaires de Rennes, 2010), 148–50, 149.

20. Moreau de Saint-Méry, *La description topographique, physique, civile, politique et historique de la partie française de Saint-Domingue*, 3 vols. (Saint-Denis: Société Français d'Histoire d'Outre-mer, 2004), 1: 106. Gautier, *Les Sœurs de solitude*, 148.

21. Moreau de Saint-Méry, *La Description . . .* , 1: 104.

22. Dominique Rogers and Stewart King, "Housekeepers, Merchants, Rentières: Free Women of Color in the Port Cities of Colonial Saint-Domingue, 1750–1790," in *Women in Port: Gendering Communities, Economies, and Social Networks in Atlantic Port Cities, 1500–1800*, ed. Douglas Caterall and Jodi Campbell (Boston: Brill, 2012), 357–97, 360–65.

23. Moreau de Saint-Méry, *La Description . . .* , 1: 85.

24. Michel-René Hilliard d'Auberteuil, *Considérations sur l'état présent de la colonie française de Saint-Domingue*, 2 vols. (Paris: Chez Grangé, 1776–1777), 2: 73.

25. Garrigus, *Before Haiti*, 40. In the 1760s children or women with children were 55 percent of all slaves freed in notary records in Cayes, Saint-Louis, and Nippes (60). Arlette Gautier found that from 1721–1770 women or children comprised almost 75 percent of slaves freed. Gautier, *Les Sœurs de solitude*, 172–77. According to the Martiniquean planter Pierre Dessalles, Martinique and Guadeloupe had similar statistics, with women being manumitted at a rate significantly higher than men. Pierre Dessalles, *Histoire des Antilles*, 5 vols. (Paris: Librairie-Éditeur, 1847), 5: 39. Also see this volume, 230n15.

26. "Ordonnance du Roi, concernant l'Affranchissement des Esclaves," 24 October 1713, in Moreau de Saint-Méry, *Loix et constitutions des colonies françaises de l'Amérique sous le vent*, 5 vols. (Paris: Moreau de Saint-Méry, 1784–1790), 2: 398–99.

27. Bernard Moitt, *Women and Slavery in the French Antilles, 1635–1848* (Bloomington: Indiana University Press, 2001), 160–63.

28. There is evidence that some women of color felt attachment to their white male sexual partners. For example, in Petite Rivière freed *négresse* Jeanne made the brother of her *patron* (here potentially connoting "man of the house") her universal legatee "in recognition of the good turns that she had received from him and his family." The document refers to her as "the former slave of his [the universal legatee's] brother." "Testament de Négresse Jeanne," 7 April 1779, Notary Grasset, DPPC NOT SDOM 881, ANOM. Similarly, Cécile Mahautière, a free *quateronne* who lived in Port-au-Prince, left her estate in its entirety to one Monsieur Jetier, the procureur of the plantation on which she lived. "Testament," 1 March 1777, DPC NOT SDOM 435, ANOM.

29. "Arrêt du Conseil du Petit-Goâve, touchant le Baptême des enfants, et l'exécution d'un autre Arrêt du 7 Janvier 1727," 10 January 1737, Moreau de Saint-Méry, *Loix et constitutions*, 3: 464; "Arrêt du Conseil de Léogane, contre ceux qui négligent de faire Baptiser leurs Enfants," Nov. 14, 1742, ibid., 3: 716; "Ordonnance des Administrateurs, touchant le Baptême des Enfants," 11 October 1743, ibid., 3: 768.

30. Parish records, Croix-des-Bouquets, Saint-Domingue, 85 MIOM 46 and 85 MIOM 47, ANOM.

31. A later law did indeed prohibit mixed-race children from taking the name of their white father. "Réglemente des Administrateurs concernant les Gens de couleur libres," June 24 and July 16, 1773, Moreau de Saint-Méry, *Loix et constitutions*, 5: 448–50.

32. Garrigus puts interracial marriages at 20 percent of all religious marriages in the 1760s in the south province of Saint-Domingue. Notarized marriage contracts of interracial couples comprised 8 percent of the total. Garrigus, *Before Haiti*, 178.

33. On links of godparentage across lines of color, see King, *Blue Coat or Powdered Wig*, 13, and chap. 10.

34. Malick Ghachem, *The Old Regime and the Haitian Revolution* (New York: Cambridge University Press, 2012), 86–87.

35. King, *Blue Coat or Powdered Wig*, chaps. 9 and 10, and Garrigus, *Before Haiti*, 48.

36. Marie-Anne-Suzanne Liège was born in 1733. Parish records, Saint-Barthélémy, GG 250, AMLR.

37. Cauna says they were married in Bordeaux on 17 August 1757, but gives no source for this information. Cauna, *Au temps des isles à sucre*, 45. They must have married before 1757 because their first child was born 27 May that year, and the baptism record clearly indicates the child is legitimate. Baptism of Aimé-Paul Fleuriau, 28 May 1757, parish records, Saint-Barthélémy, GG 280, AMLR.

38. *Aimé Benjamin Fleuriau* and *Madame Fleuriau, née Marie Anne Suzanne Liège*, 1756, private collection, England. For more information on these portraits, see Neil Jeffares, *Dictionary of Pastellists before 1800* (London: Unicorn Press, 2006), 400; Joseph Baillio et al., *The Arts of France from François Ier to Napoléon Ier* (New York: Wildenstein, 2005), 217–18. They may have married in 1756, and the pastels are their wedding portraits; Marie-Anne-Suzanne Liège's has the date 20 September 1756.

39. See Cauna, *Au temps des isles à sucre*, 46. The street is now known as rue Gargoulleau.

40. Ibid., 46.

41. Ibid., 47.

42. Matthew Gerber shows that by the eighteenth century courts often upheld the bequests

of fathers to illegitimate children. Gerber, *Bastards: Politics, Family, and Law in Early Modern France* (New York: Oxford University Press, 2012), 153–83. However, customary law guaranteed no support for illegitimate children, and their parents had to make special testamentary provision for them to inherit even minimal bequests. Even legitimate mixed-race offspring were increasingly deprived of inheritances. For example, in 1773 the Conseil supérieur du Cap-Français ruled that the legitimate mixed-race offspring of Jean Guerre and Petite-Nanon could not inherit an estate their father had inherited thirty years before. Gerber, *Bastards*, 167–68.

43. Compared to 30,000 free people of color who lived in Saint-Domingue around 1789, that year only eleven people of color were registered as living in Paris, and none in Nantes, Bordeaux, or La Rochelle. Over the course of the eighteenth century, Noël finds a total of 1,145 free people of color in Paris; 1,010 in Nantes; 1,449 in Bordeaux; and 680 in La Rochelle. Erick Noël, *Être noir en France au XVIIIe siècle* (Paris: Tallandier, 2006), 281, Document 11.

44. Farther down the social scale, free people of color did marry in France. Although there were no examples in La Rochelle of formerly enslaved women marrying white men, white women did occasionally marry men of color who had formerly been enslaved. For example, former slave Monréal stated in the 1777 Police des Noirs survey in La Rochelle that he had married a white woman. "État des noirs libres qui sont en France," 1777, 352, ANOM. Jean Nicolas, a man who identified himself in the Police des Noirs survey as a *mulâtre* and a native of India, married a white woman named Marie-Anne Perraud. "Déclaration du Nommée Jean Nicolas, Mulâtre," 18 September, 1777, Colonies F1B4 Dossier VI, ANOM. This information is repeated in "Registre Contenaient les déclarations des noirs, mulâtres, et autres gens de couleur, en conséquence de l'Édit du Roy du 9 août 1777," B 258, ADCM. On marriages between white men and women of color in colonial Saint-Domingue, see Garrigus, *Before Haiti*, 63–64; and King, *Blue Coat or Powdered Wig*, 181–83. Marriage between wealthy free women of color and white men did occasionally take place in France. Garrigus points out that two of Julien Raimond's sisters married well-off Frenchmen, one in Bordeaux and one in Toulouse. Garrigus, *Before Haiti*, 1. Martinique, Guadeloupe, Louisiana, Île Bourbon, and Île de France all had laws prohibiting interracial marriage by the 1720s, but Saint-Domingue did not. Yvan Debbasch, *Couleur ou liberté: le jeu de critère ethnique dans un ordre juridique esclavagiste* (Paris: Librairie Dalloz, 1967), 46–50.

45. "1 nègre, le Sr. Fleuriau," "Registre de sa Majesté commencé le 23 mars 1753 et fini le 14 avril 1757," August 2, 1755, B 6086, ADCM. Very few slaves came from Banguia, also called Bandia. David Geggus, "Sugar and Coffee Cultivation in Saint-Domingue and the Shaping of the Slave Labor Force," in *Cultivation and Culture: Labor and the Shaping of Slave Life in the Americas*, ed. Ira Berlin and Philip Morgan (Charlottesville: University of Virginia Press, 1993) 73–98, 81.

46. "1 nègre, le Sr. Fleuriau," "Registre de sa Majesté commencé le 23 mars 1753 et fini le 14 avril 1757," August 2, 1755, B 6086, ADCM. Fleuriau states that he and Hardy had arrived in France the month before; they seem to have disembarked 31 July 1755.

47. "Registre de sa Majesté du greffe du l'amirauté commencé le 14 avril 1757 et fini le 20 octobre 1760, " 15 September 1757, and 20 August 1760, B 230, ADCM.

48. For further discussions on the Ordinance of 1762 and the legal case that brought it about, see Sue Peabody, *"There Are No Slaves in France": The Political Culture of Race and Slavery in the Ancien Régime* (New York: Oxford University Press, 1996), 72–75; Dwain Pruitt, "Nantes Noir: Living Race in the City of Slavers" (dissertation, Emory University, 2005), 74–76.

49. Ordinance of April 5, 1762, B 5592, ADCM.

50. On how free people of color recorded their freedom, see Laurent Dubois, *A Colony of Citizens: Revolution and Slave Emancipation in the French Caribbean, 1787–1804* (Chapel Hill: University of North Carolina Press, 2004), esp. chap. 15; Garrigus, *Before Haiti*, 83–84.

51. There are other instances of free people of color taking offense at being mistaken for dependents. Garrigus gives an example of a free woman of color who entered into a business partnership with a white man, and found it "deeply galling" to be mistaken for his servant. Garrigus, *Before Haiti*, 60.

52. Voltaire, for example, describes the different races as different species. Voltaire, *Essai sur les moeurs et l'esprit des nations et sur les principaux faits de l'histoire depuis Charlemagne jusqu'à Louis XIII*, 2 vols. (Paris: Garnier Frères, 1963), 1: 6–9. A long tradition of justifying slavery by portraying Africans as supposedly suited for slave labor dates at least back to the seventeenth century. Many subsequent works draw on the text of the Dominican Du Tertre, who asserts that enslaved Africans "suffer almost no fatigue . . . one feeds them as one wishes, one pushes them to work as beasts, and one wrenches from them one way or another until their death all the work of which they are capable." He continues, "When one treats them with gentleness, and when one feeds them well, they count themselves the happiest people of the world." Jean-Baptiste Du Tertre, *Histoire générale des Isles de S. Christophe, de la Guadeloupe, de la Martinique et autres dans l'Amérique* (Paris: Jacques Langlois, 1654), 2: 493, 496–97.

53. "Registre pour recevoir les déclarations des nègres, négresses, mulâtres et mulâtresses qui sont dans cette ville de La Rochelle, suivant les lettres de M. L'Intendant," 1763, 352–19, AMLR. Fleuriau's claim that Hardy was training as a saddler seems specious; he made no such claim in any of his Admiralty declarations.

54. "Hardy," 19 August 1771, parish records, Saint-Barthélémy, GG 309, AMLR.

55. "Registre pour recevoir les déclarations des Nègres, Négresses, Mulâtres & Mulâtresses," 1763, 352, AMLR.

56. Ibid.

57. *Dictionnaire de L'Académie Française*, 4th ed., 2 vols. (Paris: Chez la veuve de Bernard Brunet, 1762), s.v. "créole."

58. "Livre de Comptes," 1777, 1Mi 255, ADCM.

59. Pierre Boulle similarly argues that colonial views about race influenced French ones, particularly after the founding of the Sociéte des Amis des Noirs and the Club Massiac. However, he contends that colonial ideas of blacks and whites as clearly separate races shaped French policy. Boulle, "'In Defense of Slavery,'" 221–41.

60. "Registre pour recevoir les déclarations des Nègres, Négresses, Mulâtres & Mulâtresses qui sont dans cette ville de la Rochelle, suivant les lettres de M. l'Intendant," 1763, 352–19, AMLR.

61. Garrigus, *Before Haiti*, chaps. 4–5.

62. The passenger lists for La Rochelle list Joseph and Paul Mandrox [sic] as passengers on the ship *Père de Famille*, captained by Pierre Botineau, which departed from La Rochelle 25 July 1765, bound for Saint-Domingue. They are identified as brothers and each listed as twenty-one years of age, a slight miscalculation as, according to their baptism records, Pierre-Paul would have been twenty and Joseph-Benjamin twenty-two; however, the boys were born only seventeen months apart. They were both identified as "natural sons of Sr. Fleuriau." Jean-Baptiste left France in 1773 on the ship the *Cérès*, Captain Nicolas Collett. "Passagers embarqués en France-La Rochelle," 1764–1765 and 1773, Colonies F 5B57, ANOM. Cauna refers to the sons' role in managing the plantation. Cauna, *Au temps des isles à sucre*, 5.

63. Slave women were proportionally more likely to be assigned hard agricultural labor,

which was considered unskilled, while men were more likely to engage in specialized forms of labor, including artisanal labor. See Geggus, "Slave and Free Colored Women in Saint Domingue," 261–62; Barbara Bush, "Hard Labor: Women, Childbirth, and Resistance in British Caribbean Slave Societies," in *More Than Chattel*, ed. Gaspar and Hine, 193–217, 196; and Moitt, *Women and Slavery in the French Antilles*, chap. 3.

64. Nearly twenty years later, the Ordonnance des Administrateurs, concernant les Orfévres of 15 January 1781 banned people of color from becoming goldsmiths, showing that people of color exercising this luxury trade was a point of conflict. Dominique Rogers argues that, rather than discrimination against people of color, this measure was part of an overall administrative attempt to control white society. She also points out that the Conseil supérieur of Port-au-Prince refused to register this ordinance, citing Article LIX of the Code Noir, which guaranteed rights to free people of color. According to Moreau, it was registered by the Conseil supérieur of Cap Français on 4 April 1781. Moreau de Saint-Méry, *Loix et constitutions*, 6: 92–95; Dominique Rogers, "Les libres de couleur dans les capitales de Saint-Domingue: Fortune, mentalités et intégration à la fin de l'Ancien Régime" (dissertation, Université Michel de Montaigne, Bordeaux III, 1999), 259.

65. "Registre pour recevoir les déclarations des Nègres, Négresses, Mulâtres & Mulâtresses," 1763, 352, AMLR.

66. Ibid.

67. Ibid.

68. On the delicacy of white créole women, see Yvonne Fabella, "Redeeming the "Character of the Créoles": Whiteness, Gender and Creolization in Pre-Revolutionary Saint Domingue," *Journal of Historical Sociology* 23, 1 (2010): 40–72, 45–49. Jesuit priest Jacques Bouton said of the enslaved Africans he saw in Martinique, "This miserable nation seems only to be in the world for servitude and slavery." Jacques Bouton, *Relation d'un établissement de françois depuis l'an 1635 en l'isle de Martinique, l'une des Antilles de l'Amerique* (Paris: Sebastien Cramoisy, 1640), 101. Du Tertre calls Africans "this unhappy nation, to whom God has attached as a particular and hereditary curse, as well as the blackness and ugliness of the body, slavery and servitude." Du Tertre, *Histoire générale . . .* , 2: 480. Both cited in Sue Peabody, " 'A Nation Born to Slavery': Missionaries and Racial Discourse in Seventeenth-Century French Antilles," *Journal of Social History* 38, 1 (2004): 115.

69. On European discourses about African women's productive and reproductive capacity, see Jennifer Morgan, *Laboring Women: Reproduction and Gender in New World Slavery* (Philadelphia: University of Pennsylvania Press, 2004), esp. 47.

70. On the importance of death in plantation culture, see Vincent Brown, *The Reaper's Garden: Death and Power in the World of Atlantic Slavery* (Cambridge, Mass.: Harvard University Press, 2008).

71. In the eighteenth century overall Garrigus finds an interracial marriage rate of 17 percent in the south province; that had dropped to 7 percent by the 1760s. Garrigus, *Before Haiti*, 63.

72. After their father's death, Paul Mandron in Saint-Domingue exchanged letters with his half-brother Louis-Benjamin Fleuriau in La Rochelle. Paul wrote letters on Dec. 12, 1792, Feb. 11 and May 15, 1794, and in year II of the Revolution, and letters survive from Louis-Benjamin to Paul dated year II and 11 February 1794, 1 Mi 238 and 1 Mi 239, ADCM.

73. Marie-Charlotte Fleuriau, *dite* Mandron, 1773, parish records, Saint-Barthélémy, GG 313; and Marie Mandroux, 1793, GG 354, AMLA.

74. François Lebrun, *La Vie conjugale sous l'ancien régime* (Paris: Armand Colin, 1975), 65–66. Fleuriau made an unsuccessful attempt to be ennobled, but his children successfully sought ennoblement. Cauna, *Au temps des isles à sucre*, 48–50.

75. At the end of the Old Regime, about forty thousand foundlings were abandoned in France each year. Allan Mitchell, *The Divided Path: The German Influence on Social Reform in France After 1870* (Chapel Hill: University of North Carolina Press, 1991), 100–101. Also see Pier Paolo Viazzo, "Mortality, Fertility, and Family," in *The History of the European Family: Family Life in Early Modern Times (1500–1789)*, ed. David I. Kertzer and Marzio Barbagli (New Haven, Conn.: Yale University Press, 2001), 157–188, 177.

76. A sizable minority of women did not marry—as many as 15 to 20 percent. Some families may have discouraged some daughters from marrying. Christine Adams, "A Choice Not to Wed? Unmarried Women in Eighteenth-Century France," *Journal of Social History* 29, 4 (1996): 883–84.

77. John Clark, *La Rochelle and the Atlantic Economy During the Eighteenth Century* (Baltimore: Johns Hopkins University Press, 1981), 56–59.

78. Her dowry was precisely 22,184.18.10 livres. "Dépôt du testament olographe de M. Aimé-Benjamin Fleuriau," 21 August 1787, in files of Notary Delavergne fils, 3 E 1698, ADCM.

79. On white fathers providing for children of color, see Robert Taber, "The Issue of Their Union: Family, Law, and Politics in Western Saint-Domingue, 1777 to 1789" (dissertation, University of Florida, 2015), 157–201.

80. Similarly, Natalie Zemon Davis discusses how Maria Sibylla Merian's daughters also wrote themselves into family history when one of their mother's works was published after her death. Natalie Zemon Davis, *Women on the Margins: Three Seventeenth-Century Lives* (Cambridge, Mass.: Harvard University Press, 1995), 200.

81. Fleuriau, "Declaration des Polices des Noirs," 5 September 1763, 352–19, AMLA.

82. The Catholic record says Marie-Charlotte "was buried in the Church of the R.R.P.P. Récollets, after the ordinary ceremonies in our Church and that of Saint-Saveur." Marie-Charlotte Fleuriau, *dite* Mandron, 1 August 1773, parish records, Saint-Barthélémy, GG 313, AMLR.

83. Ibid.

84. Marie Mandroux, 20 September 1783, parish records, Saint-Barthélémy, GG 333, AMLR.

85. Michel-Joseph Leremboure to Aimé-Benjamin Fleuriau, 22 March 1787, in Papiers Châtillon, cited in Cauna, *Au temps des isles à sucre*, 54

86. "Déclaration de mulâtresse Victoire," 5 October 1777, Colonies F1B4 Dossier VI, ANOM.

87. Michel-Joseph Leremboure to Aimé-Benjamin Fleuriau, 22 March 1787, in Papiers Châtillon, cited in Cauna, *Au temps des isles à sucre*, 54

88. Me. Lamauve, "Cession de bail à ferme à Jean-Baptiste Fleuriau, habitation appartenant au dit Fleuriau au Mirebalais, six esclaves," 30 November 1777, ANOM, cited in Jacques de Cauna, "Une famille transatlantique: Les Fleuriau," *Cahiers de Framespa* 9 (2012), accessed 7 November 2014, http://framespa.revues.org/1152.

89. Elisabeth claims these honorific titles were prohibited in 1781, but cites no statute for this. Léo Elisabeth, "The French Antilles," in *Neither Slave Nor Free: The Freedman of African Descent in the Slave Societies of the New World*, ed. David Cohen and Jack Greene (Baltimore: Johns Hopkins University Press, 1972), 134–71, 162. Rogers cites two arrêts of the Conseil du Cap Français of 22 February 1783 that restrict use of the honorifics "sieur" and "dame" to whites, and require that free people of color be called "le/la nommé(e)." Rogers, "Les libres de couleur,"

288–89. By 1785 even poor whites in Saint-Domingue were given the titles "Sieur" and "Demoiselle," while people of color were not. Garrigus, *Before Haiti*, 142. See also Carminelle Biondi, "Le problème des gens de couleur aux colonies et en France dans le seconde moitié du XVIIIe siècle," *Chronos* 8 (2003), 5. Biondi agrees with Garrigus that attitudes toward free people of color in the colonies began to change around 1760, with the end of the Seven Years' War.

90. Marie Mandroux, 20 September 1783, parish records, Saint-Barthélémy, GG 333, AMLR.

91. On La Rochelle's common inheritance law, see Charles A. Bourdot de Richebourg, *Nouveau coutumier general, ou corps des coutumes générales et particulières de France et des Provinces*, 4 vols. (Paris: Robustel, 1724), 4: 856–59.

92. "Dépôt du testament olographe de M Aimé Benjamin Fleuriau," 21 August 1787, in files of Notary Delavergne fils, 3 E 1698, ADCM.

93. Correspondance of Louis-Florent de la Vallière, March 1772, ADCM C8A71, folio 24. Cited in Edith Géraud-Llorca, "La coutume de Paris outre-mer: L'habitation antillaise sous l'ancien régime," *Revue Historique de Droit Français et Étranger* 60, 2 (1982): 207–59, 230–31.

94. Although in Saint-Domingue it was quite common for white fathers of mixed-race children to leave legacies to them, historians also have identified instances in which fathers left the majority of their estate to their mixed-race children of their former slaves. Tiya Miles, *Ties That Bind: The Story of an Afro-Cherokee Family in Slavery and Freedom* (Berkeley: University of California Press, 2005), 138–43; Kent Anderson Leslie, *Woman of Color, Daughter of Privilege: Amanda America Dickson, 1849–1893* (Athens: University of Georgia Press, 1995), 80–104. John Garrigus also discusses methods fathers of mixed-race children used to circumvent rules of inheritance, including *donations entre vifs*. Garrigus, *Before Haiti*, 65–66.

95. "Dépôt du testament olographe de M Aimé Benjamin Fleuriau," 21 August 1787, in files of Notary Delavergne fils, 3 E 1698, ADCM.

96. Ibid. Fleuriau perhaps felt this necessary given the recent decease of his eldest son Jean-Baptiste on 10 April 1785. Upon his death, one of his children went to live at the Bellevue plantation, another with Paul Mandron, and the last two with the widow Cambre, *née* Guimbelot, demonstrating that the ties between the Mandron and Guimbelot families continued. Michel-Joseph Leremboure to Aimé-Benjamin Fleuriau, 22 May, 31 July 1785, 1 Mi 259, ADCM, cited in Cauna, "Une famille transatlantique: les Fleuriau." *Cahiers de Framespa*. Subsequent documents created by Paul Mandron show that he acted as and considered himself the legal guardian of his brother's children. "Bail pour un Terrain pour le ne. [nommé] Paul Fleuriau," 6 January 1788, Notary Badoux, Mirebalais, DPPC NOT *SDOM 87, ANOM.

97. "Dépôt du testament olographe de M. Aimé-Benjamin Fleuriau," 21 August 1787, files of Notary Delavergne fils, 3 E 1698, ADCM.

98. Fleuriau's estate amounted to a net total of 960,033 livres, 13 sols, 10 deniers. Each legitimate child received 316,011 livres 4 sols 7 deniers after their mother's portion of the estate was deducted. ADCM, 3 E 1698, "Partage de la dite Veuve Fleuriau et ses Enfans [*sic*]," 24 September, 1787. In comparison, Fleuriau left an annual income of 120 livres to his domestic servant. ADCM, 3 E 1698, "Dépôt du testament olographe de M. Aimé-Benjamin Fleuriau," 21 August 1787, in files of Notary Delavergne fils. Based on the value of his colonial property at the time of indemnity in 1828, Cauna places the value of the Fleuriau succession at four million livres. Cauna, *Au temps des isles à sucre*, 50.

99. Martha Howell found that when women left legacies of personal property, this had the effect of reinforcing affective ties by linking them with economic ones, for often personal property had significant market value. Howell, *The Marriage Exchange: Property, Social Place, and*

Gender in Cities of the Low Countries, 1399–1550 (Chicago: University of Chicago Press, 1998), 162–67, 132–38. Similarly, Jeanne-Marie Fleuriau Mandron chose to reinforce family ties with economic ones.

100. "Dépôt du testament de la citoyenne Mandron Fleuriau," 24 November, 1793, records of Notary Farjenel, 3 E 960, ADCM. The will itself, written in Jeanne-Marie Fleuriau Mandron's own hand, was dated 24 May 1788, although it was not filed until her death five years later.

101. État-Civil, record 2148, 2E 312 456*, ADCM.

102. Suzanne Desan, *The Family on Trial in Revolutionary France* (Berkeley: University of California Press, 2004), 207.

103. ADCM 2 Mi 238. Letter from Louis-Benjamin Fleuriau to citoyen Pierre-Paul Fleuriau Mandron of 11 February 1794.

104. "Dépôt du testament de la citoyenne Mandron Fleuriau," 24 November 1793, files of Notary Farjenel, 3 E 960, ADCM.

105. "Inventoire Fleuriau Mandron," 2 December 1793, files of Notary Farjenel, 3 E 960, ADCM. She also had among her papers copies of her father's will and letters from her brothers in Saint-Domingue. The paper money she possessed was in assignats.

106. Howell, *The Marriage Exchange*, 166.

107. E.g., Leremboure to Fleuriau, 22 May, 31 July 1785, 1 Mi 259, ADCM.

108. Louis-Benjamin Fleuriau, known as Fleuriau de Bellevue, published a number of scientific treatises on geology, hydrology, mining, agriculture, and natural history. He was a member of the Academy of La Rochelle, president of its agricultural society, and a deputy of the Charente-Inférieure. For more on his biography see Christian Moreau, "Louis-Benjamin Fleuriau de Bellevue (1761–1852): Sa vie," unpublished paper, in the collection of the author (La Rochelle: Université de La Rochelle). Fleuriau's publications include "Mémoires sur de nouvelles pierres flexibles et élastiques et sur la manière de donner de la flexibilité à plusieurs minéraux: lus à la Société d'histoire-naturelle de Genève," *Journal de Physique* 41(1792), and *Notice sur le puits artésien des bains de mer de La Rochelle* (Paris?: s.n., 1834).

109. "Inventoire Fleuriau Mandron," 2 December 1793, files of Notary Farjenel, 3 E 960, ADCM.

110. Cauna, *Au temps des isles à sucre*, 55.

111. Me. Badoux, Paul Fleuriau, "Bail d'un terrain de 33 carreaux 1/3 à J.-F. Cazeau," 6 January 1788, ANOM; and letter to M. Fleuriau de Bellevue, 6 May 1788, 1 Mi 257, ADCM, both cited in Cauna, "Une famille transatlantique: les Fleuriau."

112. Jean Fouchard, *Les marrons du syllabaire: Quelques aspects du problème de l'instruction et de l'éducation des esclaves et affranchis de Saint-Domingue* (Port-au-Prince: Henri Deschamps, 1953); plates 34–37 are facsimile reproductions of this letter and its signatures. Paul Fleuriau's signature appears on plate 37. On relations between whites and free people of color in Mirebalais, see David Geggus, *Slavery, War, and Revolution: The British Occupation of Saint-Domingue, 1793–1798* (New York: Oxford University Press, 1982), 328–30. Also see Cauna, *Au temps des isles à sucre*, 55.

113. Cited in Cauna, *Au temps des isles à sucre*, 56; Cauna gives no further reference.

114. *Genèse: Journal Généalogique et Historique*, Archives Nationales d'Haïti, http://www.agh.qc.ca/articles/?id=68, accessed 30 March 2015.

115. Cauna, *Au temps des isles à sucre*, 55. Cauna is not clear on his source for this information, but it is probably ANOM, Notary Badoux.

116. On the tendency of free women of color, in particular, to reject their white father's

name, see Dubois, *A Colony of Citizens*, 251–52. Other studies of naming tend to focus on slaves, not free people of color. See, for example, Cheryll Ann Cody, "Naming, Kinship, and Estate Dispersal: Notes on Slave Family Life on a South Carolina Plantation, 1786 to 1833," *William and Mary Quarterly* 39, 1 (1982): 192–211; Trevor Burnard, "Slave Naming Patterns: Onomastics and the Taxonomy of Race in Eighteenth-Century Jamaica," *Journal of Interdisciplinary History* 31, 3 (2001): 325–46; Jerome S. Handler and JoAnn Jacoby, "Slave Names and Naming in Barbados, 1650–1830," *William and Mary Quarterly* 53, 4 (1996): 685–728.

117. Dubois identifies a similar impulse. Dubois, *A Colony of Citizens*, 251.

118. "Liste des Habitants de Saint-Domingue, qui, conformément à la loi du août, relative aux biens que possèdent les émigrés dans les colonies, ont fait passer, avant la loi du 20 décembre, au Ministère de la Marine, leur certificat de résidence, dans le territoire de la République," Reel 27, Bibliothèque et Archives Nationales de Québec, http://www.agh.qc.ca/articles/?id=32, accessed 18 November 2010.

119. Former colonists and their families continued to dream of returning to Saint-Domingue even after the establishment of the Republic of Haiti. Darrell Meadows, "Engineering Exile: Social Networks and the French Atlantic Community, 1789–1799," *French Historical Studies* 23, 1 (2000): 67–102, 71.

120. "Registre pour recevoir les Déclarations des Nègres, Négresses, Mulâtres, & Mulâtresses qui sont dans cette ville de La Rochelle, suivant les Lettres de M. L'Intendant," 1763, 352, AMLR.

121. "Déclaration pour la police des noirs," 9 August 1777; Isambert, Decrusy, and Taillandier, *Recueil général des anciennes lois françaises, depuis l'an 420 jusqu'à la Révolution de 1789*, 29 vols. (Paris: Belin-Leprieur, 1830), 25: 81–84. Also see Peabody, *"There Are No Slaves in France"*, chap. 7.

Chapter 6. Negotiating Patriarchy

1. Jean-Baptiste Du Tertre, *Histoire generale des Antilles habitées par les François, devisée en deux tomes, et enrichi de Cartes & de Figures*, 4 vols. (Paris: Thomas Jolly, 1667), 2: 506.

2. Médéric-Louis-Élie Moreau de Saint-Méry, *La description topographique, physique, civile, politique et historique de la partie française de Saint-Domingue*, 3rd ed., 3 vols. (Saint-Denis, 2004), 1: 106.

3. Emily Osborn, *Our New Husbands Are Here: Households, Gender, and Politics in a West African State from the Slave Trade to Colonial Rule* (Athens: Ohio University Press, 2011), 28, 18, 32.

4. Laurent Dubois, *A Colony of Citizens: Revolution and Slave Emancipation in the French Caribbean, 1787–1804* (Chapel Hill: University of North Carolina Press, 2004).

5. Osborn, *Our New Husbands Are Here*, 39–40.

6. Natalie Zemon Davis, *Fiction in the Archives: Pardon Tales and Their Tellers in Sixteenth-Century France* (Stanford, Calif.: Stanford University Press, 1987), 18–25, 25.

7. For example, a 1783 notary contract in Léogane shows that two men of color, Pierre Gautier *dit* Bois Savin and Théodore Lespinasse *dit* Bois Gaillard, lived outside of La Rochelle. They sold a piece of property in Saint-Domingue to a free man of color. Although their names should be included in Admiralty records of people of color in and around La Rochelle, they are not. "Vente d'Emplacement," 11 December 1783, DPPC NOT SDOM 1183, ANOM. I would like to thank Rob Taber for calling this contract to my attention.

8. In the 1763 survey, a total of thirty-four men of color and twenty-two women of color were registered as living in La Rochelle. Of these Pierre Neptune and Antoine Monréal were the

only black men (*nègres*) to make their own declarations. André and Vincent Micheau du Sexe and Marianne Sanite, all of mixed race, also made their own statements. No black women made their own statements. "Registre pour recevoir les déclarations des Nègres, négresses, mulâtres, et mulâtresses qui sont dans cette ville de La Rochelle, suivant les lettres de M. l'Intendant," 1763, 352, AMLR.

9. Similarly, Amy Dru Stanley argues that newly freed slave men made claims to freedom and masculinity through their ownership over the labor of their wives and children in the post-bellum United States. Amy Dru Stanley, *From Bondage to Contract: Wage Labor, Marriage, and the Market in the Age of Slave Emancipation* (New York, 1998), chap. 4, esp. 143.

10. "Registre pour recevoir les déclarations des Nègres, négresses, mulâtres, et mulâtresses qui sont dans cette ville de La Rochelle, suivant les lettres de M. l'Intendant," 1763, 352, AMLR; "Registre Contenaient les déclarations des noirs, mulâtres, et autres gens de couleur, en conséquence de l'Édit du Roy du 9 aout 1777," 1777, B 258, ADCM; "Déclaration du nommé Neptune Noir," 18 September, 1777, Colonies F1 B4, Dossier VI, ANOM.

11. "Déclaration du nommé Neptune Noir," 18 September, 1777, Colonies F1 B4, Dossier VI, ANOM. On Ouidah and its role in the slave trade, see Robin Law, *Ouidah: The Social History of a West African Slaving 'Port' 1727–1892* (Athens: Ohio University Press, 2004).

12. Jean Mettas, ed., *Répertoire des expéditions négrières françaises au XVIIIe siècle*, vol. 1, *Nantes* (Paris: Société Française d'Histoire d'Outre-mer, 1978), 374–75, 393, 410. Also see David Eltis et al., Voyages Database, 2009, *Voyages: The Trans-Atlantic Slave Trade Database*, http://www.slavevoyages.org.

13. Mettas, *Répertoire des expeditions négrières*, 1: 136; *Voyages*, http://www.slavevoyages.org/, accessed 2 July 2014. If this scenario is correct, the five years between Neptune's capture and his forcible departure from Africa remain unexplained. Perhaps he experienced slavery in Africa similar to that described by Olaudah Equiano, or maybe he simply left his dates fuzzy, whether intentionally or not. Olaudah Equiano, *The Interesting Narrative of the Life of Olaudah Equiano or, Gustavus Vassa, the African* (New York: Modern Library, 2004), chap. 1.

14. This was one of just 145 such revolts out of 3,373 slaving voyages on French ships over the course of the eighteenth century. *Voyages*, accessed 2 July, 2014.

15. The Cadou name also was associated with other slaves brought to La Rochelle. Pierre Cadou's (probably Neptune's owner's son) slave Charles, about thirteen, was baptized 1 April 1747; the godmother was Louise Cadou. Cadou brought another slave to France in 1775. Marie Magdelaine Therese Julie, a *négresse* of about sixteen, belonged to Cadou. She was baptized 11 January 1775 and died 17 January 1775. Parish records, Saint-Barthélémy, GG 458 and GG 369, AMLR.

16. "Recensement des nègres qui se trouvèrent actuellement dans la ville de la Rochelle," enclosed with letter of 10 December 1741 from Barentin, intendant of La Rochelle, to Maurepas, Minister of the Marine, Marine B 3 405, AN. Also see Sue Peabody, *"There Are No Slaves in France": The Political Culture of Race and Slavery in the Ancien Régime* (New York: Oxford University Press, 1996), 49.

17. Cadou did register an individual named Pierre Bossay *dit* L'Evillé in Nantes on 3 July 1739, specifying that he first brought him to France in 1729 when he was ten, likely on a ship called *Le Neptune*. B 4496, Archives Départementales de la Loire-Atlantique. Pierre Boulle has concluded that this individual was likely not the same person as Pierre Neptune. Pierre Boulle, personal communication, 11 August, 2014.

18. Letter of Minister of the Marine to Intendant of La Rochelle, 11 December 1747, Colonies B 86, AN. I thank Pierre Boulle for pointing me toward this correspondence.

19. Notary Act, Notary Fleury, 7 March 1749, 3 E 1612, ADCM.

20. "Registre de sa Majesté commencé le 19 octobre 1737 et fini le 27 juin 1744," B226, ADCM.

21. "Marriage Pierre Neptune Nègre Louise Négresse," 1 March 1756, parish records, Saint-Nicolas, GG 473, AMLR. I would like to thank Pierre Boulle for sharing this reference. "Déclaration du nommé Neptune, Noir," 18 September, 1777, Colonies F1B4, dossier VI, ANOM. Neither the baptism nor the burial records for their children have been found.

22. "Registre pour recevoir les déclarations des Nègres, négresses, mulâtres, et mulâtresses qui sont dans cette ville de La Rochelle, suivant les lettres de M. l'Intendant," 1763, 352, AMLR.

23. "Registre pour recevoir les déclarations des Nègres, négresses, mulâtres, et mulâtresses qui sont dans cette ville de La Rochelle, suivant les lettres de M. l'Intendant," 1763, 352, ADCM.

24. A number of young girls of roughly appropriate age had arrived in La Rochelle several years before, including Rosette, who arrived in La Rochelle with Dame Louise Geneviève Roy in September of 1758 on a ship from Saint-Domingue when she was only thirteen, or Nanette, who worked as a chambermaid to Widow Damien and was freed by her mistress in February that same year. She could have been any number of young slave girls who arrived in La Rochelle; she could have been born in France or even been the daughter of Louise or Neptune from a previous relationship. "Registre de sa majesté du greffe du l'amirauté commencé le 14 Avril 1757 et fini le 20 8bre 1760," 9 September 1758, B 230, ADCM, 17 February 1758.

25. Suzanne Miers and Igor Kopytoff, "Introduction," in *Slavery in Africa: Historical and Anthropological Perspectives*, ed. Miers and Kopytoff (Madison: University of Wisconsin Press, 1977), 3–81, 25. In France, the presence of children in families continued to be used as a powerful rhetorical strategy by people of color in the Restoration period. Jennifer Heuer, "The One-Drop Rule in Reverse? Interracial Marriages in Napoleonic and Restoration France," *Law and History Review* 27, 3 (2009): 515–48, 531–32.

26. This and subsequent information about Monréal's life is drawn from "Registre Conte-naient les déclarations des noirs, mulâtres, et autres gens de couleur, en conséquence de l'Édit du Roy du 9 aout 1777," 1777, B 258 ADCM, and "Déclaration du Nommé Monréal noir," 18 September 1777, Colonies F1 B4, Dossier VI, ANOM. See also "Registre pour recevoir les déclarations des Nègres, négresses, mulâtres, et mulâtresses qui sont dans cette ville de La Rochelle, suivant les lettres de M. l'Intendant," 1763, 352, ADCM.

27. Monréal only mentions this legacy in his 1763 declaration. "Registre pour recevoir les déclarations des Nègres, négresses, mulâtres, et mulâtresses qui sont dans cette ville de La Rochelle, suivant les lettres de M. l'Intendant," 1763, 352, ADCM.

In comparison, in La Rochelle, the wealthy merchant Aimé-Benjamin Fleuriau left an annual income of 120 livres to his domestic servant, which was on the high end of legacies left to servants by masters. "Dépôt du testament olographe de M. Aimé-Benjamin Fleuriau," 21 August 1787, Notary Delavergne fils, 3 E 1698, ADCM. Sarah Maza found that 40 percent of masters left legacies to servants in their wills. Servants usually inherited a small annuity, a year's worth of wages (for unskilled male workers around 80–120 livres), or a few hundred livres. Usually legacies only went to servants who worked for the testator at the time of his or her death. Sarah Maza, *Servants and Masters in Eighteenth-Century France: The Uses of Loyalty* (Princeton, N.J.: Princeton University Press, 1983), 170–72.

28. "Marriage M. Nègre et Gautier," 10 September 1759, parish records, Notre-Dame, GG 119, AMLR. His wife Elizabeth Gautier died 26 November 1760; 27 November 1760, parish records, Saint-Barthélémy, GG 287, AMLR. They had one daughter, Elizabeth, who was born on 19

August 1760; 20 August 1760, parish records, Saint-Barthélémy, GG286, AMLR. I would like to thank Pierre Boulle for sharing these references. Also see "Registre pour recevoir les déclarations des Nègres, négresses, mulâtres, et mulâtresses qui sont dans cette ville de La Rochelle, suivant les lettres de M. l'Intendant," 1763, 352, ADCM. On slave marriage, see "Déclaration concernant les nègres esclaves des Colonies," 15 December 1738, Article 9. Isambert, Decrusy, and Taillandier, *Recueil général des anciennes lois françaises, depuis l'an 420 jusqu'à la Révolution de 1789* (Paris: Belin-Leprieur, 1830), 22: 114.

29. Monréal mentioned that he had been married in every declaration he made. See "Registre pour recevoir les déclarations des Nègres, négresses, mulâtres et mulâtresses qui sont dans cette ville de La Rochelle, suivant les lettres de M. L'Intendant," 1763, 352, AMLR; "Registre Contenaient les déclarations des noirs, mulâtres, et autres gens de couleur, en conséquence de l'Édit du Roy du 9 aout 1777," 1777, B 258 ADCM; and "Déclaration du Nommé Monréal noir," 18 September 1777, Colonies F1B4, Dossier IV, ANOM. Only once was it explicitly recorded that his wife was white. "État des noirs libres qui sont en France," 1777, 352, AMLR.

30. Henry Robert gives the population of La Rochelle as 15,340 in 1767. Unpublished manuscript, ADCM, 2 J 91 (1). Levasseur puts the population of La Rochelle at 17,253 in 1787. Émile Levasseur, *La population française: Histoire de la population avant 1789 et démographie de la France*, 3 vols. (Paris, 1998), 1: 227.

31. "Registre pour recevoir les déclarations des Nègres, négresses, mulâtres, et mulâtresses qui sont dans cette ville de La Rochelle, suivant les lettres de M. l'Intendant," 1763, 352, ADCM.

32. Also see Rebecca Scott, "Paper Thin: Freedom and Re-enslavement in the Diaspora of the Haitian Revolution," *Law and History Review* 29, 4 (2011): 1061–87.

33. Sarah Maza, *Servants and Masters in Eighteenth-Century France*, 25; Cissie C. Fairchilds, *Domestic Enemies: Servants and Their Masters in Old Regime France* (Baltimore: Johns Hopkins University Press, 1984), 1–2. Henri Robert claims that there were 1,288 domestics in La Rochelle out of a population of 15,340 in 1767, about 8 percent of the population. Unpublished manuscript, ADCM, 2 J 91 (1). Robert cites no source for these numbers.

34. Although Kathleen Brown points out that in the North American British colonies the type of work a person performed defined his or her status, this did not seem to be the case in France where slaves and servants performed very similar work. Kathleen M. Brown, *Good Wives, Nasty Wenches, and Anxious Patriarchs: Gender, Race, and Power in Colonial Virginia* (Chapel Hill: University of North Carolina Press, 1996), 120–28.

35. Annette Gordon-Reed, *The Hemingses of Monticello: An American Family* (New York: Norton, 2008), 231–41.

36. For information about Jean Vivier, see Émile Garnault, *Livre d'or de la chambre de commerce de La Rochelle: Contenant la biographie des directeurs et présidents de cette chambre de 1719 à 1891* (La Rochelle: Typographie E. Martin, successeur de G. Mareschal, 1902), 17–21.

37. "Déclaration du Nommé F. Giles, Noir," 19 September, 1777, Colonies F1B4, Dossier VI, ANOM, and "Déclaration du Nommé Gilles Noir," 19 September 1777, " Registre contenaient les déclarations des noirs, mulâtres, et autres gens de couleur, en conséquence de l'Édit du Roi du 9 août," 1777, B 258, ADCM.

38. "Édit concernant les esclaves nègres des colonies," October 1716, Isambert et al., *Recueil général des anciennes lois françaises*, 21, Article 13, 125. Augustin, discussed later in this chapter, also changed owners.

39. "Nègre," 17 July 1737, "Registre de sa Majesté Commencé le 11e mai 1729 et fini le 16 octobre 1737," B 225, ADCM.

40. "Nègre," 19 October 1737, "Registre de sa Majesté commencé le 19 octobre 1737 et fini le 27 juin 1744," B 226, ADCM.

41. "Nègre," 16 April 1742, "Registre de sa Majesté commencé le 19 octobre 1737 et fini le 27 juin 1744." In contrast, Brett Rushforth identifies occasional blurring between slavery and adoption in New France. Rushforth, *Bonds of Alliance: Indigenous and Atlantic Slaveries in New France* (Chapel Hill: University of North Carolina Press, 2012), 268–69.

42. Élie Vivier declared the slave Thereze for a M. Sallette who commanded the *Flute du Roi*, on 24 February 1748. "Registre de sa Majesté commencé le 9 novembre 1747 et fini le 16 janvier 1751," B 228, ADCM. His brother Paul Vivier declared the slave Joseph for Sr Jean Baptiste Charles DeClien, lieutenant des vaisseaux and a knight of the order of Saint Louis. "Nègre," 20 October 1756, "Registre de sa Majesté commencé le 23 mars 1753 et fini le 14 avril 1757," B 6086, ADCM.

43. Garnault, *Livre d'or de la chambre de commerce de La Rochelle*, 55.

44. "Registre pour recevoir les déclarations des Nègres, négresses, mulâtres, et mulâtresses qui sont dans cette ville de La Rochelle, suivant les lettres de M. l'Intendant," 1763, 352, AMLR.

45. Laurent Dubois charts how slaves inscribed their family history in marriage contracts and other documents, and how the possession of documents could aid former slaves in their claims to freedom. Dubois, *A Colony of Citizens*, 76–80, 374–378, 249–253. François Gilles made his own statement to the Admiralty in the Police des Noirs survey of 1777, but he does not mention the circumstances of his emancipation. "Déclaration du Nommé Gilles Noir," 19 September 1777, B 258, ADCM, and idem., Colonies F1B4, ANOM.

46. The record identifies Gilles as "appurtenant à M. Caraillon," language exactly the same as that used in slave declarations to indicate ownership. 16 April 1769, parish records, Saint-Barthélémy, GG 305, AMLR.

47. Gilles made his 1777 declaration at the same time as Deday, who is discussed later in this chapter. Both originally came from Saint-Domingue. A second group of free men of color, Antoine Monréal, Pierre Neptune, and Jean Nicolas, none of whom originally came from Saint-Domingue, also made their declarations at the same time. "Registre contenaient les déclarations des noirs, mulâtres, et autres gens de couleur, en conséquence de l'Édit du Roi du 9 août," 1777, B 258, ADCM, and "Police des Nègres de France (Police des Noirs)," 1777, Dossier VI, Colonies F1 B4, ANOM.

48. For examples see "Registre pour recevoir les déclarations des Nègres, négresses, mulâtres, et mulâtresses qui sont dans cette ville de La Rochelle, suivant les lettres de M. l'Intendant," 1763, 352, ADCM; "Registre contenaient les déclarations des noirs, mulâtres, et autres gens de couleur, en conséquence de l'Édit du Roi du 9 août," 1777, B 258, ADCM; "Police des Nègres de France (Police des Noirs)," 1777, Dossier VI, Colonies F1 B4, ANOM.

49. "M. François Gilles et Elizabeth Prevost," 15 June 1772, Saint-Saveur, GG 653, AMLR; "Bapt. Jean Joseph," 3 February 1773, Saint-Saveur, GG 655, AMLR. In his marriage record, Gilles is identified as being "of the *nègre* nation." I would like to thank Pierre Boulle for sharing these references. Also see "Déclaration du Nommé F. Giles, Noir," 19 September, 1777, Colonies F1 B4, Dossier VI, ANOM, and "Registre contenaient les déclarations des noirs, mulâtres, et autres gens de couleur, en conséquence de l'Édit du Roi du 9 août," 1777, B 258, ADCM.

50. "M.[ariage] François Gilles et Elizabeth Prevost," 15 June 1772, parish records, Saint-Saveur, GG 653, AMLR

51. "Déclaration du Nommé F. Giles, Noir," 19 September 1777, Colonies F1 B4, Dossier VI, ANOM.

52. According to the Edict of 1716, slaves were not allowed to marry without the permission

of their owner. "Édit concernant les esclaves nègres des colonies," 6 October 1716, Isambert et al., *Recueil général des anciennes lois françaises*, 21: Article 7, 124; "Déclaration concernant les nègres esclaves des Colonies," 15 December 1738, ibid., 22: Article 10, 115.

53. "Déclaration du Nommée Jean Nicolas, Mulâtre," 18 September, 1777, Colonies F1B4 Dossier VI, ANOM. This information is repeated in "Registre Contenaient les déclarations des noirs, mulâtres, et autres gens de couleur, en conséquence de l'Édit du Roy du 9 aout 1777," B 258, ADCM. In France, this pattern of men of color marrying white women but white men rarely marrying women of color continued in the Napoleonic and Restoration periods. Heuer, "The One-Drop Rule in Reverse?," 525.

54. The word *mulâtre* referred to someone with European as well as African backgrounds. *Dictionnaire de L'académie français*, 4th ed., 2 vols. (Paris: Chez la veuve de Bernard Brunet, 1762), s.v. "mulâtre."

55. Three free people of mixed race had made statements in the 1763 survey: André and Vincent Micheau du Sexe, who classified themselves as *mulâtres* and listed their profession as goldsmiths, and a *mulâtresse* named Marianne Sanite. The clerk added that she was "under the direction of M. Bernon, merchant." "Registre pour recevoir les déclarations des Nègres, négresses, mulâtres, et mulâtresses qui sont dans cette ville de La Rochelle, suivant les lettres de M. l'Intendant," 1763, 352, AMLR. Jean Nicolas was the only free man of mixed race who made his own declaration in the 1777 survey. There was also one free mixed-race woman named Victoire. "Registre contenaient les déclarations des noirs, mulâtres, et autres gens de couleur, en conséquence de l'Edit du Roi du 9 août," 1777, B 258, ADCM, and "Police des Nègres de France (Police des Noirs)," 1777, Dossier VI, Colonies F1 B4, ANOM.

56. Declaration of André and Vincent Micheau du Saxe, 12 September 1763, "Registre pour recevoir les déclarations des Nègres, négresses, mulâtres, et mulâtresses qui sont dans cette ville de La Rochelle, suivant les lettres de M. l'Intendant," 1763, 352, AMLR. Also see Chapter 5 on the mixed-race sons of Aimé-Benjamin Fleuriau.

57. The question of whether or not Indians could be enslaved remained controversial well into the nineteenth century. Sue Peabody, "La question raciale et le 'sol libre de France': l'affaire Furcy," *Annales: Histoire, Sciences Sociales* 64, 6 (2009): 1305–34. Also see Peabody, *"There Are No Slaves in France"*, chap. 4, 57–71; and Joly de Fleury, de la Roue, and Collet, *Mémoire signifié pour le nommé Francisque, Indien de Nation, Néophyte de l'Église Romaine, Intimé; contre le Sieur Allain-François-Ignace Brignon, se disant Ecuyer, Appellant* (Paris: P.G. Simon, Imprimeur du Parlement, 1759), MFICHE 4–FM-12698, BN.

58. Peabody, *"There Are No Slaves in France"*, 59.

59. Ibid., 70.

60. Maza, *Servants and Masters*, 312. Customarily, masters had been considered legally and morally responsible for their servants and were invested with the authority to punish them more or less as they saw fit. However, the physical and sexual abuse of servants was increasingly frowned on, and servants themselves became less and less likely to tolerate it. A relationship traditionally conceptualized as based on loyalty gradually moved toward a more businesslike contract. In their scholarship on servants, both Sarah Maza and Cissie Fairchilds identify this as a broad cultural rather than legal change. This change does not seem to have applied to black servants or slaves, whom masters continued to treat in a way reminiscent of how white servants had traditionally been treated. Maza, 257, and Fairchilds, *Domestic Enemies*, 139, 158.

61. On the challenges of curtailing the actions of slaves in France, see Gordon-Reed, *The Hemingses of Monticello*, 175–79, 298.

62. The Admiralty registers for 1760–1772 are lost. Augustin does not appear on extant lists for 1719–1779.

63. John G. Clark, *La Rochelle and the Atlantic Economy During the Eighteenth Century* (Baltimore: Johns Hopkins University Press, 1981), 135.

64. "Édit concernant les esclaves nègres des colonies," October 1716, Isambert et al., *Recueil général des anciennes lois françaises*, 21: 122–26, Article 9, 125. Under colonial law slaves were classified as meubles, or liquid heritable assets. "Code Noir," Moreau de Saint-Méry, *Loix et constitutions*, 1: 414–24, Article 44, 421.

65. The relationship of the siblings is laid out in the marriage record of Daniel Garasché to Sara Carayon, 12 May 1767, Protestant Records, GG 709, AMLR. Also see Isaac Garasché's succession, 11 August 1770, 4 J 1610, ADCM.

66. Contract prepared by Notary Morin, 12 May 1773, 4 J 13, ADCM.

67. Meynardie to Pierre Garasché, 23 June 1777, 4 J 1610, ADCM.

68. Meynardie Jeune to Pierre Garasché, 23 June 1777, 4 J 1610, ADCM.

69. Garasché Meynardie to Pierre Garasché, 24 June 1777, 4 J 1610, ADCM.

70. Meynardie Jeune to Pierre Garasché, 23 June 1777, 4 J 1610, ADCM. Meynardie mentions the procuration in his letter of 28 June 1777 to Garasché in Cap Français, 4 J 1610, ADCM. In France, dressing hair could provide individuals with a livelihood within a relatively limited social circle made up of friends, family members, and neighbors. Mary K. Gayne, "Illicit Wig-making in Eighteenth-Century Paris," *Eighteenth-Century Studies* 38, 1 (2004): 134. Whether or not this was true in Saint-Domingue, Meynardie likely assumed his own frame of reference applied, and that many eager colonists would want to have their hair dressed and wigs made in the latest French styles.

71. Legislation increasingly put up roadblocks to manumission, although these seem to have had little effect on manumission numbers in the first half of the eighteenth century. John Garrigus, *Before Haiti: Race and Citizenship in French Saint-Domingue* (New York: Palgrave, 2006), 42. On the process of manumission, see Chapter 4, this volume. Also see "Arrêt du Conseil du cap, touchant l'affranchissement des esclaves," 28 January 1768, Moreau de Saint-Méry, *Loix et constitutions*, 5: 152–53.

72. Meynardie Jeune to Pierre Garasché, 23 June 1777, 4 J 1610, ADCM.

73. Ibid.

74. Meynardie Jeune to Pierre Garasché, 28 June 1777, 4 J 1610, ADCM.

75. On the vulnerability of domestic servants to the abuses of their owners see Maza, *Servants and Masters*; Fairchilds, *Domestic Enemies*. On people of color's preference for living in their own communities see Sandra Lauderdale Graham, *House and Street: The Domestic World of Servants and Masters in Nineteenth-Century Rio de Janeiro* (New York: Cambridge University Press, 1988), esp. chap. 3, and Elizabeth Clark-Lewis, "'This Work Had an End': African-American Domestic Workers in Washington, D.C., 1910–1940," in *To Toil the Livelong Day*, ed. Carol Groneman and Mary Beth Norton (Ithaca, N.Y.: Cornell University Press, 1987): 195–208.

76. Jacques Guibert was the cousin of Pierre Garasché and Meynardie's wife Marianne Garasché. He also had an extensive involvement in what seemed to be an informal slave trade in La Rochelle. When Rochelais residents received slaves from friends or relations in the colonies, Guibert often acted as their agent by registering them with the Admiralty. In January 1773, for example, he registered the slave Igénie, a young *mulâtresse* of about twelve or thirteen, for Madame la comtesse de Montboussier. Igénie was to learn to be a dressmaker. Registre de sa Majesté commencé le 4 julliet 1772 et fini le 19 julliet 1779, B 231, ADCM.

77. Jacques Guibert to Pierre Garasché, 26 July 1777, 4 J 1610, ADCM.

78. Meynardie Jeune to Pierre Garasché, 28 June 1777, 4 J 1610, ADCM.

79. This and the rest of Deday's story draw from "Déclaration de Noir Jean-Baptiste-André Deday," 19 September 1777, Colonies F1B4 Dossier VI, ANOM, and "Déclaration du nommé Deday noir," 19 September 1777, in "Registre contenant les déclarations des noirs, mulâtres, et autres gens de couleur, en conséquence de l'Édit du Roi du 9 aout 1777," B 258, ADCM.

80. Male servants tended to travel farther to find employment and to change employers more frequently than women. Fairchilds, *Domestic Enemies*, 63.

81. "Déclaration de Mulâtresse Catherine Mercier" and "Déclaration de Marie Jeanne Angélique Négresse," both 22 September 1777, in "Registre contenant les déclarations des noirs, mulâtres, et autres gens de couleur, en conséquence de l'Édit du Roi du 9 aout 1777," B 258, ADCM; and "Déclaration de la Nommée Marie Catherine Mercier, Négresse," and "Déclaration de la Nommée Marie Jeanne Angélique, Négresse," both 22 September 1777, Colonies F1 B4, ANOM. These pairs of documents are substantially similar, but have some important differences. First, Mercier is classified as a *mulâtresse* in the La Rochelle original and a *négresse* in the official copy in the ANOM; second, a passage heavily crossed out in Angélique's original declaration is omitted from the official version. On Mercier and Angélique, also see Boulle, *Race et esclavage dans la France de l'Ancien Régime*, 186; Pierre Boulle, "Ensuite, à La Rochelle," in *Historians' Stories from Canada*, ed. Susan Mann (Montréal: Samuel Lallouz, 2010), n.p.

82. "Déclaration de Marie Jeanne Angélique Négresse," 22 September 1777, in "Registre contenant les déclarations des noirs, mulâtres, et autres gens de couleur, en conséquence de l'Édit du Roi du 9 aout 1777," B 258, ADCM. This does not appear in the ANOM version.

83. "Déclaration de Marie Jeanne Angélique Négresse," 22 September 1777, in "Registre contenant les déclarations des noirs, mulâtres, et autres gens de couleur," B 258, ADCM. The other man of color, François Coton, was from another town and in service to a marquis.

84. On seamstresses and gender, see Clare Crowston, *Fabricating Women: The Seamstresses of Old Regime France, 1675–1791* (Durham, N.C.: Duke University Press, 2001).

85. Pierre Boulle offers an interesting and persuasive interpretation of the circumstances surrounding Angélique's slavery and eventual freedom. Her new mistress was the wife of the lieutenant of the Admiralty of La Rochelle, Harouard de Beignon. Given the 1777 Police des Noirs legislation, it would be difficult and embarrassing to explain why the lieutenant's wife possessed a slave. That, combined with the trouble and expense of sending a slave back to the colonies, may have made her willing to sell Angélique to Mercier for a relatively low price. Angélique reveals this part of her story in the crossed-out lines of her declaration. Boulle proposes that the lieutenant intervened and the story was edited. Boulle, "Ensuite, à La Rochelle," n.p.; Boulle, *Race et esclavage dans la France de l'Ancien Régime*, 186.

86. On women workers both in and outside the guild system, see Daryl Hafter, *Women at Work in Preindustrial France* (University Park: Pennsylvania State University Press, 2007).

87. The third, Victoire, was a girl of mixed race from Louisiana who had been brought to France to be educated. A pensionnaire in the Convent of the Ladies of Providence in La Rochelle, she may have been the illegitimate daughter of a wealthy colonist. "Déclaration de mulâtresse Victoire," 5 October 1777, Colonies F1B4 Dossier VI, ANOM. In comparison, eight free men of color made their own declarations. "Registre contenant les déclarations des noirs, mulâtres, et autres gens de couleur, en conséquence de l'Édit du Roi du 9 aout 1777," B 258, ADCM.

88. Many scholars have addressed the question of the meaning of Christianity for slaves.

Much of these scholarly efforts have focused on the English-speaking, Protestant Atlantic colonies, particularly slave religion and its potential to question authority in North America. Early works emphasize Christianity as an alternate source of authority, and frame the practice of religion as a mode of resistance to slavery. See, for example, Eugene D. Genovese, *Roll, Jordan, Roll: The World the Slaves Made* (New York: Pantheon, 1974); Albert Raboteau, *Slave Religion: The "Invisible Institution" in the Antebellum South* (New York: Oxford University Press, 1978); Albert Raboteau, *A Fire in the Bones: Reflections on African-American Religious History* (Boston: Beacon, 1995); Timothy Fulop and Albert Raboteau, eds., *African-American Religion: Interpretive Essays in History and Culture* (New York: Routledge 1997). More recent works on slave religion demonstrate that African, Christian, and Native American religions blended into a distinct whole, and emphasizes slaves' role in creating an autonomous culture. See Ira Berlin, *Many Thousands Gone: The First Two Centuries of Slavery in North America* (Cambridge, Mass.: Harvard Universiy Press, 1998); Philip Morgan, *Slave Counterpoint: Black Culture in the Eighteenth-Century Chesapeake and Lowcountry* (Chapel Hill: University of North Carolina Press, 1998); Michael Gomez, *Exchanging Our Country Marks: The Transformation of African Identities in the Colonial and Antebellum South* (Chapel Hill: University of North Carolina Press, 1998). Scholarship on religion and slavery in the French colonial context tends to focus on voodoo. See David Geggus, "Marronage, *Vaudou*, and the Saint Domingue Slave Revolt of 1791," in *Proceedings of the Fifteenth Meeting of the French Colonial Historical Society*, ed. Patricia Galloway and Philip Boucher (Lanham, Md.: University Press of America, 1992); Leslie G. Desmangles, *The Faces of the Gods: Vodou and Roman Catholicism in Haiti* (Chapel Hill: University of California Press, 1992); Pierre Pluchon, *Vaudou, sorciers, empoisonneurs de Saint-Domingue à Haiti* (Paris: Karthala, 1987); Joan Dayan, *Haiti, History, and the Gods* (Berkeley: University of California Press, 1995). Also see Sue Peabody, "'A Dangerous Zeal': Catholic Missions to Slaves in the French Antilles, 1635–1800," *French Historical Studies* 25, 1 (2002): 53–90, esp. 55–56. Scholars of Africa in particular emphasize the potential for slaves to overlay African religious practices onto Catholic rituals. John K. Thornton, *Africa and Africans in the Making of the Atlantic World, 1400–1680* (New York, 1992); John K. Thornton, "Les racines du vaudou: Religion africaine et société haïtienne dans la Saint-Domingue prérévolutionnaire," *Anthropologie et Sociétés* 22, 1 (1998): 85; Wyatt MacGaffey, "Europeans on the Coast of Africa," in *Implicit Understandings: Observing, Reporting, and Reflecting on the Encounters Between Europeans and Other Peoples in the Early Modern Era*, ed. Stuart B. Schwartz (New York: Cambridge University Press, 1994). Also see James H. Sweet, *Recreating Africa: Culture, Kinship, and Religion in the African-Portuguese World, 1441–1770* (Chapel Hill: University of North Carolina Press, 2003).

89. Peabody, "A Dangerous Zeal"; Robert Harms, *The Diligent: A Voyage Through the Worlds of the Slave Trade* (New York: Basic, 2002), esp. 6–11 on Pauline Villeneuve.

90. This belief spread in France as well as in European colonies, although it was more prevalent in the seventeenth than the eighteenth century. Once the Code Noir required baptism in 1685, the basis for this belief was eroded. On France, see Antoine Loisel, *Institutes coutumières* (Paris: Abel l'Angelier, 1608), 1, cited in Peabody, *"There Are No Slaves in France"*, 31; Léo Elisabeth, "The French Antilles," in *Neither Slave Nor Free: The Freedman of African Descent in the Slave Societies of the New World*, ed. David W. Cohen and Jack P. Greene (Baltimore: Johns Hopkins University Press, 1972), 141. In France's colonies the belief that baptism would lead to emancipation might have prompted the statute of 1736, which forbade priests from baptizing children as free without having proof of their mother's manumission. Moreau de Saint-Méry, *Loix et constitutions*, vol. 3, "Ordonnance du Roi, concernant l'Affranchissement des Esclaves

des Îles; et Ordonnance des Administrateurs en conséquence," 15 June 1736, 453–54. On England, see Seymour Drescher, "Manumission in a Society Without Slave Law: Eighteenth-Century England," *Slavery & Abolition* 3, 10 (September 1989): 85–101.

91. Peabody, "A Dangerous Zeal," 63; Thornton, "Les racines du vaudou."

92. Few people of color formally married in La Rochelle, although some did. For example, see the marriage record of Jacques *dit* Leveillé, who married Catherine Bouhault. 21 February 1792, parish records, Saint-Barthélémy, GG 187, AMLR.

93. Julie Hardwick, *The Practice of Patriarchy: Gender and the Politics of Household Authority in Early Modern France* (University Park: Pennsylvania State University Press, 1998), 167–72.

94. 8 January 1726, parish records, Saint-Barthélémy, GG 245, AMLR.

95. This is in contrast to the "social death" of slaves explored by Orlando Patterson. Orlando Patterson, *Slavery and Social Death* (Cambridge, Mass.: Harvard University Press, 1982).

96. 18 January 1726, parish records, Saint-Barthélémy, GG 245, AMLR.

Epilogue. Race from Colonialism to Revolution

1. Jean-François Brière, *Haïti et la France, 1804–1848: Le rêve brisé* (Paris: Kathala, 2008).

2. Old Regime plantation owners notably eyed the bottom line, yet in 1768 Belin wrote to his colonial agents, "I do not complain about my revenues." Nearly a quarter of a century later in 1792, Belin's heirs seemed to want and indeed received assurance of the profitability of their property from the plantation's manager, who expressed his confidence for "a very favorable year." Letter to MM. de la Vincendière and Gel. Berard from Belin des Marais, 16 August 1768, E 298, ADCM; St. Macary to Belin des Marais heirs, (no date) October 1792, 4 J 2915, ADCM.

3. The first letter to the heirs from the St. Macary, Baucamp, Poujé, and Michel was dated 5 June 1787. One earlier letter from the firm Majoret and St. Macary was dated 26 July 1780. E 300, ADCM. The firm had broken up by 1791, leaving full management of the estate to St. Macary. St. Macary to Belin des Marais heirs, 6 January 1791, 4 J 2915, ADCM.

4. St. Macary, Baucamp, Poujé, and Michel to the Belin des Marais heirs, 6 October 1790, 4J 2915, ADCM.

5. St. Macary, Baucamp, Poujé, and Michel to Belin des Marais heirs, 28 June 1790, 4 J 2915, ADCM.

6. *Archives parlementaires*, vol. 26 (Paris: P. Dupont, 1887), 15 May 1791, 89– 97.

7. St. Macary to Belin des Marais heirs, 16 August 1791, 4 J 2915, ADCM.

8. St. Macary to Belin des Marais heirs, 3 September 1791, 4 J 2915, ADCM. He refers to the rebelling slaves as "brigands" in, for example, his letters of (ND) October 1791, 18 January 1792, and 25 April (?) 1792, 4 J 2915, ADCM. Debien points out that colonists distinguished between "maroons," on the one hand, slaves who fled individually, often to escape the upheavals, and "brigands" or "rebels" on the other hand, who joined rebel bands. Gabriel Debien, *Les esclaves aux Antilles françaises (XVIIe–XVIIIe siècles)* (Basse-Terre: Société d'Histoire de la Guadeloupe, 1974), 468–69.

9. St. Macary to Belin des Marais heirs, (ND) October 1791, 4 J 2915, ADCM.

10. Although several concordats aimed at keeping the peace between the army made up of free people of color and rebel slaves and the municipalities of Croix-des-Bouquets and Mirebalais, they ultimately broke down and a new wave of violence ensued. Carolyn Fick, *The Making of Haiti: The Saint-Domingue Revolution from Below* (Knoxville: University of Tennessee Press, 1990), 121–27; Laurent Dubois, *Avengers of the New World: The Story of the Haitian Revolution* (Cambridge, Mass.: Harvard University Press, 2004), 119–122.

11. On how free men of color defined their own identity and positioned themselves politically, see John Garrigus, "'Des françois qui gémissent sous le joug de l'oppression': Les libres de couleur et la question de l'identité au début de la Révolution française," in Cécile Vidal, ed., *Français? La nation en débat entre colonies et métropole, XVIe–XIXe siècle* (Paris: École des Hautes Études en Sciences Sociales, 2014), 149–67.

12. For example, a free man of color was hired in 1786 to build slave huts on the Belin plantation. He worked there alongside a white carpenter for 111 days. "Compte que moy Vizeux Gérant l'haon [habitation] Belin Desmarais rendu à Messieurs St. Macary Baucamp et Ponyés Fréres negts. [négociants] St. Marc et charges de la Procuration," 23 July 1786, 4 J 2915, ADCM.

13. This echoes longstanding official views on the position of people of color. See Stewart King, *Blue Coat or Powdered Wig: Free People of Color in Pre-Revolutionary Saint Domingue* (Athens: University of Georgia Press, 2001), xviii; Yvan Debbasch, *Couleur et liberté: Le jeu du critère ethnique dans un ordre juridique esclavagiste* (Paris: Librairie Dalloz, 1967), chap. 2.

14. St. Macary to Belin des Marais heirs, 14 May 1792, 4 J 2915, ADCM.

15. Fick, *The Making of Haiti*, 121–25; Dubois, *Avengers of the New World*, 119–20.

16. Fick, *The Making of Haiti*, 118–29; Dubois, *Avengers of the New World*, 134–38.

17. St. Macary to Belin des Marais heirs, 14 May 1792, 4 J 2915, ADCM.

18. Ibid.

19. St. Macary to Belin des Marais heirs, 18 January 1792, 4 J 2915, ADCM. Port-au-Prince burned in late November 1791; two-thirds of the city was destroyed by fire. Fick, *The Making of Haiti*, 126–27; Dubois, *Avengers of the New World*, 121.

20. St. Macary to Belin des Marais heirs, 12 April 1792, 4 J 2915, ADCM; St. Macary to Belin des Marais heirs, 14 May 1792, 4 J 2915, ADCM.

21. St. Macary to Belin des Marais heirs, 25 April? 1792, 4 J 2915, ADCM.

22. Ibid. On the rebellion in the Artibonite Plain, see Fick, *The Making of Haiti*, 139; Dubois, *Avengers of the New World*, 136–137.

23. St. Macary to Belin des Marais heirs, 12 April 1792, 4 J 2915, ADCM. Geggus' research bears out St. Macary's claims; by around 1794 only sixty white adult men remained in Saint-Marc. David Geggus, *Slavery, War, and Revolution: The British Occupation of Saint-Domingue, 1793–1798* (New York: Oxford University Press, 1982), 228.

24. St. Macary to Belin des Marais heirs, 25 April? 1792, 4 J 2915, ADCM; St. Macary to Belin des Marais heirs, 14 May 1792, 4 J 2915, ADCM. Geggus refers to similar categories, although he references "bons nègres" rather than "bons sujets." Geggus, *Slavery, War, and Revolution*, 302, 307.

25. St. Macary to Belin des Marais heirs, 20 July 1792, 4 J 2915, ADCM.

26. St. Macary to Belin des Marais heirs, 25 April? 1792, 4 J 2915, ADCM.

27. St. Macary to Belin des Marais heirs, 20 July 1792, 4 J 2915, ADCM.

28. Also see Debien on how the gérant of the Maulévrier plantation passed incomplete information to absentee landowners. Gabriel Debien, *Études antillaises, XVIIIe siècle* (Paris: Librairie Armand Colin, 1956), 128–29. Geggus also points to distrust between absentee planters and "dishonest estate attorneys." Geggus, *Slavery, War, and Revolution*, 257–58.

29. St. Macary to Belin des Marais heirs, 20 July 1792, 4 J 2915, ADCM.

30. St. Macary in Saint-Marc to Belin des Marais heirs in La Rochelle, 30 April 1792, 4 J 2915, ADCM. Michel-Rolph Trouillot, *Silencing the Past: Power and the Production of History* (Boston: Beacon Press, 1995), chap. 3, esp. 73.

31. Tarin to "Ma très chère mère," New York, 12 September, 1793, AN D XXV 80, d. 785, cited

in Jeremy Popkin, *Facing Racial Revolution: Eyewitness Accounts of the Haitian Insurrection* (Chicago: University of Chicago Press, 2007), 16–17; Anonymous, *Histoire des désastres de Saint-Domingue* (Paris, 1795), note on 196–197, cited in Popkin, *Facing Racial Revolution*, 25, 177–79.

32. Gabriel Debien, "Sur les plantations Mauger à l'Artibonite (Saint-Domingue 1736–1803)," in *Enquêtes et Documents: Nantes, Afrique, Amérique*, ed. Centre de Recherches en Histoire Internationale et Atlantique (Nantes: Imprimerie Graphique de l'Ouest, 1981), 289–99.

33. Popkin, *Facing Racial Revolution*, 175–76.

34. St. Macary to Belin des Marais heirs, 14 May 1792, 4 J 2915, ADCM.

35. St. Macary to Belin des Marais heirs, 30 April 1792, 4 J 2915, ADCM. Bastien paid St. Macary a visit at the procureur's request. First the plantation's *indigoteur* came to see him, and reported that "the workshop was tranquil and occupied with the work that the moment demanded. I charged this *nègre* with telling the first slave driver to come find me next Saturday to have an interview with him, and to give him the orders that I believed necessary in the present circumstances." St. Macary to Belin des Marais heirs, 12 April 1792, 4 J 2915, ADCM.

36. St. Macary to Belin des Marais heirs, 14 May 1792, 4 J 2915, ADCM.

37. St. Macary to Belin des Marais heirs, 30 April 1792, 4 J 2915, ADCM.

38. St. Macary to Belin des Marais heirs, 14 May 1792, 4 J 2915, ADCM.

39. St. Macary to Belin des Marais heirs, 30 October 1792, 4 J 2915, ADCM.

40. St. Macary to Belin des Marais heirs, 14 May 1792, 4 J 2915, ADCM.

41. Bergé was not explicitly identified as white, but he was given the honorific title "monsieur," usually reserved for whites. St. Macary to Belin des Marais heirs, 30 April 1793, 4 J 2915, ADCM.

42. St. Macary to Belin des Marais heirs, 14 May 1792, 4 J 2915, ADCM.

43. St. Macary to Belin des Marais heirs, 27 December 1792, 4 J 2915, ADCM.

44. Dubois, *Colony of Citizens*, 167; Geggus, *Slavery, War, and Revolution*, 128. As Republican commissioners worked to crush the counter-revolution in Saint-Domingue, they inadvertently destroyed white power. Further, in April 1794, Toussaint Louverture and his forces switched sides and began fighting against the British and Spanish, likely in an effort to resist the restoration of slavery. Geggus, *Slavery, War, and Revolution*, 102, 116–18.

45. Ibid., 128.

46. One observer reports that under the British around 4,500 whites returned to their homes in 1793 and 1794. Ibid., 228. It is not clear if St. Macary was among their number. There are no records of letters from him to the Belin heirs between March of 1793 and March of 1798.

47. Darrell Meadows, "Engineering Exile: Social Networks and the French Atlantic Community, 1789–1799," *French Historical Studies* 23, 1 (2000): 67–102, 70. Meadows puts the number of refugees who went to the United States at approximately 25,000, while Ashli White estimates at least 20,000. Ashli White, *Encountering Revolution: Haiti and the Making of the Early Republic* (Baltimore: Johns Hopkins University Press, 2010), 2.

48. St. Macary to Belin des Marais heirs, 24 March 1798, 4 J 2915, ADCM.

49. Ibid. The "État General des nègres de l'habitation des MM. Les héritiers Belin des Marais en 8bre 1777" lists 205 slaves total, 4 J 2915, ADCM. According to Geggus, most slaves in the west province remained on plantations. Geggus also points out that the mere number of those remaining gives an inaccurate picture. Often able-bodied men were most likely to leave, and the elderly, sick, children, and women more likely to stay. Geggus, *Slavery, War, and Revolution*, 101, 308–312.

50. St. Macary to Belin des Marais heirs, 24 March 1798, 4 J 2915, ADCM.

51. St. Macary to Belin des Marais heirs, 28 May 1798, 4 J 2915, ADCM.

52. "Ministère des Finances-État Détaillé des Liquidations opérées à l'époque du 1er janvier 1830 par la commission chargée de répartir l'Indemnité attribuée aux anciens Colons de Saint-Domingue, en exécution de la Loi du 30 avril 1826 et conformément aux dispositions de l'Ordonnance du 9 mai suivant," 1829, Bibliothèque SOM D 64 1829, ANOM.

53. Nicole Charbonnel, "La commerce maritime à La Rochelle: La Révolution et ses précédents," in *La Rochelle, ville frontière*, ed. Michel Vovelle (La Rochelle: Rumeur des Âges, 1989), 82,88.

54. Claude Laveau, *Le monde rochelais des Bourbons à Bonaparte* (La Rochelle: Rumeur des Âges, 1988), 211–12. Also see the reproduction of the minutes of the Society in Marcel Dorigny, "Les colons de La Rochelle se mobilisent contre les Amis des Noirs: procès-verbaux de la Société des colons franco-américains de La Rochelle, 14 octobre 1789–27 août 1790," in *La Rochelle, l'Aunis et la Saintonge face à l'esclavage*, ed. Augeron and Caudron, 223–30.

55. Marcel Koufinkana, *Les esclaves noirs en France sous l'ancien régime (XVIe–XVIIIe siècles)*, (Paris: L'Harmattan, 2008), 126.

56. In general, port merchants and their representatives in Paris fought against extending rights to free people of color. Boulle, " 'In Defense of Slavery': Eighteenth-Century Opposition to Abolition and the Origins of Racist Ideology in France," in *History from Below: Studies in Popular Protest and Popular Ideology*, ed. Frederick Krantz (Montreal: Concordia University, 1985), 221–41, 32.

57. Franco-American Society to Club Massiac, 4 October 1789, Société des Colons, Series L, ADCM; cited in Laveau, *Le monde rochelais des Bourbons à Bonaparte*, 212.

58. Fleuriau de Touchelonge to du Fougerais, 3 November 1789, Société des Colons, Series L, ADCM, cited in ibid., 212.

59. Not all Rochelais adhered to the view that slavery must be maintained at all costs. Merchant Samuel Demissy, deputy to the Estates-General, joined the Société des Amis des Noirs. On Demissy, see Pascal Even, "Un armateur ami des Noirs, Samuel Demissy," in *La Rochelle, l'Aunis et la Saintonge face à l'esclavage*, ed. Augeron and Caudron, 215–22.

60. Pierre Piere et fils to Harouard du Beignon, 23 August 1789, Archives de Montbrun (Chateau de Buzay), in Laveau, *Le Monde rochelais des Bourbons à Bonaparte*, 213.

61. "Pétition a l'Assemblée Nationale par les Citoyens de La Rochelle, réunis en Sections," n.d., 3 and 6, Carton XV, Archives of the Chamber of Commerce, La Rochelle.

62. John Clark traces a long decline of the Rochelais economy, and argues that the French Revolution administered what amounted to a death blow. John Clark, *La Rochelle and the Atlantic Economy During the Eighteenth Century* (Baltimore: Johns Hopkins University Press, 1981), 233.

63. Pierre Boulle and Sue Peabody, *Le droit des noirs en France au temps de l'esclavage* (Paris: L'Harmattan, 2014), Document 7/11, 178.

64. Jennifer Heuer, "The One-Drop Rule in Reverse? Interracial Marriages in Napoleonic and Restoration France," *Law and History Review* 27, 3 (2009): 515–48.

65. Michael Sibalis, "Les noirs en France sous Napoléon: L'enquête de 1807," in *Rétablissement de l'esclavage dans les colonies françaises: 1802*, ed. Yves Bénot and Marcel Dorigny (Paris: Maisonneuve & Larose, 2003), 95–106.

66. "Mémoire sur l'état colonial de la France, à l'époque de la paix conclue à Amiens, le 4 germinal an 10," 12 germinal an X (2 April 1802), AN (Pierrefitte), AF/IV/1212, 10, 2. Cited in Boulle and Peabody, *Le droit des noirs en France*, 164.

67. Other depots were the Île d'Hyères and Île Saint-Marguerite off the Mediterranean coast. Aix had been established as a depot under the Directory; the others were added 19 August 1802. Boulle and Peabody, *Le droit des noirs en France*, Document 7/10, 178. Each depot held a company of one hundred black men, supervised by three whites. Another goal of this containment was to recruit soldiers to the Régiment Royal Africain, formerly known as the Pionniers Noirs. Half of this force perished in the siege of Gaeta in 1806. Sibalis, "Les noirs en France," 96–97; Boulle and Peabody, *Le droit des noirs*, 164–166. Also see X h 3, Vincennes.

68. Letter from Gautras, Letellier, and Garnard to the Minister of War, 8 nivose an II (28 December 1798), X h 3, Service Historique de la Défense, Vincennes. I would like to thank Pierre Boulle for sharing this reference.

69. On similar struggles over race and national identity in Sénégal and Gorée, see Guillaume Aubert, "'Nègres ou mulâtres nous sommes tous Français': Race, genre et nation à Gorée et à Saint-Louis du Sénégal, fin XVIIe–fin XVIIIe siècle," in *Français? La nation en débat entre colonies et métropole, XVIe–XIXe siècle*, ed. Cécile Vidal (Paris: École des Hautes Études en Sciences Sociales, 2014), 125–47.

INDEX

Guillemaut family, 23, 24; Françoise, 23, 224nn34, 37
Guimbelot, Jeanne, 129, 132–36, 141, 148, 151

Haiti, 155, 195, 197. *See also* Haitian Revolution
Haitian Revolution, 16, 17, 34, 154–55, 185–95
Hallays, 34
Hardy, 1–4, 17, 48, 64, 130, 138, 140–41, 142, 235n95
Head of household, 52, 143, 146; men of color as, 37, 163–65, 170, 183–84; women as, 71, 83, 88, 96, 106, 108, 112, 115, 120, 125. *See also* Household; Patriarchy
Hierarchy, 35, 67, 99, 124; between slave owners and slaves, 2, 3, 20, 106, 127; gender, 21, 165; plantation, 28, 32, 33; racial, 5, 16, 97, 110–11, 121, 146, 193; social, 16
Hilliard d'Auberteuil, Michel-René, 67, 98, 134
Household, 97, 134, 159, 199; as site for interracial intimacy, 13–15, 16–17; authority of slave owners over, 47, 66; connections outside, 50, 136; people of color as members of in France, 2–6, 24, 48, 59–62, 64, 123, 128, 129, 139, 158, 163, 167–68, 170, 173–78, 179–83; people of color as members in Saint-Domingue, 99, 100–111, 127
Housekeeper, 19, 93, 105, 134, 214n88
Huguenot Diaspora, 9, 22
Hurricanes, 11, 75
Husband: absence of, 71, 72–73, 79, 80–81, 83, 96, 112, 120; authority of, 3, 4, 49, 52, 72, 76, 86–88, 93, 97, 107, 113; financial ventures and property of, 72, 75, 77–78, 91, 94–95, 117; men of color as, 164–66, 183–84, 198. *See also* Head of household; Masculinity; Patriarchy

Île Bourbon, 171
Île de France, 167, 171, 173
Illegitimate children, 71, 89–95, 97, 131, 135–36, 137, 145, 147, 150–51, 153–54, 227n86, 238–39n42. *See also* Family; *Mulâtre*
Immeubles, 46, 77, 153; slaves as, 215n2. *See also* Meubles, Slaves
Indenture, 122, 220n1
India, 171–72
Indigo, 8, 23, 73–74, 81, 83, 115, 117, 186
Indigoteur (indigo maker), 28, 40, 256n35. *See also* Slaves
Inheritance, 34, 63, 70, 71, 72, 73, 75, 76–78, 79, 89–95, 106, 109, 117, 131, 132, 136, 138,

145, 147, 150, 153, 182, 219n55, 223n30, 238–39n42. *See also* Legacy; Testament; Universal legatee
Intimacy, 1–6, 8, 12, 13–15, 16–17, 20–21, 41, 43, 45, 47, 66, 68–69, 70–71, 89, 97, 99, 100–101, 106–11, 127, 156, 159, 168, 170, 171, 173, 174, 175, 178, 181, 184, 185, 198, 204n44

Labat, Jean-Baptiste, 30, 67
Labor, 14, 100, 108–9, 122, 159, 187, 195; as common experience, 20–21, 26; gendered understandings of, 111, 143, 158; of free people of color, 143, 170, 179, 181; of slaves, 24, 29, 34–35, 40–44, 51, 60, 99, 103, 123, 167, 176–77; of white women, 77, 95, 118; reproductive, 41–42, 158. *See also Métier*
La Rochelle, 1–3, 5, 6–12, 14, 16, 21–24, 34, 47, 48, 50, 52–65, 71–83, 84, 85, 87, 90, 91, 94, 95, 96, 109, 112, 120–27, 129–57, 158–84, 195–97, 239n43
Legacy, 19, 25, 90–94, 96, 100, 104–5, 109–11, 146, 150–52, 153–56, 166. *See also* Inheritance, Testament, Universal legatee
Legitimacy, 63, 70, 89–95, 97, 137, 145, 182. *See also* Illegitimate children
Léogane, 1, 3, 10, 11, 66, 81, 89, 92, 102, 109, 114, 121, 127, 207–8n6, 221n10, 245n7
Letters, 14, 17, 23, 85–86, 88, 186; of permission (to transport slaves to France), 50, 52–55. *See also* Credit
Liège, Marie-Anne-Suzanne, 137, 155
Lineage, 27, 77, 94, 110, 147, 150–51, 152
Lizette, 1–4, 17, 48, 64, 126, 138, 225n49
Louis XIV, 62
Louise, 162–65, 178, 181, 184
Louverture, Toussaint, 155, 194, 256n44
Loyalty, 38, 64, 67–68, 106, 124, 173, 179, 192–93, 250n60

Mandron, Jean, 129, 132, 138, 141, 142, 144
Mandron, Jean-Baptiste, 132, 149, 151, 135, 236n12, 243n96
Mandron, Joseph-Benjamin, 129, 132, 138, 141, 142–44
Mandron, Marie, 149
Mandron, Marie-Charlotte, 129, 132, 138, 141, 143–44, 146–49
Mandron, Marie-Jeanne, 129, 132, 138, 141, 143–44, 146–57, 158
Mandron, Marie-Magdeline, 132

ACKNOWLEDGMENTS
───────────

Writing a book is like taking a transatlantic voyage. You bring some baggage with the prospect of acquiring much more along the way, you struggle to make sense of a shifting horizon, and sometimes you feel a little sick. Above all, the experience of such a journey relies on one's fellow travelers. I have been lucky to make this passage in excellent company. Historians past and present have offered inspiration, mentorship, guidance, and a platform on which to build my own work. Friends, family, and colleagues have helped and supported me along the way. The people who are the subjects of this research have also accompanied me, shadowy presences that whisper insistently and sometimes seem almost corporeal. Now that I have reached the end of this expedition, it is my honor and privilege to thank those who eased my trip.

My first debt is to those who provided advice, mentorship, and models of historical scholarship. Dena Goodman offered imaginative and challenging direction and continues to be my intellectual guide to eighteenth-century France. Susan Siegfried, Martha Jones, Joshua Cole, Rebecca Scott, and Regina Morantz-Sanchez all provided mentorship and showed me how to be a historian. Jean Hébrard encouraged me to consider transatlantic contexts.

Many scholars of France and the French Atlantic have helped this project along. Sue Peabody supported this project intellectually and personally since its inception, and has consistently pushed me to ask (and answer) difficult questions precisely. Pierre Boulle generously shared his unsurpassed knowledge of the social landscape of people of color in France. At crucial points, Robert Duplessis and Robert Taber pointed me to key documents in various archives. Brett Rushforth pushed me to think about empire. Yvonne Fabella,

Elizabeth Heath, Jeremy Popkin, Denise Davidson, Clare Crowston, Julie Hardwick, Nina Kushner, Rebecca Hartkopf Schloss, Cynthia Bouton, Jennifer Sessions, Jennifer Heuer, Judith DeGroat, John Savage, Robin Mitchell, and Meghan Roberts all offered insight at critical junctures. I received stimulating feedback from various conference and workshop participants, including the Caribbean Studies Workshop, Modern France Workshop, and Center for Gender Studies at the University of Chicago; the Omohundro Institute of Early American History and Culture; and at conferences including the American Historical Association, French Historical Studies, French Colonial Historical Society, Western Society for French History, Association of Caribbean Historians, Berkshire Conference for Women Historians, and Consortium on the Revolutionary Era.

I have been inspired by colleagues at a variety of institutions over the years. Catherine Cangany, Tamar Carroll, Saskia Coenen, Jessica Fripp, Katie Hornstein, Robert Kruckeburg, Suzi Linsley, and Dan Livesay at the University of Michigan; Elizabeth Heath, Emily Osborn, Julie Saville, and Tara Zahra at the University of Chicago; Emily Sahakian, Ben Ehlers, Steve Berry, Tim Cleaveland, and Dan Rood at the University of Georgia all provided guidance, good companionship, and stimulated my thinking, while John Morrow made a research trip possible.

In France, Mickaël Augeron and Annie and Jacky Grizon made me welcome in La Rochelle. The archivists at the Archives départementales de la Charente-Maritime and the Archives municipales de La Rochelle may have wondered at the persistence of "la Américaine," but nonetheless indefatigably supported my researches. I also wish to thank the staffs of the Archive nationales d'outre-mer, the Archives nationales, and the Bibliothéque nationale.

While a transatlantic voyage may be an apt simile for a journey of discovery, I also received support for actual transatlantic trips. Research for this project has been funded by the Institut Français d'Amérique, the Society for French Historical Studies, the Western Society for French History, the American Society for Eighteenth-Century Studies, and a Chateaubriand Fellowship. I received writing support from the Willson Center for the Humanities and Arts at the University of Georgia, the University of Michigan Institute for the Humanities, and the Michigan Society of Fellows. A grant from the University of Georgia College of Arts and Sciences supported publication of the maps and images for this book.

Personal debts run the deepest, and many friends and family have sustained me over the course of this project. My parents Mary Palmer and Hugh

Palmer have exhibited unflagging encouragement for all my endeavors. David Lee has been my rudder and compass, and has supported me throughout this project. Our toddler Henry came along toward the end of this process. When he learned that I was writing a book he admonished me, "We don't write in books!" He and brand-new baby Benjamin are unsurpassed joys, and someday I look forward to teaching them that there are good reasons for writing in—and writing—books.

An earlier version of Chapter 5 was published as "What's in a Name? Mixed-Race Families and Resistance to Racial Codification in Eighteenth-Century France" in *French Historical Studies*, 33, 3 (2010): 357-85; copyright 2010, Society of French Historical Studies. All rights reserved. Republished by permission of the copyright holder, and the present publisher, Duke University Press. An earlier version of Chapter 3 was published as "Women and Contracts in the Age of Transatlantic Commerce," in *Women and Work in Eighteenth-Century France*, ed. Daryl Hafter and Nina Kushner (Baton Rouge: Louisiana State University Press, 2015).